A MIND OF HER OWN

The Life of Karen Horney

SUSAN QUINN

SUMMIT BOOKS
New York · London · Toronto · Sydney · Tokyo

Designed by Anne Scatto/Levavi & Levavi
Manufactured in the United States of America

10   9   8   7   6   5   4   3   2   1

Library of Congress Cataloging in Publication Data

Quinn, Susan.
    A mind of her own : the life of Karen Horney / Susan Quinn.
       p.   cm.
    Bibliography: p.
    Includes index.
    1. Horney, Karen, 1885–1952.   2. Psychoanalysts—United States—
Biography.   I. Title.
RC438.6.H67Q56   1987
150.19′5′0924—dc19
[B]

ISBN 0-671-47518-5

Acknowledgments

I am particularly grateful to Karen Horney's three daughters,
Renate Horney Patterson, Marianne Horney Eckhardt, and Brigitte Horney Swarzenski, for information and insights about their
mother. Another important guide in my research was Susanne
Spielvogel Trüber, who knew where to find what I was looking
for in Germany. In Japan, Misako Mizonoe was similarly helpful.
Jeff Shore led the way to key people and places and provided, by
his example, an insight into Zen. Franklin Buchanan's knowledge
of Japan and Zen was also very useful.

I gratefully acknowledge the generosity of Jack L. Rubins,
M.D., the author of *Karen Horney: Gentle Rebel of Psychoanalysis*
(New York: Dial Press, 1978), the first biography of Karen
Horney. Dr. Rubins, himself a Horneyan psychoanalyst, devoted
the last seven years of his life to research on Horney's life in Europe and the United States. He interviewed sources who were no
longer alive by the time I began my effort and gathered facts and
anecdotes that have been invaluable to me. I met Dr. Rubins only
once, in the spring of 1982. Although he was not well at the time,
he was humble and warm toward me and expressed willingness to
help with my project. After his death his family, in a similar spirit,
granted me the use of his voluminous notes and documents.

I have come to rely for wisdom and moral support on the

5

friends I see regularly in several different groups. I feel especially grateful to Evy Davis, Kathryn Kirshner, and Diana Korzenik, with whom I have met for the last eight years and who have listened so well. I am also thankful to all the members of my writers' group: Paula Bonnell, Ruth Butler, Judith Cohen, Christopher Corkery, Elaine Ford, Alice Hoffman, Sue Standing, Pam Painter, and Marjorie Waters. They have given me encouragement throughout the research and writing process and have made useful comments on the text. Fellow biographers Phyllis Cole, Megan Marshall, and Lois Rudnick have provided practical advice. I am also thankful to Richard Lentscher, for translating, to Jan Schreiber, who has read every word with care, as well as to Carol and Jim Gilligan, Tom Simons, Anna Wolff, Tony Kris, Fran Nason, Sander Gilman, Don Davidoff, and Sanford Gifford, who have made important suggestions. Thanks to Joan Hergenroeder for coming along and to Dr. Uwe Peters and Ilse Bezzenberger for their hospitality in Germany. I have relied throughout this five-year undertaking on my superb editor, Ileene Smith. Finally, I am grateful to my husband, Daniel Jacobs, whose support and wisdom have affected this project from the moment of conception and who has been my most important reader. I am thankful also to my son, Tom, who believed in me, my daughter, Anna, who spurred me on and helped with the title, and my parents, who have been encouraging and enthusiastic for so long.

To my parents,
Robert Emmet and Esther Taft Quinn

Contents

Prologue

On March 13, 1940, a New York psychoanalyst named Fritz Wittels wrote a long, angry letter to fellow members of the New York Psychoanalytic Society. "Freud's psychoanalysis achieves remarkable success in America," Wittels began. Nevertheless, the New York Society, the first and most influential in America, was threatened with "pending disintegration" because of the disruptive influence of one of its members, a fifty-four-year-old German-born analyst named Karen Horney. Not only had Karen Horney "with one sweeping gesture refuted most of the fundamentals of psychoanalysis" but she had done it "in a book written in a demagogic style and avidly read by social workers, politically minded laymen and by the critics of the *New York Times,*" with the result that "forty years of patient scientific work were thrown to the dogs." The issue, as Wittels saw it, came down to "Freud or no Freud." Either Dr. Horney should return to "Freud's principles" or she should give her doctrine a new name and teach it somewhere else, with "an educational staff of her own."[1]

Wittels' letter was the opening salvo in a battle that was to rage within the New York Society for a year, culminating, in the spring of 1941, in a report from the society's education committee. The "published writings and contentions of Dr. Karen Horney," the committee declared, were resulting in "preliminary indoctrination with theoretical and emotional orientations which are contrary to the fundamental principles of psychoanalytic education."[2] The committee therefore recommended that Horney be removed from her training and supervisory role. For Karen Horney, a founding member of the Berlin Psychoanalytic Institute, who had been teaching psychoanalysis longer than anyone else in the New York group at the time, there could be only one response to such an affront. On April 29, 1941, after the membership had voted to demote her, she got up and walked out of the New York Psychoanalytic Society, never to return.

It soon became apparent to those who stayed behind, however, that Karen Horney was not going to be quickly forgotten. Horney's departure led four other analysts and fourteen students to resign in sympathy, causing the first split in American psychoanalysis and leaving behind resentments that contributed to another major split in the New York Society three years later. Rumors and conjectures were so rife after Horney's exodus that the New York Society devoted a good part of the following year to defending itself. A statement was issued and sent to anyone with even the slightest interest in the matter, from the Rockefeller Foundation to the editors of professional journals. And officers of the New York Society traveled to other cities to explain the facts as they saw them to colleagues.

In several ways the campaign of the New York Society succeeded. Largely as a result, Karen Horney was never able to gain official national recognition for the alternative institute she founded. Furthermore, Horney's contribution has continued to be overlooked or minimized within psychoanalysis. In 1971, when a Harvard senior wrote asking the prominent New York analyst Lawrence Kubie for information about Karen Horney, Kubie wrote back: "I frankly think that you could do something better with your time than to write a senior honors thesis on someone as confused and as essentially trivial and transitory as Horney."[3]

Fortunately Karen Horney's writings have saved her from the oblivion to which some of her enemies tried to consign her. Far from being trivial or unimportant, Horney was the first, and perhaps the best, critic of Freud's ideas about women. Her early essays on female psychology have an astonishing immediacy. In such brilliantly argued papers as "The Flight from Womanhood" Horney was saying in the 1920s what feminist critics of Freud rediscovered fifty years later. Many of Horney's other ideas, which so enraged the New York Society in 1941, have since been incorporated into psychoanalytic thinking: her emphasis, for instance, on first addressing the here and now instead of diving right into the patient's past. The recent attention to the narcissistic personality in the writings of Heinz Kohut and other "self psychologists" was anticipated by Karen Horney thirty-five years ago in her books *Our Inner Conflicts* and *Neurosis and Human Growth*. Even Dr. Samuel Atkin, one of the members most adamantly opposed to Karen Horney's theories in 1941, conceded recently that Horney was "ahead of her time in recognizing psychoanalysis as a humanity rather than a rigid science." She honored Freud as "a first-rate teacher" but understood the need to extend psychoanalysis "in the direction of other social sciences."[4]

Karen Horney led a restless life, full of shifting passions and allegiances. But in one thing she was consistent: her independence of mind. She was simply incapable of accepting someone else's version of reality until she had measured it against her own experience, what she once called, in an early diary, "the delicate vibrations of my soul."[5] This was Horney's greatest strength, and sometimes her undoing as well. As a grade-school student she almost lost the love of her favorite teacher, Herr Schulze, when she voiced doubts about Christ's resurrection. But later her independence led to her become one of the first female medical students at a German university and, some years after that, one of the first people in Berlin to undergo the new treatment developed by the brilliant but unorthodox psychiatrist Sigmund Freud.

When a new orthodoxy grew up around Freud, Karen Horney was bound to play the role of challenger. And even though she may have walked out of the New York Society that night in 1941 with tears streaming down her face, she would never have recanted, any more than she would have in elementary school. In this way Karen Horney's life is of a piece. No one moment, no one relationship, explains just why this should be so. But everything in her history affirms that Karen Horney, born Karen Clementina Theodora Danielsen, could not be otherwise.

_____ PART ONE

Girlhood

Hamburg 1885–1906

1

Home

Karen Clementina Theodora Danielsen was born in Eilbek, just outside of Hamburg, Germany, on September 15, 1885.[1] She was the second child and only daughter of Berndt Henrik Wackels Danielsen, a sea captain, and Clothilde Marie Danielsen. In another family she might have grown up in the shadow of her brother, Berndt, who was blonder and three and a half years older. But in the Danielsen household Karen seems to have been almost equally prized from the start. Her extravagant name, Karen Clementina Theodora, implies great expectations. And Karen's intensity comes through even in early photographs. In one, taken when she was around two, the expectant eyes and full, downturned lips, the little raised hand, seem to command the camera to action. Her face shows keen interest in the event of the photograph, just as the white eyelet-embroidered dress, satin bows and sash, and shiny patent shoes reveal the attentions of a loving mother in preparation for it.

Berndt was the adored first child and the one with looks and charm. Karen was always understood to be the smarter one and the "character." "It was always my pride," Karen wrote in her diary many years later, "that in school I was better than Berndt, that there were more amusing childhood stories about me than about him."[2] Certainly no one knew better than Karen how to

19

attract the family's attention and concern or how to get her way.

But both Karen and her brother, Berndt, must have sensed from an early age that the attentions their mother lavished on them had a somber underside. The children were, as their mother would often tell them, her only happiness. Had it not been for them she probably would not have stayed in her unhappy marriage or even, she sometimes implied, gone on living. So Berndt and Karen had to bear the weight of this grave responsibility for their mother's happiness. Though they were loved, their childhood would have been more carefree if their parents had loved each other.

The marriage had inherent difficulties from the start. Wackels, as he was known in the family, was a steamship captain on the pioneering Kosmos line, and a forty-four-year-old widower at the time of his marriage. "Sonni," as Clothilde was called by all who knew her, was only twenty-eight. Such age differences were not unusual in nineteenth-century Germany. But in addition to bridging the age gap, Sonni had to become a stepmother to four nearly grown children by Wackels' previous marriage. These four were forever taking Wackels' side against Sonni. And Sonni, for her part, probably favored her own two much younger children, Berndt and Karen.

There were temperamental differences as well. Wackels was usually absent, but when he came home he made his presence felt. A zealous Lutheran and a devotee of the fiery local pastor, he often delivered sermons around the house. Sonni, on the other hand, was more impressed with the prognostications of fortune-tellers than the word of the pastor. Secular heroes, particularly the Austrian emperor Franz Josef, had excited her as a girl. And her one great love had been a German officer who died in the Franco-Prussian War.

Underlying the disharmony in the marriage was an important difference in class. Wackels was the son of a Norwegian watchmaker, Lars Jorgen Danielsen. Born in Bergen, he had originally been called Berenth Henrick Vakkels Danielsen, but he had Germanized the name to Berndt Wackels sometime after taking a job as a seaman in Germany.[3] By age thirty-seven he had risen to the rank of captain and was piloting steamships out of Hamburg across the South Atlantic and through the Strait of Magellan to South America's most distant ports. This was dangerous and pioneering work. Indeed, Captain Danielsen was one of the first to complete the route from Hamburg to the west coast of South America and Central America under a German flag. His ships carried railroad parts to ports in Chile and Peru, and, later, farther up the coast, in Costa Rica and Guatemala, returning with copper, tin, and saltpeter to supply industries in Europe.[4] Between 1873 and 1904 he piloted six ships, of increasing size, around the Horn and back, over and over again.[5] The journeys were long, each lasting about six months. They required not only nautical skills for navigating large ships through difficult waters but leadership as well. On each journey he was in command of a crew of about forty men.[6]

Admirable as Captain Danielsen's accomplishments might be, however, the fact remained that he was a seafarer. Sonni came from a family that had prospered from seafaring without taking the same risks. Her father was Jacob Joseph van Ronzelen, a Dutch-born architect whose name bespoke noble ancestry. (A "van" from Holland would be equated in Germany with a "von" and was a coveted sign of a propertied past.) Born and trained in Amsterdam, van Ronzelen, while still in his twenties, oversaw construction of the port of Bremerhaven, one of the great seaports of the Hanseatic trading alliance. Twenty years later he built a second port, larger and more modern than the first. Van Ronzelen held the title of Surveyor and Director of Harbor Construction for Bremerhaven. A street in Bremerhaven bears his name; his oil portrait hangs in a local museum.

Sonni was the product of van Ronzelen's second marriage, to a woman of aristocratic stock, Marie von Camerer. The second Mrs. van Ronzelen, however, died in childbed two weeks after Sonni's birth. So Sonni was raised by a stepmother, van Ronzelen's third and last wife, Wilhelmine Lorentz-Meyer.

It is quite possible that Karen Danielsen's early ambitions, so unusual in a girl of that time, were inspired by this unusual grandmother, Wilhelmine Lorentz-Mayer. Minna, as she was called in the family, was educated by her father alongside her seven brothers. She studied physics and Latin, subjects that were usually a male preserve, and throughout her life she maintained an interest in astronomy. There is no evidence that her stepdaughter, Sonni, received a similar education. But there is little doubt, given this background, that Sonni's marriage to Captain Danielsen was a sizable step down the social ladder. Jacob van Ronzelen, a man who, according to a contemporary, was "hated by the liberals for his aristocratic outlook," would not have been pleased with the match.[7]

Sonni's father was long dead by the time of her marriage to

Wackels, however, and all her siblings had left home. At age twenty-eight Sonni was in danger of remaining single for life, forced to live out her days in the family house or in one of the "homes" run by charitable organizations for the many women in similar circumstances. In nineteenth-century Germany it was often better for a woman to compromise than not to marry at all and be permanently dependent on relatives. Certainly employment was nearly unthinkable. It was a time too when women far outnumbered men in the population. In 1867 in Bremen, for instance, more than half of those women between sixteen and fifty were unmarried.[8]

Besides, Wackels would have cut a fine figure in his captain's uniform. He was a man of action, vigorously handsome, with a bushy blond mustache and large rounded features. His churchgoing, unusual in a sea captain, added to his refinement. Or so Sonni may have felt when she married him in 1881.

Wackels, for his part, seems to have been content with the marriage. Probably his expectations were rather simple: he was a conventional man, fond of his comforts and fully expecting the woman of the house, in her God-given role, to provide them. He may have complained and bullied, but he relied on Sonni to take care of him.

However she may have felt in the first years of marriage, Sonni's unhappiness eventually became so unbearable that she did something almost unheard of among women of her class in that time and place: she walked out. But that was nearly twenty years after Karen was born. In the interim the relationship between Sonni and Wackels had one saving grace: the captain was almost always away at sea.

It is likely in fact that Captain Danielsen was at sea on September 15, 1885, when his daughter, Karen, was born. He made two trips round the Horn that year, and since each lasted five months, he may well have received news of Karen's birth by telegram in a South American port. He *was* present at the christening, which took place two months later at the Danielsen family church, the Friedenskirche.[9] But for the most part Karen and her brother, Berndt, grew up in a fatherless home. In fact, thirteen years later, when Karen began keeping a diary, she made it sound as though she had no father at all.

"How I come to be writing a diary," she begins, "is easy to explain: it's because I am enthusiastic about everything new, and I have decided now to carry this through so that in later years I can better remember the days of my youth.

"Now," she continues, "for a short introduction, the following: we, i.e., mother, Berndt, who is now 17 years old, and I, live in Eilbek, Papenstrasse, to be precise. My best friends are Tuti and Käthe. We are in the second class at the Convent School. Our favorite teacher is Herr Schulze; he teaches us our German lessons, history, and religion."[10] Among the important people of her life her father is nowhere to be seen. It isn't until more than a year later that he finally appears in a diary entry, and then because he comes home from sea and breaks in on "our idyllic life."[11]

In family photos Karen, her mother, and her brother appear in various combinations. The captain is always absent. The one time in the diary when Karen's father is included in a happy family scene is Christmas of her fifteenth year, and it is only because of the general goodwill required by the occasion. "Christmas Eve is almost over," she writes. "The lights on the Christmas tree have burned down long ago. My beloved Mother is sitting with brother Berndt at the piano. . . . Father (today all bitterness is to be banned) is running from one thing to another and enjoying everything like a child, especially the goodies. Mother had the charming idea of surprising us with a genuine Norwegian Julklap [punch]."

Among the gifts Karen received that Christmas were a Negro boy doll that she had "ardently longed for" (such dolls were in vogue in Germany at the time) and a new diary, in which she promptly made this first entry.[12] It was her second diary—a cloth-covered one in green with the word *Tagebuch* impressed in silver script on the cover. Of better quality than the first, cardboard-covered one, it had the advantage of possessing a lock, making it safer for private thoughts. Since these were the most frequent focus of her diary entries, the lock was particularly welcome.

Occasionally Karen's diary-keeping—which she continued intermittently until she was twenty-six—did have the straightforward purpose she assigned it at the start—to "remember the days of my youth." But mere record-keeping never interested her for long. The facts—grades in school, family events, names, and dates—nearly always prompted her to reflect on how she felt about them. When she had her hair pinned up for the first time at thirteen, she told her diary how grown-up she felt.[13] When at fifteen she found herself wishing to play with dolls again, she noted that this was a surprising inclination in someone old enough to be

"Sie'd" like a grown-up in school.[14] While she may well have been "enthusiastic about everything new," it was her own internal discoveries that interested her most.

There *is* a feeling in the diaries, however, that life holds thrilling possibilities. And while this is a reflection of Karen's personality, it coincides with the pervasive mood in turn-of-the-century Hamburg, a mood that was to have a profound effect on Karen's destiny. Had it not been for the social ferment of the 1890s and the resulting pressure for women's rights, she might never have been able to study at Gymnasium and go on to medical school. And that social ferment grew out of the transformation that was taking place in the social fabric of German cities.

Karen Danielsen came into the world just as Hamburg was steaming into the industrial age. During the ten years after her birth Hamburg Harbor was transformed into the third largest international port in the world. The half-timbered houses that had lined the narrow canals of earlier days were unsentimentally torn down, beginning in 1888, in the interests of broadening and deepening the Elbe River basin, which formed the port. The sailing ships, which had created a picturesque forest of masts in the old harbor, were outnumbered in 1899 by smoke-spewing steamboats. Inland from the harbor, whole sections of the old city were torn down to make way for new, steam-powered industry. Electric trams replaced the horse-drawn railway on city streets. In the center of town an imposing new city hall—still the pride of Hamburg—was rising block by granite block. Its scaffolded clock tower, visible from every quarter, must have heightened the inescapable feeling that Hamburg was a city on the move.[15]

Eilbek, the town on the outskirts of Hamburg where the Danielsens lived, was a product of the rapid growth. Ten years before Karen was born it was a country village, connected to the city by the Eilbek Canal, one of the many veins of water that flowed to Hamburg's watery heart. By 1899, when she began her diary, Eilbek had become a city of about 25,000 with a regular train connection to the metropolis.[16] The Danielsen family, like many of the inhabitants of Eilbek, lived in a large, elegant apartment. Sixty-four Papenstrasse, where they moved when Karen was a young girl, was in a rather typical corner building, with one wing extending along Papenstrasse and the other along Hirschgraben. The Danielsens lived in an apartment that took up an entire wing of the third floor and offered views, from elegant wrought-iron balconies, of the park across the street. The building's style was elaborate: no window or door was unornamented, and no roof lacked gables and cupola. But in fact this Danielsen apartment, the third they lived in in Eilbek during Karen's first thirteen years,[17] was a relatively restrained example of the current style. An adjoining street was sometimes called "Soup Tureen Street," because the ornate cupolas on the buildings looked like the heavy soup tureens that might appear at Sunday dinner on the tables of Eilbek's prosperous inhabitants.[18]

Elsewhere such architecture, with its extravagant flights of fancy, was called Victorian. But in Germany it was Wilhelmine, a reflection of the increasing influence of the Prussian emperor. Germany at the turn of the century was a confederation of independent states, all jealously guarding their powers and resisting control of a central authority. Not all the states in this federation, however, were equal. Prussia, by far the richest, largest, and most powerful, was ruled by a monarch who was at once the king of Prussia and the German emperor. And in 1899 an energetic young monarch, Kaiser Wilhelm II, ascended to power with the determination to consolidate Prussian might and instill fervor for the German fatherland in all the quasi-independent states of the confederation.

Hamburg, as one of the cities of the Hanseatic League, had a long and proud history of independence from the Prussian monarchy and from the rule of kings in general. When Kaiser Wilhelm made his ceremonial visits, members of the Hamburg Senate proudly wore their civilian black cutaways and silk top hats, providing a sober contrast to the plumage of the Kaiser and his entourage. Nonetheless the young Kaiser's frequent visits stirred German nationalist sentiments even in republican Hamburg. When the Kaiser's coach and four paraded through the streets, schoolgirls in long white dresses and straw hats lined the way, paying homage as "maidens of honor."[19]

Even Karen Danielsen was caught up, reluctantly, in the general adulation. "Such is life," she lamented to her diary in English in January 1901. "I am supposed to recite a dreadful, rumbling poem for the Emperor's birthday on Saturday. I've resisted as long as I could, but I must get at it; dreadful."[20] Such public idolatry would never be to her liking. Besides, she had her own, more deserving, heroes to worship. Foremost among them was her teacher at the Convent School, Herr Schulze.

It may well be that Karen began her diary because she needed a place to unburden herself about her growing passion for "him," a pronoun she uses with quotes to distinguish her beloved Herr Schulze from other mortals. Certainly Herr Schulze is the central subject of nearly every entry, including the first. "Last year," she explains, "we had German with Frl. Schöne, whom Tuti and I were also crazy about, though we like Herr Schulze much better still, because the way he treats us is so charming."[21]

Five days later she is ecstatic about a visit she has made with her mother and girlfriend Tuti to visit Herr Schulze, who has been convalescing at his home in Reinbek. "It was *heavenly* yesterday," she writes. "On the road to Reinbek, we picked flowers for 'him,' poppies, camomile, and pretty weeds. When we arrived in Reinbek, he was not home yet, but 5 minutes later he came. Oh, that feeling, as he stepped into the room! What bliss to look into his beautiful eyes. I believe I won't forget that moment very easily. He shook our hands again and again, saying: 'Dear children.' . . . We both believe we may conclude from a few words of his that he will invite us sometime. Oh, how lovely that would be!"[22]

Four days after that she sends Herr Schulze an anonymous gift of six bottles of wine, signing, "From someone who has the sincerest wish to see you well soon."[23] When she is away from him, even on a July vacation at the ocean, she pines. "My being away from school for 4 days is very hard for me, as Herr Schulze is back. Today my thoughts lingered alternately on him and on Langballigau, our destination."[24] When she is near him the smallest privilege delights her. "Yesterday," she writes in August, "we made a lovely class trip to Venttorf. At the station I sat opposite Herr Schulze, then I carried his coat, which I enjoyed very much."[25]

A photograph from around this period catches Karen as she moves from childhood into womanhood. Standing opposite her is Sonni, looking quite young and shapely. A corset has given her the fashionable "monobosom" look under her embroidered black dress. Her hair is pulled up tight into a braid on top of her head. Next to her stands Berndt, a tall and debonair young man in white tie and formal black satin suit, looking very much like his mother and almost old enough to be her husband. On the right is Karen. She too is formally dressed in a black satin dress with grown-up details — a ruff at the neck, finished off with a brooch. But her hair is still in a single fat braid, ending in a bushy tail drawn forward over her shoulder. And the pleated bodice of her dress hangs loose, whereas her mother's nearly bursts with fulsomeness.

Even in a still photograph it is easy to guess the young Karen's intelligence and seriousness, qualities that undoubtedly endeared her to Herr Schulze. Less obvious perhaps was her passion. Did Herr Schulze know what exquisite pleasure he provided by allowing this intense young girl to carry his coat? One can imagine her walking along behind him on the class trip, carrying the bulky coat worshipfully over her arm, perhaps even holding it fervently to her cheek when he wasn't looking. Since Herr Schulze was, by Karen's account, an excellent and sensitive teacher, he probably recognized Karen's condition as a classic schoolgirl crush. Perhaps he also suspected that Karen was seeking an alternative in him to her own father, whom she found it so difficult to love.

Karen's real feelings toward her father during this period were probably more complicated than she could easily admit. When she mentions him at all in the diary, it is in adamantly negative terms. But in fact Karen, like all children in divided marriages, had had to take sides at an early age. And since her father was so distant, often physically and always emotionally, it is not surprising that she took her mother's side. Forty-five years later, in her book *Our Inner Conflicts,* she would write of the child who "may find himself in a situation that threatens his self-confidence—in short the very core of his psychic existence." In such a situation, she notes, the child's "first attempts to relate himself to others are determined not by his real feelings but by strategic necessities . . . he has . . . to devise ways to cope with people and to manipulate them with minimum damage to himself."[26] As the quarrel between her parents escalated, this was increasingly Karen's position.

"It must be grand to have a father one can love and esteem," she writes in December of her fourteenth year, "and when the 4th Commandment does not confront one like a terrifying specter with its 'thou shalt _____.' I can't do it. I can't respect that man who makes us all unhappy with his dreadful hypocrisy, selfishness, crudeness, and ill-breeding, etc."[27] There is something suspiciously adult about this condemnation. In particular, "crudeness" and "ill-breeding" sound more like words Sonni might use in complaining about her husband than those a daughter would choose in writing about her father.

What few glimpses we have of Wackels through other eyes suggest that, no matter how unpleasant he might have been, he was not in command at home the way he was at sea. When Karen really wanted to go to Gymnasium or when she and Sonni hatched plans to move to the nearby town where Herr Schulze lived, Wackels could be "got round" by Sonni. Wackels, whom the others called "the old man" behind his back, seems to have played the fool more often than the villain.

The worst times seem to have come when Wackels' children by his first marriage were in the house. Then the marital quarrel escalated into a battle, with Sonni, Berndt, and Karen squaring off against Wackels and his other children.

> The summer of 1900 was the finest I've had so far [Karen wrote in her diary in November of that year], for we were living in Reinbek.... Our summer house was charmingly situated. In front of the house, meadows and woods, behind it the Bille, a little stream where I could swim in good weather.... But this glorious life was to have a sudden end. In the beginning of September my stepsister Astrid, with her 5-year-old daughter, came to stay for 5 weeks. She had behaved very badly toward Mother in the past. Our idyllic life was over. It went well enough so long as Father wasn't there, but when he came in the end of September, all hell broke loose, and up to now it has been getting worse rather than better. Astrid incites him against Mother. There are daily scenes. It finally got so bad that Berndt and I didn't let Mother out of our sight for a moment.[28]

Yet Karen is troubled by her complete alienation from her father. Because he is a religious man, and because she is wrestling with religious doubt, her inability to love God the Father and her near contempt for her *own* father are seen as two parts of the same sin. That New Year's Eve she writes:

> I look back on the past year with gratitude to God and man. But bitter self-reproaches press upon me too. Unkindness, lack of self-control, my unbelief, making fun of the holiest things, exaggerated enthusiasms, and serious offences against the 4th Commandment [Honor they father and thy mother]. For the New Year my resolutions are: 1. to stop mockery, even if I unfortunately don't possess a child's faith any more and no other faith has taken its place; 2. to learn to suppress my moods and tempers—to behave equably; 3. to try to fulfill the 4th Commandment, at least outwardly. Today I read in a book that one should honor one's father not for his personal characteristics but to honor the authority God has vested in him. But it is awfully difficult.[29]

It is easier by far to honor Herr Schulze, whose authority and theology are more congenial. "Today, we had a splendid religion lesson again," she writes in the spring of 1901. "Herr Schulze is not totally liberal . . . but so nicely in the middle between orthodox and liberal, inclining somewhat more to the latter." Herr Schulze seems to bring religion down to a human scale. Discussing the concept of the Holy Trinity, the idea that Father, Son, and Holy Ghost are both one and three in one, he explains, "They are just as much one as the *various* powers in a person are one, as: willing, feeling, perceiving, etc." It was natural, given her interest in observing her own complicated internal life, that Karen should be attracted to such psychological analogies. "It was heavenly," she concludes of their discussion, "and he was heavenly. It's so touching, how he responds to all my questions. He is my inner God. I am afraid that when I no longer have him as a teacher, I may go astray."[30]

Not everyone in Hamburg was as preoccupied with theological questions as Karen Danielsen. It was, in fact, a period when religion was more often discussed in connection with politics than with inner faith. The Protestant Evangelical Church (as the Lutheran Church in Germany was called after 1814) was governed by secular heads of state. As a result it was at once an arm of conservative politics and religion. In such large cities as Hamburg the ideas of Karl Marx, as enunciated by the Socialist Workers Party, were attracting followers among intellectuals and in the working class. They in turn linked religion with the oppressive power of the Prussian state. Protestant pastors, in their view, were nothing but "black police."[31]

Even in the middle class, not all families took their religion as seriously as the Danielsens. Most parents in Hamburg, a thoroughly Protestant city, took the trouble to observe the conventions: baptism of babies and confirmation for fifteen-year-olds. But these rituals were often *pro forma,* as in the case of a young man confirmed at Karen Danielsen's church in Eilbek in 1905. "I had enjoyed a good upbringing," writes Albert Goetz in a reminiscence of his confirmation at the Friedenskirche, "but on the point of Christianity my parents and especially my dear father... were extremely liberal. I was so far removed from Christian knowledge that I thought the words above the altar in our Friedenskirche, 'He suffered in order that we might have peace,' were a blasphemy. I didn't have an inkling of Christ's crucifixion for us." For young Albert Goetz the confirmation instruction rounded out a liberal education. "I learned, for the first time as a fifteen-year-old Gymnasium student, the various Christian ways of thinking and learned to know and understand the questions of life, of political, social and religious outlook, from the point of view of Protestantism."[32]

Such an intellectual grasp of religion was not enough for Karen Danielsen. Two years before confirmation classes even began, she was troubled by her inability to *experience* faith. "In spiritual matters," she writes in her very first diary entry at thirteen, "I feel *very unworthy,* for although I am steadily growing up, I do not yet feel the true need for religion. A sermon can overwhelm me and at times I can act accordingly, but prayer . . . spiritual poverty—in a word."[33]

Empirical and down to earth, she struggled with the miraculous elements of the Christ story. How, for instance, could Christ be God's son? When her brother, Berndt, gave her an explanation that helped her to accept Lutheran doctrine, she was genuinely grateful. She wrote in her diary a few weeks later:

> Berndt really is a fine fellow. Yesterday he again enlightened me on several things that were not clear to me. Up to now it has been the personality of Christ that was the most unclear. Although Herr Schulze has taught me about it, it seems to me to make no sense that Jesus should be God's son. Berndt told me: Christ is and always will be the greatest among all men, because the divine element, the thing that is embedded in every human being, was much stronger in him and so he stood nearest to God. And he is here still (spiritually of course)— one has to think of resurrection in a spiritual sense anyway. With this explanation a heavy burden fell from my heart, for I could not imagine, could not love, such a mixture of God and man. Now Jesus had become much dearer to me.[34]

However much Karen wished to believe, she also knew that she was *supposed* to believe. Her father, when he was home, required piety. And even in his absence, other eyes were upon her. If she walked half a block east from her apartment on Papenstrasse she confronted the tall spires of the slender brick Friedenskirche, the pride of the Eilbek congregation. And along the way, either on the street or in the sanctuary, there was a fair chance of encountering her father's friend, the energetic leader of the congregation, Pastor Nikolai von Ruckteschell.

Pastor von Ruckteschell was a man of impressive and unusual reputation. Before coming to the Friedenskirche he had risked imprisonment for his faith as a pastor in the Baltic region of czarist Russia. Apparently the czarist regime tolerated the German Protestant minority in the region only as long as they didn't seek converts. But when Pastor von Ruckteschell administered Lutheran communion to a Greek Orthodox Christian, he was nearly sent to

Siberia. Only the intervention of a grand duke saved him.

In Eilbek, as in Russia, Pastor von Ruckteschell sought converts everywhere. Despite his own blue blood, he professed egalitarianism. In order to lure the working class away from Socialist meetings, he set up "Friday evenings," where workers came to discuss grievances, and he insisted that "the heart of man is the same under every coat and vest." Von Ruckteschell was also a lover of literature. He invited the young people of the congregation to "classical evenings" at his house. Together they would read Goethe's *Faust* and engage in "free and easy conversation"[35] about *Faust* and life in general. But von Ruckteschell's greatest triumphs occurred in the pulpit on Sunday mornings. "His great eloquence," one churchgoer remembers, "combined with deep piety to make one of the most well-known and beloved preachers in Hamburg. Sunday after Sunday his church overflowed. The altar room, the aisles, the church steps, every standing place was taken."

"In his church," another churchgoer remembers, "no one slept, and when he made the sanctuary resound with *Faust,* in order to underscore his words, then women, men, old and young, held their breath."

Pastor von Ruckteschell's confirmation lessons, like his sermons, were much sought after. One boy's parents chose Pastor von Ruckteschell after shopping in parishes all over Hamburg. "When I was first introduced," remembers one student, "...the dear von Ruckteschell put his hand on my head and said in his unforgettable Baltic dialect, 'Now, my dear boy, it will all come to pass!' It seemed to me as if the spirit of the Lord had convulsed my body. I was electrified! No man had ever spoken or dealt with me in such a way before. The confirmation hours were the goal and the joy of the whole week for me."[36]

Even Karen's beloved Herr Schulze shared in the general admiration for the pastor, as Karen noted in her diary. "He [Herr Schulze] too, has great respect for Pastor von Ruckteschell, our splendid minister in Eilbek," she wrote. What *really* interested Karen, however, was where Herr Schulze sat when he came to church on Sunday mornings. "We now know where he usually sits," she reported to her diary, "up in the choir loft, though we'll have to find out whether to the left or to the right."[37]

Although Karen Danielsen gave lip service to the popular view of Pastor von Ruckteschell, she knew him too well to idolize him. For one thing, he was a friend and religious mentor to her father, whose faith she dismissed by turns as naïve and hypocritical. Furthermore, when there were disputes in the Danielsen family, the pastor apparently felt no compunction about entering in on the side of the captain. Just how self-important and overbearing these two might be as a team, with God on their side, is suggested by a surviving photograph. In it the pastor is sitting in a rose arbor enjoying a cigar with Wackels and another prosperous-looking parishioner. All three wear cutaways, vests, high collars, and white ties. Perhaps it is a special occasion, since they also sport boutonnières. Wackels and the other parishioner stand flanking Pastor von Ruckteschell, who sits back in a comfortable chair, bearded chin lifted high so that he stares haughtily down at the camera. In the manner of a great man at ease, his legs are crossed, one foot dangling in air and the other resting on a small round pillow, placed on the ground for that very purpose.

When Karen began attending confirmation classes she quickly decided that Pastor von Ruckteschell was no match for Herr Schulze as a teacher of religion. On Christmas Day of 1900 she wrote:

> I've been going to church in the mornings. Unfortunately this winter I will have to go whenever Pastor von Ruckteschell preaches, because I am to be confirmed at Easter. My religion is in a desperately sad state at the moment, I am stirred by questions and doubts that probably no one can solve for me. Was and is Christ God? What is God? Is there resurrection? Is God personal? Is he a God of love? Confirmation lessons don't make it any clearer for me. I see this now with deep disappointment. Only the religion lessons with Herr Schulze, my idolized teacher, bring me some light.[38]

No doubt Karen discovered in confirmation classes what others had found out elsewhere about the pastor: there were limits to the good man's liberality. Though he encouraged the workers to speak their minds at his "Friday evenings," he objected strongly when some in attendance expressed contempt for the celebration of the hundredth anniversary of the birth of Kaiser Wilhelm I. Such unpatriotic sentiments were not allowed.[39]

In his dealings with young people the pastor—who had twelve of his own—was even less forgiving. The mere hint of a flirtation between boys and girls of the confirmation classes enraged him beyond all reason. There was, for example, the incident involving three boys who were lingering around the park across from the church at dusk, chatting to pass the time until their confirmation class at six. The pastor, who had issued a strict order not even to go *near* the park, walked over with his blood boiling and decreed, "From this day on, you are not my confirmation students!"

This sudden expulsion prompted an outcry from the boys' parents, but the pastor defended his decision as the only means to combat a growing menace. "For some time," he wrote, "we have had a terrible nuisance in our city park in Eilbek, which has become a rendezvous point for youthful gangs, who through wild and shameless carrying on have brought a bad aura to this place and disgusted decent people. Unfortunately, one sees not a few upper-grade students in the gangs, which attack young girls, who for their part are openly willing to let it happen to them, in fact go to the park in crowds willingly seeking this experience."[40]

The park disturbances that so exasperated Pastor von Ruckteschell took place several years after Karen's confirmation. Had they occurred in her own time, she probably would have taken part with relish. The controversy might have added some excitement to the classes; as it was she found them boring as well as disappointing. Earlier, when her friend Tuti had taken classes with a "very liberal-minded minister,"[41] it had caused a quarrel and rift in their friendship. She explains in her diary: "I was at the time rather narrow-minded in matters of faith. (I really had never reflected much about such things.)"[42] But at fourteen she seeks broader, less literal, interpretations of Scripture than either her father or Pastor von Ruckteschell would countenance. She is attracted to the ideas of the liberal "Pastor N.," whom she hears about from her friend Anita. "I heard from Anita, who is to be confirmed by Pastor N., that Christ's miracles were in part added in later writings and in part can be explained, for example, his healing of the sick through the power of his personality and the firm belief of the people in him. . . . Pastor N.'s confirmation lessons must be very interesting. I wish ours weren't so horribly dull."

Powerful fathers on earth, Wackels and Pastor von Ruckteschell, thwarted Karen's attempts to love a heavenly father. Only Herr Schulze, the one good father surrogate, provided a way to belief. Ultimately, though, even Herr Schulze felt the lash of Karen's growing skepticism. The day after hearing a "heavenly lecture" by Anita's Pastor N. on the meaning of the Old Testament for the modern Christian, she managed to anger her favorite teacher. "Something dreadful happened today," she wrote in January of 1901. "I'm afraid my adored Herr Schulze is angry with me." The class had been discussing the "(so called) proofs Paul cites of Christ's resurrection, namely that he appeared to various people (after his death) and also to Paul. I dared to express the view that Paul had been in an overwrought nervous condition and so imagined he saw this luminous vision. I implied that this was really no proof of Christ's resurrection."

Apparently this was too much, even for the liberal Herr Schulze. "I don't know if he misunderstood me or what, but in short, he got quite excited and said, slapping his Bible shut, that we could just as well busy ourselves with something else . . . and delivered a severe sermon to me. It is true that he didn't address himself specifically to me, but of course it was meant for me. If I were not still totally dumbfounded, I should long ago have despaired, for the consciousness of the feeling that he is angry with me is terrible. I think I shall be very much embarrassed at his next lesson."[43]

By the day of her confirmation, April 26, 1901, Karen had become a self-avowed hypocrite. "My day of confirmation was not a day of blessing for me," she wrote in her diary. "On the contrary, it was a great piece of hypocrisy, for I professed belief in the teachings of Christ, the doctrine of love, with hatred in my heart." As in the past, her unbelief was fused in her mind with her anger toward her father, who happened to be home for the event. This anger was now augmented by an immense dislike for Pastor Ruckteschell. Leading up to the confirmation were "indescribably difficult days provided for Mother and us by the master of the house and by Pastor R. I don't want to write about it, for pen and paper would rebel against writing down anything so coarse and mean, committed furthermore by Christians (even orthodox ones). But it is conceivable that I could . . . hate the Pastor."[44]

Because of Pastor von Ruckteschell's large following, Karen's confirmation class was huge: one hundred and two girls filed into the Friedenskirche in their white dresses that day to be confirmed.[45] But for Karen it was not a day of triumph. "I long for the faith, firm as a rock," she wrote, "that makes oneself *and others* happy. I hardly dare to love Christ, he who was love, the pure one, although he stands before me as a glorious ideal. I hardly dare to pray, for I don't want to be hypocritical. Until I feel strong enough to pray sincerely and to act accordingly, I would rather not pray at all."[46]

Karen Danielsen never overcame her religious doubts, or gave up her longing for a faith transcending reason. More and more, however, her search for deep and true experience changed from a religious into an intellectual quest. Reading and study, which she pursued with the encouragement of Herr Schulze, became her Holy Grail. "School," she wrote in her diary after a particularly difficult period at home, "is the only true thing after all."[47]

2

School

Later in life Karen Horney told several people, including her daughters and a *New York Post* reporter, that she had traveled to South America as a nine-year-old girl on one of her father's steamships. It was on this trip, Karen told one daughter, that she saw and tasted bananas for the first time. There is reason to doubt this story, however. For one thing, there is no mention of such a trip in her diaries, even though it would have lasted six months and caused a major interruption in her schooling. And how could Karen, a young woman so alive to new experiences, keep an adventure of such proportions entirely out of her diary, even after the event?

Furthermore, it seems unlikely that Captain Danielsen, a man of the utmost propriety, would have approved of such a plan. Karen would probably have been the only female on board, along with a crew of about forty rough-and-ready sailors, given to spells of cursing and drinking. Surely the captain's friend Pastor von Ruckteschell would have advised against putting a young lady in their midst.

Then too the voyage was often rough and dangerous. Steamships at the turn of the century were still relatively new and unsophisticated. Until 1889 ships under sail predominated in Hamburg commerce, and steamships were often equipped with sails for insurance. And for good reason. The early steam engine required prodigious amounts of coal, so fueling stops were essential. And fires and explosions on board the coal-fired behemoths were not uncommon. During the first thirty years after transatlantic steamship travel began, in 1848, 144 steamships were lost at sea.[1]

The route Captain Danielsen traveled held its own unique challenges. He captained six ships over his thirty-one years, heading them down and across the South Atlantic to Montevideo, in Uruguay, where they stopped for coaling, then proceeding by way of the inside passage through the Strait of Magellan, one of the most treacherous routes in the world.[2] "By the time the inside passage is reached," as a contemporary naval officer noted, "the chances are it will be thick and unsettled, with every prospect of a foul gale. When the storm breaks it is tremendous; in no other part of the world do winds blow harder or seas rise higher; lofty ships carry low sails hereabouts, and steamers frequently have to lie to."[3]

Even though it seems unlikely that young Karen Danielsen made this long and difficult trip with her father, her claim suggests that, for all her anger at him, there was a part of her that wished to be close to him and to see the wide world he knew. "What someone thinks he remembers from his childhood," as Freud noted in an essay on Leonard da Vinci, "is not a matter of indifference" but can "cloak priceless pieces of evidence about the most important features of his mental development."[4] There is no doubt that Karen traveled to the New World many times over in her imagination. She would have had her father's stories to take her there. Even the severe Captain Danielsen must have told tales of such an astonishing land, so utterly remote from the civilized conventions of Hamburg life. Perhaps he told of the mountainous glaciers of blue and green ice that he passed by in the Strait of Magellan or of the flora and fauna he encountered in port: lion monkeys and parrots, roses and exotic flowers in a profusion unknown in Europe. Probably, like most seafarers, Captain Danielsen brought back souvenirs: a piece of buffalo-horn carving or one of the highly prized ponchos made by the women of Chile from the coat of the guanaco, a species of llama. The captain might have told of human encounters astonishing to the European mind. In Brazil, black slaves were still being bought and sold at auction. In Tierra del Fuego, the wild land at the southernmost tip of South America, it was still possible to encounter naked Indians traveling in canoes who would come up alongside European ships offering sea-otter skins in exchange for tobacco.[5]

Whatever Karen learned from her father about the world beyond Hamburg was greatly augmented and embellished by her own imagination and by reading. Storytelling became a means of escaping when her father made life at home difficult. "I tell myself stories all the time, now more than ever," she wrote in January of 1901. "This story-telling is really awfully funny. I imagine what I would like to have. As chief characters appear my crushes and myself. The theme of the stories is similar, but each time I weave in whatever I have experienced or read." This description of her fantasy life is immediately followed by a comment on harsh reality: "Father is very hard to get on with now. He complains about everything, meals, clothes, behavior. Then he delivers conversion sermons, says endless, rather stupid, prayers every morning, etc."[6]

Karen's best-loved resource for her flights into fantasy was the stories of a German adventure writer, Karl Friedrich May. Karl May's books, which began appearing in Germany in the 1880s, were set in exotic places—some in May's version of the Near East, others in North Africa. But the most popular, and the ones that most intrigued young Karen Danielsen, were set in the American West. May, who had never visited the United States, provides such American-sounding place names as Antelope Hills and Fort Union, as well as the requisite good guys—a white man who has earned the nickname Shatterhand because of his lightning draw and aim with a gun, and an Indian named Winnetou, a noble savage capable of swimming faster, creeping through woods more softly, and covering his tracks more deftly than any other mortal. Together Shatterhand and Winnetou take on the evil forces and triumph—repeatedly.

May's white protagonist, Shatterhand, is a German, ridiculed as a "greenhorn" from the moment he arrives in the Wild West. Yet his European education—and rifle practice—allow him to outsmart all his enemies, to the surprise of the locals. And what seems to amaze everyone most of all is that he has learned the better part of what he knows from *books*.

The bookish Shatterhand's triumphs would have had a particular appeal for Karen Danielsen, who often felt powerless in the face of the quarrels at home and used books as a means of escape. Her favorite character, however, seems to have been the young Apache warrior Winnetou, who had learned all he knew in the wild and who became the German-born Shatterhand's blood brother.[7]

By the time she was fifteen Karen Danielsen had already perceived that the Karl May books were simpleminded. Other books, as she noted in her diary, had more lasting appeal. "Among the numerous books I have got hold of there are only a few that keep me fascinated for any length of time.... Books that do can carry me away enraptured; I read them once, twice, after a short time again—and again." Among these books she includes the historical novels of Joseph von Schefel and Felix Dahn—long, detailed, romantically colored sagas of German antecedents, based on Roman, Ostrogothic, and medieval history. In these books too she finds heroes. Interestingly, she is particularly attracted to the Emperor Julian in Dahn's three-volume historical novel *Julian the Apostate.* Julian, who lived from 331 to 363 A.D., was the last Roman emperor to oppose Christianity. Karen writes breathlessly of her enthusiasm for him. "Julian—I'm always furious when people speak contemptuously about him. His personality has always interested me, and now since I have read Dahn's book, I'm all aflame with enthusiasm about him. He has become my 3rd historical enthusiasm. I have set him beside Brutus and Napoleon."

But even in the midst of her excitement about her new reading discoveries the Karl May books remain her comfortable old favorites. She writes:

I think I can say that the novels I have read haven't done me any harm. Some of course fascinated me for the moment—the next day I didn't think about them any more... my favorites are the Karl May travel novels. After having read... and heard a lot that's clever, those are really the nicest sort of thing one can read—even when one is tired out. 1. They are not love stories, 2. they are not so awfully stupid, 3. they are *very exciting,* 4. they are nicely stimulating and humorously written—whether everything happened the way he writes it, I don't care.[8]

Young Karen's sentimental attachment to the Karl May stories persisted. Thirty years later one of the few childhood keepsakes she brought with her to America was a pennant emblazoned *Winnetou.*

Winnetou and Shatterhand had staying power because they invited the young Karen Danielsen not just to imagine them but to *become* them in fantasy. The emperors Napoleon and Julian might inspire, but they were, after all, real historic figures, and male ones at that. Winnetou and Shatterhand were total fictions, and even though they were males, their indifference to romance and their nonviolent methods rendered them sufficiently neuter to appeal to girls as well as boys. Alone or with her fellow Karl May enthusiasts Erik and Tuti, Karen could indulge in her own versions of the Winnetou and Shatterhand adventure by the hour. With Tuti, a lifelong friend whose full name was Gertrud Holmberg, Karen even swore "blood brotherhood *à la* Karl May." "We very carefully slit a finger," she wrote later, "till a microscopically small drop came out, diluted it with water, and drank, brrr. . . . "⁹

It may well have been this long-standing habit of imagining that allowed Karen during these same years to envision a path for herself that had been uncharted by any German female before her time. Certainly when she wrote in her diary of the future she planned for herself, she seemed to have an almost visual sense of herself in it. As in a Karl May story, she was there, playing the role. In July of 1899, while sick with the flu during a family vacation on the North Sea, she writes that "a very nice Doctor Dugge took care of me. Once when we were taking a walk he told me a whole lot of things about the study of medicine. Now I see my goal to study medicine more clearly before me. First years of splendid but strenuous work, then being able to serve mankind through curing diseases. When I was younger, it was the large amount of money I would then possess that attracted me, now it's something else, something more precious."¹⁰

The entire plan is laid out so matter-of-factly that it seems perfectly sensible; but in fact for a woman to become a doctor was almost as improbable as one of Winnetou's feats of daring. To begin with, at the moment she wrote, there was not even a Gymnasium course for girls in Hamburg. Without the six-year Gymnasium training there was no chance of taking and passing the *Abitur,* the necessary preliminary to university admission. Furthermore, in 1899, there wasn't a single university in Germany that admitted women. Yet in her imagination she was already Dr. Karen Danielsen, out there in the world curing diseases and saving lives.

In August of the same year, when Berndt returned to Gymnasium, Karen wished in her diary that she could take his place. But instead of dwelling on her envy, she turned to the fantasy provided by an amusement park in the city, billed as a "Mountain Trip in the Tyrol." "Yesterday we climbed the 'Tyrolese Mountains'. . . .

Now people are even building mountains. It is magnificent. It is supposed to remain 5 years." Then, returning to her own dream for the future: "And how far along will I be in 5 years? In the Gymnasium?"[11] A week later her mother writes to Hannover, a few hours from Hamburg, where Gymnasium classes for girls have recently become available. Once again Karen's mind races forward to the moment of fulfillment. "I wanted to go right away to the Gymnasium for girls," she writes, "in my thoughts I was there already."[12]

Then reality comes crashing in. "I had not taken Father into account. My 'precious father' forbade me any such plans once and for all." And yet young Karen never lets reality dampen her spirits for long.

Of course he can forbid me the Gymnasium, but the wish to study he cannot. My plan for the future is this:

1. Stay with Mother till Michaelmas (i.e. 29 September), and then take my 1st exam.
2. From Michaelmas 1901 to Easter 1902 to Paris.
3. From Easter 1902 to 1905 to Wolfenbüttel [for training as a teacher].
4. A couple of years as a teacher or tutor and preparing myself for final exams and medicine, on my own hook.
5. And ultimately: doctor.

You see, dear diary, Fate will have an easy time with me, for I prescribe everything for him.

Karen's plan to enter teaching, the only profession truly open to women, would probably have been deemed admirable and sensible by her father and other adults. But to travel to Paris at sixteen, a young girl alone, and live there for seven months? To study medicine "on her own hook," take the state exams, and become a doctor? These two plans were equally wild and improbable. Most unrealistic of all, of course, is the idea that she will "prescribe everything" for fate. Only in her own imagination does she have such power.

Yet, while she could not order fate around, she did seem to have it on her side. Had she been born even a year earlier, she might have lived a very disappointed life. But as it happened, Germany was changing just quickly enough to accommodate her. The 1890s in Germany were a time of social and political ferment. Bismarck had just been forced to retire, and earlier laws forbidding Socialist activity had lapsed. The society was becoming more urban, more industrial. And as conditions became more crowded and difficult, the impulse for social reform spread.

Among those who began to agitate for a change were women. German women had even less power in their society in the 1890s than their European and American counterparts. At home the wife was not viewed by civil law as a "legal person." She could not take a job or sign a contract without her husband's permission. She had no legal say in decisions about her own children. She couldn't enroll the children in school. Even if she earned money, as women increasingly did in this period, it was not hers to keep but her husband's.

In public life too women were considerably less well off than their contemporaries in other Western countries. As in most nations, they were unable to vote. But in most parts of the German Empire they were also forbidden to participate in public meetings. This law was forcibly applied in Prussia, where political meetings at which women dared to speak, or were merely in attendance, were broken up by the police.[13]

The philosophy that underlay this uniquely discriminatory system was well articulated by Kaiser Wilhelm II. Speaking at Königsberg in 1910, he said:

> Our women...should learn that the principal task of the German woman lies not in the field of assemblies and associations, not in the achievement of supposed rights, with which they can do the same things as men, but in quiet work in the house and in the family. They should bring up the younger generation above all else to obedience and respect for their elders. They should make it clear to their children and their children's children that what matters today is not living one's life at the expense of others, achieving one's own aim at the expense of the Fatherland, but solely and exclusively committing all one's mind and strength to the good of the Fatherland.[14]

In other words, any woman with aspirations for herself was selfish and unpatriotic. In a militaristic society women were expected to produce only soldiers and little mothers.

Beginning in the 1890s, some dissenting voices were beginning to challenge this catechism of the ruling elite. In 1895 a Socialist, August Bebel, introduced a motion in the Reichstag to grant suffrage to women. That same year a feminist newspaper, *Die Frauenbewegung* (The Women's Movement), began publication in Berlin. *Die Frauenbewegung* sought to unite the various classes and

interests that had emerged in Germany. The first editorial promised to give equal attention to the "battle for equal education,"
essentially a middle-class struggle, and the "battle for equal pay,"
which was of greater concern to working-class women. "The spiritual and material situation in which [woman] finds herself," declared the new paper, "will be described in these pages."[15]
Women's organizations, which had previously limited themselves
to charity work among the poor, began to lobby for their own
interests in the 1890s. The more impatient among their ranks
broke off and formed new, more radical organizations.

The first fruits of this new militancy came in the area of
women's education. Until the 1890s public education for girls was
virtually nonexistent in Germany. Unlike the boys' Gymnasium,
which received government support, secondary education for girls
was private and focused on home economics, child care, religion,
perhaps elementary pedagogy, with "aesthetic" subjects thrown in.
Until 1894, when the first Gymnasium for girls opened in the relatively liberal southern state of Baden, it was not possible for a girl
to take a college-preparatory course of study in German.[16] It
would be another seven years before any German university admitted women to degree programs.

Even a family of means had few educational options for daughters. "I attended the best possible schools in my youth," wrote the
German feminist Hedwig Dohm in 1873, "and they were the most
terrible possible."[17] Many middle-class girls attended *höhere Töchterschulen* (literally, "upper daughter schools"), where they learned,
as the German essayist Fanny Lewald noted in 1870, too
little of too much.

People say to us women that our knowledge is superficial, and they're
entirely right—but the way in which we are taught in the "higher
Töchterschulen" (the mere name is already an insipidity) is designed to
make us superficial. In a few years, with only slight effort, we're supposed to learn what young men are allowed ten or twelve years for and
what's more we're supposed to perchance become piano virtuosos between our eighth and fifteenth years, learn English, French and Italian,
draw from nature, become experienced and practiced in fine handwork
and household skills. Since that is a clear impossibility we are given a
little bit of everything and we come out of the schools as one emerges
from a fifteen-course dinner: overstuffed and at bottom not satisfied;
full of fancies, full of self-overvaluation and with a true terror of our
ignorance if one fine day the harsh reality of life's necessities should

intrude on us and, with its pale earnest face, call out: "My elegant Fräulein! My pure Salon vision! Take care of yourself now please in the real world!"[18]

By the 1890s progressives in German society were starting to respond to such criticisms of girls' education. Certainly the Convent School, where Karen Danielsen began studying at about thirteen, provided a lot more serious courses than the finishing school of Fanny Lewald's complaint. Karen even managed to get herself excused from what training there was for future ladies of leisure. "I am excused from technical subjects at my doctor's wish," she writes. "I was very glad about this too, since I am very clumsy at drawing and needlework."[19] Since Karen's health seems elsewhere to be perfect—certainly her eyes and fingers work well enough for piano lessons and even for sewing outfits for her favorite doll—one suspects the doctor's excuse tells more about her priorities than her health.

Fortunately the Convent School placed the emphasis on academic subjects: not only French and English but history and natural sciences. Most important, the teachers at the Convent School seem to have encouraged their girls to take themselves seriously. It was there that Karen began to think that she might put her intelligence to some good use. "Earlier, when I was still in private school," she reflects in her diary, "I did not think about the future at all. Then, when I went to the Convent School, I wanted to become a teacher. Then I went beyond that, and wanted to study."[20]

What Karen means by "private school" here is mystifying, since the Convent School, like most girls' schools of that period, was undoubtedly a private school as well, struggling along without official status or support. Although "Convent" suggests some church involvement, it is more likely that the school was simply named after its location on Convent Street, a block away from Karen's home. All of this, however, is pure conjecture, since the Convent School, unlike boys' schools of the same period, leaves no trace of its existence in the public records of the Hamburg State Archives.

A vivid testimonial to life at the Convent School is provided, however, by the diaries of Karen Danielsen. There the special events of the Convent School are duly noted: a class trip by steamer on the Elbe to a country town, a school celebration for Goethe's hundred and fiftieth birthday. But it is often small occurrences at school that prove most exciting, particularly when they involve an unexpected brush with a male teacher. "The great event in school today," Karen writes in June of 1899, "was that we were photographed. Frl. Schöne stood in front of me, Dr. Dietrich sat beside me. I don't really know whether I'm glad about the second fact."[21]

In her studies anything less than an *A* is considered a terrible failure. "Thank God I got an 'A' on my English homework," she writes. And a few months later: "I got only 'B+' for my essay, which makes me pretty mad, but nobody got an 'A' and that consoles me somewhat."[22] At times she can be generous toward those for whom school is more difficult. When her friend Tuti has trouble with French, she tutors her with dramatic results. "I got an 'A' on my French test," she reports, "and, what is better still, Tuti also got an 'A,' for the first time, I believe."[23]

At other times Karen's charity sounds false and condescending, as when she discusses her classmate Lisbeth H., "the stupidest and worst in our class. She has got herself all snarled up in lies and bad behavior, poor child. How sorry I am for her."[24] Later Karen even has an argument with her friend Tuti about the Lisbeth H. problem. Tuti, it seems, has been "too harsh with her and then I feel morally obligated to protect her. That makes Tuti angry with me. . . . I act according to, 'What Jesus has given me is worthy of love.'"[25] But Karen can't sustain such an angelic pose for long. A few weeks later she reports that "Lisbeth H. is not coming back, fortunately for her and for us."[26] So much for Christian charity.

Even at fourteen Karen's idealizations of people are tempered by an innate realism. Her thumbnail sketches of her teachers already show her to be a keen observer of humankind.

We really have awfully nice teachers [she tells her diary]. I'll describe their characters for you.

1. Herr Schulze, for history and religion. Heavenly, i.e. interesting, clever, quiet (almost imperturbable), naive, liberal views, not petty, a little too exact and thorough, trusting (almost too much so), selfless, charming father and friend, lovable, ironic, interested in us, his pupils, kindly disposed, etc., etc. . . .

2. Dr. Dietrich, for geography and natural sciences. Treats us like recruits, rather rough, quite handsome, rather boring lessons, not pedantic and fussy, extremely unfair, outside school very jolly and nice, natural, vain, and severe.

3. Dr. Karstens, for German. Frl. Emmerich's favorite, moderately good lessons, fussy, strict, frightfully precise in correcting composi-

tions, a hair-raising declaimer... polite, fair. Speaks peculiarly, for instance "g" sounds like "j."

4. Frl. Banning, for French (the ladies should have come first). Angelic, charming, interesting, clever, lovable, not strict, natural, opposite of pedantry and fussiness, unfortunately nervous, at times rather shy, delightful, like a sensitive plant (I believe it comes from nervousness).

5. Frl. Emmerich, class teacher for English. Very nice, clever, interesting, obliging, pretty fair, coquettish (with Dr. Karstens), trusting (rather too much), somewhat untidy, careless, the nicest classroom teacher one could imagine.[27]

Enamored as she often is, Karen manages still to see weaknesses as well as strengths in all her beloved subjects. Another adolescent diarist might limit herself to one or two adjectives per teacher. Karen, like a portraitist, adds one tint, then another, to bring the picture to life. One can almost see the untidy Fräulein Emmerich flirting with the frightfully precise declaimer Dr. Karstens. Or the vain, handsome Dr. Dietrich, who treats the girls like recruits, calling the class to attention. One can almost see too the quiet smile of the diarist, collecting her impressions at her desk in the corner.

At least two teachers at the Convent School seem to have noticed that Karen Danielsen was worthy of special attention. Herr Schulze, her first love, encouraged her to read in a depth unusual for a fifteen-year-old. When someone gives her a history book she immediately decides to exchange it for Herr Schulze's recommendation: "Beitzke's *Freiheitskriege* [Wars of Independence], three fat volumes only for the years 1813 to 1814. My mouth is watering already, it's going to be such a pleasure."[28] Herr Schulze, at least, wanted more than a superficial drawing-room education for bright girls.

The second important mentor at the Convent School was the "rather shy, delightful" Fräulein Banning, who taught French. As with Herr Schulze, Karen was infatuated with Fräulein Banning's person, more than her teaching. "I think I shall die of enthusiasm," she wrote in February of 1901. "Frl. Banning has been added to Herr Schulze. But she really is charming. For the last few days I have been taking my poetry album [a sort of autograph book in which friends entered sentiments] along to school, to have it inscribed by her. But I don't find the courage to ask her."[29]

Fräulein Banning was the first woman to make Karen's list of real-life and literary heroes. And she was the most timid—"a sensitive plant," in Karen's words. But Karen's crush on her came at a time when her own courage was about to be tested. In December of 1900, Gymnasium classes for girls were offered in Hamburg for the first time. And in January, after a period of intense lobbying in the Danielsen household, Wackels was persuaded to allow Karen to attend. Karen's dream of Gymnasium was coming true after all. It was natural at such a time for Karen to seek a mentor more like her—a woman, to begin with, who had a career and an independent life. And as much as she admired boldness in her fantasies, the prospect of breaking new ground by attending Gymnasium classes for girls probably made her feel at least as timid as Fräulein Banning.

The first announcement of a plan for girls' Gymnasium classes in Hamburg appeared in the *Hamburger Fremdenblatt* and other newspapers in the city in December of 1900.[30] The goal of the classes, which were to be given under the auspices of the Hamburg Association for the Furtherance of Women's Education and Women's Study, were twofold. First, to give girls the education necessary to pass the *Abitur* at the end of five years; second, to "give girls an education that is the equivalent of that boys receive in a Realgymnasium"[31] To enter, students had to have completed nine years of a girls' school or pass an entrance exam.

No sooner had the announcement appeared in the papers than dissenting voices were heard. Such radicals as Lida Gustava Heymann criticized the Gymnasium classes as imitative and superficial. They were nothing more than a cram course, Heymann protested, which provided, in the shortest time possible, just enough Greek, Latin, and math to get girls through the *Abitur*. Heymann and her group, Frauenwohl (Women's Welfare), wanted far more comprehensive change. Shortly after the Gymnasium classes were announced, Frauenwohl proposed a school for girls that would truly reform education. *Their* school, called the Reformed School, would have a freer atmosphere. Passing the *Abitur* would be a mere corollary of the main goal: the full development of the child. Eventually the Reformed School would be coeducational. Separate education, the radical reformers believed, could never be equal. And sexual stereotypes would never be eliminated until men and women were educated together.[32] "Here," wrote one reformer, "where they strive with one another in the same direction and see each other develop, here they could learn to believe in one another, and to truly respect the opposite sex."[33]

Frauenwohl tried hard to attract Hamburgians to its reform plan.[34] But in the end only a few families were ready to send their daughters on a coeducational adventure in which passing the *Abitur* was a secondary consideration. Indeed, there were many in Hamburg who thought girls' Gymnasium classes, which copied boys', were too dangerous a departure.

One month after the announcement of Gymnasium classes for girls, an editorial in the *Hamburger Fremdenblatt* declared:

> We are not of the opinion that boys' and girls' schools should be organized in exactly the same way. Though we fully agree that the spiritual capacity of both sexes is the same, the same is not true of the goals and the receptivity for particular subjects. To instruct boys and girls on the same level, with the same method, with the hope of reaching the same goal, is generally viewed as a psychological and pedagogical monstrosity, which will, most importantly, bear bitter fruit in our community and family life. We require a different history and geography for our daughters, a different mathematics and natural science than for our sons and also we ought to handle the instruction in German and foreign . . . languages differently, in harmony with the female perceptive faculty.[35]

A few families, however, welcomed the chance to provide promising daughters with the same courses long available to sons. In the eight days following the first announcement in the Hamburg papers a number enrolled their daughters. They were particularly pleased, according to one newspaper report, that girls wouldn't have to travel to other cities anymore to get a Gymnasium education. "Many parents," according to one newspaper report, "greet this preparatory establishment for university with joy, since it offers them the chance to give their studious daughters the same education their sons receive, without their having to leave the parents' house at an age when they most need to be at home."[36]

News of the girls' Gymnasium classes reached the Danielsen family at a time already alive with new prospects. Berndt was about to finish Gymnasium, take the *Abitur*, and then leave home, for the first time, to do his military service. Karen was on the brink of confirmation at the Friedenskirche. And the family was about to move from Eilbek to the idyllic, semirural village of Reinbek, some kilometers farther from the center of Hamburg. The Danielsens had moved three times during Karen's first fifteen years but always in Eilbek and always on the same street.[37] The move to Reinbek, where they had spent the previous summer and where Karen's adored teacher Herr Schulze lived, was more drastic. It is difficult to imagine why the move was made. The captain would be leaving his familiar church and his friend Pastor von Ruckteschell. Sonni, in her unhappiness, may have liked the idea of a change. But the only person with an obvious motive for urging the move was Karen. When the decision was made she was ecstatic. "Heavenly!! Heavenly!! Heavenly!!" she wrote in her diary on January 9, 1901. "We're moving to Reinbek, too marvelous. How glad I am. I'll tell 'him' tomorrow. What will be the expression on his face?"[38]

The very next day she learned about the Gymnasium classes. "I'm furious at myself," she wrote. "No sooner am I happy about Reinbek when another wish comes up in me, a burning desire. For in Hamburg a Gymnasium course is beginning at Easter, 4 or 5 years leading to the Abitur. I'd like to get there at Easter. Oh, wouldn't that be wonderful!! But Father..."[39]

Over the next nine days talk of Gymnasium filled the house. On the same day Karen heard the news three of Sonni's friends "came one after the other... to work on Mother to send me to the Gymnasium. Mother spoke with Father afterward. He doesn't seem opposed to the matter itself, for him it's a question of money. So my chances have improved enormously. Besides that Berndt heard a lecture on 'the woman question' by a gentleman who greatly praised the Gymnasium for girls." Afterward Berndt told Wackels "the whole lecture." Aunt Clara was primed as well, so that when Wackels went to visit, she "will work on him too. Today Berndt is going to a lady who can inform us about admissions, age, courses, etc. I believe more and more that I 'must' get there."[40]

The next day she has more facts. "My chances for the Gymnasium are getting better. I already know more about it. It's five years and begins with Obertertia [ninth grade]. We don't need to know any Latin or mathematics. Once Father has digested the monstrous idea of sending his daughter to the Gymnasium, Mother will talk with him further. He is approachable now."[41]

After six days her impatience had made her vitriolic.

This uncertainty makes me sick. Why can't Father make up his mind a little faster? He, who has flung out thousands for my stepbrother Enoch, who is both stupid and bad, first turns every additional penny he is to spend for me 10 times in his fingers. And we did make it clear to him that he has to feed me only as long as I attend school. Once I have my diploma I most certainly don't want another penny from

> him. He would like me to stay at home now, so we could dismiss our maid and I could do her work. He brings me almost to the point of cursing my good gifts.[42]

Was her father treated to a taste of Karen's outrage—a cold stare or an angry look? Or perhaps even sharp words? In any case, the next day he granted his permission.

"It's really true" she wrote on January 19, "at Easter I'm going to the Gymnasium. Father has just decided, when Mother handed him a document drawn up in verse, in which I promise that after I graduate he need do nothing for me. Oh, how happy I am!! And thankful!! First to the good Lord, for the fine gifts, then to Mother for her warm intercession and the way she handled it, then to Father for this permission!! Hurray!!"[43]

Now that her sights were raised, the Convent School began to seem disgracefully easy. She suddenly found it "unbelievable" that she had gotten an *A* for an eight-page paper she had "rattled off in two hours" on the last day.[44] And yet, while it was easy enough to dismiss the schoolwork, the people of the Convent School and the meaning the place had acquired in her life would be much harder to forget. The Convent School had been the "one true thing" in her life, the place where she could escape from her parents' unhappiness, where she found people worthy of her respect, even idolatry. There was Herr Schulze, of course, her "inner God." And Fräulein Banning as well. And there was, increasingly, a belief in her own "good gifts," gifts they had helped her to discover. Not surprisingly, Karen's last two months at the Convent School were taken up with the task of saying goodbye.

Sometimes she acknowledges her sadness. "School gets finer every day," she writes toward the end of February, "and more divine, alas, when I think that I can only enjoy it for 3 weeks more (boo-hoo!!)."[45] She writes of how much she will miss her teachers: "Ah, how divine he is," she writes of Herr Schulze. "And now I only have 19 more lessons from him. This thought is dreadful to me."[46]

Interspersed with these laments, however, are descriptions of a series of quarrels with her teachers, quarrels suggesting that Karen may have been trying not to care. Karen had gotten in trouble before at the Convent School but never as frequently as during these last months. It was in this period that she infuriated Herr Schulze by telling him there was no proof of Christ's resurrection.

A few weeks later, only a week after declaring her crush on Fräulein Banning, she managed to anger her as well. First she left her exercise book at home, and "as this was the second time" it had happened, Fräulein Banning "became so annoyed that she postponed the writing of the composition." Two days later Fräulein Banning assigned a theme that Karen considered "quite out of my line, though to be honest, I must admit that I could have done all right if I had wanted to. But I didn't in the least want to, and I made no effort." When Fräulein Banning saw that Karen wasn't writing, "she shook her wise head right at me, so that I finally wrote three little sentences. Then I went back to doing nothing. Angrily and abruptly she told the class to hand in the compositions since some of us were just wasting time. During the lesson she treated me very coldly. I did have a bad conscience. At 11 o'clock I went to her to ask her what extra work I should do. She coolly told me and then said: 'Tell me, Kaya, why didn't you write?' As I was silent, she continued: 'Honestly now, you just didn't feel like it.'"

Karen explained that she didn't like the theme topic, to which Fräulein Banning responded, laughing, "But unfortunately one can't always do what one likes, and to get to the heart of the matter, I will tell you what I think. You were being obstinate!" With that, Fräulein Banning walked off, leaving Karen "standing there deeply hurt by this expression, which one really uses only when speaking to children, but also depressed and sad that 'she' was cross with me."[47]

In the case of Herr Dietrich, the science teacher, Karen managed to provoke a fight that eliminated the necessity for goodbyes. Writing retrospectively in April, under the heading "Difficult and Eventful Days," she describes her set-to with Herr Dietrich.

Saturday the 16th of March we had a physics lesson with Dr. Dietrich. He was fixing an iron plate for an experiment and laid it down all crooked. Hertha suddenly said: "It's crooked." Käthe: "It's quite crooked." I: "It's altogether crooked." He was furious and lectured us severely. Brrr!! I.e., I couldn't help laughing. He was frightfully angry with me. I thought it was all over, but not on your life! Tuesday we peeked into the record of our marks, and there stood beside an "A" for my conduct, a "B" from Dr. Dietrich. This left me fairly cold. The last lesson was Dr. Dietrich's. So the gentleman began to give me a sermon on my lack of apology. He said he would give me a "C" for conduct. I already knew better because I had seen the "B". I did apologize after class, because I hoped he would give me an "A" after all, and in this I was not mistaken. But now I had enough of this bad business, I didn't want any more lessons with him.

By a variety of subterfuges, including coming late and claiming illness, Karen managed to avoid the last four classes.[48]

Thus Karen demonstrated just how little she cared about Dr. Dietrich and his discipline. With Herr Schulze, whom she cared for more, she managed a more amicable parting of the ways. "I think I shall always be fond of him," she wrote of Herr Schulze, "even if other crushes command my emotional energies. Herr Schulze is for me a point of rest in the confusion, in the restlessness of life, to which I cling in thought. From now on he is just my real friend, for as teacher I saw him last at the farewell party on the 23rd of March."[49]

When Karen went to visit him after her confirmation and thank him "for everything he had given me in these last years," Herr Schulze was "charming as always." "He said, 'Don't mention it. It gave me such pleasure to work with you, and I learned a lot in the process.'" That evening he came to see her and bring back her poetry album. "He wrote something in it for me, playing on the idea that I must now be called 'Karen' [as opposed to Kaya]. I was frightfully pleased with it."[50]

Judging from the space Karen gives it in the diary, the leave-taking with her new love, Fräulein Banning, assumed an even greater significance than that with Herr Schulze. Fräulein Banning seems to have been, more than anyone else at the Convent School, the person the fifteen-year-old Karen fastened on to help with the transition to Gymnasium. Fräulein Banning was the one who tutored her for extra hours in French so that she'd be ready. "She explains all the rules with the patience of an angel," Karen wrote. "Alas, my heart bleeds at the thought of having to lose her."[51] As a woman, Fräulein Banning could also help with questions of how to look, how to act: when Karen had to recite a poem for the kaiser's birthday, it was Fräulein Banning who practiced bowing with her. And when Karen paid the traditional visit to Fräulein Banning on her birthday, the event is immortalized in her diary.

March 15, 1901

Frl. Banning

Today is "her" birthday, the birthday of Frl. Banning. Happy day, on which she saw the light of the world, etc. I don't want to indulge in sentimentalities. Well, I carved for her a frame for a photograph and brought it to her this morning. I got to her house at 7 minutes to 8, and the maid announced me. At last I was led into her very prettily arranged room.

I: Good morning, Frl. Banning. Hearty congratulations.
SHE: Good morning. How kind of you to come.
(She gives me a kiss! I give her the carved frame.)
I: Please forgive me for this invasion so early in the morning.
SHE: Unfortunately I can't ask you to stay, for I haven't had my coffee yet. (She opens the packet and thanks me for it.) But your photograph belongs in here. Am I not getting that?
I: (Stammered something.)
SHE: Promise me. But keep the promise too. You only have one more week at school. But you'll come and see me at school or here, won't you?
I: Most gladly.

I don't remember what more we said. I'm afraid I have adored her terribly. Anyway I was blissful as I trundled home. I burst into tears on my way for joy and sorrow that I shall be losing her soon now.[52]

From their farewells it is easy to see why Herr Schulze and Fräulein Banning were Karen's favorite teachers. How sensitively each of them has managed to leave her with a sense of their admiration and expectations of her! Herr Schulze tells her that she must no longer be the little girl Kaya but the young woman Karen. And Fräulein Banning, by requesting a photograph, leaves Karen with the feeling that she is a pleasure to behold, a person to be prized for her appearance as well as her intelligence.

Perhaps the teachers were responding to cues from Karen. After all, what must Karen have had in mind when she presented Fräulein Banning with an empty picture frame? Certainly in her diary there are signs that Karen is beginning to want not only to adore but to be adored in return. In the past she may have been content to carry Herr Schulze's coat or his flowers. But now she is beginning to want more.

"Why? Why is everything beautiful on earth given to me, only not the highest thing, not love! I have a heart so needing love, the words apply to me too: To love and be loved/is the highest bliss on earth. Only the first is granted me. Yes, I love Mother, Berndt, Herr Schulze, Frl. Banning, etc., with all my heart. But who loves me??"[53] Karen asked her diary these questions on February 20,

1901, just five weeks before beginning Gymnasium classes in Hamburg. Over the next five years she would discover how much more difficult it is to love and be loved than to worship from afar.

3

"Karen Hamburgensis"

In the spring of 1901 the train to Hamburg assumed a new importance in the life of Karen Danielsen. There had always been trips to the city with the family—to visit Hamburg's elegant shops, for photography sittings, for dinner at Aunt Clara's. With her family she had stopped for refreshment at the Alsterpavillion—the ornate restaurant Hamburgians compared to a Dutch tiled oven—and watched boats bobbing about in the Alster, the big lake at the center of the city. The harbor too would have been familiar from school and family outings along the Elbe, a popular bourgeois pastime. But when Karen began attending Gymnasium classes she became a young lady who daily traveled the thirty-two minutes[1] into the city alone. Until now she had been accountable to someone for every waking hour. Sonni, Herr Schulze, Pastor von Ruckteschell, all had watched over her tenaciously. Now for the first time the Hamburg train was transporting her out of the protected atmosphere of home into the anonymity of a big city. In the streets of Hamburg no one watched her. She in turn was free to look and look again. A Latin epigraph, entered in the frontispiece of one of her diaries, captured this new phase of her life. It read, "Vidi, audivi, legi, feci [I watched, I listened, I read, I acted]." It was signed, "Karen Hamburgensis."[2]

"Karen of Hamburg" was free to discover the great city in all its diversity. She must have walked along the fashionable shopping streets bordering the Alster, observing the graceful ladies promenading under the double protection of hats and parasols, sometimes on the arms of men in Prince Albert suits and silk top hats. But she also went to the museum, attended concerts at the Musikhalle, and above all went to the theater. There she saw Sarah Bernhardt play Schiller and marveled at her "complete command of every movement, every nuance of her voice." She left the theater, as she wrote afterward in her diary, with "a calm quiet feeling of happiness... happiness about such perfection in art."[3]

Behind the obvious symbols of Hamburg's commercial might —the big steamers of the world that docked in the wide harbor and the monumental granite offices of the shipping giant Hapag along the Alster—there was another, more humble Hamburg. Walking, or riding on the platform of the electric tram, one could glance into courtyards of crooked, crumbling half-timbered houses, filled with hanging laundry and the children of large, poor families. At the "Pots and Pans Market" on the Elbstrasse, Jewish merchants shouted Yiddish among themselves as a crush of traders, sailors, and housewives gathered around bargaining for cheap goods with abandon, in the manner of customers at an Oriental bazaar. Karen discovered streets only a few blocks away from the docks where prostitutes catered to the needs of sailors from around the world and husbands from the local middle class. Now, traveling and exploring alone, Karen was free to imagine every possibility. There was even the chance that *she* might be drawn into the action. As she sat on the tram, her eyes might meet those of a passionate stranger. If a conversation were to follow, who would know? Once, as she told her friend Alice, a gentleman *did* follow her on a Hamburg street, though she considered him "impudent" and ignored him.[4]

School paled beside the possibilities now unfolding before her. Right at the beginning she described Gymnasium in her diary as "overwhelming, bewildering" and noted, "I'm only beginning to learn what 'learning' means."[5] But her enjoyment had become grown-up and dispassionate, qualified with "rathers." After three weeks at Gymnasium she was finding Latin and mathematics "rather dry," though she liked them both "quite well." Arithmetic was "rather difficult" for her as usual. She enjoyed the other subjects more, especially German grammar, once the dullest, "now enormously interesting because it has become a broader study of the German language."[6] Even her good grades at the end of the

term failed to excite her, although "everyone said I had the best."
"Well," she concluded, "one's first record in the Gymnasium is
always rather amusing. An 'A' only in history." Better than the
grades, she told her diary, were the monetary rewards that she got
for them, probably from Sonni: three marks for the grades themselves, another three marks for a hat, on which she spent two,
leaving her with four marks for a "perfectly great book."[7]

The old Karl May fantasies were now looked on with amusement as the stuff of childhood. She remembers how she and Tuti
swore blood brotherhood back at the Convent School: "Oh dear,
when one is still young."[8] Crushes too began to lose their appeal in
the new world of the Hamburg Gymnasium. Only when she saw
Herr Schulze or Fräulein Banning did longing "grab with all its
claws."[9] Later, when she went to visit Herr Schulze on his birthday, she found him "horribly boring."[10] When new crushes came
along, Karen gave in to them reluctantly, all the while telling her
diary—which she now called "Kitten"—[11] that she found herself
rather silly. "After Easter," she wrote, "I firmly resolved to go in
for no more enthusiasms, and since then I've already done so a
number of times. . . . Yes, I confess it honestly—I am a stupid
Backfisch with my eternal crushes."[12]

Backfisch, which means literally a fish ready for baking and carries implications of maturity slightly beyond "teenager," is a favorite term in this period. And indeed Karen gives more and more
signs that she is ready for baking—ready for the heat of love and
tired of platonic crushes. By the end of the first term at Gymnasium she is beyond crushes on the teacher. "My favorite subject
now is mathematics," she writes. "And accordingly I have a crush
on Dr. Bohnert? No, Kitten, you've miscalculated this time. I do
like him very much, but a crush?? No, that's something else . . .
just think, I have now entered into a state that you will hardly
understand. I haven't a crush on anybody. That would be miraculous?—but it's true." Perhaps, she guesses, this results from "the
beneficent influence of mathematics" or from being so "old and
sensible." She is, after all, "already 16."[13]

In a pair of photographs taken at Gymnasium, Karen sits at a
table surrounded by ten classmates and a male teacher. Her braid
has been replaced by a very grown-up bun, planted on top of her
head. Her face has thinned, and the intense, almost melancholy,
seriousness of earlier photos has given way here to a mischievous
half smile. The pictures were apparently snapped in a hurry: Karen
and her friend in the foreground are out of focus, and several heads

are blocked out. But they catch Karen's animation as photographs rarely do. In one the girl next to Karen is whispering something in her ear about someone off-camera whom Karen is eyeing with amusement. In the other Karen's friend has assumed an innocent look and stares straight ahead, but Karen is still glancing off, amused, toward the off-camera distraction. The other girls, in contrast, appear to be concentrating on having their pictures taken.

The photographs could serve as a metaphor for Karen's state of mind during this period. Her intense interest had shifted from text to subtext, from what was going on in the classroom to what was going on between classes, after classes, and behind the teacher's back. Classmates, rather than teachers, now became the objects of her fascination. Some intrigued her—like Gertrude Piza, for instance, who had already had a year of Gymnasium in Hannover and who had "a clever, impressive face,"[14] and A. Loewenthal, who "has something dazzling about her, yet unsympathetic."[15]

She was most attracted, it seems, to the girls who were most daring. There was Lisa B., "an interesting *Backfisch* type. Gets crushes on many people like mad, is pretty and rich, but a little superficial, I think."[16] Despite her doubts, Karen was soon joining in Lisa B.'s subterfuges. "In school," she wrote that first summer, "we are carrying on. In English class for instance, I did nothing today but read *die Berliner Range* [The Berlin Tomboy], consumed pears, plums, chocolate, and candy." Lisa B., it seemed, was "the most mischievous." The teacher, Frau Grube, in fact, told Lisa she was going to have her dismissed from English and French.[17]

Karen's most important friend during this period was Alice Hennings. Alice had been at the Convent School with Karen, and they had shared a crush there on Fräulein Banning. But for some reason the friendship didn't flower until Gymnasium, where Karen was immediately struck by Alice's "bright wit."[18] In the beginning their love of Fräulein Banning bound them, and they went to visit her together. But within a year they were united against teachers in a battle for Alice's survival at Gymnasium. In February of 1902 Karen wrote: "Heavy clouds are obstructing the clear sky. Alice, my dear Alice, that child of Nature, who has indeed grown strange through a love-starved youth and wrong upbringing, has been, if not exactly thrown out, nevertheless forced to leave at Easter on account of bad behavior. And what bad behavior? Well, yes, she was unruly before Christmas. Since then she has pulled herself together very much." Apparently Alice had made a remark during class that "these super-clever pedagogues made into a big affair. That means they expect a person to change completely in a few days on command. Oh, cruel tyrants!! How I hate them! How could I ever have a crush on a teacher."[19]

A delegation went to plead with the school's director, Professor Doctor Gustav Wendt, on Alice's behalf. Apparently Professor Wendt showed mercy, because Alice and Karen remained school companions for several years after the threatened expulsion.

Aside from school conspiracies, the subject on which their relationship turned during this period was sex. During the first year Karen, Alice, and others started a newspaper called "A Virginal Organ for Supervirgins," a title that, with its double emphasis on virginity, was a dead giveaway.[20] Virginity, after all, is rarely mentioned except by those who are thinking of giving it up.

It was only a matter of months before Alice provided Karen with her first bite into the "apple of knowledge," confirming her "dark suspicion [of] what that business with the 'stork' was all about."[21]

The momentous conversation, as reported by Karen—complete with dialogue—in her diary, took place on a Monday in February of 1901. It began with Karen telling Alice about the "impudent gentleman" who had followed her. Alice grinned at Karen's indignation and said, *"Sancta simplicitas,* what's wrong with that? Did you go with him?"

Karen looked at her in surprise. "Would you do such a thing? Go with a strange gentleman?"

Alice: "That all depends on how they look. If they look decent and nice, why not?"

Karen: "Don't tell me you meet them half-way?"

Alice: "Hm, not exactly, but if it's something special one walks a little slower, or looks in a shop window or something of that sort."

Alice then went on to tell Karen that as a matter of fact she and Lisa had had such an experience the night before, when they had gotten caught in a downpour with only one umbrella between them. They had waited and waited for a streetcar, but it hadn't come. Then suddenly "a gentleman" had come rushing toward them—"very handsome, very elegant, about 40"—and said they'd better come with him into a café until the rain let up. Feeling "very enterprising and jovial," they took him up on the offer, consumed cakes, and had a fine time. The handsome gentleman turned out to be a writer and, what's more, entirely smitten with Lisa! "He said we were the only sensible girls in the whole of Hamburg," Alice told Karen. "Oh, you know, one joke after another. At first quite innocent. Then he asked me what I thought about love between women, just think how shocking."

Karen innocently (or pseudo-innocently) inquired what could possibly be wrong with girls loving each other, as she and Alice did. Alice countered that that was *not* what this writer fellow, identified simply as B., had had in mind. She then proceeded to give "a long explanation of perversion."

Once that was out of the way, Alice went on to say that in fact Lisa liked B. too and wanted to meet him again that same night. To which Karen replied that she didn't find that very nice behavior, although she didn't know what Lisa might do. To which Alice rejoined, "Now little Karen, don't pretend to be so stupid. If L. goes to his room with him and he asks her, then she will do it, and that of course would be frightful."

Karen was dumbfounded. "No, Alice, it isn't possible. Do you really know these things? I believe I've misunderstood you. You mean L. would do the worst thing a girl can do?"

Alice responded: "Why not? It comes awfully easy. I almost did it myself once." Then Alice gave her an account of the time a man had tried to seduce *her*.

Finally, after a silence, Karen came back: "But if L. were to get a baby..."

To which Alice, implying (or pretending to have) some knowledge of birth control, replied, "Oh, she won't be that stupid," and added, "Actually I don't believe that she'll do it."

Karen was amazed. "I thought such things didn't happen at all in our circles." To which Alice replied with a laugh, "In masses." And then, providing yet another shock, Alice added, "A girl in our class did it—and even with her father."

Karen was "speechless with horror" but not so stunned that she couldn't listen as Alice filled her in on the details of the incest, including the name of the girl.

Thus far Alice had managed to cover lesbianism, seduction, and incest. She had one last shocking topic to address: prostitution. There was an actress, one Frau Doree, who performed in the Hamburg theater and whom both Karen and Alice admired. Now Alice told Karen that "she used to be crazy too. Had one after the other. But what does it matter?" In another theater group there was an actress who had a different man every night until the other members of the troupe had become indignant. But the director had defended her, pointing out that at least she didn't sell herself.

This led Alice right into a description of "those creatures who sell themselves for little money. It was my first glimpse," Karen told her diary, "into that miserable business, prostitution."

That afternoon Karen tried to make small talk at her Aunt Clara's house but was completely preoccupied with the "whole dreadful knowledge" she had acquired all at once from Alice earlier that day. Soon after, in a final blow to her naïveté, Alice told her that Lisa had indeed become B.'s lover. "I say," said Alice, "it's horrible, but I now feel that there's nothing wrong with it." Karen countered with indignation. "How *can* you, Alice, it really is the worst thing one can do." Alice shrugged her shoulders.[22]

There is probably a rule about such conversations as this one Karen had with Alice: they take place only when the listener is ready, and indeed eager, to receive the knowledge they impart. Karen was clearly at that juncture. Indeed, even before Alice's initiation, she had surely known that sexual intercourse, not the stork, brought babies. After all, it was she who pointed out that Lisa might "get a baby" if she went with the gentleman. What was probably new, and definitely shocking, was that girls "in our circles" were contemplating sex before marriage.

Karen's shock, however, didn't last very long. Less daring girls might quickly repress the "dreadful knowledge" and the sexual excitement it aroused. Or they might position themselves until their wedding day on the higher ground Karen initially took with Alice. But Karen, characteristically, followed her passion and her curiosity instead. In the year following the momentous conversation, she set out to discover everything she could about love and sex.

For information she went to her old friend Tuti, former Karl May blood brother, now engaged to be married and therefore "initiated." Whether this meant Tuti had experienced sex or merely had received some adult's orientation lecture is not clear. Biological studies were another source: during this period Karen read Bölsche's *Love Life in Nature* and *Bazillus-Apeman,* by her own admission for this purpose. She developed "a preference" as well for walking in the streets where prostitutes sold sexual favors to the men of Hamburg. And for more sociological detail there were the novels of Maupassant, which Lisa brought to school and Karen devoured during class, and Zola's *Nana,* the story of a beautiful courtesan to the French upper class.[23] It must have been the sensuality of *Nana* that intrigued Karen most, as when Zola describes his subject standing naked before a mirror. "Nana was all covered

with fine hair, a russet down made her body velvety; whilst the
Beast was apparent in the almost equine development of her
flanks, in the fleshy exuberances and deep hollows of her body."[24]

More stimulating even than *Nana* was the work of a poet who
created a sensation in Germany in 1901 with a "little book in the
nude" called *On Cyprus*. The poet, who wrote under the pseudonym
Marie Madeleine, produced torrid verses about "loosened passions"
and "lusts that will not brook delay" that set off a war within Karen
between her senses and her intellect. Karen had a suspicion that
Marie Madeleine's work might be "artificial," "overflowing fantasy." "One's senses," she noted, "exult at her poems in unbridled
delight. One's intellectual nature turns away in disdain."[25]

Marie Madeleine, who later became the Baroness von Suttkoff,
was just Karen's age, seventeen, when she wrote *On Cyprus*. Although turn-of-the-century German critics were shocked by Marie
Madeleine's precocity, the poems suggest a young woman who,
like Karen, was obsessed with sex as an idea rather than as a reality. They are full of surging—"the crimson wine of eager life ran
riot through each tingling vein"—and of climaxes—"I felt my
senses sway and leap/Like sinuous tongues of wind-blown flame."
They often involve a woman whose desire pulls her inexorably
downward into some sort of degradation, as when the poet wishes
to dissolve into the arms of Lucifer. And there is, almost always, a
painful denouement, after the lover grows indifferent. "Some
touch of pity still might lift/Your heart to me could you behold/
My broken body cast adrift/On bitter waters, dead and cold"[26]
What is missing in the poems, and probably in Marie Madeleine's
experience as well, is a flesh-and-blood lover. These are works,
Karen noted, of "undefined longings, blurred."[27]

As a result they served Karen's fantasies, in her uninitiated *Backfisch* state, better than Zola's stark realism. When Marie Madeleine
wrote, "The beating of my heart is all I hear,"[28] she could be describing Karen's agitated, lonely state as well as her own.

In reality, as Karen lamented, "there is nothing in the world so
immaculate as I! Not even the tips of my fingers have been
kissed." But in her fantasy she was "a strumpet." "In my own
imagination there is no spot on me that has not been kissed by a
burning mouth. In my own imagination there is no depravity I
have not tasted, to the dregs."[29]

Karen dates her awakening to sexual reality from the day of the
momentous conversation with Alice, and there is no reason to

contradict her. But enlightenment would have come, with or without Alice's help. Indeed, it was impossible for an intelligent young woman in Hamburg during these years to avoid the facts of sexual life. For Hamburg, beginning in 1901, had become the target of a campaign by Frauenwohl, the radical wing of the feminist movement, to abolish prostitution. This group within Frauenwohl, called the Abolitionists, held protest meetings, made public pronouncements, and generally attracted as much attention as possible to the base passions of men, which, they emphasized, brought about not only the evil of prostitution but also rape and other forms of sexual exploitation of women.

That Karen knew about this debate is evident from one reference in her diary. But it would be safe to assume that she knew even without the diary proof. She couldn't have avoided reading about it: it was a cause both celebrated and derided in every German newspaper and, ultimately, in the Reichstag. In fact, given the enormous turnouts of young women at the meetings of the Abolitionists, it seems likely that she attended at least one of them.

The originator of the Abolitionist movement in Hamburg was Lida Gustava Heymann,[30] the daughter of a prosperous coffee merchant and Hamburg senator. Heymann inherited much of her father's wealth at the time of his death and proceeded to make use of it in charitable work for women: a day nursery, a cheap lunch club for single women, an organization for actresses, and a society for female service employees. By 1898, however, Heymann had turned from good deeds to social protest. Along with other radical feminists, she wanted to put an end to prostitution, an institution she believed to be perpetuated by the state.

The government of Hamburg regulated prostitution through a system known as *Bordellierung,* which involved placing prostitutes in large brothels that the police controlled through the brothel keepers. Such a system came close to being a government-run vice trade and was a natural target for the Abolitionist zeal of Lida Gustava Heymann and her followers.

In 1901, the year Karen began Gymnasium, Heymann and the International Abolitionist Federation launched their Hamburg campaign by filing suit against a brothel keeper, distributing leaflets, and holding public meetings to protest Hamburg's role in prostitution. "Women have remembered their rights," declared Lida Gustava Heymann; "they want to be human beings, and to be a human being means to fight for our rights."[31] Such impassioned pronouncements earned Heymann the title of *das verrückte Frauen-zimmer* (the crazy female) from her detractors.[32]

Hamburg was one of the few cities in the empire where women had the right to assemble for political purposes. But in 1902 the Hamburg police put a stop to all meetings of the Abolitionists, claiming they offended public decency and endangered public order. Predictably, the ban added fuel to the Abolitionists' fire; they merely moved their meetings to the adjoining city of Altona, drawing larger and larger crowds. The Hamburg *General Anzeiger* reported that "the electric tramway carries wagons filled to over-flowing with women from Hamburg to Altona, and the women feel themselves more and more at home and entitled to speak out at these meetings." The Abolitionists, the newspaper observes, would probably not have aroused so much interest with women "otherwise not so strongly moved by such a burning interest in public affairs," if they had been allowed to hold meetings without police interference in Hamburg.[33] As it was, the numbers in at-tendance continued to grow. About 750 women attended one gathering at which Heymann talked on sex education. A crowd of 900 turned out when the Abolitionists protested the acquittal of men involved in the gang rape of a young girl in the Hamburg suburb of Blankenese.

Despite all the attention, the Abolitionists were unable to make even the slightest change in the Hamburg system of *Bordellierung*. They did, however, provoke a public discussion of sexual morality in which, for the first time, the woman's voice was heard.

Karen's attitude toward the Abolitionist movement must be gleaned from one oblique reference in her diary. In February of 1904, shortly after the Abolitionist debate was taken up in the Reichstag, Karen "happened" to find a passage in a book which she wrote down in her diary. It was written in the voice of a woman degrading herself before a man. "Let me grow small, quite small alongside you," goes the incantation, "oh, be the strong man, the big man, the healthy man, the superior human being in whom I can lose myself completely." On it goes in this vein: "Force me to my knees, dearest. For I am a woman ... for just this proud, free independently thinking woman there is no sweeter lot than to be allowed to worship, to bow down in love. Oh, dearest — will you be my master?" Karen finished off the diary entry with one brief but telling quip. The passage, she noted, was "something for Lida Gustava Heymann!"[34]

This brief moment of irony foreshadows Karen Danielsen's

modus operandi in her later psychoanalytic writing. Something bothers her about the essentially puritanical position of Heymann and the Abolitionists. The Abolitionists saw men, and men's unbridled desires, as the sole cause of sexual exploitation in the world. And women, by their lights, were innately incapable of deriving much pleasure from sex. Karen's way of evaluating this Abolitionist position was the one she would continue to use throughout her life: she tested it against her own experience. And because her fantasies and sensations told her that women do experience desire, she poked fun at the Abolitionist position. The fantasy of total male dominance clearly attracted her: it was what she liked in the Marie Madeleine poems, and it may have been what prompted her to walk the streets of prostitution in Hamburg. And while she may not have understood *why* she was attracted, she knew there was more to female sexuality than was dreamt of in the Abolitionist philosophy.

What intrigued her (and this too was a harbinger of things to come) were not so much the *public* questions of morality that the Abolitionists addressed as the private ones, not what was right in general but what was right for the individual woman. How could she be true to her longings and her principles at the same time? This question was not one the Abolitionists cared to deal with. But there were others who started out in the Abolitionist movement yet shared Karen's preoccupation with individual morality. In this same period they broke away and formed the League for Mutterschutz (League for the Protection of Mothers), an organization whose concerns were much closer to Karen's.

The founder and leading light of Mutterschutz, Helen Stöcker, had a life history and sensibility much like Karen's. Stöcker, who was born in 1869, had rebelled like Karen against the narrow religious restraints of her family, then had gone on to study and ultimately travel to Switzerland to obtain a doctorate. Her principal intellectual influence was Nietzsche, whose philosophy she understood as a call to women to live life to the fullest. She credited Nietzsche with replacing the "old life-denying ascetic morality of the Church Fathers," who saw sexual love as "something sinful" and woman as "lowly and impure," with a "life-affirming morality" that frees human beings from guilt and "sanctifies their love." In the beginning this led Stöcker to argue that middle-class women should live life to the fullest by marrying, having children, *and* pursuing education and the professions. But following an unhappy affair with a married man, she began to question the

institution of marriage. Marriage, she declared to an assembly of
women's organizations in 1903, was a form of "sexual subjection."
In a patriarchal society it led to the growth of prostitution on the
one hand and the stigmatization of unwed mothers and illegitimate
children on the other. Stöcker called for an end to patriarchal laws,
"replacing brutal despotism with the consciousness of responsibility, prostitution with love."[35]

Such ideas were considered outrageous by most of the respectable middle class in Wilhelmine Germany. But by 1905 Stöcker,
whose particular charge as head of the League for Mutterschutz
was to improve the lot of unwed mothers, had the support of
many leading liberals of the day. Unlike the Abolitionists, the
league included male members—a professor of medicine who
dealt with venereal disease, a sexologist, a scholar of prostitution,
as well as many leading feminists. Sigmund Freud was attached to
a sister league in Austria.

While it flourished, from 1905 to 1910, the League for Mutterschutz advocated a "new morality" that included many of the demands of the women's liberation movement of the 1960s. They
wanted "free marriage," sanctioned only by the consent of the man
and woman. As novelist and cofounder Heinrich Meyer put it, "If
physical union is the expression of spiritual communion and true
love, then it is moral."[36] They wanted women to be informed
about contraception and free to choose abortion. Motherhood,
they argued, "should no longer be forced on women by threats of
imprisonment, but consciously and responsibly *chosen*."[37] And in
general they wanted women to be as free as men in their personal
lives. Such unconventional ideas had caused their advocates in
other countries to be ostracized by the mainstream women's
movements. What made Germany unique during this period was
the extent to which Helen Stöcker and her group were accepted. In
this regard the women's movement in Germany was more advanced, in a brief period from 1905 to 1910, than any other. And it
was with this "new morality" group within the women's movement that young Karen Danielsen's sympathies lay.

It is not clear how much Karen was directly influenced by the
ideas of the League for Mutterschutz. She definitely heard of the
league a few years later when, during law school, her brother
Berndt was asked to offer his opinion at a meeting of the Hamburg
branch.[38] She was also profoundly impressed by the work of a
Swedish writer named Ellen Key, who influenced the Mutterschutz group and was herself a cautious advocate of "free love."

Furthermore, she probably knew Helen Stöcker later, since Stöcker joined the Berlin Psychoanalytic Institute at a time when Karen was one of the few female members. But it seems unlikely, since Stöcker didn't really begin to propagate the Mutterschutz ideas until 1905, that Karen knew about them as early as 1903, when she was developing her own views on sexual morality.

Yet Karen arrived independently at many of Mutterschutz's conclusions. Like Stöcker, she took Nietzsche as text, interpreting his dictum "Der Frauen Ehre ist Liebe" (The honor of women is love) to mean that the "more completely, unrestrainedly" a woman gives herself to the man she loves, the "higher she stands."[39] Like the League for Mutterschutz, she wished for a generation in which all children would be born of love, when there would be no shame in admitting a pregnancy out of wedlock.

By far the most pressing question for Karen, one which occupied her for "weeks, even months" after her conversation with Alice, was whether it was "wrong to give oneself to a man outside of marriage or not."[40] Karen's answer to this question, as developed in her diary entries, is a testament to her talent for argument. She makes use of Luther's thesis that it is, after all, not outward form but inner conviction that matters. "When will we stop judging people by what they *do*?" she asks, in the rhetorical mode of a preacher. "What they *are* is the only criterion. There is no question that a woman who gives herself freely to a man—aware of the step she takes and all its consequences—stands infinitely higher than the thousands of girls who marry the first comer in order to marry." Furthermore, sexual behavior is hardly an adequate measure of morality. "Altogether too absurd, judging a person's character exclusively from his attitude toward sex. Much more important is, for example, his attitude toward the truth." There are, she concluded, two preeminent moral laws. The first is "Thou shalt not lie." The second is "Thou shalt free thyself from convention, from everyday morality."[41]

The pain of her parents' unhappy marriage gives Karen's ruminations a bitter personal stamp. It was surely the unhappy outcome of Sonni's marriage to Wackels that led her to the conclusion that "a girl who gives herself to a man in free love stands morally way above the woman who, for pecuniary reasons or out of a desire for a home, marries a man she does not love."[42] One "comes to know," she writes, sounding older than her seventeen years, "how few marriages are really good ones." Among the large circle of couples she knows, she can think of only two that are happy.

What's more, one of those couples is "pretty limited," while the other is "very superficial." As for the rest of the marriages: "What a mess!"[43]

There was a particular reason at this stage of Karen's life for her vehemence: conditions at home had gone from bad to worse. In May of Karen's first year at Gymnasium, Wackels informed the family that he probably would be staying home for the next eight months while waiting for construction to be completed on a new ship that he would captain. "Delightful prospect," Karen noted ironically in her diary.[44] By June she writes of "fatiguing daily excitements" caused by her father's presence, and of her mother's suffering.[45] Wackels, in her view, is simply unbearable. He is "low," "stupid," "materialistic," "without self-discipline and self-respect," and a hypocrite besides, a Christian with his "mouth" but not in his "actions."[46] In August, Sonni is "down again," made "ill and unhappy" by the quarreling. Karen wishes in vain that she could do something for "Mutti, my all." "If only she had, as I do, some sort of school or other means of distraction," Karen laments. She herself often leaves in the morning "with tears in my eyes," but always returns "cheerful."[47]

Karen's way of coping with the unhappiness at home had always been to put it behind her when she walked out the door, to direct all her thoughts and emotions toward some beloved object. At the Convent School there had been Herr Schulze, then Fräulein Banning, and of course school itself. Now that she had grown beyond crushes on her teachers, she longed for and needed a new passion. For a brief period during her second year at Gymnasium, it was theater. Suddenly she announced "a new era of world history." School, which had taken precedence over declamation lessons, now "hardly dare[d] present itself as a competitor without making itself ridiculous." She was in fact, "going on the stage!!!!"[48] She would begin her career just as soon as, in deference to Mutti, she had completed enough schooling so that she could fall back on teaching as a profession.

Karen's sudden decision to become an actress was influenced by an actor at the Court Theater named Herr Schrumpf, who had just become her declamation teacher and had convinced her, in a tête-à-tête over coffee, that acting was "the right road for my life."[49] Herr Schrumpf briefly replaced Herr Schulze as the "he" in the diary. He was "handsome, big and very bright," and taking lessons with him left Karen "swimming in bliss."[50] Then too a career in theater was a way of declaring her independence from

Sonni, who was "totally opposed" to the idea.[51] Theater was not an entirely respectable trade—actresses were known to be wild—or a dependable one. This must have added to its attraction for Karen, who was in the mood to defy convention. In any case, it was to be her life. In a year and a half, she predicted, "school will have vanished totally from the earth and I will be living for art and art alone."[52]

But the passion for art turned out to be short-lived, a mere postponement of the more exciting and terrifying prospect of romance. Ever since the conversation with Alice, Karen had thought day and night about falling in love with a man. But what she knew of marriage made her wary. How could she fulfill her desires without winding up a prisoner in a marriage like her parents'? At seventeen her solution, on paper anyway, was to flee convention in favor of a *"spiritualized great sensuality."* Not for her the "petty bourgeois" values of her family. Rather, she would choose the "riotous sensuous exuberance" of the Greeks in their Dionysian festivals.[53] She would find a truer, deeper faith: maybe she would become a pantheist, a monist, an atheist. "Perhaps I'll become an orthodox Jew," she ventured defiantly. *"Qui lo sa?"*[54] In the process she would put all the quarreling and hypocrisy of her "Christian" home behind her in favor of the genuineness of passion. "Passion," she declared, "is always convincing."[55]

4

First Love

When Karen began a new diary in the winter of 1903 she compared herself to a sea captain "who leaps from his safe ship into the sea," who "clings to timber" and lets himself be "driven by the sea's tumult, now here, now there," not knowing "where he's going."[1]

That Karen chose to describe herself as a sea captain, like her father, signaled her confusion about who she was and who she wanted to become. Much as she scorned her father, there was a part of her that still identified with the boldness his life represented. And yet, at the same time, the sea captain of her metaphor lacked the control required of a real-life captain. Rather than taking command in stormy seas, he allowed himself to be drawn into them, into the sea of emotion, where he was tossed hither and yon by giant waves of feeling. This sea captain behaved more like Karen's mother than her father.

Karen didn't seem to know herself what exactly was causing these tumultuous feelings—only that she was seventeen and full of "disordered turmoil" and "chaos."[2] It was, as she noted, a "time of transition."[3] She was between passions: no longer in love with school or with the stage, but not yet in love with a man. In such times it was harder to block out troubles at home or her own sadness about them. When she was younger, she writes, she used to have a dream that the floor gave way and her bed sank, slowly at first and then faster and faster. Now she often had the same feeling, "but not in my sleep... I lose ground under my feet— desolate chaos surrounds me." Was she the only "young person," she wondered, who had such feelings? As though she were a spectator she wrote, "I often wonder whether I'll make it."[4]

She felt powerless to write the script for the next phase of her life. Again the sea-captain metaphor reflects her conflict. On one hand, she would like to be active, like a captain, in shaping her destiny. That was the old impulse, declared at fifteen, when she planned to "prescribe everything" for fate. But the wish for control was powerfully opposed by a desire to be swept away, "plucked from the night," as in the Marie Madeleine poem, by a Greek demigod, a "daemon with giant wings superbly spread."[5]

On Christmas Day of that year Karen's daemon appeared. His name was Ernst Schorschi. He was twenty, two years older than Karen and yet "almost a boy"[6] in experience. He had "luminous young strength"[7] and a "sunny sparkle"[8] in his eyes. It is not clear why he was spending time at the Danielsen house that Christmas; perhaps he was a friend of Berndt's from school or military duty. What is certain is that Karen Danielsen on Christmas Night lay in her bed wondering if Schorschi was as fond of her as she was of him. That this was "love, the dawning of young first love's happiness, didn't occur to me." Then the next day "as he covered my tear-stained face with kisses, as I kissed him, it all seemed... so natural, as if it had always been so." Before, she had "yearned madly for love, my whole being dissolved in this one great longing,"[9] but it had been purely abstract. Now it was real, and it was happening to her.

For the next two days she and Schorschi were a couple, waltzing gaily around the Christmas tree, admiring a painting of Mary Magdalen in the Kunsthalle, walking around the Alster, kissing in the Reinbek woods. Then he left on the train for Berlin. "I was so blissful, so divinely happy in my half unconscious enjoyment," Karen remembered later. "And he too was happy."[10]

For Karen at eighteen the two days of love with Schorschi constituted a momentous, life-transforming event—"the accolade."[11] In her diary poetry took the place of prose. On New Year's Eve, when the rest of the family went out to hear a sermon, she stayed home, unwilling to have her mind cluttered with "conventional last-day-of-the-old-year thoughts," and wrote a poem called "Awakened to Life."

Till now eagerness, striving, anxious seeking for some inner hold
Now divine rest.
Till now chasing after happiness in every form—now exultant hap-
    pinesss, heavenly joy in my heart.
Till now only half alive with the constant, reproachful question in
    my eyes of whether this is really living,
This everlasting monotony?—
Now full, whole life, joy of life in my veins down to the littlest
    fingertip.
I thank you, old year, for having wakened me out of the twilight in
    your dying days.
I love you, dear year of 1903, because you have given me the high-
    est and best we human beings can have—love.[12]

Karen's joy was short-lived. Walking in the Reinbek woods,
Schorschi "thought of eternal love," while she "didn't want anything but the moment and didn't think of the future."[13] Once
Schorschi left Reinbek, however, the roles were reversed. Schorschi wrote one passionate letter, which arrived two days after he
left. But in Berlin he soon moved on to other excitements. Karen,
back in Hamburg, "thought only of him the whole long winter,
every minute, every hour."[14]

For the first time Karen's diary becomes tedious. Like young
lovers generally, who manage to redirect all conversations back to
their loved one, Karen's entire world becomes Schorschi. As she
herself notes, "One's thoughts all gather around one focal point,
around 'him.'" This has the effect of shutting out other concerns.
For if "he is my thought day and night, how shall other thoughts
have room?"[15]

Written mostly in verse, the lovesick diary entries of this period
are full of theatrical touches. When she asks Schorschi, rhetori-
cally, "My love, my Baldur, my joy: do you no longer think of
your little friend in Hamburg?" one can almost see her as the
vamp, stretched out on a divan with a long cigarette. "My heart
quivers in a torment of doubt," she writes, echoing the vibrant
style of Marie Madeleine.[16] What's more, her claims for the two-
day love encounter seem exaggerated. It is, she writes, a "far
greater chapter of one's life" than confirmation, leaving school, or
"losses by death."[17]

But while the passion seems exaggerated, her pain at rejection is
inescapably real. Until Schorschi returns in March, Karen clings to
the hope he still loves her, writing repeatedly in her diary the refrain "It is still the blossoming golden time/It is still the days of the

roses."[18] But when Schorschi arrives, the "dreadful knowledge" comes to her that he has "become indifferent."[19] As they walk together he alludes casually to the first passionate letter he wrote, shortly after their brief romance. "That first letter," he says cruelly, "was never written." Karen nods and smiles, "as though it went without saying, but inside me something tore in two."[20] There is one "frosty" kiss of farewell at the train station, and "a few cool sensible words of good friendship, etc."[21] Soon, she notes realistically, "he will have forgotten me."[22] Karen's first reaction is to think of suicide. "Death, where is thy sting?"[23] Then indignation: "Does he feel so superior to everything, so grand, so aware of his invincible power, that he thinks he need not say a word to me when he appears as a stranger?"[24]

Words of genuine anguish pierce through the melodrama. For a while she can forget everything, then "it comes again, the grey ghost that crushes the nerves of my life with its bony hand."[25] Often, she writes a month after the parting, "I have such a cramp about my heart that I would like to cry aloud, imagining that I cannot endure it any longer."[26] Only nine months later does she dare to read Schorschi's first letter again without fear of "inner revolutions." Even then the letter produces a "flutter of happiness" followed by "deepset bitterness."[27]

The bitterness was surely compounded by Karen's inability, or refusal, to express a single word of anger or sadness to Schorschi. Even before she met him she had made a vow to herself to suffer in silence. Though she might "groan," and "weep with despair and pain," she resolved to "look happy when someone comes in the room." Her reason was one of pride: "If I show my suffering, it calls forth sympathy." Since "sympathy hurts and humiliates me," no one is to know when she is suffering.[28] That March, when Schorschi visited, Karen remained true to this earlier resolve. She "wept through the nights" and in the daytime "laughed with him and rejoiced in his springtime beauty."[29] She felt he was "offensive and coarse" when he put his arm around her without feeling any affection. Yet she couldn't say anything. "I would rather have bitten off my tongue than say to him: 'I'm so fond of you, what have I done that you act so distantly toward me? Do you not love me any more?'"[30]

Inside, Karen might feel hatred: "Oh you, how well I can hate/ Watch out!/Love—hate, *one* emotion really/Indifferent toward you I cannot be."[31] But the outward resolution of the Schorschi affair couldn't have been more sedate and civil. A year and a half later, when she met Schorschi at a train station for a brief chat, she had convinced herself of her indifference. "I behaved naturally with him, like a comrade. Of course, the obligatory bouquet. Still a delight to see him. The old feeling completely extinguished, forgotten."[32]

In the end, Karen's painful first experience with love provided consoling proof that wounds heal, life goes on. But at the same time the rejection left her more cautious, less willing to act on emotion alone. The love for Schorschi "came over me like an elemental force, like a storm." There had been "no reflection," "no hesitation," only "total giving in to an immense emotion."[33] She had been like the captain who jumped into the sea. Never again would she leave herself quite as vulnerable. A new respect appears in the diaries, after the Schorschi affair, for self-examination, a new distrust of the "wild turmoil of the senses." Increasingly Karen tried to guide her ship, rather than let it drift, through the stormy emotional waters in which she seemed always to travel. If there is no free will, she notes in her diary, we are free to "just drift along" without need to "ponder, should I do this or that?" But, she argues, "we simply *cannot* live without reflecting."[34]

The romantic verse that had filled page after page of her diary gave way to notes on Ellen Key and Spinoza's *Ethics*. Spinoza argues that "happiness is absence of all influences from outside that threaten self-preservation." One should not surrender to "the force of external things," such as "the desire to please, voluptuousness, intemperance, greed and sensuality." "Where intellect is hampered by passion," says Spinoza, "suffering remains."[35]

It was not the first time a rejection had propelled her toward study and examination. Even before Schorschi, during her second year at Gymnasium, she had tried to join a class in dissection offered at another school and had been turned down. Her solution was to substitute herself as subject. "I shall take myself to pieces. That will probably be more difficult, but also more interesting."[36] It is not clear *why* Karen couldn't join the dissection class, but it seems likely that the class was offered at a boys' school and unavailable to her because of her sex. Characteristically, however, she didn't rail against the unfairness of the system. Instead she turned to the one territory that was truly her own and to which no one could deny her access: her own internal life. The resolve to "take myself apart" shines like a beacon into her future, anticipating her life's work. Four years before she began reading Freud, ten years before she began her own psychoanalysis, forty years before she advocated self-analysis in a book of that title, Karen Danielsen was already writing about taking herself apart, about trying to understand her behavior in a systematic fashion.

The Schorschi affair heightened her resolve. At the end of 1904, a year afterward, Karen toasted the previous year as "a good tough friend to me." It let the flowers of first love wither, but it "gave me other flowers, not so fragrant, not so touchingly sweet and delicate, no, they were spicier and stronger." Out of rejection came her resolution to do "hard *work*," including "deep absorption in the natural sciences and philosophy, penetrating into the greatest poets and thinkers" and, at the same time, "to learn how to listen to the delicate vibrations of my soul, to be incorruptibly *true to myself* and fair to others, to find in this way the right measure of my own worth."[37]

More and more her diary entries reflect this wish to listen carefully to her feelings, to try to understand her actions rather than act on impulse. She was no longer content to declare herself madly in love. She was now breaking feelings down into smaller parts, dissecting them: what she felt versus what she thought, what she felt a week ago, a day ago, as opposed to what she was feeling that day. Her poetic outpourings about her love for Schorschi stand in contrast to her first entry about her new friendship with a young musician named Rolf. "Am I already in love again? Can I still love? Can one give one's whole heart away twice? Is there a difference between loving and 'being in love'? Or is there only the one great flame that burns in our soul?" She is confused by conflicting sisterly and sensual feelings: "I love you like a sister, Rolf, like a friend who only wants the best for you." Yet "other feelings" are "mixed with this pure love . . . a consuming longing for you comes over me, a wild turmoil of my senses."[38]

Karen's relationship with Rolf was the subject of endless soul-searching of this kind. She wrote about Rolf while she was with him, and she wrote even more after they had parted, in an attempt to understand what had gone wrong. All in all, her account of the Rolf relationship runs to seventy-six diary pages. As she acknowledged, writing about Rolf served at times to "fill out the yawning emptiness inside."[39]

It was not the first time that Karen had used writing as a ritual means of consoling herself. Four years earlier, when she had felt so tossed about by her unfulfilled desires, she had written out dozens of love poems in her diary. And the long account of her relationship with Rolf was crowding out another painful reality. In August of 1904, while Karen was writing it, Sonni decided to leave Wackels. To leave one's husband, taking the first step toward divorce, was a bold act for a middle-class woman in that day. In Thomas Mann's *Buddenbrooks,* which chronicles the life of a wealthier North German family, a divorce is a disgrace, no matter how justified by circumstances. "It lies like a weight on my heart, to know that I have besmirched our name," Toni Buddenbrooks tells her brother Tom, "even if it was not any fault of mine. You can do whatever you will, you can earn money and be the first man in the town—but people will still say: 'Yes, but his sister is a divorced woman.'"[40]

Separated but not yet divorced, Sonni moved with Karen and Berndt to Bahrenfeld, a suburb on the other side of the town, where she struggled to make ends meet by taking in boarders. Karen, perhaps to avoid her family worries, became so thoroughly absorbed in recollection of the Rolf affair that she barely mentioned this difficult and momentous event in her diary. Even after she graduated from Gymnasium and began medical school, she continued for a time to write about her love for Rolf to fend off her loneliness, not unlike the way she had once told herself Karl May stories.

And yet, unlike the infatuated poetry of the Schorschi period, the long story of her relationship with Rolf remains deeply absorbing. Because she is trying to "write quite honestly, without mental reservations,"[41] her account provides a vivid picture not only of her relationship with Rolf but of the difficulties that will recur in relationships to come. Through the story we also learn of the wider world of young intellectuals in Wilhelmine Germany. And in Rolf and Karen's struggles with conventions and prejudices we learn something of the attitudes that surrounded Karen in turn-of-the-century Hamburg.

Karen's first meeting with Rolf, or Rudolf, as he was more formally named, came about quite by accident on a fine Sunday in April of 1904. It was a day for "light spring dresses," but Karen was wearing black and a doleful face. The doleful face came from "after-pains" of her first love of Schorschi, the black blouse from her performance in a Lenten passion play. Rolf stopped by the Danielsen house that day with one Herr Rehtz, a poet Karen knew, and inquired about renting a room. He was about twenty, with dark-brown curly hair, "snow white teeth," and "such a pretty face" that Karen was initially "horrified." Karen was further put off by the suspicion that Rolf "had had his hair curled." All in all, his "shameless hairdo" and his delicate face led her to the conclusion that he was "one of the dandies[42] who frequent the Jungfernstieg." When she learned that the room rental wasn't going to work out, she was relieved, for she found him "unsympathetic."[43]

A little later, after Rolf had found a room elsewhere in Reinbek, they met one morning as Karen was "sauntering back and forth on the good old Reinbek platform," waiting for the train to Hamburg. Their ride into Hamburg together that day was the first of many. The trip from Reinbek, Karen noted, takes thirty-two minutes. "When one multiplies them and also adds the waiting time in Reinbek and the walk through Repsoldstrasse [to Karen's Gymnasium], it amounts to quite an impressive number of full hours." In those hours the friendship "sprouted and ripened slowly, steadily."[44]

In many ways Rolf was a kindred spirit. Karen, who was usually shy and reserved with strangers, found herself talking to him right away "as if I had known him for a long time."[45] When he told her about his "depressed moods," she understood him well because, she observed, "I knew the condition myself."[46] Rolf was an open book, at least as vulnerable as she, "pure from the ground up."[47] After the painful rejection by the devil-may-care Schorschi, Rolf was much safer, a soul mate who was at least as likely as she to suffer in love.

And yet Rolf was in some ways a more dangerous choice. Unlike Schorschi, who had charmed Karen's mother as well as her, Rolf was anathema to the family—definitely not the sort of young man one wished for as her future husband. For one thing, he was a penniless music student. His days revolved around his voice studies with one Frau Pennarini and a variety of inconsequential jobs he did to make ends meet. He was alienated from his family and particularly his mother, who, Karen explained, "was offensive to him because of her superficiality and falseness." Rolf's friends were poets and intellectuals who read Nietzsche in cafés and scoffed at convention. All of this, however, while troublesome to Karen's family, wouldn't have made him *persona non grata* at the Danielsen house. What really rankled was the fact that Rolf was a Jew.

Interestingly, Rolf's Jewishness doesn't seem to have been a problem right at the beginning. He came to Reinbek on several Sunday afternoons and joined in merriment with Berndt and his friends. Once, in an exuberant mood, they all brewed a wine punch and "marched, singing and dancing, in goose-step around

the lawn, Berndt in the lead with the tureen and we coming along
behind with the glasses." Afterward the eight of them "went
through Reinbek arm-in-arm, dancing in circles around the good
old Reinbek peace oak."[48] But the family attitude changed when
they discovered that Rolf was not only a Jew but a Jew who saw
no need to play by the conventional rules.

After they had gotten to know each other fairly well, Rolf asked
Karen to go with him to a lecture in Hamburg given by the Free
Association of Artists. The lecture was "rather insignificant," but
afterward Rolf invited her to join him and some friends at a café.
"I found this somewhat improper," Karen relates, "but naturally I
went along."

That night, sitting at a little table by the window upstairs at the
Hôtel de l'Europe, Karen listened in "mute admiration" as Rolf
and his friends, Walter Singer and Martha Deucker, "a young girl
in simple black," talked about modern literature. Walter read aloud
from Nietzsche's *Zarathustra,* "the sound of which was new to me
and gave me insight into an unsuspected world of happiness."
They left the hotel reciting a joyous poem by the North German
contemporary poet Theodor Storm, "Oktoberlied":

> The day is ours, this whole day,
> let's gild it, yes, let's gild it
> The blue days are dawning,
> and ere they flow away
> we would indeed, my brave good friend,
> enjoy them, yes enjoy them.[49]

The evening had already been a revelation to Karen. But on the
way home her conversation with Martha challenged her old assumptions about class. Martha was not like the other young girls
she knew. Her father, as Karen later explained to a friend, was a
warehouseman, "the philosopher among the workmen." Walter
Singer had first met Martha when she was working as a maid in
his house and had noticed her "because of her extensive knowledge
and her thirst for learning." Now Martha was a salesgirl who
"used all her free time to satisfy her drive for knowledge," and
impressed Karen by reciting the opening words of a contemporary
novella. As a result of meeting Martha, Karen began to think more
about the question of class. "Real class differences," she wrote to
her friend Tuti, "do not lie in money but in the development of a
cultured, educated mind, and in this regard Martha is far superior

to most girls of her class."[50] Several years later she went further, observing that she got on "quite easily" with women of "lower social standing" because "women don't really belong to any class, they all belong to one. Much sharper boundary lines with men."[51]

Karen's mother, however, did not take kindly to these egalitarian views. The following Sunday, when Rolf came to visit with Martha in tow, the reception at the Danielsen house was "frosty." "Martha," Karen noted, "has nothing fine in her social manners, one recognizes the shopgirl in her." At this point the family's dislike of Rolf—"anti-Semitism and the rest"—surfaced. "A big scolding afterward," Karen recalls, "impudence on the fellow's part to come along with his floozy, etc." Anti-Semitism was usual in the middle class of that time. However, the Danielsens seem to have been willing to tolerate Rolf until he challenged their sense of propriety by bringing along Martha, with her "shopgirl" ways. Perhaps that reinforced a familiar stereotype of Jews as grubby and coarse. (Berndt later married a woman who was half Jewish, thus suggesting that he made distinctions between some Jews and others.) Sonni forbade Karen to bring Martha to the house. And after that day Rolf was "as good as outlawed." The next time Rolf came to visit, Berndt and his friends treated him so rudely that he never returned. Because she could see his "vulnerability," Karen never told Rolf that the reason for Berndt's rudeness was his "repugnance" at Rolf's Jewishness. But the family's rejection of her friend placed Karen "in sharp opposition to the others, so that I drew closer and closer to Rolf."[52]

Karen had been feeling discontented with her family even before they ostracized Rolf and Martha. For years her father had been the enemy, the object of all her wrath and indignation. But now she was beginning to feel that Sonni and Berndt were "limited" (a favorite word of this period) as well. In her relationship with Rolf she saw the opportunity to follow her moral commandment, "Free thy self from convention."[53] She longed, as she told Rolf, "to get out into that purer atmosphere" away from the constraints of this "good-middle-class family life." Berndt, in particular, had "inoculated" her with a "utilitarian morality."[54] Rolf, on the other hand, "unconditionally placed what he held to be right above practical utility." He was "a person in whom the practical was subordinated to ideas, a person to whom all conventionality meant nothing, an idealist, in short, but not of the cheap variety who enthuse over a lot of fine slogans and never get beyond that."[55] She was particularly impressed by Rolf's insistence on total honesty. When his mother sent him a basket of fruit, he announced, "One may not accept any present from people one despises!"[56] and gave it to the landlady. Another time, when he was gloomy while the rest of the party was gay, he insisted he "had a right to his moods, and... didn't like to and wouldn't play-act."[57] For Karen, so used to covering her anger with compliance, such behavior was refreshing.

Even though they claimed indifference to convention, however, Rolf and Karen's courtship couldn't have been more deliberate and careful. In part, the need to proceed clandestinely slowed things down. When Karen wanted to meet Rolf she had to make up a story at home: once she claimed "with beating heart"[58] that she was going with Alice to meet their old crush Fräulein Banning, another time it was an excursion with Alice to the zoological gardens. When all else failed, she fell back on physical complaints. Once, when it was "raining in torrents," she claimed she had to mail a letter, then explained her long absence with a "whopper" about having had "something of a fainting spell" on the way back from the mailbox. This lie, she noted, left her with "a rather uneasy feeling."[59] When she and Rolf were together, Karen was never entirely free of the "breathless fear of meeting anyone."[60] Walking home from the Reinbek station after an outing one day, it seemed "perfectly natural" to take Rolf's arm. "When I thought someone I knew was coming toward us, I quickly let go of his arm." But when the danger was over "my arm willingly slipped under his."[61]

What Karen feared even more than the danger of being seen, however, was the danger that her feelings might take over and leave her as vulnerable as she had been when she fell for Schorschi. As long as she and Rolf were friends, she felt in control. But in her view, falling in love meant relinquishing one's freedom. "The feeling that binds me to Rolf," she insisted in the early days of their relationship, "is much deeper, more valuable—but it is not that elemental passion.... Toward Schorschi I feel as woman only, toward Rolf as human being."[62] She envied the total control of the Swedish writer Ellen Key. "She does not seem to know any sensual excitement, any sensual longing of which she would be intellectually ashamed in other hours." Probably, Karen concluded, almost wistfully, "her senses do not inflate her imagination, as mine do so often."[63]

In the beginning it seemed natural for the relationship to be platonic. Karen viewed Rolf as a "teacher," who opened a "new and more noble view of the world before my eyes." Like the schoolteachers she had adored earlier, Rolf became the object of emulation. When he didn't like her hat, she "tore it up bit by bit so that it was unusable," then went out and bought a straw hat of the kind *he* wore.[64] Even after they grew closer, Rolf didn't generate the same sexual excitement as other men. Of course their attraction had "something to do with the senses—every contact between man and woman has."[65] But the bond was grounded in understanding: she felt "at home" in "his soul," as though he had been, in Goethe's words, "either sister or my wedded wife" in some past life.[66] At other times, when he was depressed, she felt maternal. In the end, however, her attachment to Rolf, based as it was on understanding as well as sensuality, proved more powerful than her first love. As time went on, the clandestine nature of the relationship, "that tremulous and provocative feeling of danger,"[67] only made it more desirable.

Looking back on it in her long reminiscence, Karen recounted the small increments in intimacy. There was the day's outing with the Free Association of Artists to the home of Detlev von Liliencron, a venerated lyric poet of the era. It was on the train there that Karen "rumpled up" Rolf's curls for the first time.[68] Another time, after Karen had managed to sneak out to a bon voyage party for Martha, several people were offering to walk Karen home when Rolf suddenly said "in quite commanding tones: 'I'll take you home!'" This otherwise unremarkable statement took on great significance because Rolf used the intimate form *Du* for "you." "I was quite taken aback, for we did not use the 'Du' to each other."[69] On still another evening, after they had visited the zoological gardens together, Rolf proposed that they get off one stop before Reinbek and walk home through the woods. It was dark in the woods, so that Karen was "scared and pressed close to him," all the while listening to his account of *I Pagliacci*. Once, when she stumbled, Rolf said he wished she had fallen "so that he could have helped me." Such tentative endearments led her to remember the evening as "marvelous."[70]

Before long she went to visit Rolf at his room in Reinbek because he "wanted to play me something." This was not a proper thing for a young lady to do, but "through association with Rolf the last remnants of 'the young lady' had disappeared." Rolf sang for her and played the overture to Wagner's *Tristan* while she lay on the floor and "gave myself up completely to enjoying the music."[71] Afterward, when Rolf walked her home, she realized for the first time that he loved her.

As they grew more serious they began to look for a place where their embraces wouldn't be noticed. Frau Meyer, Rolf's landlady, had objected strongly to Karen's visit to his room. And of course Rolf couldn't come to her house. So one evening, four months after their first meeting, they arranged to rendezvous at the forester's house in the Reinbek woods. As they walked toward the Lovers' Beech a quarrel arose. "I think he wanted to take a stick away from me. We struggled with each other, and suddenly I felt his breath close to my face. Half startled and half instinctively, I put both my hands before my face. He let me go." Presently they sat down at the edge of the wood, where the meadow ran steeply down to the stream, the Bille, and talked "about forbidden pleasures and the enjoyment of stolen goods." Suddenly Rolf said, "A stolen kiss is also lovely" and kissed her. "Quite shy, quite gently, quite uncertainly."[72]

Thus commenced a new and particularly troubled phase of the relationship. Right away, when Rolf kissed her, Karen felt "disconcerted and sad...a shadow had fallen across our delightful relationship as friends." This understandably put Rolf into a depressed mood and set him to making, with "a sort of gallows humor, one stupid joke after another." Finally, feeling sorry for him, she "took heart" and kissed him "with energetic determination." This, however, didn't cheer him, since he felt she had kissed him out of pity. Karen, however, arrived home happy. "I stood before the mirror and looked into my excited face and saw myself as something new."[73]

When Karen met Rolf the next Sunday by the churchyard, she had nearly convinced herself they hadn't kissed. Rolf "had become more of a stranger" to her—"the intimacy had vanished." And yet they chased each other around that day until her hair came down, and "he loosened it altogether so that it fell free."[74] That night Rolf—remembering their earlier intimacy, no doubt—insisted on leaving their friends at a bar and taking a walk. When they sat on a bench to rest he began to kiss her passionately. Karen, however, "remained perfectly passive." "Only when he hurt me did I remonstrate." While she "half lay, half sat," Rolf kissed her incessantly, as though he were "parched with thirst." Throughout it all she felt "nothing, not the least bit," except "displeasure at my uncomfortable position and his too vehement passion."[75]

Whether because of Rolf's insensitivity or her inability to express her feelings, the two seemed always to be out of step. Karen often felt "desire" when she was away from him, but when she was with him she was "cool and not at all in love."[76] When they went into the Saxon wood and "played around" in the bilberries, staining her white sailor blouse, her senses were "hardly awakened." As a result, when he asked to kiss her breast, she was "quite astonished and embarrassed." When she refused, "he did not press me further."[77]

There were to be many more such awkward moments, with Rolf advancing on an unwilling but mute Karen. They culminated, in the summer of 1904, in a wild confrontation in Rolf's room. As the two of them stood looking out the window at a lovely view of the churchyard and the Böcklein trees, Karen wondered aloud what the landlady thought of her for visiting a man's room. Rolf, inferring that such a visit implied a sexual liaison, answered, "And would it be so bad if that were so?" After they had eaten "cozily" and Rolf had played and sung for her, Karen announced she wanted to catch the nine o'clock train. But Rolf begged her to stay. A "wild scene" unfolded. Rolf tried to undo her dress, then threw her down on his bed, so that she saw "his hotly glowing eyes close to mine." She yelled at him, "Beast!" Eventually Rolf stopped. "I did not want to be desired by him," Karen recalls. "I did not desire him."[78]

After that evening the relationship settled into a more tender mode. She would go to his apartment in Hamburg (where he was now living), have tea, and listen to him play, usually from his enduring love, *Tristan*. Then they would sit side by side on his "shabby sofa," he, with his head on her shoulder, lamenting the suffering caused him by a "cold, mendacious world," and she trying to "drive away the black shadows."[79] Rolf's foiled attempts to seduce her were now referred to only indirectly in Rolf's words "You know, Karen, that you owe me thanks."[80] This was a sort of code, current at the time, which meant that the man had shown restraint in his sexual advances and that the woman should be grateful to him for keeping them under control. Karen agreed that she "owed" Rolf "many thanks."[81] Despite evidence to the contrary, Karen wrote, "I would surely have become his lover if he had so desired."[82]

The reasons Karen *didn't* become Rolf's lover are interesting to contemplate. There was, of course, the obvious one: Rolf was simply unable, except on rare occasions, to "inflame" her "senses." Rolf "did not kiss well," she noted. His "was at bottom such a chaste nature that he too found himself in strange waters."[83] Karen was understandably wary: premarital sex went against everything she had been taught and held the real danger of pregnancy besides.

There was a wide gap, certainly, between Karen's advanced views on the subject of sex before marriage and her experience. "Even if I *knew* anything about sexual relations in those days," she wrote, looking back, "it was just an external knowledge and nothing personal."[84] And yet at the same time she faulted Rolf later for not being more forceful. A man, she noted, "must take the sure lead." Only then can a woman have "full enjoyment." "I was then more child than woman—but he could have awakened what was slumbering in me."[85] Rolf, she would note on another occasion, "was not strong enough to hold me."[86]

Rolf certainly appears to have had his difficulties with women. But with Karen it seems clear that he couldn't have won. In this, her first long-term and in-depth relationship with a man, the sea metaphor of her earlier diary entry was played out. On one hand, she wanted to experience abandon, to be tossed about in the stormy seas of passion, under the the "sure lead" of a man who would be skillful enough to "awaken" her, "strong enough to hold" her. But she also wanted to be a captain, in control of her own destiny.

The passive role in sex was, after all, what she had been taught to expect by her culture and by the books she had read. Women who openly expressed desire were either brazen or prostitutes. Young ladies such as Karen didn't initiate, they merely reacted. It was the man who aroused the woman, bringing her to a point at which she abandoned her better instincts and gave in, against her will, to passion. "A man," she wrote, "wants a woman calm and superior to these low instincts," since "everyone loves that which is higher." As in the "old song about the vanity of man," he wants to "conquer, always to conquer" and "will accept nothing that is given to him."[87] The man conquered, the woman surrendered. And when, out of some noble sentiment, the man restrained himself, the woman "owed him thanks."

Much as she longed for love, Karen had too independent a nature to play the passive role assigned to the female in this script. She wanted, needed, to be her own master. Some of her bitterest arguments with Rolf, for instance, were over money. She "couldn't stand his paying for me." She felt so strongly about this that when Rolf refused four marks she claimed she owed him, she mailed the money to a mutual friend. Rolf turned the entire affair into a joke. On the train the next day he spread out "an enormous form" in which he had "artfully figured out that *he* still owed *me* something."⁸⁸ The argument about money kept recurring, however. To Karen it was not a joke but an expression of her intense need to be free from entangling and potentially painful dependence.

And yet, as Freud would argue, those feelings we defend against are often the ones with the greatest potential to dominate our lives. Karen's need for others, her near total dependency on others to fill an inner emptiness, was a repeating theme throughout her life. She tended, in this period, to put dependence in sexual terms: if only she could rise above desires of the flesh, she could keep control of her life. "To be free of sensuality," she wrote, "means great power in a woman." It was the only way to be "independent of a man." Otherwise, in "the exaggerated yearning of her senses," she will "drown out all feeling of her own value. She becomes a bitch, who begs even if she is beaten—a strumpet."⁸⁹ But Karen's need to be in love, to have some one person in her life who mattered above all others, was more than a need for sexual fulfillment. It arose from greater depths. Without someone else, she feared losing her own sense of identity and of purpose.

The enormity of this need became apparent when, after Rolf and Karen had been close for a year and a half, he announced that he was leaving Hamburg in order to pursue his voice studies in Graz, Austria. Karen wrote in her diary that his leaving made her feel "homeless."⁹⁰ But as in the past, Karen kept her hurt to herself. Though "everything inside went into a tight knot," she didn't "have the courage" to say so and told him only that she was happy for him. It was Rolf who went into a depression, torn "to pieces" by his "unhappy temperament."⁹¹ But after he had left, in October, just a month after her nineteenth birthday, she grew more and more disconsolate.

For a while she was able to keep him with her as an almost physical presence. "Often, quite suddenly, I see him vividly standing before me... then the vision is gone again."⁹² Or on the way to tutoring "little Olga" (a job she had apparently taken on to help Sonni in her straitened circumstances) she "had conversations" with Rolf, "as though he were walking beside me."⁹³ She relied on his correspondence so much that "if the mail doesn't bring the expected letter, I feel suddenly quite weak and miserable."⁹⁴ But after a while Rolf's letters and imagined presence weren't enough. Even before Rolf left, she had begun to feel that the days on which she didn't see him "seemed empty."⁹⁵ Now that he was gone she felt "paralyzing fatigue and apathy."[96] If Rolf had not gone away, Karen wrote afterward, her "life would have been chained fast to his." But her need for an intense relationship with someone close by made it impossible after a while to hold out for Rolf. "If he had stayed," she wrote, "I would have remained faithful to him. But in his long absence my senses did at last awaken."[97]

Over the winter there were temporary distractions from her loneliness—the deepening of her friendship with Martha and a trip with an aunt named Selma to Switzerland. On a path in Chamonix, feeling "utterly lonely and deserted," she "felt protected" in the thought of Rolf, the "one person who loved me."[98] But by July she had found another. His name was Ernst and he was the new boarder with Sonni, Berndt, and Karen at their apartment in Bahrenfeld.

Karen threw herself into the new relationship with her usual intensity. She loved Ernst "madly," she told her diary, and her longing for him was "so strong that I think I can hardly breathe anymore."[99] In retrospect, she understood that Ernst was "built of coarser stuff"[100] than Rolf. But in August of 1905, when Karen traveled to Berlin to visit Rolf, Ernst was so much on her mind that she told Rolf about him. Rolf, who shared Karen's tendency to rush to extremes, immediately concluded, "You're in love with him." Karen tried to explain that she wasn't sure herself. But Rolf replied "almost tonelessly": "Then it's all over between us." As they traveled around Berlin trying to enjoy themselves, Rolf pressed for assurance that Karen "loved" him, was not just "fond" of him. This she "*could* not give him." But in the final hours, heated by wine, Karen told Rolf what he wanted to hear and allowed him to express his boundless passion. "I no longer had myself under control," she wrote. "I let him do what he wanted." What Rolf wanted is never made clear. Whatever it was, it didn't prevent her from catching the six o'clock train back to Hamburg to meet Ernst. "Every moral concept must have been lacking in me at that moment," she writes, indignant with herself. "How was that possible!"[101]

Yet there were several reasons why Karen might have preferred Ernst over Rolf at the time. For one thing, he was *there,* in Hamburg; with him she wouldn't have to endure that feeling of emptiness. Then too, though he wasn't good-looking, she was so attracted to him that her "senses ran ahead of love." With him, as with Schorschi, she felt "elemental passion."[102]

But more important still, Karen was on the threshold of the choice of her lifetime. A few months hence, in the spring of 1906, she would graduate from Gymnasium and take the *Abitur*. If she passed, she would be in a position to become one of the first women in Germany to attend medical school. But this choice was daunting: she would have to leave Hamburg, live alone in a strange city, and battle the odds as a female in the unwelcoming male environment of a German university.

Ernst represented the other, more familiar, option: marriage and family. Rolf was not an acceptable marriage candidate in the eyes of the family. Nor did he seem inclined to take such a conventional step at that point in his singing career. When Karen thought of Rolf in the future, she imagined a joyous reunion on the street after he had become "a great singer" and she "a doctor of whatever Nature has in mind for me."[103] But with Ernst, middle-class, non-Jewish, mildly intellectual, she could imagine doing what Sonni had in mind when, passing a couple with a baby, she told Karen, "Look there, the picture of your future."[104]

As she prepared to face the unknown, there was a part of Karen that wished Ernst would rescue her with marriage. "Two questions are agitating me all the time," she wrote in December of 1905. "The one is: Graduation? Berlin? Study? And the second is: Ernst??" Of the two the second interested her more, since "of course, I am first of all a woman." Perhaps, she imagined, there would come a moment when Ernst would take her in his arms and say, "We just can't do without each other!" And yet she "wouldn't like to become his wife, in any case not now," because, she believed, "there is still a lot in me that is only waiting for the waking call to come forth." Unsure about her feelings—sometimes she thought he was her "great love," other times a "charming amusement"—she waited for Ernst in a moment of passion to provide an escape by "binding" her to him through his love. "I often feel: if he doesn't take hold now, before I go, it is all over; I mean, then I will get over him, gradually, out there in the big world."[105]

But if Karen had *really* wanted to get out of going to medical school, she wouldn't have chosen Ernst as an alternative. Ernst, as it turned out, was a man who couldn't decide: give him any proposition, and he would say "on the one hand...," but "on the other hand..."[106] Karen, in fact, was eager by this time to try sex. But Ernst, with "his timidity, his respect for propriety,"[107] worried about being seen by the neighbors. Karen might well have asked if her choice of Ernst, who was hardly the man to stand in the way of her medical studies, was accidental.

There is no evidence that Karen had yet read the writings of

Sigmund Freud. But she was becoming increasingly aware of the role of the unconscious in seemingly chance occurrences. "I recently read somewhere," she wrote around this time, "that the unconscious in people stands in the same relation to the conscious as the entire mass of water in a pond to the greenery swimming on the surface."[108] How much, she wondered, had she charted the course of these relationships without knowing it? Did the fact that she "never could or would" talk with Rolf about his Jewishness "perhaps unconsciously erect a partition between us?"[109] And what of the "chain of events, every single one of which looked as though its purpose were to separate me from Rolf," just after she had realized, while walking in Chamonix, that she "belonged to" Rolf? "*Were they all chance?* Was it a chance that just on my return home—a week before I was to see Rolf again—I met Ernst? That we made that tour through the heath together and slept in the haystack?"[110]

The story of Karen's relationship with Rolf had one last stormy chapter. On the Saturday after they met in Berlin, a "half-insane" letter arrived from Rolf. He was in Hamburg, "longing for love and death close to each other." Karen met him at the train station, "sobbing, his whole body trembling." He still "would have nothing to do with my being fond of him." He wanted to kill both Ernst and himself. The next day, feeling calmer, Rolf swore he wouldn't "do anything silly," kissed her twice "with the force of his desperation and his passion,"[111] and left. Shortly after, Ernst grew less attentive. But by that time it was too late for Karen to win Rolf back; he wrote, in answer to her plea, that he was "done with" her. When they met again in Hamburg, "he let me feel that I was nothing to him anymore."[112]

This time, Karen suspected that there was something in *her* that made being alone especially painful. "Deep in me," she wrote, "is a terrible, a disconsolate emptiness."[113] Such insight didn't keep her, however, from continuing to search for the magic solution. "One person! Is that asking so much? Oh God, how shall I go on enduring this emptiness?"[114] Ernst, she had concluded, "is not the man to whom I belong." Nor was Rolf the "one who must come."[115] At times she decided she must "first be quite, quite alone, to be prepared for the one. But will he come, will he come?"[116]

In the meantime there was the "pressure, the dreadful pressure," of the *Abitur*. Though she doesn't take much space in her diary talking about it, it is clear that passing the *Abitur* was even more important than finding her true love. "If I don't pass the exam——! Then I'm finished. Then I can't go on living." However, as she confidently noted, the thought of failure was "only a phantom that leers at me from time to time." She was, in fact, "clever enough to learn a great deal in life."[117]

That spring she passed the *Abitur*. And on Easter Sunday she left Hamburg on a train bound for the University of Freiburg, traveling "with a thousand anxious expectations, into an unfamiliar life."[118]

PART TWO

University Life

Freiburg and Göttingen

1906–9

5

"Myself in Every Part"

During one of the periods of depression she experienced later in Berlin, Karen Horney daydreamed in her diary about a return to Freiburg, the small university town in South Germany where her medical studies began:

> Freiburg, a nameless longing steals, steals into my heart when I think of it. I believe I would kiss the earth of the Schlossberg [an adjacent mountain] if I set foot upon it, I would go into the Cathedral and kneel down and rejoice in my heart and pray thankfully to—well, to some being my naive heart needed at that moment, just to be able to say thanks. I would even take pleasure in the black clerics again. I would go to Wiedersheim's course and hear how he says: "Commilitonen!" [fellow students]. And all the fountains, the many-colored tower gates, the narrow winding streets—ah, Freiburg![1]

The two years Karen Horney spent as a medical student in Freiburg, from 1906 to 1908, were among the most exhilarating of her life. In Freiburg the pleasure in work she had experienced in Hamburg Gymnasium classes developed into a "deep pure joy" that was "free from the material...suprasensual."[2] At the same time the medical-school years brought her into full enjoyment of her sensual self. The little girl who had tried to get out of gym classes became, in Freiburg, a woman who reveled in hiking and skiing in the surrounding mountains of the Black Forest. In Freiburg too Karen's adolescent sexual gropings gave way to full and pleasurable sexual relationships. The exuberance breaks through in her diary in the Freiburg period. And when, as happened during good times, she stopped writing in it, she put her diarist's energy into a long correspondence with Oskar Horney, her future husband, that is even richer in enthusiasms—for medical school, for new ideas, and for the dances and all-night parties of student life.

Just getting to Freiburg was a triumph for Karen Danielsen. It meant she was on her way to fulfilling point five of the plan, set down in her diary six years earlier, of becoming a doctor; in Germany in 1906 that was an unusual achievement. And in Freiburg she was away, for the first time in her life, from the squabbling between her parents, which kept on even after they had separated. She was away too from family constraints. No longer did she have to concoct stories if she wanted to meet a boyfriend, or worry about chance encounters with relatives on one of her rendezvous. Hamburg was not only a twelve-hour train journey away;[3] in ambience it may as well have been in another country.

But for the fact that they spoke roughly the same language and belonged to states that were loosely allied within the German Empire, the inhabitants of Freiburg and Hamburg in 1906 had very little in common. Hamburg was a modern commercial port city of half a million, situated on a flat coastal plain and surrounded by water—a city as rainy in climate and as proper in comportment as London.

Freiburg was a sunny little city of forty thousand, a mecca for hikers, who fanned out from there onto the mountain trails of the surrounding pine-carpeted Black Forest, and for students, who had been coming to study at the University of Freiburg, one of the oldest in Germany, since it had been founded in the fifteenth century. Unlike Hamburg, Freiburg had retained some of its fifteenth-century flavor. Cold water from the mountains still flowed in sparkling open streams (*Bächle*) along Freiburg streets. Peasants, wearing traditional regional dress, brought their vegetables down from the surrounding countryside each morning for sale in the market square.

In Freiburg all the buildings of town and university were dwarfed, as they had been since the Middle Ages, by the colossal presence of the Catholic cathedral. The russet sandstone spires of the Freiburg *Münster*, one of the loveliest and grandest Gothic cathedrals of Europe, towered over the cobbled streets and stone buildings of the town, with their ornately carved and richly painted façades. Even when you didn't see the cathedral in Freiburg, you heard it. During the day, in the shaded courtyard·of the nearby university, in the arched hallways and stark lecture halls where Karen and her fellow medical students learned anatomy, the great bells of the cathedral penetrated every quarter hour. At night the bells competed with the drunken singing of students on the Kanonenplatz or sobered revelers coming out of smoky, ancient taverns surrounding the cathedral square.

The cathedral at Freiburg, with its Gothic tower and lovingly carved saints, crowning the entry, represented a church of celebration, of soaring faith, which was more in tune with young Karen Danielsen's mood than the forbidding faith of her father. The stern moral preachings of Pastor von Ruckteschell would have seemed out of place in a pulpit illuminated by the glorious jeweled light of the cathedral's rose windows.

The cathedral was merely atmospheric, however, since Karen's "Christian period," as she called it, was behind her. Of more immediate appeal was the social atmosphere of Freiburg, compared with Hamburg. Less attention was paid in the South to the formalities, and more time was devoted, among Karen's new friends, to the active appreciation of good food, of beer, and of the local Gutedel wine. In the university atmosphere of Freiburg, she noted, a "charming comradely relation between men and women students" replaced the "unnatural formal intercourse between young people of different sex in the better social classes!"[4]

Karen Danielsen, who had already tasted the excitement of Rolf's "intellectual world" in Hamburg, embraced what Freiburg had to offer within a few months of her arrival there. Just after she moved, in April of 1906, she wrote in her diary that she was "mortally unhappy to be so totally alone"[5] and went on to console herself, as she so often did, by writing a "story"—this one a continuation of the long saga of Rolf and Ernst. But before long the brooding over what might have been with Rolf gave way to a gleeful account of an evening at one of the restaurants in the mountains surrounding the city.

On July 14th the commemoration of the academic-social society was celebrated at the Dattler. There I got acquainted with Losch [nickname for Louis Grote]—and the Hornvieh [nickname for Oskar Horney]. We [she and Losch] danced a Française together, neither of us knowing it—we threw rose-leaves at each other on the veranda, which was decorated with colored lanterns...we went arm-in-arm down the Schlossberg at three in the morning and out to the suburb of Gunther-stal. And suddenly somebody was walking beside us, telling one story after another—it was the little Hornvieh. Somewhat later we sat on Hornvieh's balcony, dangling our legs and laughing at each other, happy and surprised, not understanding our being together there at all. And then it was all the way up the steep road to the Solacker hill in dancing slippers and ball dress. Up there we lay in the sun and gradually our eyes fell gently shut.[6]

Thus began, on a carefree summer night in Freiburg, a lasting three-way relationship. Although Oskar Horney, or "Hornvieh," as she called him, would later become her husband, she fell in love with her fellow medical student Louis Grote, "Losch," first. The evening after the all-night romp she and Losch returned to the Dattler alone. "And he kissed me, and I felt that he was strong and that joy of living and strength burned in his kiss, and I came to love him. The last two weeks of the semester we were always together, with the exception of a few nocturnal hours. We drank tea for hours at my place or visited the Hornvieh, or it was an evening of music, or we went walking. All permeated by a serene careless joy of life."[7]

Karen Danielsen's fourth diary, begun in 1904, slows to a halt after this entry. But at the same time her correspondence with Oskar Horney gains momentum. There are sixty-two surviving letters from her side of the correspondence, written over a period of ten months between July of 1906, when Oskar left Freiburg for Braunschweig to work on his Ph.D. in political science, and March of 1907, when he returned. In the beginning the letters are in her newly acquired comradely student mode. But they soon grow into long and increasingly frank discussions of the people in Karen's life—of Karen's mother, Sonni, who arrives in Freiburg and sets up a household after Karen's first semester, of Losch, of Karen's good friend from Gymnasium days "Idchen" (Ida Behrmann), who comes to live with her and her mother.

During this long-distance phase of their relationship Karen idealizes Horney as someone wiser, more dispassionate, somehow above the complicated tangle of relationships she is struggling with. Thus it is easier to confide in him. And, probably at Oskar's suggestion, Karen comes to use the letters as a diary substitute, putting down her ideas, her insights, and, sometimes, her feelings. Of course, as she points out, writing him letters is *not* the same as keeping a diary. "Yes, I find it highly sensible, letters in diary form," she writes. "The business has only one hitch: assume I am in a very pronounced mood one day and write it down. When I go at the letter again, perhaps I read over what I wrote. And the letter strays into the waste-basket. Anyway that's the way it will be mostly," especially if she should "put down everything in the sense of my mood."[8]

Karen's self-censorship may have made things sound even better than they were. But the pleasure she expresses is convincing. "I write you only about enjoying—but my life is now just *one* enjoyment. Now? No, really always. It is as though everything has turned into enjoyment in my hands. Perhaps because everything I do—or almost everything—I attack intensively. Whether learning chemical formulas or making a pudding or reading something beautiful or being out in the open—profligate epicure, eh?"[9]

Curiously, the one thing Karen rarely discusses in her letters to Oskar from Freiburg is her reason for being there: the study of medicine. Often when she does mention medicine she sounds cavalier: "Today for the first time," she writes Oskar, "skipped a lecture. Wiedersheim was demonstrating an abdominal situs and rummaged around voluptuously in the intestines. I bore it very bravely. Yes, really! Nevertheless we preferred to go to the café and then up the Schlossberg. It was fine. Below, fog thick enough to cut. Above, ice-clear. And he is such a dear, Losch!"[10] So she moves quickly from the blood and guts of an anatomy class to levity on the mountain. Only rarely, in her later letters to Oskar, does she reveal, without joking or apology, how deeply engrossed she is in medical school. But in her diary she writes, in her customary end-of-the-year summation: ". . . if I were to read this some day in later years, I would get no correct impression of the year 1906 if at least one more point were not mentioned: I am getting fonder and fonder of my studies and my working power is borne on the wings of joyousness in work."[11]

Her days in class and in the labs are so long that "afterward a feeling of blessed weariness comes over you, almost like a slight champagne tipsiness."[12] Since writing Oskar provides an escape from all that, her reticence about her studies is understandable. Then too, although her course load includes as much chemistry, anatomy, physiology as in modern medical training, she seems to manage her work with relative ease. By her second year she is coaching Losch and another male classmate in chemistry and placing bets with them that she will do as well as or better than they

will in the final physics exam. Such confidence leaves little doubt
that medical school is going splendidly. And indeed Karen completes the required course work at Freiburg (the first half of the
four-year German medical education) in the shortest possible time,
passing the state written exams in March of 1908, just two years
after she began.

But some of Karen Danielsen's reticence about her medical studies may have derived from another source: the general disapproval
the German establishment felt toward women in universities.
After all, Karen was not just another smart medical student. She
was a smart female medical student. And if medical studies get
short shrift in her letters to Oskar, the fact of her being a *woman*
studying medicine gets no mention at all. It is intriguing that, in an
early card to Oskar, she signs herself, "Karen Danielsen, *stud.
med.*," an abbreviation for the widely used Latin designation *studiosus medicinae*.[13] By abbreviating it thus, Karen didn't have to
make the necessary gender change to *studiosa medicinae,* a rare species indeed in Germany of 1906. Like most breakers of societal
barriers, Karen preferred not to draw attention to herself, to become, as much as possible, one of the boys.

So we see and hear her putting aside girlish ways. "Then anatomy *in vivo*," she writes to Oskar describing her courses, "which I
had objected to for a long time out of embarrassment—but one
has to deposit little-girl feelings outside the door of anatomy. Most
of it is probably acquired prudery, which has little to do with
modesty and is hardly justified."[14] Indeed, in the time-honored
tradition of medical students, she soon comes to enjoy shocking
laymen with her callous attitude toward human remains. "I have
an embryo at home in alcohol," she writes to Oskar, "which we
with parental pride call Idchen's [roommate Ida Behrmann's]
youngest brother—well, I dissected the said embryo. Hornvieh,
why aren't you an M.D.? It's a failure in your character! Indeed it
is! Now *if* you were an M.D. I would expound to you with full
particulars why I am ecstatic about this embryo. You are certainly
thanking your Creator that you don't need to listen to that?!"[15]

Some male bastions, however, presented an even greater challenge. One of the most telling photographs from this period shows
Karen Danielsen flanked by six male fellow students. All are posing in their Sunday best: the men wear suits with vests, string ties,
or sashes; Karen wears a long black skirt and dignified white shirtwaist with flowing white tie. Each man carries a potent symbol of
German university life, the dueling sword, or *Schläger*.[16]

Obviously the dueling brotherhood is one Karen could not join. Instead, in this picture she has found a way to emphasize her uniqueness. The men all stand with swords, concealed in walking sticks, resting rakishly on their right shoulders, left hands resting on hips, faces turned to the camera with expressions of mock gravity. Karen, without sword, stares at the camera with a deadpan expression. Tucked under her left arm, also staring, is a grinning, hollow-eyed skull.

Did she suggest holding the skull in this picture? Since she owned a skull (a gift on her twenty-first birthday), it seems quite possible that she did. In any case, it was a clever remedy. Empty-handed in this picture, she would have been the odd woman out, the one who didn't belong to the fraternity. With the skull she becomes the centerpiece. It is an example of her knack for transforming a potentially unwelcoming environment.

Karen Danielsen's ability to adapt, to become one of the boys, tends to obscure how unusual it was for her to be in medical school at all. In fact, German universities were the last in Europe to admit women to medical studies. Until 1900 no women were admitted as matriculating students. It was possible in some universities for women to sit in as auditors. But even this privilege was reserved for women who had the proper credentials and depended on the indulgence of particular professors. Among the few women who audited university classes before 1900, many were foreign: some Americans, many Russians. "Female outsiders sitting in the same lecture hall with men," notes historian Peter Gay, "seemed more tolerable to the all-male university establishment than having one's sister, or one's friend's sister, sitting there."[17]

The pressure on German universities to grant degrees to women resulted in large part from the success of the liberals in establishing Gymnasia for girls. Once girls had gained access to the classical Gymnasium education long available to their brothers, the inevitable next goal was a university degree. And because the first Gymnasium for girls in Germany was established in Karlsruhe, the seat of the relatively liberal Grand Duchy of Baden (one of a loosely joined, separately governed confederation of German states), Baden was among the first states to confront proposals for opening classes to female students at its universities, in Heidelberg and Freiburg. In 1900, after several years of sidestepping and vacillation, the education ministry of Baden ordered the "trial" matriculation of women at its universities. Freiburg then became the first university in Germany to graduate a woman.[18]

Not everyone on the all-male faculty at Freiburg, however, accepted the ruling of the ministry with equanimity. Some professors would not let women into their classrooms. So in April of 1900, two months after the law was passed, the ministry had to issue a second ruling to the effect that separate is not equal. "The Baden Ministry holds," read the edict, "that the Freiburg Medical faculty's proposal for setting up separate classes and laboratories for women is not allowed.... It is not permitted to refuse female students participation in certain lectures or parts of lectures because of the views of the affected professor."[19]

Because Freiburg and Heidelberg were the first universities in Germany to open their doors, women attended them in rapidly increasing numbers from 1900 on. And within the universities, medicine was by far the most popular professional choice. Medicine had the advantage of placing women in the familiar role of care giver. In addition, there was a belief among some feminists of the period that, for reasons of modesty, women had a right to treatment by others of their sex. In 1900 there were 5 women enrolled at the University of Freiburg, all in medicine. By 1904 there were 20 women in medicine and 30 in the university altogether. By March of 1906, when Karen Danielsen signed her name in the great book of registrants, she was one of 34 women entering medical school.[20] Yet women remained a very small minority: out of a total of 2350 students at the University of Freiburg that spring only 58 were women. And even in 1906, despite rulings from Karlsruhe, a few professors refused to accept women in their classes. Karen does not record any rebuffs. But one woman doctor who finished at Freiburg in 1910, two years after Karen Danielsen left, remembered a certain full professor who pressed a book covering his specialty into her hand and urged her to study it well before she took the state exam. It was all he could do, he explained, since he simply could not allow her to attend his lectures![21]

The arguments against higher education for women in Germany were anthologized by Arthur Kirchhoff in an 1897 volume entitled *Die akademische Frau*. Kirchhoff asked many university professors from every discipline to write brief essays on the woman question; his results provide a revealing sampling of attitudes of the time. Of the thirty-eight medical-school professors from all over Germany who were asked whether women should study medicine, only a handful were unequivocally positive. One professor, Franz von Winckel, of Munich, had worked extensively with women students from other countries. He asserted that "even the tenderest among them cheerfully stayed on hand right up to the end of difficult operations. Many," he insisted, "have from here gone to appointments in hospitals in their home countries and have taken official positions, many have developed large practices. I know of only one who does not live from her practice. Many have married and have become happy mothers, without giving up the profession they love."[22]

Dr. von Winckel, however, was a rarity. Most of the professors insisted that medicine was no place for a woman. For one thing, their bodies wouldn't stand it. A professor of anatomy, Karl von Bardeleben, wrote:

> In my opinion women don't have the physical strength for really serious study, maybe for philosophy, theology, history, teaching or mathematics—but not for the natural sciences and least of all for medicine.... Already through study in the girls' schools [*höhere Töchterschulen*] they are sitting too much, often in slanted and crooked positions, which results commonly in harm to the spine, the chest and the pelvis, as well as the circulatory system and abdominal region. What will happen through serious study in the girls' Gymnasium and University!

Warming to the subject, Dr. von Bardeleben continued: "The disturbance of study will naturally affect menstruation with its accompanying symptoms, especially in puberty. As for the practice of medicine as a profession one must consider the lesser strength of women, the weaker skeletal structure, the smaller capacity of the heart—as well as menstruation, eventual pregnancy, childbirth—menopause, nervousness, hysteria, etc." Besides, Dr. von Bardeleben points out, tipping his hand a little, the situation in Germany is entirely different than in Russia and America, where they need more doctors. "Here we already have enough or too many."[23]

Another outspoken opponent, Dr. Georg Lewin, asserts that true womanhood will be sullied by medical studies. Dr. Lewin, a professor of internal medicine, claims that "a woman who is informed about the sexual parts not only of the woman but of the man and who can speak without blushing about the mystery of sexual acts will, if she doesn't repel men altogether, always leave them cold."[24]

Apparently the medical establishment's dim view of women in medicine was shared even by cognoscenti, as cartoons in *Simplicis-*

simus, a satirical magazine of the period, attest. One such cartoon is titled "Fräulein Doctor." In it a short, dark-haired young woman (the lady doctor) sits impassively on a sofa, head on hand, cold eyes staring straight ahead. A young man kneels on the floor with his head thrown passionately onto her lap. "You're mine at last!" cries the young man. "I can hear your heart beating at my words!" Says she: "You're wrong dear, it's the abdominal artery."[25]

Another cartoon suggests women are too frivolous for medical studies. Titled "Frauenstudium" (Women's Studies), it shows a spinsterish female medical student examining a young woman who has slipped her underclothing off down to the waist. A white-bearded professor, standing beside the young patient, quizzes the female student: "Candidate, what strikes you about this patient?" The female candidate replies: "That she is wearing silk underwear."[26] The cartoon is intriguing on two levels. There is the obvious implication that women just aren't serious enough to see beyond satin and lace. But there is a subtler, more vicious, implication as well: the female medical student is a particularly old-maidish and unattractive specimen, and she ogles the nubile young girl's naked breasts through her spectacles in a way that suggests a secret sexual attraction. There was something unnatural, in the eyes of the German public, about a professional woman. The unspoken word, of course, was "lesbian."

Indeed, the argument that seemed to have the most resounding effect in Germany was that female professionalism was unnatural. *Kinder, Küche, Kirche* were the solemn responsibility of German women, linked in many minds to the birthrate and to the military and moral might of the German nation. Men and women had separate roles; and a woman was meant to be at home, supervising the household and bearing and raising the children. Max Planck, queried in 1897 when he was on his way to becoming one of the world's leading physicists, maintained that room should be made in universities for the occasional female who demonstrates a great scientific gift. But, he added, "one cannot emphasize enough that nature itself has prescribed to woman her vocation as mother and housewife."[27] In newspapers and magazines of turn-of-the-century Germany, ads for boarding schools for young women proliferate, all promising training in the womanly arts: cooking, handwork, household management, painting, music, foreign languages, even "science." Some courses culminated, poignantly, in an exam and a degree.[28] But it was a degree good only for finding a husband—and no guarantee even of that.

As women's dissatisfaction with their separate "destiny" grew and the pressure for admission to universities increased, the opposition's arguments often turned vicious. Women who became professionals, some argued, were not real women at all but a kind of man-woman hybrid—just the sort of bony, cold, and aggressive freak featured in the *Simplicissimus* cartoons. Of all the arguments against rights for women, this was—and remains even now—the most insidious: that the woman who goes after and achieves what she wants will lose some essence of womanhood in the process. And of course the most troubling implication of this argument is that she will lose her capacity to be a good mother to her children.

In turn-of-the century Germany even women who wanted a university education took these arguments seriously. The novelist Ricarda Huch, who went to Switzerland for university study and obtained a degree there in 1892, wrote an essay, "Regarding the Effect of Study and a Profession on the Personality of the Woman," in which she argued that a woman's previous education and professionalism did *not* result in her bearing unhealthy children.[29] Even to Huch this was not self-evident.

Like Ricarda Huch, Karen Danielsen seriously pondered whether womanhood was compatible with intellectual achievement. On New Year's Eve in 1906 Karen began a notebook that she titled "Ego." Here, over the next several years, she made notes on the reading she did for her own curiosity and pleasure: on the novels of Turgenev and Zola and—later—on some of her first reading of Sigmund Freud. But the early pages of the black-and-white-speckled copybook contain careful outlines of treatises on the dangers of female emancipation. She quotes Otto Weininger on "The Emancipated Woman": "All women who really strive for emancipation are sexual intermediate forms . . . all the so-called important women are either strongly masculine or imprinted by man or overestimated." Real liberation for woman, Weininger maintains, can come only when she frees herself from "her greatest enemy: her femininity."[30] It is easy for us now to dismiss such misogynous theories. But it was not easy for Karen Danielsen. "Have you read Weininger?" she asks Oskar in a letter written around this time. "The man impresses me frightfully in part and I am looking for points of attack. He confuses me at the moment because he brings forward so many really plausible observations in support of his thesis. But it cannot, must not, may not be like that."[31]

For his part, while he seems to have been generally supportive of Karen's aspirations, Oskar about this same time sent Karen an article from a journal which presented similar arguments in less strident form. It is written by Albert Reibmayr and is entitled "The Biological Dangers of Today's Emancipation of Women." Karen's notes on the article and her subsequent discussion of it in a long letter to Oskar reveal the genuine trouble these ideas were giving her. In the "Ego" notebook her notes are straightforward: Up until now, Reibmayr says, woman's biological task has been to educate men in the spiritual realm. Men took care of intellectual development, women of emotional development. As a result of this long-standing division of labor, argues Reibmayr, organic changes have occurred. Women's logical capacities are not as developed as men's. Reibmayr maintains that it would be a terrible thing to alter this division of labor. Who would provide sensitivity training? he asks. And furthermore, intellectually active women would be less likely to have children. No, concludes Reibmayr, a healthy national culture must be a male culture, and the uneducated woman is ultimately more powerful, as a mother, than the educated one. In conclusion, Reibmayr trots out all the code words: home, family, husband and children, hearth—the woman should return to them all so that she can be truly effective. In other words, the hand that rocks the cradle rules the world.

In a letter to Oskar in mid-January of 1907 Karen responds to Reibmayr's thesis. "The article naturally interested me very much," she told him. "I will try to say briefly what I think about it." In the first place, Karen begins, Reibmayr "neglects the economic question." Conditions have changed, and women must now earn a living too. Reibmayr is right, however, that women will never be able "to achieve intellectually what men do. Lies in the nature of the matter—women are too involved in the sexual—children! etc." Women's emancipation "won't bring any direct advance in the life of the mind (science, art)." On the other hand, Karen continues, the relation of the sexes to each other would not be harmed by women's new freedom. On the contrary, "the *general level* of culture rises... women will begin to reflect, even if it only means at first that they grasp the phenomena of custom, religion, personality, etc., etc., *as problems,* and cease looking in a limited way on what is given as if it were sacred." As for the argument that women's education will lead to fewer births and fewer soldiers for the German nation, "it will *always* be only a small percentage of women who work at such a highly intellectual level that their capacity for motherhood would suffer, and then after all it really does not depend on a few people more or less!"

Here we see young Karen Danielsen arguing, once again, from experience. Because of Sonni's humiliating situation, in which she has to depend for sustenance on a man she despises, Karen is acutely aware of women's need for economic independence. And from her own development she knows that education leads to critical thinking. But experience has not yet instructed her on the other questions—namely, whether women can "bring any direct advance in the life of the mind" or whether motherhood and intellectual pursuits are compatible.[32] On these points she accepts Reibmayr's opinion. But in years to come her life will prove him wrong.

Given the attitudes toward accomplished women which surrounded her, it is not surprising that Karen, wanting to seem appealing, soft-pedals her excitement about medical school. Even when she does mention her studies to Oskar, they are linked with some frivolity: after a twelve-hour day of hard work she curls up on the sofa and listens to Losch play Chopin. After watching Wiedersheim rummage in the bowels, she and Losch bolt class and go to a café on the Schlossberg. Dissecting the neck muscles is followed by a walk up Solacker Hill. And a reference to "eye-ology" (presumably ophthalmology) is dropped into a charming little discussion of summer clothes: "I sat me down at a sunny window and fixed myself up a summer hat . . . the whole presentiment of summer lies in it, in the straw, the ribbon, the flowers."[33]

As a woman in male territory she had learned well how to improvise. In a *Weinstube* she could be a hearty comrade. At other times she could become a young woman possessed of the expected "feminine" qualities of her time, capable of spending an hour sitting in a sunny window trimming a summer hat. By the time she had reached medical school Karen had become acutely aware of her facility for slipping in and out of roles. "I automatically give myself differently to different people," she observed in a letter to Oskar and proceeded to list various people in her life and summarize their views of her. To "the old aunts in Hamburg" she was a "nice, clever, modest young girl"—"clever" because she was in a university. To Professor Wendt, the director of the Hamburg Gymnasium, she had been "brilliantly gifted; but irregular, unreliable, given to extreme moods, and boundlessly arrogant, honest." Sonni, she conjectured, saw her as "good at the core" but possessing "extravagant ideas," "rather cold-hearted," lacking in "self-

control, not likeable," and having an "exaggerated feeling of independence." To Idchen she was "all feelings," and to various others
she had met in Freiburg she seemed "careless" and "gay," with a
"tendency to 'bum around.'"

The problem, as Karen understood it at twenty-one, was that
the old roles she'd played—for aunts, for teachers, for her mother
—lacked breadth. What she needed were relationships in which
she could give her whole self: "Now I 'love' the people to whom I
can give myself out of inner necessity (without reflection!), give
myself in every part (or could give) as I am."[34]

But this solution raised yet another question, the most troubling
and difficult of all: Who exactly was the self in "myself in every
part"? Beneath all the roles, where was the real person? "There's
still such chaos in me," she wrote Oskar toward the end of the first
semester in Freiburg, "still so little firmly outlined. Just like my
face: a formless mass that only takes on shape through the expression of the moment. The searching for our selves is the most ago-
nizing, isn't it?—and yet the most stimulating—and one simply
cannot escape it. And when once again one stands helpless: what
are you?"[35]

It is a question she returns to often in various ways in her
letters to Oskar. It is a question one can often read on her face
in photographs: she looks at the camera inquisitively, as though
asking, "What will you find here in this face?" She feels herself
to be not one but many: "I'm always bad on properly taken
photos," she writes Oskar. "You would have to snap me 50
times in succession and present the thing as a movie."[36] At the
same time that she seeks self-definition, though, she fears it.
Again, speaking of a photograph, she writes: "That you like my
picture naturally pleases me. But every picture has its dangers,
because it compels one to fix and nail fast the conception one
gets of the person too one-sidedly." Characteristically, she relies
on others to judge the picture. "Are those here content with my
expression? Yes, very."[37]

At this period in her life Karen sought to know herself through
relationships. She had a desperate need for the regard and affection
of others to ward off the self-dislike that often overtook her. Writing Oskar about the picture she concluded that the others loved
her because of "my nature, as I am in other respects neither amusing, not complaint, nor pretty, nor 'afflicted' with any other characteristics worth aspiring to."[38] But the love and admiration of
friends, as important as it was, always left her hungering for some-

thing more—some relationship that would make her feel whole. In Freiburg much of Karen Danielsen's time and energy were taken up with the restless search for a love that would reveal herself to herself.

She had come to Freiburg by train on Easter Sunday of 1906, probably in the company of her classmate and friend from the Hamburg Gymnasium Josine Ebsen. Josine and Karen were destined to follow similar paths: both became psychiatrists, and, in later years, members of the Berlin Psychoanalytic Institute. But although they signed their names one after the other in the University of Freiburg register that April,[39] they lived separately.[40] Karen took a room on Friedrichstrasse, just a few blocks from the university, and proceeded to feel miserable, longing not so much for home as for past friends and loves. "Never will I forget those first days here," she wrote in her diary at the end of the year, "days full of desperate loneliness, of the disconsolate feeling of being forsaken."[41]

By July the lonely days were over. First she became "good friends" with Hans Bender, presumably a fellow student. "And no sooner was it better," she writes, "than I already wanted more, wanted something for heart and senses."[42] Then came the fateful night at the Dattler, when Losch and Hornvieh entered her life. In the beginning it was Losch, the "tall fellow," she was "in love" with.[43] From photographs it is easy to see why.

Louis Grote—Losch—had certain things in common with Karen Danielsen. He had come to Freiburg from Bremen, a North German port city like Hamburg, and he was just one semester ahead of her in medical school.[44] That Losch was a serious musician, as Rolf had been, might have touched Karen as well. But Losch's immediate attraction has been preserved in photographs: he was a young man who, from all appearances, felt genuinely pleased with his good looks. Whatever his conflicts—he was torn, for instance, between medicine and a career in music—Losch was a man who felt comfortable in his skin. To Karen, who repeatedly wrote of her plainness in her diary, this must have been impressive. In every group photograph from the Freiburg years, even the silly ones, the eye is drawn to the handsome Losch. It is not just the large, strong features but the proud carriage and, above all, the sense of style. Losch obviously cared about such things. His mustache, with the neat separation at the center and the pointy waxed ends, has had attention. The three-piece suits, with their double-breasted vests in subtle checks and stripes, have been selected with

care. The wave in the thick shock of honey-colored hair falls perfectly from the part. And he manages the right look for every
occasion. When Karen poses with her fellow medical students and
their dueling swords, it is Losch who leads the parade, sporting a
dashing silk cummerbund.

Even when others wilt, he always manages to look debonair.
There is one delightful sequence of photographs of Losch, Karen,
Idchen, and an unidentified fourth on a hike somewhere in the
Black Forest around Freiburg. In the first photograph all four have
waded into a rushing stream to pose together on a rock. The
women's outfits look wildly impractical for such an outing: ruffly
white blouses, buttoned to the neck, ankle-length flared skirts,
and, perched on top of their rolled-up pompadour hairstyles,
ladies' hats. The men wear knickers and sport walking sticks,
more appropriate gear for the vigorous hike this turns out to be.
Losch, however, looks most stylish of all: with walking stick in
one hand, cigar in the other, a little billed cap perched way back on
his thick hair, knickers, and matching Norfolk jacket. Of the four
he alone has kept his shoes on, so that his ribbed knee socks and
ankle-height blucher shoes complete the look.

By the time of the second photo it is clear that many more miles
have been walked and decorum has been thrown to the winds.
Everyone looks tired. The women's hats have disappeared, deposited perhaps beside some rock along the trail. Gone too are the
men's jackets, along with the high, stiff collars and the ties. Karen
sits, her face flushed from sun and exertion, on a log carved out to
serve as a watering trough for animals. Idchen stands barefoot,
sleeves rolled up to reveal bare arms, wisps of hair escaping their
pins. The unknown male's hat has gotten rumpled and his shirt is
unbuttoned. Only Losch, in a tidy white shirt and wide sus-
penders, remains fresh and unmussed.

Karen admired Losch's inward harmony as well. "Losch as a
whole person is much more coherent than I," she wrote Oskar.
"His whole thinking goes in only one direction, which one might
call that of natural science (in its deeper sense). Philosophy (especially theories of morality) and similar jocularities he basically (almost instinctively) rejects, because they don't suit him."[45]

Because they had different sensibilities they complemented each
other. "I am smarter at more abstract things, e.g., physics, and he
is in general quicker at understanding concrete things like anatomy." And then too there was the physical attraction: "He gives

my senses such a measure of nourishment that they do not upset my inner equilibrium through pangs of hunger. Is that cynical? I don't really know. You may criticize."[46]

The very fact that she is discussing her relationship with Losch in letters to Oskar, however, suggests that Karen is not entirely satisfied. She keeps coming back in her letters to the fact that she and Losch inhabit different worlds, that "there are sides to me that are incomprehensible to him and hence in part unsympathetic— that is, tritely put, that I think about and grapple with things that one cannot touch and put under the microscope like a beetle or some other insect."[47]

For those other things, and particularly for her self-searching, she turns to Oskar, whom she sees as the heir to Rolf in her life. "What Rolf awakened in me is being brought to life again by Hornvieh," she writes in her diary. "How shall I say it briefly? The reflecting about myself perhaps, about the deeper springs of my ego, the search within."[48] In the beginning Karen views Oskar Horney as Losch's and her special mutual friend, "our little Hornvieh."[49] Three years older and in the midst of writing his doctoral dissertation in political science, Oskar is in fact a practical man destined for a career in business. But because of his interest in ideas, he is seen by Karen as an explorer of unknown, perhaps deeper, realms—he has plunged into "the immeasurable waters of philosophy,"[50] something Karen plans to do when her medical studies ease up.

Then too, while he has some of her father's sternness, Oskar, unlike her father, is someone you can joke around with. "What a pedant you are," she writes at one point. "I'm throwing the whole bowl of my abhorrence into this sentence."[51] At first Karen's letters are taken up with the sort of friendly ridicule exchanged between drinking companions—an example of the "comradely relation" that, she maintains, is possible "between men and women students." In Germany such comradeship requires nicknames. Because the name Oskar defies nicknames ("I find it incredible, my dear," she writes, "that you acquired such an unqualifiable... name as 'Oskar'"[52]), "Horney" becomes the basis for "Hornvieh." *Hornvieh* is a collective noun meaning "horned cattle," but it also can mean, in colloquial speech, something like "blockhead." But whether dubbed by Karen or by earlier acquaintances, "Hornvieh" would probably not have taken offense; in a formal society such rough jocularity bespoke close friendship.

So too did Karen's frequent teasing in the letters about Horney's Ph.D. research, admittedly on a subject that invited humor. The exact title of the dissertation was "The Socioeconomic Value of Municipal Wastes." She calls him "dung beetle" and urges him to finish quickly with his "dirty business" so he can return to Freiburg.[53] "When," she asks, "will we be able to stop having to think immediately of our little *Hornvieh* at every manure pile?"[54]

In looks, Oskar Horney was no match for Losch. Where Losch managed always to look well turned out, Horney managed only to look stiff. He stood ramrod straight, a posture inherited from his righteous schoolteacher father. He had a rather small head, high cheekbones, and a slightly receding hairline. His small rimless glasses and goatee made him look prematurely professorial. When he tried to look casual, posing for the camera in an open smocked white shirt, he looked only uncomfortable and poorly shaven. In the begining Karen wasn't physically attracted to him. On that first evening the three had walked to Oskar's apartment, where she had fallen asleep on the couch. "Yes, and I was lying on Hornvieh's sofa" she writes in her diary, "and awoke because something was very gently stroking my cheeks—it was the little Hornvieh; but I was annoyed at that, for I was in love with the tall fellow who had fallen asleep among the cigarettes and books on the balcony."[55]

Even if she had found him attractive, a relationship with Oskar would have been impossible during her first year at Freiburg, because he left shortly after she had met him to continue work on his Ph.D. thesis in Braunschweig. But no sooner had Horney left Freiburg, in the summer of 1906, than Karen began to wish for his humor and wisdom. Karen tells her diary of her happiness with Losch during a vacation in Fallingbostel that September: "Then came the happy days on the heath with Losch. The bond between us became stronger, more intimate . . . to the mere *being in love,* friendship was added, *loving.* His strong love for me is something infinitely calming, making for happiness."[56] But happy as she was, she wrote Horney in a postcard of invitation: "Beloved Hornvieh, do let us hear from you for once, old fellow! Can't you come here for a bit? Losch is here too.—I would so frightfully like to hear you laugh again. And to philosophize with you, with Losch one just can't talk sense, as you know. . . . Now we are going out rowing with lanterns. And anyway it's ideal here. Write at least, do you hear? Hearty greeting and kiss from your Karen." To this

enthusiastic outpouring Losch added in a playful pique: "I've heard
so much about you and your laughter. Come along with
it!—?!!Losch."[57]

A week later, sitting "enthroned high up on a pair of weathered
stone veterans" on the North Sea, she writes Oskar a letter: "I look
forward terribly to seeing you again and above all to listening to
you—God, what beautiful hours those were on your balcony in
Günthersthal! Do you remember?—when you explained to me
how you had come to an understanding with those various big
question marks. You know, I have found so few people with
whom I could have conversed about deeper-lying things, and
therefore I am the less likely to forget those hours."[58]

Increasingly Karen saw Losch and Horney as having separate
roles in her life. She looked to Horney for understanding, to Losch
for pleasure and affection. In her letters to Oskar, Karen makes her
relationship with Losch sound like puppy love: "He is a *dear*.
Under his cheekiness there is something pure, childlike, it is the
artist in him. And that indestructible freshness—on the heath we
naturally romped around like two young dogs."[59] But in her diary
it is clear that the attraction is sexual. By the end of the first semester she writes: "Our being in love . . . developed into a passion
whose impact was too strong for us. But then, luckily, the day of
my departure had come."[60]

Some of the excitement—and sense of danger—Karen felt about
her relationship with Losch may have been conveyed to the family
back home in Hamburg when she returned there during the semester break in August.[61] One can easily imagine Karen, in a de-
fiant moment, making some offhand remark about her "passion"
to Berndt, or perhaps speaking of it in confidence with Sonni.
Whatever the cause, Berndt and Sonni became increasingly
alarmed around this time about Karen's wildness. Neither mother
nor son approved of such a middle-class young girl as Karen engaging in premarital sexual relations. With abortion available only
to the wellborn and birth control unreliable, pregnancy was a
likely outcome. Even Karen, writing of her "too strong" passion,
understands the dangers as well as the attraction of sex for a young
girl of her time. Sonni, who often said she had tolerated her marriage only because of her ambitions for Karen and Berndt, feared
perhaps that her impulsive daughter might in a moment of passion
sabotage her career in medicine.

Beyond such practical concerns Berndt and Sonni worried about

appearances. By the standards of the day Karen's behavior in Freiburg had been outrageous. Staying out all night with two men,
going to one man's apartment and falling asleep on a couch, inviting men, without a chaperone, up to your apartment for tea—
such things were simply not done by a middle-class girl in 1906. "I
was a frightfully dissipated rascal in those days,"[62] Karen noted.

Such behavior was thought by the family to be typical of Karen.
She was forever trying to break out of the usual social restraints.
Other women of her time protected their skin from the sun; when
she went into the mountains she soaked it up until she became a
deep, dark brown—the color of the fabled Winnetou. Back in
Hamburg after her first semester, she complained, "Oh God, little
Hornvieh, I am now in such a petit-bourgeois atmosphere of *'respectability'* [in English], young-lady manners, maid-servants—and
talk about clothes—oh, I naturally move around in this milieu
appropriately and converse exhaustively about whether Hirschfeld
or Feldberg makes better suits. In the long run such an atmosphere
always makes me restless, to the point of turning somersaults."[63]

Sonni and Berndt both lamented her unladylike lack of moderation. "Sonni," Karen confided to Oskar, "operates with the
word 'healthy' a great deal. That is all well and good, but it involves a disregard of everything that goes beyond the ordinary
measure. . . . Generally speaking: she is not free from the mistake,
frequent enough, to be sure, of setting up a norm meant for everybody. 'Only nothing too much!'—a little friendship, a little work,
a little idling, etc."[64]

Worried as they were about Karen's behavior on her own in
Freiburg, Sonni and Berndt were probably even more worried
about money. In the fourteen months since the separation the financial situation of Sonni and her children had grown increasingly
precarious. Wackels, always penurious, was their only substantial
source of support, and he had become unpredictable since Sonni
had left him. When he did send Sonni an allowance, it was very
small, and the same was true for Karen and Berndt. Karen had to
pay by the course for medical school[65] and so did Berndt for his
law studies in Hamburg. And living expenses were a problem,
even though both Berndt and Karen seemed to watch every pfen-
nig. It was largely out of this concern that in the fall of 1906
Berndt, Sonni, and Karen devised an unusual plan: Sonni would
go to live with Karen in Freiburg.

In Freiburg, Sonni could keep an eye on Karen's love life. More important, she could take in boarders, who would help to support them. The plan was made more appealing by the fact that Ida Behrmann, Karen's friend at the Hamburg Gymnasium and the daughter of a prosperous insurance executive, was coming to Freiburg that fall to study at the university. Idchen, financed by her father, would be Sonni's first boarder. Joining them—and this surely at Karen's invitation—would be Losch. "Just think, my dear," she wrote to Horney, "Losch will live with us too!! What do you think of that? It has its two sides, doesn't it? But now on the heath we have become much closer and are, I believe, on the way to becoming a pair of good comrades. Perhaps it will happen. We also have just about the same work—that is probably a factor not to be underestimated."[66] For Sonni there was yet another advantage to the plan: it would take her far away from Hamburg and the husband she now referred to in her letters as *"this* man."

Sonni traveled to Freiburg several weeks before Karen in order to find an apartment with adequate space for herself and her three boarders. The apartment she found couldn't have been commodious: it was on the third floor, above a notions shop, at 12 Sedanstrasse, a few blocks from the university. The landlady, who lived in time-honored tradition over her shop, is listed in the Freiburg address book of 1907 as "Julius Streit's widow." The renters on the fourth and fifth floors were widows too. Only "Frau Clothilde Danielsen" appears in the address book as still attached.[67] And she of course was a married woman in name only.

It is hard to imagine an atmosphere less conducive to gay abandon than an apartment house full of single matrons above a shop for seamstresses. Yet right from the beginning the jolly young boarders seem to have loved Sonni's choice. In November of 1906 Karen wrote to Oskar:

> ... it is always inexpressibly cozy. For Mother is here and she knows not only how to cook well, but above all how to spread about her a fluid atmosphere of coziness. And then our living room! When one first comes in, one thinks one has always lived in it. ... And then we four are all so fond of one another, each individual of each individual. So that the thought of our home has something infinitely calming, so that one is happy when one comes home after a lecture. I missed that so much, this—how to say it—this atmosphere of tenderness about me. ... The question of going home for Christmas is pretty well solved, because my "home" is now here. In Hamburg there is only my father. And I have no contact with him.[68]

For Karen the Freiburg household seemed the answer to a dream of a happy family life she had never known. In another letter she wrote Oskar:

> Our home is often like a doll's house:
>
> Sonni—the stepmother
> Losch—the husband
> Karen—the wife
> Idchen—the daughter
>
> A tantalizing little idyl. A lot of dear people.[69]

The phrase "doll's house" inevitably calls up the Ibsen play by that name. But of course Ibsen's *A Doll's House* describes an artificially cheerful place that falls to ruin when true feelings are expressed. Perhaps Karen, who knew Ibsen well, already had intimations of the tensions to come. But for the time being everyone seemed to view the arrangement with great optimism.

Quite apart from the financial benefits she brought, Idchen was seen by everyone as a wonderful addition to the mix. "You know I find it very nice," Berndt writes Sonni from Hamburg, "that Idchen lives with you. A little bit of Karen's intensity is made milder."[70] From the beginning Idchen assumed the role of frothy opposite to the fiery Karen. Idchen, Karen wrote Oskar, was "awfully cunning"[71] and managed to get by in German and history on a minimum of study. For weeks before *Fasching,* the pre-Lenten carnival celebrated in the Catholic South, Idchen and Karen—novices in such carryings-on—worked gaily on costumes that became essences of their roles in the "family." "Evenings," Karen wrote Horney, "we sew on our costumes of colored patches. We started out with the same material and the same purpose and it is significant that Idchen's dress is turning into a beggar *princess* dress and mine more a gypsy dress."[72]

When *Fasching* came around that February, Idchen posed for a photograph in her beggar princess costume. In it she leans gracefully into the frame of the picture as though suspended in the midst of a waltz turn. There is the hint of a mischievous little smile on her face—a reference to her costume. The costume is a happy hodge-podge: a little beggar in the boldly ripped sleeves and disheveled flower pinned to the bosom, quite a lot of princess in the long, elegantly cut ball gown, finished off with a sequined bolero that adds a touch of gypsy as well. Her prettiness is of the wholesome kind: delicate features in a round face, creamy skin, thick hair done up in a roll and crowned with a Spanish comb. She is tall, with a good figure, nicely nipped in (with the help of a corset) at the waist. With or without costume, there is something regal in her carriage. No wonder that, as Karen writes Oskar, she has "half Freiburg so far as concerns masc. gen. at her feet."[73]

At first Karen delighted in Idchen's gifts, so different from her own. To Oskar she described Idchen as "enchantingly graceful and coquettish, one of those conscious coquettes who is fully aware of every little charm, loyal to herself and to me in the subtlest ways, utterly lazy, very touchy, and as she admits herself, quite cowardly, frivolous—and the whole mixture *perfect* in its own way, and there is a great charm in it too."[74] Sometime later she wrote, "What makes her valuable to me is above all her being honest with herself—so few people are that."[75]

In the beginning she and Losch grew closer too, living under the same roof. "Losch and I—I had almost been afraid we would get 'fed up' with each other living together; but the bond has only become firmer, more solid through it."[76]

There were to be many good times during the year and a half the "family" lived together at 12 Sedanstrasse. But the idyllic atmosphere lasted only a few months. By the first Christmas, in fact, Karen was showing signs of disenchantment with the place she had so hastily pronounced to be her real home.

6

Courtship and Marriage

As she had vowed, Karen spent that first Christmas in her new "home" in Freiburg. But Losch and Idchen returned to their real homes elsewhere. So she and Sonni were left behind, probably joined briefly by Berndt from Hamburg. Two days after Christmas, Karen was writing to Oskar from an inn in the Black Forest, where she was entirely alone. As she had often done before, she wrote to keep herself company. This time it was not just the writing that gave solace but the conjuring up of flesh-and-blood Oskar to sit by her side.

27 December 1906

Hornvieh, dear one, little one,

You know, I am quite alone this evening. . . . And I seem to myself so helpless among all those strangers. Now I have fled to my room. So, now the Hornvieh has sat down beside me—you see I am no longer so disconsolate—now we will have a chat. And what would we be talking about if you were really here? I try to imagine how you look—but I only remember that from time to time your unruly "forelock" [in English] fell over your brow and that always looked so tremendously funny.

Thus begins a very long letter, written in a room so cold that she interrupts it halfway through to run outside to get her circulation going. "I am really beginning to freeze," she complains. "Come along, Hornvieh, let's run up and down outside a couple of times." And then, returning to her letter:

> So, here we are again. And now it is quite comfortable here. Whee, how cutting the cold was. The snow crunched under every step. Perfectly light. Moonlight. The big white flat areas were quite ghostly, and behind them the pine tree tops. It should be lovely to walk through the snow-covered woods now. Perhaps, no surely, down to the Feldsee [a lake nearby].—But quite alone? Naa, much too timid.

The bulk of the letter is an appreciative description of each of the members of the "doll's house." There is Sonni—"emotions like a child, strong in hating and loving," "touchingly selfless"; Losch, with his "rich emotional life" and ability to "lose himself in his music"; Idchen, "amusing, lively and quite unusually graceful in mind and body." It is as though she is gathering the dream of family warmth around her like a featherbed.[1]

But when she continues the letter the following evening, with limbs aching after a day of skiing, she reveals that there is some trouble in paradise. In fact, there is tension about Oskar, who has become, distant though he is, the third member of a romantic triangle.

Karen's concern about this had no doubt been heightened by a recent letter from Oskar in which he asked her to clarify her feelings about him. In the beginning Karen had found Losch's and Oskar's rivalry amusing and, no doubt, flattering. "The funniest thing," she wrote in her diary of their first meeting at the students' ball, "was the jealousy of my little ones [Losch and Hornvieh], and how I finally managed to reconcile them by making the tour to the Jägerhäusle."[2]

Now that both men were growing more serious and asking her to choose, she was uncomfortable. She resented Losch's claim to exclusivity. At the same time she was unnerved by Oskar's request. From her room in the Black Forest inn she wrote:

> Your letter—yes, now I will try not to be afraid of you any more. The thought that you want to be my friend makes me happy. You know that you can be, no, are a great deal to me now. And there again is

your fate, of which you spoke in your first letter to me: to give to
everyone more than is given to you. For what am I to you! Losch
cannot help me there. What does he think of your letters? I have
shown him practically nothing of the last ones, for I had the feeling
they had been written for me alone. At first he was—jealous! Now I
think he has understood that you are taking nothing from him, for
what you are to me he cannot be at all. And yet he would rather have
me entirely to himself. And if he wasn't fond of you too, he might be
just as glad if you did not exist. I understand that perfectly well—but I
can't change it.[3]

Two weeks later, back on Sedanstrasse, the cold loneliness of
her room in the Black Forest has been replaced by a warmth she
finds oppressive. "It often seems to me," she writes Oskar, "that I
am living all the time in overheated rooms here, as though I would
suffocate under all the love and care surrounding me."[4]

Increasingly the letters to Oskar become her escape. They grow
longer, more frequent, and more open as well. She abandons the
toujours gaie pose and allows Oskar to see her moodiness, her genuine faults. "I have so often thought of writing you," she confides
to Oskar on February 5, 1907, "and yet I preferred to get off 10
letters first saying nothing to indifferent people. Probably that fear
again of giving too much, of spiritual undressing—or perhaps because I have a dull suspicion that I could hardly manage to clothe
in words what is oppressing me." She goes on to confess that even
though "I have everything, everything, haven't I, that a person
could ask in order to be happy—satisfying work, love, home,
natural surroundings, etc.," she frequently feels, "What is this all
for? You see, quite ordinary sophomoric *Weltschmerz*! And I, I'm
almost ashamed to have it. It sounds so incredibly immature. I
have to smile at myself—and that doesn't get rid of it."[5]

She continues to add to the letter, without sending it, for the rest
of the month, giving Oskar a good sampling of her ups and
downs. Four days later she is so low that she feels "it is impudent
to write you today. It is as though one went into the living room
in dirty boots."[6] Four days after that, Ash Wednesday, she has been
to two balls celebrating Fasching and has concluded "that probably
not much is the matter with me." She has clearly been enjoying
herself. "Yesterday we were out late dancing in the Festhalle. And
it was frightfully common there. The atmosphere stifling and
heavy with wine fumes and kissing... it intoxicated me, infected
me—and I was not better than all the others. And you must not
think me better than I am—that's why I have to tell you all this.

Perhaps there is a bit of the hussy in all of us."[7]

But nine days after that when she writes again she is caught in the vicious circle she suffered from in later years: depression, which makes her too tired to work, followed by self-reproach, a sense of worthlessness. "You must be patient with me now. I think I have been utterly flattened out lately; a sultry feeling tells me so, the yawning emptiness in me and the disgust. I *believe* I *could* amount to something pretty good. But not like this; this way I'm going backward." There had been talk of meeting in Hamburg. But, she tells Oskar, "I am not coming *now*. I am so tired. I look forward to their all being away, need badly to be alone with myself again." She concludes the letter: "Hornvieh, write me now—so that I have someone once more to whom I can look *up*. If you would come now! Farewell, your Karen."[8]

But Horney doesn't come. Nor does Karen come to him for another four months. Both seem to sense that a meeting holds risks. For Karen it might mean abandoning the fantasy that Oskar is the longed-for ideal man, the person who understands her completely and will give her inner peace. Horney, though surely flattered by it, has already sensed the dangers in this idealization.

In comparison to the idealized Horney, Losch, and all others with whom she shares daily life, suffer. Their inferiority becomes a convenient rationale. "I do not love Losch," she writes Horney not long after the letter in which she declines to visit. "I believe one can only love that which one recognizes as superior."[9]

Dropped matter-of-factly into the letter, this hardly sounds like a painful change of heart. Her *not* loving Losch is made to seem obvious and inevitable. And yet she *had* loved Losch, with a genuine passion, only a few months before. Something had changed. For one thing, probably no man could live up to her expectations. Living in the same house with Losch, working with him on cadavers and in classes, Karen was too close *not* to see his imperfections. But her haughty claim that "one can only love that which one recognizes as superior" has a hollow ring. One suspects she is trying not to care.

And indeed a careful reading suggests Losch has in fact been moving away from *her*. "Toward the end of the semester we were once on the point of breaking up," she tells Oskar. "He began going to the café day and night and in consequence was quite utterly limp in his non-café life. Well, those are the cares of married life. But I do believe the mutual ill-humor that stemmed from it will die down in the course of centuries."[10] The facetious tone here tries unsuccessfully to mask hurt feelings. The rather pointed sexual reference (the most explicit in these letters) makes it sound as though Losch is nothing to her but a sexual convenience who was falling down in performance of his duties. But in fact he is more to her, as she reveals at other moments. And while she may well be bored with Losch some of the time, she is also terrified of being hurt, and especially of being left. The mere possibility of abandonment sends her scurrying for protection, declaring that she didn't love Losch anyway because she couldn't look up to him.

Her declaration of non-love is accompanied by a burst of activity outside the "doll's house." She starts going to the theater again and embraces it with even more than her usual intensity: "I hadn't seen a play for two years," she writes Oskar, "and earlier on the theater was my all, my home, my passion—and the thing took such hold of me that in the intermission I asked my companion not to talk. *On revient toujours à ses premiers amours.*"[11] With Losch away for the spring break touring the mountains of the Harz region, she sets out "with a young fellow as amiable as he [is] insignificant"[12] on two tours of her own in the surrounding Alps, which are covered with five or six meters of snow. "It was pretty strenuous on account of the snow. But glorious. . . . Yesterday our resting place was a little pine wood, snow all around, on a slope—in it a little round clearing in full sun, moss-covered, with a few great stones; and my only wish was to lie there for my whole life, staying in the sun."[13]

When she writes of Losch again, a protective shell surrounds her. She seems to have convinced herself that the only real issue is her dwindling affection for *him*. "I got a long letter from Losch yesterday. I had that feeling of guilt toward him again, because I do not love him as he loves me. He writes so beseechingly. I know he needs me very much now. . . . He is struggling sincerely to become a whole person, to conquer the vacillation between art and science that has prevented him from getting anywhere—in any field. I will write him soon. I know I can make him happy with a few words.—Bah, a horrid thought comes to me: is it only this sense of power that stirs me?"[14]

In early April, as her relationship with Losch languishes, her correspondence with Oskar reaches a new level of feeling. When Oskar sends her poems he has written about a past love, Karen responds tenderly and emphatically:

I hardly dare speak of what you have confided to me. Surely it is something sacred for you! But I *thank* you! The poems—such deep distress rings through them—why couldn't you make her happy? Do you believe a woman's suffering can be so great that a man's love could not encompass it? You must have loved her differently from the way she loved you—one hears that in your "Song of Farewell" ("Give me once more"—). How remarkable, that love and suffering lie so close to each other. Perhaps it *must* be so, because becoming *one* is probably just an illusion and we want to make it into a reality. . . . Tell me more about her—if it is not too hard for you to speak of this woman who brought you such great happiness and so much anxious suffering. . . . That you sent me the poems! They are a part of you—and so I will protect them devoutly. I won't speak of them any more; perhaps that would only hurt you.[15]

In the letter enclosing the poems comes the news that Oskar may have difficulty meeting her as planned in the summer. She responds, "Now maybe nothing will happen about your coming in summer!! You are copying me—promise and then thumb your nose. Otherwise *I* will certainly come in August. But this time no backing out."[16] As the letters become more frank and open, the thought of meeting face-to-face seems to daunt both correspondants. "I am frightfully shy," Karen writes, "—don't laugh, Hornvieh!—I really am. Only not with the few people with whom I feel at home at once—and even there it is still a long time before I have sounded out enough terrain. I have already spoiled a great deal with this not-being-able-to-get-out-of-myself (oh!). But naturally it isn't as bad in writing as orally."[17]

The correspondence allows for intimacy at a safe distance. With Losch, there are no such geographical protections. And many of the fluctuations in her feelings toward him during this period are linked to her complicated feelings about closeness and distance. On one hand, when he goes off to the cafés day and night, she puts up a protective shell and declares she doesn't care about him. But after his absence on a tour of the Harz she is ready to risk being his "girl-friend" again and meeting his demands for exclusivity. When Losch gets angry because she is writing a letter to Horney, she dutifully tears it up and passes on the reason to her correspondent. "It was a matter between Losch and me," she explains to Horney. "May I talk about *that* with *you*? Isn't that a sort of—deception?"[18]

But three weeks later she is feeling hemmed in again after a four-day trip to the Vosges (a chain of mountains that begins in

Alsace) with Losch, Idchen, a friend named Venus, and, probably, Sonni. They all seem to have gotten too close for comfort.

"It is blasphemy to be five on a trip in the Vosges," she writes. "Two at most, or at least two *at best* assuming that the two are attuned to each other. The way it's best to go to the theater alone. There must be no break in the mood, and one should not have to spend part of one's strength eliminating—mentally—the others.... Losch measures Nature only by the yardstick of the grandiose—a good Alpine view can drive him wild with enthusiasm. He has no sense of the idyllic." Karen feels "admiration for the grandiose, it *elevates* me," but prefers the quieter beauty of the Lac de Corbeaux. "Only that moving, silent beauty, that deep, smiling peace, as, for example, this little lake exhales it, makes me *happy.*"[19]

Karen seems to be in constant conflict with the others about group activities. "I find that so long as it doesn't do the others real harm," she writes, "each one should do what seems to him best.... I do not see the sense of demanding that in disputed cases I should join the majority.... What do you think? Is this lack of *esprit de corps* a real lack on my part or is it justified?"[20]

By June she has come to feel hounded by the others on this point of togetherness:

> There are moments when I hate the others—a mild feeling of contempt seldom leaves me. And then—this belongs to it—it practically lies in the nature of the case that the three stand together against me in all and everything. Not that they don't love me. On the contrary: I am the one who receives the most love from the others, and a "friend" actually spoke today of a Karenocentric system. These external irritations come from a difference of principle in the concept of living together, about which I have already written you, but which I can now formulate better. Losch says that when three want something and the fourth doesn't, the fourth should in any circumstances acquiesce (in all social doings, amusement, etc.)! I say it doesn't matter *how many* want something, but what the individuals want. For example, if the others want me to play cards with them and I am working, work takes precedence. Now Losch is just as convinced of his own viewpoint as I am of mine. In consequence of which I am daily obliged to hear that I am unkind, single-track minded, that I "always" separate off, and want something special for myself. Well, let them talk! But this eternal nonsense really does make me unkind in the long run.[21]

Forgotten now are Idchen's charms and Sonni's selflessness. Now both are shocking hypocrites. Idchen, for example, is leading on a "rather dreamy and poetic" young man whom she has no real interest in, answering his letters "into which he apparently put his deepest thoughts and feelings" in his own florid style.[22] As for Sonni, while she is "at bottom a good person," she is "in ethical things... incredibly inconsistent and thoughtless.... She often used to spur us on in lying to the old gentleman [Wackels], while at another time she would insist to us that lying was something bad."[23]

Her brother, Berndt, too is a disappointment, perhaps in part because of the anti-Semitism in the Rolf affair but also because of a more recent brother-sister quarrel: Karen apparently refused to lie to Sonni for Berndt, who wanted to go off on a romantic weekend, and Berndt in turn denied a similar request from Karen. "Hornvieh, my brother—he was formerly my idol. Recently he has given me a chance to look into the depths of his soul. And I saw abysmal meanness and an ignoble disposition. It was so low that I was quite stunned and kept thinking only: it is impossible for anyone to be so mean. And my brother at that! It is too long to tell you the story. I felt bruised all over. Losch says this probably comes of my 'always going around with such ideal people, like Hornvieh.'"[24]

Perhaps Losch was being sarcastic. In fact, Horney could remain ideal just as long as she didn't "go around" with him. As her disillusionment with the others grew, her adulation of the far-off Horney reached new heights. "Hornvieh, if I didn't have you— I already feel almost safe, just writing to you."[25] Horney's letters become talismans, acquiring magical powers:

> But now I must have another letter from you. Yes indeed. I remember when your last came. I had just waked up, and it lay on my heart like a mountainous burden that my dentist would be torturing me in a few hours. And then Sonni brought me your letter. Whereupon the barometer of my mood shot up and even the dentist appeared to me in a milder light. And when I got to him trembling, he thought we could leave things as they were for the present. I could have embraced him with delight—I'm an infuriating coward where such murderous instruments are concerned![26]

In August, after many false starts, Karen and Oskar made definite plans to get together. This time there really was no backing out. As the time of their meeting approached, however, Karen served notice that there were other men besides Oskar in her life. In June, Karen wrote Oskar full of "inner jubilation"[27] because

Rolf, after two years of silence, had written, wishing to renew
their friendship. She was making plans to meet him in August as
well. And then, as she and Losch were about to part for the summer, they too started to get along better. So by the time she left
Freiburg, on July 31, Karen had plans to see not only Oskar but
two others—Losch in Hildesheim and Rolf on Lüneburg heath.
Her mother would have seen this as wildness. But it was also a
way of staving off disappointment if Oskar Horney didn't live up
to the advance billing she had been giving him.

The suspense had been building for nine months. In May she
had written, "You know, I see it coming: we shall have so much to
tell each other that we will be wrapped in deep silence."[28] Five days
before her departure she was optimistic:

> My dear, I am delighted that I can stay with you. I have such a horror
> of hotels when I am alone in them. I shall surely recognize you?! Yes, I
> think when I see you I will know that it is you—and then the mem-
> ory-pictures that had gone to sleep will awaken again. Yes, you are
> quite right: what we shall talk about together is only a secondary con-
> sideration—the fact in itself is precious enough. I also don't believe
> that our being together will in principle alter anything in the concep-
> tion we each have of the other. But it will become more plastic, more
> alive. My dear, how glad I am. O Lord! Frightfully! . . . Your Karen[29]

Somehow, Karen reconciled the idealized Oskar she had known
from afar with Oskar in the flesh: that summer the relationship
made the transition from friendship to passion. In October, Oskar
returned to Freiburg to complete his Ph.D. thesis. The two became nearly constant companions and, probably, lovers as well.
The fact that no diary exists for the period of these last two semesters in Freiburg suggests that it was an engrossing, happy time for
Karen. So too do Sonni's letters to Berndt from Freiburg. For
Sonni it was quite the opposite: she complained bitterly to her son
of Karen's neglect and coldness. Like Karen, Sonni hated to be left
alone. And during this final semester in Freiburg, as she wrote to
Berndt, she was left day after day.

All of Sonni's surviving letters seem to have been written at
fever pitch. They are full of exclamations and underlined words,
and, invariably, many complaints. The idea that life isn't worth
living comes up more than once: "In general these days I have only
one wish," she writes Berndt that winter, "if only life would come

to an end, it is now *so* useless and I am in the way of myself and others!"[30]

After Oskar Horney returns to Freiburg, she complains most of Karen's neglect:

Here I have hardly anything for the heart, especially this winter, it is getting terrible, I have days and hours where I can hardly bear this outer and inner loneliness. Especially when I don't feel well. . . . It's possible that it's my own fault, I don't know. . . . Also I have been too considerate, too modest and generous, and I misled others into a healthy selfishness by being that way. And also, the very annoying and never-ending housework. To make it short, I often feel *terribly* down and degraded. I'm only there to clean, cook and darn and patch, the others go their way and this winter they only come for the meals and I'm not even supposed to ask when they go out when they will be back. The mornings alone to piddle around I don't mind, but the afternoons and mostly the evenings I can hardly bear it. They are nice and sweet with me, but their egoism has something very hurting, especially from Karen who is my *own* very beloved child and who should have more heart and sense and understanding for me. . . . It was a little easier during the first two semesters, because the four of us held more together and they stayed home four or five nights out of seven. . . . Now Karen is not there *at all,* since Horney is here. In the morning an hour or two, in the afternoon and evening she is with him. So if she *wants* and *loves* she has time for everything. I asked once for a *half* hour—she snapped at me! Now I admit that she and Horney really enjoy being together and should take advantage of it, that they mean a lot to each other and give a lot to each other—but there we are again with Kaja's thing about moderation! Myself I really think highly of him, and I know of *no one* who could have such a good influence on Karen; but say for yourself, does she have to run over to his place so often and *every* evening, be there until 10 or 10:30? I know about everything —so couldn't they stay once or so with me? But that's Kaja, not Horney, because he is very charming with me.

Idchen, she complains, is just as preoccupied with *her* boyfriend. And Losch is constantly going to concerts "for inspiration" or studying with friends. "And why am I doing this?" she asks. "Basically so that Idchen gets away from home and Karen has a sort of stabilizer in me." But now Karen's "partner-changing is ending— and she knows what she wants and is basically a very independent nature who can manage without me. There are times when she is *so* nice and reasonable and considerate—but then again she is so

without understanding and ego, ego, ego." Sonni ends her letter
by begging her son "not to worry about me, I just *had* to let it out.
Here I don't have *any*body with whom I can talk, no social acquaintances, nothing."[31]

Berndt's letters to Sonni are as breezy and light as Sonni's are
heavy and histrionic. Often they read like a hurried conversation
over breakfast—a jumble of incomplete sentences and unfinished
thoughts. Sometimes he seems to be speaking private family language, as when he calls his mother *Mudding*—a playful version of
the usual *Mutti* (Mommy). In general the language is idiosyncratic
—full of youthful slang, coined words and phrases, and sometimes
a little Plattdeutsch (the Low German dialect spoken around Hamburg) thrown in for good measure.

The inner preoccupations of Karen's letters to Oskar never surface in Berndt's correspondence. Berndt's "recipe," as Karen noted
some years earlier in her diary, is not to "yield to any conjectures
about final things."[32] His concerns are practical, down to earth.
Should he choose the matching or the contrasting colored vest (at a
greater price) for the new suit he's having fitted at Dykhoff? Bodily events are regularly reported: indigestion comes and goes,
hangovers result from late-night carousing, his mustache has been
shaved, revealing a comic white shadow. In their unselfconscious
detail the letters provide a lively picture of a young up-and-coming
law student and man-about-town in Hamburg. Parties, weddings,
weekend tours into the countryside, nights out on the town—all
are chronicled for Sonni's benefit. The overwhelming preoccupation of the letters, however, is not pleasure but money: how much
money Sonni needs, how much he can get from Wackels, how
much he can make, what Karen should try to get from a rich aunt,
and so on.

The principal target of Berndt's financial schemes is his father,
Wackels, referred to in his letters to Sonni as *der Alte* or, slightly
more respectfully, *le vieux*. Since Sonni left, Wackels has continued
to live in the same place in Reinbek, cared for by a series of wife
substitutes: a daughter by his first marriage and housekeepers.
Wackels wants Sonni to come back and has been using money as a
weapon—not sending her support money in Freiburg and, apparently, holding out the promise of money if she returns.

Sonni, however, is adamantly set against even writing to
Wackels, let alone returning. When Agnes, one of Wackels' daughters by his first marriage, writes asking her to return, she explodes:

How someone, being on a certain moral level and knowing me a little bit, can ask *that* from me I absolutely don't understand. If the old man were fragile, confined to bed and needing care, then maybe one could think about this. No, no, no, no—better to live a poor life with strangers than to go back to slavery and to *this* man. My God, don't ask this of me—if I took up the fight courageously when you started studying, to make your education and a later career possible, so now when I only have to think about myself, I'm not going to let *despair* drive me into his arms. As he said at the time, he could hurt me most deeply and sensitively through my children, by refusing money [for the children's education]—so now I need him even less and even if he promised me golden mountains and a comfortable future—you can look at my stubbornness as obstinacy or sickness—I would rather be dead.[33]

This angry standoff has left Sonni and Karen living on the edge. They survive on what the boarders on Sedanstrasse bring in, plus a small allowance Wackels sends Karen. And Wackels is always threatening to cut off even this.

This is the situation in July of 1907, when Berndt perpetrates one of his schemes. He tells Sonni to compose a letter to him "which I would give to the old man, saying you're not clear about what you want to do in the future, but need to allow yourself a little more time. If the old man had a letter from you, if you showed a little more consideration, then he would be willing to give you more money and all our difficulties would be a little bit softened and we would be on the way to more prosperity." As an afterthought he adds, "The letter must not look like you want something."[34]

Sonni writes the letter and Berndt takes it out to Reinbek with him on one of his visits to Wackels. Berndt gives the letter to Astrid, a stepsister, who shows it to Wackels. Wackels, extracting from it the hope that Sonni might return one day, is pleased. Berndt reports back to Sonni: "Our goal is reached for the first time. . . . Regarding money I asked the old man this time to send you the monthly money directly in order to have a faster settlement, so you get 150 marks probably Tuesday."[35]

Berndt's manipulation of his father's emotions seems cruel. But amid all the scheming there are poignant hints that Berndt has another, unacknowledged, agenda: bringing the family back together again. "The old man still hopes that you are going to come back," he writes Sonni in the spring of 1907. "He became a lot more human. He doesn't want to send Karen money anymore, as long as she only writes when he does."[36] Some weeks later, when Karen is making plans to pass through Hamburg on her way to Sweden for the summer break, Berndt writes: "Karen has to plan a longer stay in Reinbek [with her father], and has to write more often to the old man. There's too much at stake. You really have to realize that. In the long run I cannot make up for your sins of neglect.... You must be more careful in your own interests. You have to take the given conditions into account!"[37]

That summer, when Sonni becomes ill on a vacation in Switzerland, Berndt writes with advice: "Please eat well and not only little bites, you have to have a proper warm meal. And how is it with your sleep now? Please please let me know soon and in detail about you.... Unfortunately you don't write about whether I should send you the extra costs immediately or only with your monthly money. Please let me know." Then he adds: "Today you will probably get a letter from the old man, he is really sorry about your sickness and asks me if he should send you the money for September a little earlier. But I said no, he should rather send you some extra for a bottle of wine.... You should thank the old man with a postcard, could say you feel too tired to write more."[38]

Conventional and narrow-minded though he is, Berndt has important virtues. He seems to be the only person in the Danielsen family who has a practical overview. His concern takes the form of action, not only on Sonni's behalf but also on Wackels'. Berndt may ridicule *der Alte* in his letters to Sonni, and yet, just as he worries over Sonni's problems, he worries over Wackels'—negotiating with a troublesome landlord, interviewing for a housekeeper. In his relationship to Sonni it is he who takes on the role of provider Wackels has abdicated. *Someone* has to think about where the next meal is coming from. And if it weren't for Berndt, who in this volatile family would?

When the parents act like children, the children often take on adult roles early. Certainly this was true in the Danielsen family, not only of Berndt but also of Karen. Berndt carried the provider burden in this role reversal, but the emotional burden was on Karen. Although Sonni took on the important and exhausting task of homemaking—cooking, cleaning, and running a boarding-house besides—she relied on Karen for emotional support. When Karen, in the last semester at Freiburg, withdrew into an intense relationship with Oskar, Sonni felt enraged and betrayed.

Sonni's unhappiness, and the heavy weight it carried in her children's lives, were not new. When she was fifteen Karen wrote in her diary, "Mother is ill and unhappy. Alas, if I could only help my 'dearest in the whole world'—How miserable you feel when you see your loved ones suffer."[39]

Berndt's reaction to Sonni's outpourings of unhappiness was usually a pep talk. Or he would try to cheer her by sending money or promising money for the future. But he rarely came to visit. There was always some reason—the time was too short or he was too busy—why he couldn't come to Freiburg. To Sonni's letter complaining of Karen's desertion he replied, "My poor Mommy, how sorry I am that you are going through so many difficulties.... Don't let yourself be pushed down and don't lose courage. Stay cheerful. It's only a matter of time! And Christmas we should not let fall through; I could probably make it even if it's only eight days or so; wait and see."

No sooner has Berndt mentioned a visit, however, than he starts to back off. "But one thing you should think about and thoroughly, is it reasonable that I should come for such a short time, and I ask this question *only* for one reason, that maybe afterwards you would feel too lonely if I'm gone after such a short time?? Please think about it so that I can see what I can do."[40] Berndt prefers to lend emotional support from a distance.

Both children hope to rescue their mother through their accomplishments. On Sonni's birthday that spring, not long after her unhappy letter from Freiburg, Berndt writes: "So, my Mommy, I wish you the very best in your new year, that you become younger and stay as flexible and that the year will bring you *lots and lots* of nice and good things. I can contribute to that today, or at least begin. Are you still in bed? If not sit down first!"[41] Berndt goes on to tell his mother that he has passed his law exams and has the promise of a job in a good firm. He has actually taken the exams a few days early so that he can announce it to Sonni on her birthday.

With Berndt a junior lawyer and Karen on her way to becoming a doctor, Sonni can now look forward to a time when her children can take her in and provide for her. Indeed, when the Freiburg household breaks up, she proposes coming to live in Hamburg with Berndt. But Berndt wants no part of it: "You know *I* would find it very nice if we could live together, also if you would come to Hamburg even without living together. But the first thing is out of the question because of the money.... And nonsense because my position is *at least* for a year very insecure. What would happen if it didn't work out and you didn't find anything else?"[42] The truth is that Berndt is leading a gay bachelor life. Even if his position were secure, living with his mother would cramp his style. And so when Karen leaves Freiburg for Göttingen, Sonni, either unwilling or not invited to join her, goes instead to Stockholm to stay with her stepdaughter Agnes.

Among medical students in Germany it was the custom to "migrate" during medical training—taking classes and clinical training in two or more places. After completing the two years of classroom work and passing the required state exams Karen chose to travel to the University of Göttingen, not far from Hannover, in north-central Germany, for clinical work. She went there to be near Oskar, who seems to have been spending the year in Braunschweig, near his parents' home in Hessen, not far from Göttingen.

In Göttingen, Karen would have been asked for the first time to play the role of doctor rather than student, observing initially and then participating in clinics in obstetrics and surgery and practicing her diagnostic skills. In Göttingen too she and Oskar were really free for the first time to be together as much as they pleased without feeling qualms about Sonni and without distracting memories of old loves and alliances.

Thinking later in Berlin about whether she would like to go back to Freiburg or Göttingen, Karen concluded: "I still would go to Göttingen, perhaps because I crave an indifferent milieu, because I want only something friendly, quiet, peaceful—and not go see some memory laughing out of every corner, and not to think on every path I take: I used to walk here with this one or that one, here we kissed, here we picked raspberries, here we drank winepunch."[43]

Still, Sonni's unhappiness, far away in Stockholm, must have weighed on Karen. Things had gotten worse for Sonni after Freiburg. Wackels, perhaps because he realized that Sonni *wasn't* returning after all, had cut off Sonni's funds altogether, prompting her to request a divorce. Her attempts at earning money herself had fallen through. Her ads in the *Daheim* offering her services as a companion had gotten nowhere, and she wasn't having much luck finding work as a translator. For the first time she spent Christmas away from her children. She wrote from Stockholm that she was feeling sick and discouraged.

Ten months after her departure, Berndt and Karen acted in concert to rescue her. Berndt's way, predictably, was to exact a financial commitment from Wackels. On New Year's Day of 1909 he wrote Sonni the good news that the old man had promised in writing to send her 900 marks (in 1909 the equivalent of $215 in American currency), to be paid in quarterly installments.[44] At around the same time Oskar and Karen invited her to come to live near them in the Harz Mountains. On New Year's Day, Oskar wrote, "My Sonning, it is good that we're going to have you here a week from now! Those must have been terrible weeks for you— The new year shall and will be better. Everybody who loves you is going to take care of that." Karen added a postscript: "My Sonning, I am sooo much looking forward to seeing you!... You shall be happy again.... Your Kaja."[45]

The next fall Karen and Oskar announced that they were planning to marry. The announcement was greeted by everyone in the family as just the thing for Karen, since Oskar was a stabilizing influence. Berndt wrote to Sonni that it proved Karen "is now somehow a social creature....[46] "Poor Oskar really has to go through a lot with Karen," he writes some months later, "but I feel with you how glad you can be that the direct and primary worry about Karen is taken away from you and that on top of that you get such a son-in-law."[47]

Karen would have balked at the idea that she needed constraints. But perhaps she too was attracted to Oskar's solidity. Like Berndt, he was down to earth. Before Sonni came to stay, it was he who figured out and meticulously relayed the train schedules, just as Berndt had done before him. Unlike Losch, who was torn between music and medicine, Oskar seemed to be clear that he wanted to prosper in business. Oskar was steady: he had proved that as a correspondent. And he had been tolerant when she had loved Losch, never withholding his attentions. Oskar was tolerant too of new ideas. Not many men, in Germany in 1909, were ready to marry a woman of ambition such as Karen.

Equally important, Oskar seemed to best fulfill Karen's wish to be understood "in every part." It was in her letters to him that she had felt free to talk of her "unremitting, ever more refined self-observation that never leaves me, even in any sort of intoxication."[48] She believed Oskar could know and understand her. "*Because* you understand the good in me, I have a burning wish that you should know me wholly, wholly. Why is it so unutterably beneficial, the thought that somebody besides myself knows me??"[49] Perhaps Karen believed that if she gave herself to Oskar, his steadiness would somehow steady her, shielding her from "those sluggish days" when "everything goes askew" and "I slip out of my own hands."[50] Thirty years later, in *Self-Analysis,* she would write about the futility of placing the "center of gravity entirely in the 'partner,' who is to fulfill all expectations of life."[51] But at twenty-four that lesson was yet to be learned.

While it is impossible to know fully why Karen chose to marry at this stage of her life or why she chose Oskar as a marriage partner, it is true that marriage solved many practical problems at once. There was, first of all, the ever-present money problem. Oskar was an ambitious man with good prospects: at the time of their marriage he was beginning a promising career with a prewar industrial giant, the Stinnes Corporation in Berlin. As Berndt, ever practical, wrote his mother, "*Quant* à money—the question 'when' was only a question of money—so I think they must have thought about it thoroughly."[52] To sweeten the pot, Wackels would add a modest dowry of two thousand marks. Even more important, the marriage promised to provide Sonni, for the first time since she had left Wackels, with a secure and socially acceptable home.

In this way Karen would be achieving another goal she had set for herself nine years earlier. It was then, during a particularly unhappy time in her mother's life, that she had resolved to provide a new home for her. "If only she [Sonni] is spared for Berndt and me," she wrote, "so that later on she can lead a friendly life with the two of us—when Berndt is a lawyer and I am a teacher. It is probably just as well that one cannot lift the veil of the future, and so can go on hoping."[53] Now that Karen had exceeded those early expectations and become a doctor, it was possible to fulfill the wish, with a husband, instead of a brother, at her side. Through her marriage Karen would now be able to provide the "friendly life" for her mother, and for herself, that she had dreamed of at fifteen.

————————————PART THREE

Berlin

1909–32

7

Psychoanalysis

Berlin in 1909, when Karen and Oskar settled there as newlyweds, was a city yearning to become cosmopolitan. The public dream, as a visiting English journalist noted at the time, was Berlin as *Weltstadt,* a world city in a class with London, Paris, and Rome. "The more noise, sky-signs, kinos, cafés, pickpockets, sins, the happier [Berlin] is," Edward Edgeworth asserted. "By being a world city Berlin confutes the old, resented charge that it is a town of soldiers and bureaucrats, a tedious provincial nest of order and virtue."[1] As a Gymnasium student in Hamburg, Karen Danielsen had believed in Berlin's modernity; her first plan had been to go there to medical school. But the Berlin of her imagination was more modern than the reality. In fact, she would not have been welcome at the University of Berlin in 1906. Prussia, the most reactionary of the German states in its policies toward women, didn't admit them to universities as degree candidates until 1908.[2]

Berlin before World War I was a hybrid, a city both provincial and sophisticated, both radical and extremely conservative. Unlike the established world cities, Berlin's dominance was based not so much on a rich cultural past as on the recent military successes of Prussia, which had ballooned in the aftermath of the Franco-Prussian War into a sprawling German state dwarfing all others in size and wealth. Further, the Hohenzollern Kaiser Wilhelm, who

135

resided at the imperial palace in Berlin when he wasn't off on one of his many junkets, was a singularly shallow and intolerant autocrat. He despised the innovative art that flowered around him. And since the Kaiser liked to express his opinions (it was said of him that he approached every question with an open mouth[3]), the imperial taste was well known to the general public.

To Richard Strauss, whose operas and symphonic poems were creating international excitement, he proclaimed all modern music "worthless," because "there isn't an ounce of melody in it."[4] The Impressionist paintings of Max Liebermann and the drawings of Käthe Kollwitz, depicting Berlin's poor and homeless, were dismissed by His Majesty as "art from the gutter."[5] When political protest reared its threatening head in the theater the Kaiser was indignant. *The Weavers,* Gerhart Hauptmann's dramatization of the plight of poor weavers in Silesia, prompted the Kaiser to cancel the subscription of the imperial box at the theater where it appeared. He also advised the army and navy to stay away from the theater, which had succumbed to un-German tendencies.[6]

Fortunately the Kaiser's views on art could not prevent Berlin artists from performing and displaying their works, nor Berliners from appreciating them. Unable to gain access to official showings, Liebermann and others formed the Secessionist group and set up a gallery on Berlin's modern thoroughfare, the Kurfürstendamm. And Hauptmann's *The Weavers* became a great success in part *because* the Kaiser inveighed against it.

In politics too the Kaiser met with powerful opposition. In fact, it was as though Berlin were not one but two cities. On one hand, it was the city of the Kaiser and his court, whose gala dinners and charity balls were chronicled daily in the newspapers and followed by thousands in the middle class who dreamed of moving up into the Prussian aristocracy. On the other hand, it was the city of August Bebel, heir to Karl Marx and leader of the international Socialist movement. The Socialists' cry "Berlin belongs to us" was a fact by 1903, when 61 percent of the voters in Berlin were Social Democrats. Imperial Berlin was also the red city.[7]

Paradoxically, the artistic daring and leftist sentiments of which the Kaiser so heartily disapproved were a direct result of the proindustrial policies of the empire, which had turned Berlin into a boomtown in the years following the Prussian victory over the French. In the *Gründerjahre* (founding years) of the late nineteenth century Berlin became a major industrial center, attracting in particular chemical, electrical, and other enterprises developing out of new technology. By 1900 the new industry had produced dozens of new millionaires and thousands of urban poor. At the same time Berlin had grown diverse, attracting peasants from the East and tripling its already significant population of Jews. There was building everywhere. In the east, north, and south poorly constructed apartment houses, so crammed with people they were accurately called "barracks" (*Mietkaserne*), could not be built fast enough to meet the housing needs of the working class. The nouveau riche, of whom there were many in Berlin, erected lavish homes to the west, along the Kurfürstendamm. The style of choice was eclectic international: an Assyrian palace might rise beside a mini-Versailles or an Italian villa. The pace and the newness reminded Europeans of America. Berlin was a city with an *Amerikanisches tempo*,[8] or, in the words of one of its leading industrialists, Walther Rathenau, "a Chicago on the Spree."[9] And like American cities, it made up in industrial might and size what it lacked in culture and history. By 1909, when Oskar and Karen arrived there, Berlin was the most thickly settled city in the world and an industrial power equal to any other in Europe.

In some ways Karen and Oskar Horney were typical of the new middle-class arrivals swelling the population of Berlin. Oskar, the son of a small-town schoolteacher, came, armed with a Ph.D., to make his fortune in the new Berlin industry. He and Karen married in Berlin, apparently with a minimum of ceremony, on October 30, 1909, and settled, as middle-class couples would, on the fast-growing west side of town. In the 1910 Berlin *Adressbuch* they appear to be boarders in a boardinghouse on Schweinfurthstrasse in Dahlem. It seems likely that they chose the neighborhood because Oskar had begun work in nearby Steglitz in the offices of the coal baron Hugo Stinnes. Oskar rose quickly within the growing Stinnes empire. In the 1910 *Adressbuch* he is listed only as a Doctor of Political Science. But the following year the second title of General Secretary, describing his position at Stinnes, has been added. By 1911 the title has yielded concrete results: Oskar Horney has moved to his own apartment in the modest middle-class neighborhood of Lankwitz.[10]

From these three entries in the Berlin *Adressbuch* a contemporary Berliner could have sketched in a typical life. Here was a young man on his way up in the corporate world, moving from boardinghouse to apartment house, from degree to title. By his side, no doubt, was a Frau General Secretary; wives, invisible in the phone book, were identified socially by their husbands' titles. Together the young couple were probably planning a comfortable future: children would arrive, they would move on to ever more luxurious apartments or even a villa (as Berliners called private homes with land) on the outskirts of the city. Frau General Secretary's task would be to preside over a large household of servants, including nannies for the children and perhaps even a chauffeur if things went really well. If they had social ambitions, this typical Berlin couple might well use their growing fortune to trade up the social ladder. A daughter, with the promise of a large dowry, might win the most coveted prize of all, a reserve officer. A son might marry into a family with "von" in its name, or at any rate one with more breeding than cash.

Such a couple might well appear in the novels of Theodor Fontane, keen observer of middle-class mores in Wilhelmine Berlin.[11] Karen and Oskar Horney, however, were a new and quite different sort of bourgeois couple. There would be children and nannies, a villa, and even for a time a chauffeur. But there would never be a Frau General Secretary devoting her entire energies to advancing her husband and the family. Instead there would be a woman of many parts, a wife and mother who also had a life of her own as Dr. Karen Horney. To make matters even more unusual, her life as a *doctor* would be subdivided too. Karen had decided to specialize in psychiatry, but for a reason that she had to keep secret from her medical-school teachers. During the day she was a student doctor, undergoing orthodox training in a series of psychiatric clinics in Berlin. But after hours Dr. Horney pursued another kind of training, as a patient and student of Freudian psychoanalysis. It was probably psychoanalysis that led her to specialize in psychiatry and not the other way around.

And yet her interest in Freud's new ideas could have nothing to do with her medical studies. Psychoanalysis was frowned upon by the medical establishment and would continue to be for years. "The medical profession, including psychiatry," as one early student noted, "had no use for psychoanalysis."[12] During her final year of medical school at the world-renowed Berlin Charité, Karen Horney studied under an important figure in German psychiatry at the time, Karl Bonhoeffer. Bonhoeffer, by all accounts, was mild in his disapproval of Freud. Not so Theodor Ziehen, head of the psychiatry department. When Karl Abraham, the only trained Freudian in Berlin, presented a paper to the Berlin Neurological Society in 1909, Ziehen responded by cutting off all discussion and delivering instead a "short but furious attack." The rest of the psychiatrists in attendance, according to Abraham, greeted the paper with "those well-known supercilious smiles." The only medical colleague who took an objective view, Abraham reported, was "a surgeon who wandered into the room by mistake."[13]

Ziehen's hostility, and the generally unreceptive attitude of German psychiatry toward psychoanalysis, had to do with recent history. Psychiatry was a latecomer to German medicine: the first state exams in psychiatry as a specialty weren't administered until 1904. In the early nineteenth century, psychic life had been viewed in Germany as the province as much of philosophy as of medicine. The psychiatric literature during much of the nineteenth century was influenced by German Romanticism, by *Naturphilosophie,* a mystical pantheism that viewed all nature as possessing a single soul. Romantic psychiatry, as it has been called, was speculative and often moralistic and theological as well. Observation of behavior had little part in it.

But in the late nineteenth century, as better facilities for the care of the insane developed in Germany, psychiatrists turned increasingly from speculation to examination of cases. By the end of the nineteenth century, in fact, the pendulum had swung to the opposite extreme. Successes in experimental science, particularly the success of Hermann von Helmholtz in measuring nerve impulses, had made a profound impression. German psychiatry, as taught and practiced in medical schools and clinics, saw all mental aberrations as caused entirely by organic changes. There was no place in academic psychiatry then for the view espoused by the Romantic psychiatrist Ernst von Feuchtersleben that "mental disease" derives "neither from the mind, nor from the body, but from the relation of each to the other."[14] Instead psychiatrists operated with the dictum that "mental illness is brain illness [*Geisteskrankheiten sind Gehirnkrankheiten*]."[15]

The author of this much-cited pronouncement was Wilhelm Griesinger, a psychiatrist whose rise coincided with the establishment of psychiatry as a branch of medicine in Germany in general and at the Berlin Charité in particular. Griesinger, who was named to the newly created chair in psychiatry and neurology at the Charité in 1865, viewed psychiatry and neurology as a single branch of medicine, no different from other branches in its reliance on physiology: all mental aberrations, in this view, originated at a "locality," a "cerebral center," in the brain. Nonmedical and "particularly all potential and ideal conceptions of insanity," declared Griesinger, were "of the smallest value."[16] This approach reached its apotheosis in the writing and teaching of Munich psychiatrist

Emil Kraepelin. Kraepelin considered psychiatry to be a laboratory science, in which the clinician's task was to observe and catalogue facts. The patient, in this approach, was a collection of symptoms more than a person. Not he but his *disease* was under scrutiny, just as if it were a rash or a lung infection. Kraepelin's methods yielded useful results: from studies of thousands of case histories he compiled a careful system of classification of diseases, parts of which have endured in psychiatry to this day. But Kraepelin, and others in German medical psychiatry, felt confident that they had arrived at ultimate truth. "We are not presumptuous," Kraepelin wrote in 1917, "in stating that we have discovered the approach to be followed henceforth in psychiatry." No wonder Sigmund Freud once described Kraepelin as "Super-Pope."[17]

Freud's ideas were bound to be unwelcome in such an atmosphere. His earliest major work, *Studies on Hysteria,* which appeared one year after Kraepelin's text on classifications, gave particular cause for alarm. For one thing, Freud made use of hypnosis, a technique perfected by Charcot and French psychiatry and considered by German medical men to be theatrical and inexact. Hypnosis harked back to old Romantic and mystical elements, threatening psychiatry's recently won respectability as a medical science. Equally unwelcome was the subject matter of Freud's exploration: hysteria. "Hysteria," a word that derives from the Greek word for womb, was generally thought to be a woman's complaint, manifesting itself in a vast array of symptoms from headaches and fainting spells to numbness and paralysis. Hysteria, as Freud noted, behaves as though anatomy did not exist.[18] And since hysterical symptoms, with their tendency to come and go and to travel around the body, were difficult to ascribe to organic causes, German psychiatrists of the period tended to dismiss hysteria as malingering or even, because it had been studied by Charcot and Janet, as a disease more common among the degenerate French. Those who tried to explain hysteria usually blamed it on heredity. Kraepelin, for instance, considered it an "inborn psychopathic peculiarity" and thus a "degenerative," incurable disease. The idea that Freud, using the decidedly dubious technique of hypnosis, could produce a dramatic cure in a woman suffering from an almost equally dubious disease was not likely to win much support in Berlin and Munich.

By 1899, when the far more ambitious *Interpretation of Dreams* appeared, Freud had discovered that he didn't need hypnosis to induce the free association necessary to his explorations with patients. Freud himself dismissed hypnosis as "hackwork and not a scientific activity," recalling "magic, incantations and hocus-pocus."[19] Still, the taint of hypnosis and its hocus-pocus stayed with him. Nor did it help, in a society with powerful strains of anti-Semitism, that Freud was a Jew. "Rest assured," Freud wrote to Abraham in 1908, "that, if my name were Oberhuber, in spite of everything my innovations would have met with far less resistance."[20]

But Freud knew that the greatest resistance to his ideas sprang from a deeper source. He sought "not merely to describe and to classify phenomena, but to understand them as signs of an interplay of forces in the mind."[21] This was a proposal, he suggested, as humbling to human pride as the theories of Copernicus and Darwin had been in earlier periods. From Copernicus man learned that he was not at the center of the universe, from Darwin that he was descended from apes rather than that he was a being apart. Freud's theories deprived man of mastery of his own interior house: powerful unconscious forces, according to Freud, could engulf ego and will.[22] In Freud's approach the patient was no longer a specimen, separated from the physician by his disease. The patient's difficulties were, rather, induced by experiences not entirely unlike the doctor's. Perhaps this was the most disturbing of all Freud's disturbing ideas. In *The Interpretation of Dreams,* after all, Freud used himself as a research subject. The idea that the examining eye, trained so assiduously on the patient's external symptoms by Kraepelin, should be focused instead on the inner life of not only the patient but the doctor must have caused many German psychiatrists to close their minds, with a shiver, to the possibilities of psychoanalysis.

For some time the only exception among psychiatrists in all of Berlin was Dr. Karl Abraham. Abraham was thirty when he arrived in Berlin in late 1907 to embark on a career practicing psychoanalysis. He had grown up in Bremen in a prosperous Hanseatic merchant family and had studied medicine at several universities, including Freiburg, before coming to Berlin to do postgraduate work in brain pathology at the Berlin Municipal Mental Hospital. He stayed there for four years or, as he later wrote to Freud, until the rigidity and orthodoxy of "Berlin medical circles" sent him searching for a freer atmosphere in Zürich. "No clinic in Germany," Abraham wrote, could have offered "a fraction" of what he found working with Karl Jung, one of Freud's earliest disciples, and Eugen Bleuler at the Burghölzli clinic in

Switzerland.[23] It was there, where Freud already had a small following, that Abraham began a correspondence and friendship with "Professor Freud," as he respectfully called him, that was to continue for the rest of his life. In 1907, when Abraham grew frustrated with his prospects for advancement as "a foreigner in Switzerland," it was to Professor Freud he turned for approval of his plan to set up a practice in Berlin. "I should like to ask for your recommendation," Abraham wrote Freud, "should you ever have the opportunity of suggesting a doctor to undertake psychological treatment in Berlin. I am fully aware of the difficulties I shall encounter and I should therefore also like to ask your permission to turn to you for advice if necessary."[24]

Freud's reply was encouraging but realistic. He had been unable in the past, he wrote, to recommend a physician when patients asked for one in Germany. "But if such cases recur this year I shall know what to do." Might he refer them to Abraham as his "pupil and follower" in Germany? "You do not seem," he notes "to be a man to be ashamed of that description." Freud warns Abraham, however, of "the hostility with which I still have to struggle in Germany." He advises Abraham against trying "to win the favour of your new colleagues, who are primarily like those everywhere else and then a whole lot more brutal on top of it." Instead Abraham should "turn directly to the public." Wryly, Freud adds that "at the time when the campaign against hypnosis was at its most violent in Berlin, a very uncongenial hypnotist named Grossmann quickly built himself up a big practice. . . . So one should have the right to expect that with the aid of psychoanalysis you should do even better."[25]

Arriving in Berlin in December of 1907 without a university appointment, Abraham had little choice but to take Freud's advice and rely on the public. He did, however, have one influential Berlin connection—a psychiatrist named Hermann Oppenheim, who was related to him by marriage. Had Oppenheim not been a Jew, he would probably have held the chair at the Berlin Charité. As it was, he had an important reputation as the author of a widely used text, *Diseases of the Nervous System,* and as the head of a private clinic. In his textbook Oppenheim wrote that the psychoanalytic procedure was "questionable" and raised "weighty doubts." Yet he described Freud as a "gifted physician" and gave an accurate account of what went on in Freud's consulting room.[26] More important for the survival of psychoanalysis in Berlin was Oppenheim's predilection for referring some of his most difficult patients to Karl

Abraham. In the beginning, at least, Oppenheim's referrals were what put bread on the Abraham table. "I am quite pleased," Abraham wrote Freud early in 1908, "with the beginnings of my practice. Oppenheim has sent me two cases of obsessional neurosis. In one of them, where all other methods have failed, Oppenheim has in fact asked me straight out to try your method!"[27]

It may have been Oppenheim who steered Karen Horney in Abraham's direction. After passing her exams she worked for a year as an assistant in Oppenheim's polyclinic. It seems more likely, however, that she learned of psychoanalysis through one of her avant-garde friends, among whom there seems to have been a contagious fascination with it. We know from Horney's diary of this period that she began analysis with Abraham sometime early in 1910. We know too that her friend Idchen, by then living in Berlin, and a medical student Oskar knew from back home, Karl Müller-Braunschweig, went into analysis then as well. Thus it seems likely that this trio is the one Abraham had in mind when he wrote Freud, on April 28, 1910, of acquiring three "new treatments" in "a strange way." "One of your former patients," Abraham went on to explain, "has introduced analysis here to a small circle of neurotics. First of all a very intelligent young woman arrived [this would be Karen]; she is doing very nicely in her treatment, and soon sent her best friend [this would be Idchen], then some days ago she sent another friend who once discussed treatment with you in Vienna [this would be Karl Müller-Braunschweig, who had been not long before in Vienna].[28]

Once Karen had discovered psychoanalysis, it became *the* intellectual and emotional pursuit in her life. A new diary, which she started after a two-and-a-half-year hiatus, became an extension of her analytic sessions with Dr. Abraham; her childhood, her dreams, her sexual life and longings—all were examined now through the lens of psychoanalysis. Her "Ego" notebook, heretofore a wide-ranging collection of notes on everything from the novels of Turgenev to the philosophy of Hume and Kant, suddenly acquires a single focus. At first there are neat, careful notes on the papers of Jung, then of Abraham, then of Freud. Then the tempo quickens; instead of textual notes there are lists of articles: by Freud, Jung, Rank, Janet, Adler, Binswanger. Soon Karen abandons all attempts at coherence. The notebook becomes a place to scribble in a combination of rushed script and shorthand, whatever strikes her in her pursuit. "Mouth—erogenous zone" is a typical entry. Or, "Leaving in a dream=dying." As she becomes increasingly involved, the barrier between the personal and intellectual life breaks down. An anecdote about Oskar appears in the "Ego" notebook, used thus far only for notes on reading and lectures. She tells of her jealousy when Oskar flirts with the wife of a couple they know and concludes that she suspects Oskar of wishing to have an affair with the wife because *she,* in fact, has such wishes toward the husband. The whole thing is written hurriedly, half in shorthand, under the heading "Projection of one's own desires onto someone else."[29]

Karen Horney continued in analysis, probably going for six sessions a week (the usual schedule in Berlin at the time), until the summer of 1910. Such a brief treatment, lasting less than a year, was the rule rather than the exception in those early days of psychoanalysis. After she had left, however, Horney continued to use the tools of analysis to try to understand her continuing fatigue and depression. "The analysis," she wrote to Abraham a year later, "shows one one's enemies, but one must battle with them afterward, day by day."[30] Six months after that letter Horney was participating in Abraham's evening seminars. Abraham wrote appreciatively of her to Freud in February of 1912: "At our last meeting we enjoyed a report from Dr. Horney about sexual instruction in early childhood. For once, the paper showed a real understanding of the material, unfortunately something rather infrequent in the papers of our circle."[31] In April she wrote for the first time in her diary of conducting an analysis, with one Frau von Stack. "Whether she'll get something out of the analysis I don't know. I certainly will!"[32] After five years and more analytic cases Horney's mastery of the Freudian method was manifest in a lecture she delivered, "The Technique of Psychoanalytic Therapy."[33]

The lecture, given in 1917 before interested nonpsychoanalysts who were members of the Medical Society for Sexology, appears to have been Horney's "coming out" as a Freudian. Until she got her degree in 1915 she was understandably cautious about discussing Freud's ideas in the psychiatric clinics where she trained in and around Berlin. Even Karl Abraham, certainly associated by everyone in Berlin with Freud's ideas, knew better than to use them in a thesis he was writing in a bid for an appointment at the university. Instead, as he told Freud, he was working on an organic theme, "associations in normal old age and in mild cases of senile dementia." It would be, he predicted, "a good old Prussian piece of work, exploring well-trodden paths. If only it would also open up the path to the University!"[34]

Nowhere is the caution of the Freudians more apparent than in Karen Horney's dissertation, "A Case Report on the Question of Traumatic Psychosis." It was completed in 1915, five years after she had plunged wholeheartedly into psychoanalysis. Yet there is nothing in the entire thirty-page endeavor, or in the bibliography, that could link Horney with Freud or Abraham. On the contrary, everything about it suggests that she is a faithful and serious disciple of her advising professor, Bonhoeffer, and of the Kraepelinian approach. She had chosen a subject—the development of a psychosis following a blow to the head—that was very closely related to Bonhoeffer's work on psychoses brought on by external causes. The choice allowed her to list Bonhoeffer six times, more than any other single author, in her bibliography. Clearly this was a thesis designed to please.

The case Horney describes is that of a fifty-seven-year-old man named Paul Perl, who came to the Lankwitz Berolinum, a private mental hospital where she was working at the time, in the spring of 1912. Until February 8, 1912, Mr. Perl had been a healthy man; he had prospered as the owner of an underwear factory, survived a first wife, married a second, and fathered three children. Then, on February 8, he fell and hit his head, after which he complained of a headache. Nothing more happened until eight days later, when he complained again of pain and had a brief episode of unconsciousness. Two weeks later he suddenly became irrational: he played cards wildly, insisted he had to go to see the Kaiser, and may have had hallucinations as well.

It was at this point that his family had brought him to the Lankwitz Berolinum. At first Mr. Perl was both euphoric and completely out of touch with reality: one moment he was a horse trader to the Kaiser, dealing only in thousands of marks, another moment a soldier, then a chief doctor in the military. Two weeks after admission he seemed to improve briefly. But then he began on a long and gradual downward spiral: he became insulting to those around him, he had less and less sense of time and place until he no longer knew the year, he talked less and less, and spent more time in bed. After a year and nine months in the hospital he could speak only isolated words, could not swallow solid food, and was incontinent. In February of 1913, two years after the head injury, he contracted pneumonia and died.

In many ways Horney's approach was like the method of a modern psychiatrist. First, the taking of a careful history. Then the physical exam; here we get a single glimpse of Horney practicing her medical skills—looking at the eyegrounds, thumping the chest. This was followed by a series of questions designed to determine Mr. Perl's mental status. Does he know the date, the place? Does he have insight into his illness? How long can he remember a five-digit number? Does he understand distinctions: between Prussia and Germany, between a lie and an error? Can he explain a proverb, such as "The early bird gets the worm"? Such questions, designed to test different areas of mental operation, are still used as a tool in diagnosis.

In another way, however, Horney's case report is very much a product of its time: it deals almost exclusively with diagnosis rather than treatment. This was the hallmark, and the great weakness, of the Kraepelinian approach. The outcome of mental illness, according to Kraepelin, was predetermined by natural law. "Our ability frequently to predict what will happen keeps us from falsely assuming," he wrote, "that our treatment will appreciably alter the outcome of the disease.... We must openly admit that the vast majority of the patients placed in our institutions...are forever lost."[35] As historian Hannah Decker points out, "A Kraepelinian clinician confined himself to observation, description, diagnosis and prognosis. Done well—which they were indeed—that...was all that could reasonably be demanded."[36]

Such an approach may have been realistic, but it was also discouraging. What incentive was there for a patient to work at getting better if his fate was predetermined? And the doctor too was forced into passivity. Horney in her treatment of Mr. Perl can only conduct the same mental-status exams, at regular intervals, and watch Mr. Perl come up with increasingly feeble answers. In addition, the method was impersonal. There are little hints in Horney's thesis that human exchanges between doctor and patient did take place. At one point Mr. Perl, unable to answer a difficult question, winked at the *"Mädchen"* (presumably Karen Horney) taking notes in order to get her to help him. But whatever went on informally, the psychiatrist's official role was only to watch and wait—and then, after the disease had played itself out, to sift diagnoses.

Except for the case report itself, the dissertation is taken up entirely with this question of diagnosis. In the end Horney concludes that the patient was suffering from a form of dementia, a disease characterized by memory loss, confusion, severe disorientation, and sometimes, as in Mr. Perl's case, a habit of making up a past to compensate for the one beyond recall. But the more puzzling question raised by the case was the question of cause. Was the head injury, with its rather mild aftereffects, responsible for this very severe deterioration? Or was there, as Horney proposes, a preexisting disposition to illness? Might Mr. Perl, even without the accident, have developed some form of senile dementia? The patient showed signs when first examined of hardening of the arteries. Might the head injury, at the most, have accelerated the process? Since an autopsy was refused, there was little physiological evidence to go on. But Horney concluded on the basis of her observations that the dementia resulted from both the patient's predisposition, which was the underlying cause, *and* the trauma, which was the catalyst. [37]

The conclusion is cleverly balanced and presented. And it addresses a long-standing issue in psychiatry. Particularly in wartime, the question of how much a soldier's postwar problems are caused by trauma and how much by a predisposition to psychological difficulties comes up again and again. And yet it is hard to imagine that Karen Horney found her treatment of Mr. Perl, or the writing of the dissertation about it, very satisfying. In fact, it seems highly unlikely that she would have chosen to become a psychiatrist if it had meant spending her working days diagnosing and prognosticating à la Kraepelin.

Her energies and her natural inclination had always gone in a very different direction. Kraepelin, a man who didn't read poetry because it was too subjective, could hardly ignite a young woman who for years had written out page after page of poetry, in ornate Gothic script, in her diaries. Nor could a system that set out so carefully to delimit, to define, have much appeal to someone who had been looking, ever since her dialogues with Herr Schulze about religion, for answers to all-embracing questions about the meaning of existence. Most importantly, medical psychiatry, as taught at the university, had little to do with what interested her most: inner psychic life, or as she put it at nineteen, "the delicate vibrations of my soul."[38] But this was what "dynamic psychiatry," the new psychiatry of Sigmund Freud, was all about. That Karen Horney was destined to be a part of it was perhaps foretold at the Gymnasium when she vowed, after having been refused entry to a dissection class, that she would dissect herself instead and that, in fact, it would probably be more interesting.

The dissertation, her first and last paper in the Kraepelinian mode, served its purpose; with it she completed her last requirement and became an M.D. Her next paper, "The Technique of Psychoanalytic Therapy," delivered two years later before the

Medical Society for Sexology, might have been the work of a different person. Long, complex sentences had given way to simple constructions. Not a single word or concept in the paper was beyond a layman's grasp. In part this was because she was speaking before a group of non-analysts; sexologists, doctors interested in human sexual behavior, tended to be more sympathetic than knowledgeable about psychoanalysis. More important, she was no longer operating within the bounds of received psychiatric wisdom. Like other early Freudians, most notably Freud himself, she had a need to inform and persuade others which produced a vivid style—rich in analogy and anecdote, carefully paced so that no one would be left behind. It was the style of a speaker who wanted to make every friend she could for her point of view, a style that remained throughout her life one of her greatest assets.

First, she tells her audience of sexologists, we must understand the critical differences between Freud's early, groping explorations and the current method. Not only, she points out, has Freud long since dispensed with hypnosis, he has also thrown over the old emphasis on "abreaction." It used to be that the entire focus was on the *symptom* the patient presented—a paralysis of an arm, for instance. The analyst would start from the symptom and "retrace [the] steps to its origin without looking left or right." The situation is different now: "We worry less about symptoms and rather take our departure from the psychological surface, wherever it may be." The idea is that the symptom will disappear "as long as we penetrate deeply enough into the unconscious."

To illustrate the change, she turns, as Freud so often did, to archaeology: "We may compare psychoanalysis with the excavation of a buried city, in which we assume the existence of valuable historical documents." Using the old method, we would dig only in the places where we suspected the documents to be. With the new method, "we would wish to uncover the whole settlement, i.e., the whole unconscious, and would remove layer upon layer of earth inside of the entire perimeter." The goals of the old approach were less comprehensive: the patient would reach emotion-laden events in the past, there would be a release of a "strangulated" affect, an "abreaction," and the symptom would disappear. Since the abandonment of hypnosis this "purely symptomatic" form of treatment has expanded into an exploration of the "finer mechanisms of neurosis."

Horney proceeds to give the sexologists a description of technique that could still serve the uninitiated as an introduction to the psychoanalytic method. "How," she asks, "does the physician obtain knowledge of the unconscious?" Through the patient's associations. He must say "everything that occurs to him, no matter whether he considers it trite, ridiculous, absurd, indiscreet or, most important, whether it might be embarrassing to him." This "turning off of all conscious critiques of the associations, the so-called psychoanalytic basic rule," is "not an easy thing to do, as will become evident to anyone who tries it." The associations, even when they do come, are usually "distorted by a kind of censorship that anxiously watches over the illicit unconscious wishes to keep them from reaching the light of day." There is a "resistance against the reemergence into his consciousness of the repressed piece of memory. After all, he did not repress the underlying wishes for nothing, but because they were incompatible with the rest of the content of his conscious mind."

Here Horney makes the surprising claim that the physician's arriving at an understanding of the "unconscious instinctual forces" is the easy part of psychoanalysis. Freud and others have given us tools, through the study of dreams and symbols, for extracting meaning. We know, for instance, that "in general there is a repressed wish behind every anxiety." When a woman is overly concerned about her husband, worrying whenever he is delayed by minutes, "frequently leaning over him at night to make sure that he is still breathing," we may suspect that she "harbors intense but repressed death wishes against her husband."

"But," Horney continues dramatically, "even if I could interpret the patient's whole unconscious mental activity from his statements, this would not help him one iota." Here she employs another analogy. It is, she explains, "as though the patient had locked his unconscious instincts, like strange animals, behind a high wall over which he no longer can look." The patient no longer "knows" the animals but "is bothered and frightened by their noise." The physician, on the other hand, "is able because of his knowledge to distinguish the different voices, to identify the animals and to whom they belong." But even if the physician were to tell the patient what animals were behind the wall, it wouldn't change the situation for the patient. Rather, the analyst and patient must take down the wall, the "resistance," brick by brick, so that the animals can get out. Once the instincts, hitherto walled away, are admitted to consciousness, the patient may "affirm them, reject them or sublimate them."

It is not clear how many patients Horney had treated in psychoanalysis by 1917, when she delivered this talk. But when she stresses the critical role of resistance and transference, she sounds as though she had learned from her experience, including her mistakes. "A resistance that has been overlooked and an unrecognized transference may easily lead to failure in therapy," she asserts, "while an incorrect interpretation tends to correct itself." Everything that hinders the progress of the analysis, she explains, is resistance. We can assume resistance is present "when a patient arrives late, when he does not show up at all for insufficient reasons; when nothing occurs to him . . . when he no longer dreams or when he produces dreams of such a volume that their accounting occupies the whole hour, when he complains for half an hour about the lack of progress . . . when he suddenly begins to talk about the furniture, etc." Insights already gained can later be denied as well—"one of the reasons," she notes wryly, "why psychoanalysts are just as hard to analyze as other mortals."

Particularly in her discussion of the concept of transference Horney seems to be speaking not just from the text but from her own and her patients' difficulties. Every person, she explains, has certain "unique tendencies" that determine to a certain extent "the character of each new relationship" and that will be repeated in the analyst-patient relationship. At first a moderate transference is favorable for progress, but in time it "becomes the most powerful weapon of the resistance," partly because the patient "feels embarrassed, at least consciously, about telling the doctor when tender or hostile feelings toward him rise to the surface." The result is often silence. Often too the patient wants to fulfill the transference wishes rather than analyze them. "It is therefore mainly in the area of the transference," she concludes, "that the battle between the patient's unconscious and the physician is fought, the patient trying to realize those wishes that he unconsciously directs onto the physician, while the physician in turn forces him to content himself with insight only."

Horney's first public effort as a Freudian, later published as a thirteen-page paper in *Zeitschrift für Sexualwissenschaft,* differed sharply from her dissertation. The dissertation dealt with an organic brain syndrome, observed in a hospital; the talk addressed the treatment of neurotics familiar to doctors from their office practices, if not from their family life. The dissertation was dispassionate, given to abstraction, and fatalistic. The talk was engaging, anecdotal, and optimistic. Psychoanalysis can't change "constitution," can't give a person "new arms and legs," but it can "liberate a person whose hands and feet were tied so that he may freely use his strength again." Such promises are a far cry from the old "degenerative disease" model.

Yet, as different as they are in nearly every other way, the dissertation and the talk have one thing in common: both are true to an orthodoxy. The dissertation of course operated within the old framework, the talk within a new, controversial one. But even within the fledgling psychoanalytic movement there were already departures from the strictly Freudian approach. Alfred Adler's disagreements with Freud had surfaced in 1910, and Karl Jung's three years later. Freud's anger over what he considered to be misuse of his ideas by former followers erupted in a 1914 paper entitled "On the History of the Psycho-Analytic Movement," in which he asserted that "psycho-analysis is my creation."[39]

In her 1917 talk Karen Horney twice took Freud's side in this struggle. She noted that she must limit the scope of her presentation, then added: "The restriction which you will regret the least is that I shall follow in the main Freud's own views and that I will only briefly mention divergent procedures such as those of the Zürich School [Jung]." Later she takes up Freud's point that the Jungians are not really practicing psychoanalysis. The Zürich school "without justification continues to call its method 'psychoanalysis'" even though it has strayed into moral education.

If anything, Horney sounds even more convinced of the therapeutic value of psychoanalysis than Freud. Insight, she claimed, an understanding of the instinctual forces at work, would lead almost inevitably to a better life. "Many a marriage," she told the sexologists, "that might have foundered because of the neurosis of one of the partners has become healthy through analysis." Moreover, many factors that were believed to be constitutional are no more than "blockages of growth, blockages which can be resolved."[40] There is little in Horney's first Freudian work that would mark her as a potential rebel within psychoanalysis. On the contrary, she must have seemed in the eyes of her analyst and mentor Karl Abraham to be a welcome new addition to the Berlin circle. She not only was bright and articulate, she also was willing to place herself squarely and publicly in the Freudian camp.

It would be another five years before Horney's next paper, another nine before the signs of her own original vision would appear in her public work, and many more after that before she would begin to question Freud's basic assumptions about the origins of neurosis. But already in the privacy of her diary she was far less optimistic about the efficacy of psychoanalysis in her own case than she sounded in her talk to the sexologists. Her analysis did help her with certain sexual inhibitions. And when she told the sexologists that "many a marriage" had been saved, she may have been thinking, with hope, of her own. Through analysis, she declared, the patient becomes "able to direct all his forces toward his marital partner, forces that previously were fixated upon infantile models." But in her diary she was less confident that *understanding* the psychological history of the situation could lead to change. One day, struggling with the temptation to escape her marriage, she wrote, "How does the insight that this is a repetition of an infantile pattern help, after all?"[41] This doubt, the basis of a parting of the ways years later, had its origins in Karen Horney's difficulties in applying psychoanalytic ideas to her life as a young wife, mother, and doctor in imperial Berlin.

8

Love and Work

One of the happiest photographs of Oskar and Karen taken during this period shows them on some special day, dressed to the nines and posing with friends at a Berlin photographer's studio. It must have been summertime when the picture was taken: the men are in straw hats and the women in long white dresses. The photographer has assigned the group to what looks like an Oriental setting: an exotic tower is painted on a backdrop behind them, and two of the party have been seated in front of the others on a bamboo bench. All the women are wearing astonishing large hats. Karen's, a cartwheel crowned with a shirred band and buttons, floats airily above her radiant, sun-flushed face. Oskar stands by her side jauntily smoking a cigar.

Karen and Oscar's companions on this occasion are an adventurous lot. Opposite Oskar, sporting a pinstriped suit and walking stick, is Karl Müller-Braunschweig, another of Karl Abraham's first analysands. Müller-Braunschweig was a friend of Oskar's from boyhood in Braunschweig (thus the name, adopted to distinguish him from other Müllers). In time he would become a member, with Karen, of the Berlin Psychoanalytic Institute. Also along for the occasion was his wife-to-be, Josine Ebsen, who had gone to medical school at Freiburg with Karen and would also become an analyst. Seated next to Josine in the picture is Lisa

Honroth, who wrote sketches and stories, under a variety of pen names, for Berlin newspapers. Standing behind her in a straw boater is her very tall, bearded husband, Walther Honroth, an architect who studied archaeology with the great Burckhardt and traveled to Egypt in 1912 with the expedition that brought back the beautiful three-thousand-year-old bust of Nefertiti.[1]

Altogether there are four men and five women in the photograph. All appear to be in their twenties and thirties, and all are in a holiday mood. Perhaps the picture is occasioned by some momentous event—a wedding, or an engagement party. But the group is not taking the photo session very seriously. There is an untranslatable German verb, *bummeln,* which describes the mood of the picture rather well. To *bummeln* is to loaf about, at a leisurely pace, staring in shop windows, inhaling the air, laughing and joking with friends. On several occasions in her diary Karen writes of her wish to *bummeln* in Berlin. This day may be one of the few on which she did.

There are other jolly group snapshots from this period—mostly of friends gathered to eat and drink in the huge high-ceilinged dining rooms of cavernous Berlin apartments. With friends Karen always seems to be enjoying herself. But there is also a photograph of her sitting alone, which tells another story. She is pregnant in the picture and wearing a matronly high-belted dress to accommodate her new shape. Her hands are folded resolutely in her lap, and her eyes are averted, sadly, from the camera. Her mouth is tightened and pulled downward, as though having her picture taken were an affliction. Judging from the diary she kept during this period, this photograph comes closer to expressing the way she felt much of the time.

Sometimes she described her unhappiness as "a great exhaustion" and "inclination to passivity that increases to a longing for sleep—even for death."[2] At times there were "spasms of sobbing"[3] and once in a while physical symptoms—stomach pains that made her think she had ulcers. Or she would feel "oppressed, feel a tightness in my throat"[4] and her heart would pound. Although she doesn't use the word often, it seems clear that she was depressed, often to a point that made it impossible for her to function. This was particularly alarming to a woman of her drive and ambition. "I need an abnormal amount of sleep and hence have little capacity for work," she lamented. "This is my greatest worry. Were it just a matter of the 2 or 3 hours of afternoon nap and the 10-hour rest at night—but that isn't the whole story: all the rest of the time I am not really fresh, tire quickly when studying so that I have to exert willpower repeatedly to keep on studying for my exam."[5]

At the time of this complaint Karen was nearly seven months pregnant with her first child. Undoubtedly much of her fatigue and inability to concentrate had to do with her pregnancy. But she rarely mentions real-life events, and when she does, she doesn't credit them with much power to affect her mood. Instead, because of her new-found interest in psychoanalysis, she always looks for internal explanations. But it should be said at the outset that during this period, real life made staggering demands. Within the six years after Karen Danielsen came to Berlin and married Oskar Horney she became a mother, completed her final clinical year of medical school at the Berlin Charité, passed all her state clinical exams, wrote a dissertation in psychiatry, and, after hours, pursued her interest in the new theories of psychoanalysis. It is hardly surprising that she sometimes felt what she once described to Dr. Abraham as a "general disinclination."[6]

And yet it does often seem that life's difficulties played a less important role than her own conflicts. Her greatest unhappiness seems to have occurred in what should have been the honeymoon period of her marriage to Oskar, before real-life burdens accumulated.

Karen's marriage to Oskar would have been considered by many of her contemporaries to be a triumph. Oskar was that rare man in Wilhelmine Berlin who was willing to tolerate ambition in a wife. His own executive position at Stinnes practically required conservative political views. In the same year he began work there Hugo Stinnes, who was fast becoming the dominant force in the German coal industry, aided and encouraged the Berlin police in a strike-breaking action against coal miners which killed two and injured scores of others.[7] Obviously any sympathy Oskar might have had for the workers' cause, or for Socialism (with which it was linked), wouldn't have gone over well at work. But in fact Oskar's heart was probably pro-empire and anti-Socialist anyway. What was not conservative, however, was his choice of a wife. Since single women outnumbered men three to two, a man with Oskar's prospects might easily have found a wife who was more conventionally inclined.

Oskar's ability to earn a good living was also a godsend. In a society in which women paid sizable dowries to marry a good earner, Karen had managed with next to nothing: the two thousand marks that Wackels contributed was unimpressive even in those times—the equivalent of perhaps two months of Oskar's salary at Stinnes. Now, for the first time since Sonni had left Wackels, Karen could enjoy financial peace of mind and, even more important, peace of mind about her perpetually unhappy mother, who could now come to live nearby. On the surface at least Karen had good reason to be absolutely ecstatic when, in October of 1909, she married Oskar Horney. As Berndt observed, Karen's marriage to Oskar promised to make life "more secure for everybody."[8]

But of course the very security that Berndt and other conventionally minded Germans prized was likely to make Karen uncomfortable. "There is nothing more unbearable," she noted, "than the thought of disappearing quietly in the great mass of the average, nothing more fatal than the reproach of being told one is a nice, friendly, average person."[9] Marrying Oskar and settling into a comfortable middle-class existence threatened to make her "average," at least in some respects. More important, she had never felt at ease depending on a man for support; and in the early years in Berlin, while she studied, she had to rely on Oskar. Emotional dependence on one man, even one such as Oskar, whom she admired, always had made her uneasy as well; in the past, it had sent her looking for another, almost as insurance. These same impulses quickly reappeared, perhaps with even greater force, after she married Oskar. And when she looked ahead she saw, with uneasiness, the prospect of others' dependency on her.

In May of 1910 Karen's father, Wackels, who had been ailing for some time, died at the age of seventy-four. Sonni was now more dependent than ever on her children. Even though she was now living near Karen and Oskar in Berlin, she seems to have complained regularly that they neglected her. "Perhaps," Karen conjectures, "I would be better off if she were not here. Wherever she is, she is always discontented—why should I, why should my baby, suffer from this? . . . She has a depressing effect even on Hornvieh."[10] Bearing children, which Karen and Oskar seem to have assumed was the inevitable next step, promised to tie Karen down far more than Sonni or Oskar could. "Perhaps it is going to be for me as it would be for a person who has always regulated the course of his day to suit himself and then comes into an institution where every hour is fixed by an authority." The baby might be "a tyrannical authority that would rob me of my golden freedom."[11] There were also sexual difficulties. She describes herself as "frigid"[12] at one point in her relationship with Oskar.

Whatever the sources of her depression, there is no doubt that it was powerful, even debilitating. And within a year of her marriage to Oskar she went to see Dr. Karl Abraham in search of relief from the "dull pain," as she wrote in a poem, "which paralyzes the wings of my soul."[13] How much her analysis with Dr. Abraham helped is an open question. Years later she reportedly told colleagues that it had been useless. At the time, however, her diary entries suggest that the work with Dr. Abraham produced insights that brought, in her words, "release from the repression." Through analysis she was able to bring some of her negative feelings—toward Oskar, toward Sonni, and toward childbearing—to the surface. Some of her most severe symptoms lifted. In particular, her relationship with Oskar became "sexually harmonious."[14] Her severe attacks of fatigue lessened too, and she experienced "a definitely increased self-assurance . . . together with less shyness and less tendency to defensiveness toward others."[15]

In February of 1911, less than a year after the death of Wackels, Sonni died quite unexpectedly, of a stroke. But even though Karen's nervous symptoms "re-established themselves" following Sonni's death, it was "with not nearly the old acuteness."[16] Around the same time she also began to have positive feelings about the coming birth of her first child. Of course some of these improvements might have occurred over time even without the analysis. Karen herself suspected that her illness might be "cyclical." Perhaps, she conjectured, it was "something given, unchangeable, so that on the whole it can probably be mitigated through analysis but never eliminated by it"?[17]

Whether or not they were therapeutic, there is no doubt that the sessions with Abraham changed forever her way of viewing herself and others. Her new analytic approach is evident in the diary she kept during this period. The who, what, when, and where of the past have been supplanted by a newly urgent question, *why*. In the early entries, while she is still in analysis, her paragraphs often begin, "Dr. A. says," then go on to record and embellish his interpretations. "Dr. Abraham says we must now have patience," she writes, and, "Dr. A. thinks this comes from my first childhood impressions."[18] In the second, longer section of the diary it is she who analyzes—her dreams, her behavior, her feelings. The analytic method has brought her to a new level of understanding. Consider, for instance, the link she makes between her own need to "shine" and her mother's. "Sonni is just like that," she notes. "She has to be first everywhere, uses every available means to put herself in the foreground, make herself interesting: hence her craze for giving presents, her grand bearing, her desire to command in the house; hence her having managed to make me, even up to my 18th or 19th year, look upon her as perfection itself."[19] Sonni's volatility has now lost some of its power. "None of her changes of mind or attitude surprise me any more, for all her arguments take on a kind of rigid monotony: that she is always putting herself aside, sacrificing herself, and yet people owe her *some* consideration."[20]

From the insights Karen gains critical distance:

> In the end, of course, I cannot but sympathize with her and her fate, the fate of an aging woman who stands alone in the world without love, who has never had any gratification and is now morbidly seeking for expressions of affection from those nearest to her—insatiably— who doesn't know it is her discontent that never lets her rest and instead is always seeking satisfaction in external relationships that make her feel uncomfortable after a short while, who has a strong feeling for what she should be like and tries with every available means to maintain this fiction before herself and others... but in so doing becomes an almost intolerable burden to everybody.[21]

In the past Karen had only worried and complained about Sonni. Now, with the help of analysis, she is able to see some of herself in her mother and to see her mother's situation with new empathy.

In her 1917 talk before the sexologists Karen Horney mentioned three factors that contribute to success in analysis. The first two, "the slowly developing intellectual interest in the procedure" and "the conscious wish to become free from the suffering of the neurosis," are everywhere evident in the diaries of this period. Evidence of the third, a successful "resolution of the transference" to the analyst, is more elusive. It may have been in the area of transference, that process by which, in Freud's words, "a whole series of psychological experiences are revived, not as belonging to the past, but as applying to the person of the physician [analyst] at the present moment"[22] that the analysis with Dr. Abraham faltered. True to analytic expectations, Karen developed a positive transference to Abraham. She writes of wishing to be a special patient, of imagining that "Dr. A. asked permission to write up my case scientifically and publish it—this would obligate him to study all the expressions of my neurosis with a special, almost 'affectionate' care, and in return for my being his subject of scientific research, he would treat me for nothing at all."[23] She liked going to analysis, was "happy in the morning when it occurs to me on my way to college that today I am to be there at 10:45 instead of 1:30."[24] She believed, as she wrote in a poem, that she had held nothing back: "Now I have poured out to you/ my inner pain and soul's torment. . . . All the wild wishes that ever stirred/ my daring dreams, my secret aims/ you know them all, my soul is yours."

But there is something not entirely convincing about this poem; it has the melodramatic quality of an earlier era, when she was swooning over Schorschi and Marie Madeleine. If she had given herself over entirely to the analysis with Abraham, why did she need to do so much analytic work in the diary? And to what extent were her feelings—her fantasies, for instance, about being a special patient who didn't have to pay—actually stated to Dr. Abraham? More significant, what about negative feelings? Did she tell Dr. Abraham that she had, as she writes in her diary, "not only positive feelings toward him . . . but also the resistance, a certain aversion"?[25] Did she tell him that at times she harbored "doubts about the whole method"? Perhaps she did. But perhaps, instead, she resisted giving herself over completely to the process, just as she resisted other deep entanglements. Her natural inclination, in psychoanalysis as in other arenas, was to do it on her own.

For several years after she left analysis she considered returning for further work. The question "Should I go back to Dr. Abraham?" was a recurring theme in the diary of these years. She even went so far as to write a letter telling him she was coming at four on a particular Saturday afternoon. But the letter was never sent. Characteristically, she decided instead to work it through herself. "I do believe that he can't help me," she concluded two years after leaving the analysis, "with the exception of the momentary help, which is conditioned by the transference. But that I should be able to deal with in myself alone."[26]

If Karen Horney didn't place her faith entirely in Dr. Abraham, perhaps it was partly because the analytic interpretations he proferred, and which she seemingly accepted at the time, never *felt* quite right. Freud wrote that the patient's "conflicts will only be successfully solved and his resistances overcome if the anticipatory ideas he is given tally with what is real for him."[27] In reading Karen's diary of this period one is often left with the impression that what "Dr. A." says doesn't fit with her experience. Often the theory seems to have been designed for someone else—specifically, for a female hysteric whose father was a dominant presence and who had no outlet for her libido, either in sex or in the rest of her life. On Karen Horney such a theory often seems an ill-fitting suit.

There is, for instance, the matter of Karen's father. It seems very likely that Karen cared more for her father than her loyalty to Sonni would allow her to admit, even to herself. In the early years, before she began her diary, she may have been even fonder of him. Certainly it is interesting in this regard that her profound depression coincided with his death in May of 1910. Whatever her positive feelings toward her father, however, they were covered over and surely outweighed by angry and bitter ones. Yet Abraham seems to stress only Karen's attraction to her father, the Oedipal attraction that was the cornerstone of Freud's theory.

"Dr. A. thinks," she writes in her diary, that "I got my erotic ideal" from the "time when I loved my father with all the strength of my passion." This in turn explains her attraction to "brutal and rather forceful men" and to the wish to "blend in with the will of a man who has set his foot on my neck." Oskar was the choice of her conscious "I"—"a man of fine intelligence and discerning kindness," but her "instinctual life rebels," wishing for a man with more of the "beast of prey" in him. Oskar, she notes, is "always self-controlled. Even when he forces me to submit to him—it is never savagery or animal brutality—he is at all times controlled, he is never elemental." While this is ideal for marriage, "something remains in me that hungers." In contrast, she cites the time she fought with Rolf until he forced her to her knees "and after that to lie on the floor, imperiously demanding a kiss as the reward of victory." Then "a crimson glow almost engulfed me and in that instant I loved him."[28]

Even though Karen found fantasies and play in which she was overpowered sexually exciting, her overall relationship with Rolf was hardly that of victim to sadist. Nor did Ernst, the other man she cites as an example, strike one as "brutally egoistic" and "coarsely sensual" when she wrote of him during their brief affair. Nor does it seem plausible that she is discontented in her relationship with Oskar *only* because her "instinctual life" isn't entirely satisfied. She has been discontented too many times before in relationships with men. In the same way, her "first love" for her father appears to be but a small part of the story.

What *seems* to have been left out of the analytic exploration ("seems" must be stressed since there is no way of knowing what Karen left out of her diary) is the powerful reality of Wackels' absence throughout most of her childhood. As a sea captain he was almost always either away or preparing to leave. Nor was he a particularly warm or accessible man when he was home. If there was a strong attraction, there must also have been strong feelings of disappointment, abandonment, even rage. Furthermore, her mother's unhappiness must have added to her lost, lonely feelings.

Some years later Karen pointed out that the patient "whose need for love has remained largely unfulfilled moves toward every new person, including the physician, with expectations of being loved," transferring onto the doctor "not only conscious emotions such as liking, trust, etc., but also unfulfilled and unconscious loveneeds." It is an observation based on her experience in treating others. But it also describes her own wish to find, in a father substitute, what she missed at home. Similarly, when she writes that "next to tender desires, and sometimes even covering them up, are hatred and defiance, thirst for power and destructive impulses directed against the physician,"[29] she might be writing of her own transference onto Dr. A. of feelings she had toward her father. Had the meaning of her father's absence and remoteness been explored, it might have led to a different understanding of her inability to settle down with one man (or, for that matter, to trust the analysis). Perhaps it was the fear of being left, as she had been left by her father, which kept her on the move. One way to avoid being abandoned, after all, was to be the abandoner, becoming like her father in the process. And this in turn was better than becoming like her mother—unhappy, unfulfilled, and victimized by life.

Another early analytic patient of Karl Abraham's, Sandor Rado, has said that analysis in those days "was not the study of the life of a person, digging out what the turning points, what the problems were. . . . It was a search for opportunities to apply certain Freudian insights . . . castration complex, Oedipus complex, narcissism, oral eroticism, anal eroticism . . . the patient's production was very soon oriented by that, because he saw that what is fruitful is if he talks about these matters." For Rado, as probably for Karen Horney, "vitally important events and turning points . . . took place in my life which never came out."[30] What often gets in the way of such explorations is the insistence that the libido is the source of all neurotic conflict. Freud, having discovered the importance of sexuality to neurosis, couldn't see beyond it, at this early stage, to anything else. Abraham and Horney accepted Freud's dictum that, as he wrote in "A Case of Hysteria" in 1905, "Sexuality is the key to the problem of the psychoneuroses and of the neuroses in general. No one who disdains the key will ever be able to unlock the door."[31] Important as Freud's discovery of this "key" was, the insistence on it as the *only* one resulted in serious blind spots. Freud's treatment of Dora in "A Case of Hysteria," for instance, overlooks the way in which Dora is misunderstood and used by the adults around her, including not only her father but also Freud. Because of his focus on libido issues Freud sees Dora's hysteria as the result only of her own sexual guilt.

Similarly, in reading Karen Horney's diary of this period one often feels that sexual explanations are overstressed and sometimes just plain wrong. In explaining her exhaustion, for instance, Abraham falls back on that old bugaboo masturbation. "Dr. A. says that with onanists, after the excitement into which they work themselves, a state of exhaustion usually remains." While masturbation "plays no great role" in her life now, she surmises that "as a child I probably did it freely." What's more, "later on, in place of physical self-stimulation came the mental: the telling of stories. In its effects this is comparable to the physical stimulation. Here too exhaustion follows after the excitement." Even though this sounds farfetched, the next leap in the argument is even less believable. Although she doesn't tell herself stories anymore, her unconscious wants that "of which the fatigue is the result."[32] *Ergo* the exhaustion. The idea that storytelling is a form of masturbation and that it causes the exhaustion seems absurd. It was not as though Karen were escaping from reality into some other dream life. If anything, she could have used a little less of real-life pressure, a little more of fantasy. And the suggestion that masturbation is harmful reminds us that psychoanalysis still clung to some Victorian myths.

A related myth, which took longer to die out, was also visited on Karen in her psychoanalysis. This was the idea that there are better and worse kinds of female orgasm. Clitoral orgasm, brought on by manual stimulation, was considered by Freud to be the immature precursor of adult female sexuality. Only neurotic adults continued to experience clitoral orgasm. "In cases of what is known as sexual anaesthesia in women," Freud wrote, "the clitoris has obstinately retained its sensitivity."[33] Vaginal orgasm, achieved in the act of intercourse, was the grown-up and healthy kind. Karen applied this standard to her own sex life and concluded that the reason she enjoyed clitoral stimulation more than coitus was that she was still clinging to immature, masturbatory tendencies. In the mind of the neurotic, she concluded, "coitus is a poor sub-

stitute for masturbation."[34] Even though she had found clitoral
stimulation satisfying before marriage, she "felt a terrible shame
about it later on. I would not for the world," she writes in her
diary, "admit that this sort of pleasure gives me more satisfaction
than the normal sort."[35] With marriage there was of course no
reason (except her pleasure) for continuing such practices. Paradoxically, the analysis that was supposed to free her from guilt
made her feel more guilty, encouraging her to derogate what
seems to have been for her, as it is for many women, an important
avenue to sexual satisfaction.

Probably the most important shortcoming of Karen Horney's
analysis with Abraham was its failure to address her compulsion
to move in and out of relationships with men. Both analyst and
analysand recognized that Karen had a roving eye. She had, Dr.
A. told her, "a wish to throw myself away, prostitute myself—
give myself to any man at random." Dr. Abraham suggested
this was a masochistic wish to "be subject to another, to let
oneself be used by the other"—a wish related to her early attraction to her father. Abraham told Karen that her prostitution
wishes were not unusual. "He pointed out to me," Karen wrote,
"the interest all middle-class women take in prostitution." Furthermore, he told her that she had "revealed this complex to
him on the first day" through the "symptomatic action" of leaving her handbag (a symbol of female sexuality because of its
opening and shape) in his office.[36] Here he added, in a departure
from confidentiality, that he had another female patient in whom
these wishes were so strong that she had left her purse behind
not once but *three* times.

The assumption of the analysis seemed to be that such wishes to
give oneself to "any man at random" never went beyond fantasy.
While this may have been true for Abraham's other female patients, it was not entirely true for Karen. In her diary she recalls an
experience with a man who didn't know her name.[37] And she
writes of "the pleasure it gives me to be spoken to on the street."[38]
Even when she was involved in more depth, there was a pattern of
having more than one relationship at the same time and of desperately needing at least one relationship all the time. And in general,
her relationships with men started well and ended badly. Even at
the time of her analysis, less than a year after her marriage, she was
having trouble staying faithful to Oskar, just as she had in the past
had trouble with commitment to any one man.

But at this early stage psychoanalysis was more concerned with repression than with acting out. And neither Karen nor Dr. Abraham saw her restlessness as the problem. Abraham at one point did ask her to "isolate" herself from her circle of friends. Perhaps he sensed the possibility that she would start an affair that would drain her energies away from the analysis. His main reason for making the request, however, was probably to facilitate the transference. "If I think of myself as living alone—all my wildest wishes would twine around him," Karen notes."[39]

If anything, the analysis provided Karen with a rationale for what she called at one point "vagabonding" (*vagabundieren*).[40] If frustration of sexual needs was at the root of neurosis, a good love affair might provide the cure. After all, as she noted, a monogamous relationship "always goes against the grain of the subconscious." *"Only guilt feelings toward repressed wishes,"* Karen wrote and underlined in her diary during this period, *"have an inimical influence on life, restrictive, making for illness."*[41] When she wrote this she was involved in an affair, justifying it because "that great electric feeling"[42] was missing in her marriage.

As in the past, the affair was with a friend of Oskar's and placed her in a triangle. This time the friend was Walther Honroth, an architect who had known Oskar in his youth in Braunschweig and who was married to Lisa Honroth, a woman Karen liked very much. Lisa Honroth was an extraordinary woman for her time. She had grown up in Silesia, the daughter of a Jewish lawyer, and had come to Berlin to embark on a career on the stage. She was quite short and rather plain—definitely more likely to be cast in character roles than as a leading lady. But, in any case, acting was not an acceptable career for a married woman, even so "modern" a woman as Lisa. And so, lacking a university education, she fell back on her native intelligence and literary gifts and wrote little essays and stories for such Berlin newspapers as the *Berliner Tageblatt* and *Vossische Zeitung*. Berlin newspapers of the period were a source not only of information but of entertainment: sentimental poems, serialized tales of love and adventure, could all be found in the *feuilleton* sections of the city's abundant dailies. It was here that Lisa, writing under such pseudonyms as Li Ho, found a way to supplement the family income. She was adventurous as well as bright. She followed Karen into psychoanalysis, which she continued for about five years. When her husband, Walther, went to Egypt as chief architect on a major archaeological expedition, she left her two-year-old child behind and joined him for three months.

When Karen met Lisa, in January of 1911, she felt an immediate sympathy with her.[43] "I liked Lisa better than any woman I have met for a long time," she wrote afterward in her diary. "She is unsophisticated, has an honest burning interest in all questions she comes up against, be it politics, child care, art matters, the woman question, the theater . . . In all, a great capacity for deep sentiment and a general warm-heartedness."[44] Walther, Lisa's husband, is barely mentioned. But within a year, sometime after the birth of her first child, in March, Walther became the object of Karen's driven devotion.

Walther was Lisa Honroth's physical opposite. He looked, with his full beard and large, robust build, like a man in the pink of health. But in fact he suffered from a long-term kidney ailment from which he was to die only a few years later. Karen's assessments of him swing from one extreme to the other, depending on her mood. At times he is fascinating,[45] at other times, an insincere coward.[46]

Whatever Walther's faults or virtues, it is clear from her diary that Karen is, in her own neurotic way, crazy about him. "Yesterday evening," she writes after they break up, "I was cold and offensive toward Walther on the telephone, and I felt good about it. Vengeance for my injured pride. And what's more: I wanted to excite him. I thought *if* he still loves me he will not be able to bear it when I treat him coldly and contemptuously. Just as I couldn't take it from him."[47]

It is not clear exactly why or how the affair ended. Everyone in the foursome seems to have known it was going on. Oskar appears to have been remarkably magnanimous about it. And in fact there is even a hint that there was an attraction between Oskar and Lisa—though nothing to suggest they acted on it. The four remained friends afterward, even moving next door to each other in the same apartment house in Lankwitz.

Psychoanalysis was only one of the cultural currents that made such extramarital experiments acceptable in Karen's Berlin circle. Gustav Regler, writing of Berlin days, recalls talking with his up-to-date friends about "free love and how simple all these problems were if one cast off the old bonds and discarded the notion of possessiveness in love."[48] Regler was actually writing of a time after the war, but his description fits Karen's very advanced circle ten years earlier. The Honroths and Horneys seemed to enjoy the exhilarating feeling that they were the children of a new age, leaving stuffy Wilhelmine morality behind. Lisa and Walther Honroth's daughter Rita has observed that there was a general atmosphere of "openness, tolerance, and laissez-faire: friendships continued, appearances were observed, and social intercourse did not seem to be interfered with by any other kind."[49]

Nonetheless even such "modern" and tolerant couples had possessive feelings, and Lisa's may have been the cause of the breakup. Karen writes at one point that it is necessary for her development that she be rid of him,[50] but this is only after she had concluded that "Walther loves his peace more than me," adding, "Probably Lisa is behind that. Maybe Lisa has described my sexual demands in a harsh light and he is afraid."[51]

Even after the affair is officially over, it takes Karen a long time to give up hope of reviving it. In mid-April she is so low she considers the possibility of suicide[52] and even takes the drastic (and dramatic) risk of driving with Oskar in his open car in a thin dress in cold weather when convalescing from influenza, "all the while hoping very much that I would catch a deadly pneumonia."[53] Then, two days later, when the foursome spend a day together in Potsdam, she begins to hope that "in spite of Walther's lack of freedom . . . he loves me. His whole pleasant mood and his eyes betrayed it to me. I came happily home. . . . It was as if I still had the whole sun from yesterday in my eyes."[54]

Two months later she has begun to write about her passion for someone else. "I want to form my relationship to Carl into the finest and most beautiful thing within my power. There is only one way to do that: through the conscious control of impulses, we never want to kiss except when it is the expression of inner tenderness."[55] It never becomes clear who Carl is (there were several Carls in her life) or whether "the adultery experiment" that she proposes to him is anything more than a way of getting over Walther. "I could well love Carl," she writes, "with an entirely other intensity than Walther."[56]

Twenty-five years later the desperate, driven quality of her quest for the right man would become the basis of the description of the "neurotic need for affection" in Karen Horney's first book, *The Neurotic Personality of Our Time*. Certain drives, she wrote, "may be put to the service of affording reassurance against some anxiety, and . . . by acquiring this protective function . . . change their qualities, becoming something entirely different." To explain, she uses an analogy:

> We may climb a tree because we wish to test our strength and skill and
> see the view from the top, or we may climb it because we are pursued
> by a wild animal. . . . In the first case we do it for the sake of pleasure,
> in the other case we are driven by fear and have to do it out of a need
> for safety. In the first case we are free to climb or not, in the other we
> are compelled to climb. . . . In the first case we can look for the tree
> which is best suited to our purpose, in the other case we have no
> choice but must take the first tree within reach.

If we are "impelled by a direct wish for satisfaction of any kind our
attitude will have a quality of spontaneity and discrimination." If,
on the other hand, we are "driven by anxiety . . . our feeling and
acting will be compulsory and indiscriminate."[57]

In the spring of 1912, as Karen contemplated the end of her
affair with Walther Honroth, she sounded very much like the neurotic in this description, driven by anxiety more than desire. Taking up her diary after an eight-month pause during the affair, she
tells herself, "Walther is not the man for me. I will find a better
one. But I can never wait. I have no pride."[58] Her ability to examine her feelings, to analyze her acts, is overpowered by her need to
somehow fill the void. Here again her analysis with Dr. Abraham
doesn't seem to have been of much help. In trying to understand
her affair with Walther she concludes that Walther is like her father,
and Lisa like her mother, and that she can't get free of her attachment to them because of wanting, like the Oedipal child, to interfere in their marriage.[59] But this standard Oedipal interpretation
seems to leave a lot out.

It might have been more helpful to focus, for example, on
Karen's identification with her mother. Karen doesn't seem to per-
ceive, despite her greater understanding of Sonni, that she shares
her pattern of always seeking satisfaction in external relationships,
then quickly growing dissatisfied with them.[60] When Karen suspects that Sonni has put an ad in a Berlin paper offering to "provide for sunny twilight years of elderly or old, cultured, sensitive,
wealthy gentleman needing care, through marriage,"[61] she is angry
and upset. But she concludes that her unhappiness is caused by the
idea that her mother, who was her first love,[62] might love another.
While this is undoubtedly true, it is also true that Sonni's advertising for a man, her request to Oskar and Karen to "get me one at an
auction,"[63] must bother Karen because it reminds her of her own
pattern of searching for men who will solve her problems. "From
where will I take the strength to give him up?" Karen asks as her

affair with Walther ends. "People? Men? A new love? A new love is not readily at hand. And it is ugly to go looking. If it should be offered, I would grab at the chance."[64]

Her last entry in this, her last known diary, describes a "quiet strong feeling of happiness,"[65] occasioned by her new relationship with Carl. But the pattern of high hopes, followed by disappointment, is so familiar by now that it is difficult to share her optimism. She seems once again to be climbing the tree for the wrong reason.

"It is frequently declared," Karen Horney wrote in *Self-Analysis* in 1942, "that analysis is the only means of furthering personality growth. . . . That is not true. Life itself is the most effective help for our development."[66] It is difficult to know, after her diary ends in the summer of 1912, whether Karen Horney's unhappiness abated. Certainly the inner conflicts remained. But life, while it couldn't provide a cure, seems to have handed her a reprieve.

For one thing, the pressure of her studies eased dramatically after she passed her exams, including the dreaded pathology exam, in 1911. All that remained, then, was a dissertation, almost a *pro forma* exercise. Work, which had always been her refuge in the past, began to be once again. Even before the diary ends there are hints that her old relish is returning. She is excited about her "wonderful" analytic patient, Frau von Stack. And she likes her work at the private psychiatric hospital, the Berolinum. "I enjoy spending time at the Berolinum," she wrote that May. "I feel I'm in my groove there [literally, in "navigable water"]." Her boss at the Berolinum, Otto Juliusburger, shared her interest in psychoanalysis and was a participant in Abraham's psychoanalytic evenings. She found him "not of this world entirely" but "unbelievably loving and gentle."[67] Perhaps most important, by 1912 she had established a direction for her professional life. She was by then a member of Abraham's small group. There was no longer any doubt that she would cast her lot with the Freudians and work as a psychoanalyst.

At the same time, two momentous events, following one right after the other, transformed her personal life. The first was the death of her mother, in February of 1911. The second was the birth of her first daughter, Brigitte, in March. Sonni's death occasioned one of the few genuine expressions of remorse in the diaries. In an entry that she first dated "January," then changed to "February 14," she wrote: "This is not the first time I have written 'January' instead of February.... No wonder. If we could turn the clock back to a month ago, I would still have Sonni, all the dreadful things would not have happened yet.... Today for the first time there is a missing, a yearning, and not just the paralyzing horror at the incredibility of death." Now, she wrote, there was "a wish to make good, to show her how much we loved her, to give her all the happiness in our power, in which we have failed so badly, so badly. Had we let her feel in her lifetime all the love that has now awakened in us so powerfully, how much happier she would have been."[68] Her "feeling of guilt" about "the countless unkindnesses one did her, large and small," the "torment that this can never again be made good," all this "will always remain and ... should teach me to become kinder toward the living."[69]

Yet Sonni's death was also a relief. Her mother's demands had weighed heavily on her and Oskar. It was Oskar, using psychoanalytic theory, who pointed out that some of Karen's guilty feelings had to do with repressed wishes. She wrote:

> It comes to this. Sonni's death in many respects means a release for me; I must have wished for it in many ways and greeted it with relief. For one thing, through her hysteria—which, furthermore, must have been increased and reinforced in these last years through organic changes in her vascular system—she gave us many an ill-humored hour. Her fate in the future lay before us as a threatening question to which we found no satisfactory answer.... Given Sonni's inability to handle money, the pecuniary side eventually became critical too, though it was not our chief concern. The main thing was that Sonni presented a constant danger to my health.... When she had a stroke a further consideration entered in.

If she was paralyzed and had mental deficits, Karen and Oskar's "unavoidable duty" would have been to take her in. "Our whole life would have been altered, a black shadow would have darkened our sunny, harmonious home." This thought was so "dreadful" that Karen evaded it, thinking instead of Sonni's living alone with a nurse or just waiting "to see how things went, i.e., the wish that she might die before this question came up." When the death came, "the consciousness of guilt for all these wishes that had previously been discreetly repressed came to the surface."[70]

Besides remorse and relief Sonni's death also reawakened earlier, positive feelings for her mother, "my great childhood love."[71] Perhaps because of these positive memories and because of the imminence of birth, Karen began, around the time of Sonni's death, to see motherhood in a new light.

Until then she had gone along with the idea that the pregnancy made her unhappy because it forced her to acknowledge her femininity. "Every woman," she wrote during her seventh month, "feels herself to be primarily, as such, inferior to men. This originates from a girl's strength being less than a boy's and, according to Freud, from lack of a penis." A girl "as a rule sees her father as the stronger, controlling partner," though she identifies from an early age with her mother. Karen found ample evidence of penis envy in her own childhood. "I know that as a child I wanted for a long time to be a boy, that I envied Berndt because he could stand near a tree and pee, that in charades I played a prince, that I loved to wear pants and was happy in my gym suit... also that at the age of 12 I cut my hair off to my neckline, thus being the curly-haired prince again." Continuing to apply this logic to herself, Karen concluded that a girl "considers herself inferior" and tries to adopt as many "masculine characteristics" as possible.[72] Since "nothing is more specifically feminine than motherliness," and since "I found myself inferior, being a feminine creature, and in consequence tried to be masculine, a situation that like no other keeps my femininity before my eyes and others' must be painful to me."[73]

And yet, even as she lists all the ways in which mothering is anathema, including the fact that she never liked younger children when she was growing up, she can't help noting in passing "the intensity with which I played with dolls."[74] Nor can she, in analyzing her attachment to Sonni, ignore the pleasure she felt in being cared for by Sonni, a pleasure that may lead to joy in caring for her own child.[75] As she moves into her eighth month of pregnancy all ideas of "masculine protest" have been abandoned. On January 24 she writes:

Sunday it will be only eight weeks until the baby comes. We haven't agreed on a name yet: Klaus, Gerhard, Jürgen, Hanspeter are at our disposal, and for a girl Ulrike. I'm to have a nurse too. Things should go well now! How happy I am. I am always annoyed when Sonni begins to "console" me, that I shall soon be released. It is just the expectation and the joy in it that are now so indescribably beautiful. And the feeling of carrying in me a small, becoming human being invests one with higher dignity and importance that makes me very happy and proud.[76]

A daughter was born to Karen and Oskar Horney on March 29, 1911. They gave her Sonni as a first name in honor of Karen's mother, but they always called her by her middle name, Brigitte. Even though the birth followed so closely on the heels of her mother's death, Karen showed few signs of depression in her post-partum diary entries. Nursing the baby "perhaps strengthen[s] the longing for one's own mother," but it also produces "mutual sensual satisfaction" and "such an intimate union of mother and child as never occurs later."[77] And though there were moments when it was "easy to cry," there were others when "a hot feeling of love breaks through, an immediate sense of happiness" and "a kind of astonishment that the small thing is now my child."[78]

Another fifteen years would go by before Karen Horney wrote her groundbreaking essay "The Flight from Womanhood." In the interim she gave birth to two more daughters and saw her world transformed by a world war. But it was the pleasure and pride she had felt in childbirth, first with Brigitte, and then twice more with Marianne and Renate, which became the touchstone of her argument for an alternative theory of female development. Childbirth, according to the Freudian view, was only a substitute and partial compensation for the lack of a penis. "I, as a woman," Horney wrote in 1926, "ask in amazement, And what about motherhood? And the blissful consciousness of bearing a new life within oneself? And the ineffable happiness of the increasing expectation of the appearance of this new being? And the joy when it finally makes its appearance and one holds it for the first time in one's arms? And the deep pleasurable feeling of satisfaction in suckling it and the happiness of the whole period when the infant needs her care?" Perhaps, she suggested, women's feeling of disadvantage had more to do with social realities than with the lack of a penis.

As for men, "one must inquire whether an unconscious masculine tendency to depreciation is not expressing itself intellectually" in the depreciation of motherhood in analytic theory. After all, "from the biological point of view woman has in motherhood, or in the capacity for motherhood, a quite indisputable and by no means negligible physiological superiority."[79] We must, she argued, "get beyond the subjectivity of the masculine or the feminine standpoint to obtain a picture of the mental development of woman that will be more true to the facts of her nature—with its

specific qualities and its differences from that of man—than we
have hitherto achieved."[80]

There is a wonderful irony here. Like most women pioneering
in a male world, Karen Horney had devoted a great deal of energy
to trying to be one of the boys. And she *had* felt trapped, in the
beginning, by the undeniably feminine position in which pregnancy placed her. And yet, as a result of the experience of birth,
she felt compelled, for the first time in her professional life, to take
an independent position. It was because the experience differed so
strikingly from analytic theories that she was forced to propose an
alternative theory. Birth was too remarkable to be only a substitute
or a sublimation. In the end, because she was a truth seeker, she
couldn't deny her femininity. And it was her femininity that led
her to her first original, and important, conclusions.

9

Zehlendorf

For seven days and nights I haven't eaten.
Shot one man through the forehead with my gun.
My shin's all ravaged where the lice have bitten.
In next to no time I'll be twenty-one.
CARL ZUCKMAYER, 1917[1]

In the fall of 1918 the violence of the World War I came home to
the cities of Germany. Young soldiers who had marched off four
years before filled with patriotic fervor and devotion to the
Kaiser's cause had endured near starvation, ill-treatment at the
hands of officers, and above all, meaningless loss of life, which left
the survivors feeling deeply betrayed. One million seven hundred
seventy-three thousand young Germans had died—more than any
other nationality in the war that killed eight and a half million.
And by 1918, with talk of surrender in the air, the men on the
front lines were beginning to understand that it was all for nothing, indeed for worse than nothing.

   The violence began in Kiel, where German sailors, ordered to
launch a near suicidal attack on the British fleet, turned on their
admirals instead. They raised the red flag of revolt over their idled
ships, marched into Kiel, and seized control of the city. Soon after,
sailors took over Germany's largest naval base, at Wilhelmshaven;

others marched on the town hall in Hamburg, then Cologne. In Munich a leftist coup declared a "Bavarian republic." And on November 9 a general strike was called by leftist groups in Berlin.

Berlin had already had its share of unrest. The previous winter, when the food ration was cut to one thousand calories per person, strikes and riots had broken out. But on November 9 thousands milled in the streets, descending first on the Reichstag, then on the heavily guarded palace of Wilhelm II. The crowds were united in one thing: they demanded the abdication of the Kaiser and an end to the Hohenzollern reign. But when the Kaiser, hidden away in Belgium, finally abdicated, Berlin became the arena for many more months of demonstrations and street warfare over what should happen next. Mobs of the disenchanted—soldiers, unemployed workers—did battle with government soldiers and with each other. Throughout it all, the trams of Berlin continued to run and the cafés and bars stayed open. But Berlin, in the words of contemporary diarist Count Harry Kessler, "had become a nightmare, a carnival of jazz bands and rattling machine guns."[2]

On the west side of town, where Karen and Oskar Horney lived with their three young daughters, the streets remained quiet. But even in the affluent west it was impossible to ignore the events of January 1919, when the Communists seized key outposts and took control of the city, only to be crushed in a bloody counterrevolution led by Freikorps units sympathetic to the old order. In the end, when the moderate voice of the Social Democrats prevailed, Berlin was still too volatile to serve as a capital for the new regime. The Social Democrats, led by Friedrich Ebert, repaired to Weimar, the hallowed birthplace of Goethe, a hundred and fifty miles away, to write a constitution for the first parliamentary government in Germany's history.

In 1918 the Horneys too moved out of the city, to a house of their own in the new suburb at the end of the streetcar line called Zehlendorf. The turmoil in Berlin must have made the bucolic setting of 15 Sophie-Charlotte Strasse look particularly inviting. The house was at the very end of a street, with no other houses in sight, facing a wooded park with a pond and a hill big enough for sledding in winter. In back there was a huge yard, which could accommodate swings for the children, a croquet lawn, and vegetable and flower gardens besides.

Architect Paul Mebes, himself an advocate of retreat from the noisy city, had built the house. In his influential book *Um 1800* (To 1800) Mebes had decried the excesses of apartment-house "gables, towers, bays and columns," of the "incomprehensible ornament [that] has taken possession of every last square foot of building façade" on Berlin's Kufürstendamm.[3] Mebes called for a return to the craftsmanship and "simple style of our fathers" in the early nineteenth century—a modernism based on history.[4]

The Horneys' house in Zehlendorf was a lovely embodiment of his philosophy. On the outside it was an unassuming stucco, with tiled roof and upper story. The front door was painted with brightly colored "folk" designs. The interior was filled with light from many windows—a welcome change from the dark, over-decorated, and cavernous rooms of Berlin apartments. The layout of the rooms was asymmetrical. And the vaulted ceilings, the surprising nooks and crannies, the odd turns of the staircase banister, made it a house unlike any other. Above all, it welcomed in the out-of-doors: there was a large patio just outside the dining room and a balcony just off the sun-filled master bedroom.

Houses like the Horneys' were unusual in Berlin. For the most part only the very wealthy and the nobility lived in private houses, or villas, as Berliners called them. And while the Horneys' house in Zehlendorf was modest in comparison to the grand villas of Charlottenburg, it was nonetheless an impressive sign of affluence. There were other signs as well. There was a sizable staff—not only a cook and maid but several housemaids, a ladies' maid, and a gardener. There were luxurious automobiles, and soon after the family moved in, a garage was built to house them. A chauffeur was engaged and moved into nearby quarters. And there was an English governess, who taught the girls the names of the garden flowers in her native tongue. The Horneys were prospering.

Karen Horney's income undoubtedly contributed to their new affluence. By then she was spending all her time practicing psychoanalysis—seeing patients in the city in the morning, then returning home in the afternoon to see more patients in the front room of the Zehlendorf house. But psychoanalytic fees alone would not have afforded such luxury. It was the spectacular postwar rise of Oskar Horney's boss, Hugo Stinnes, that made the Zehlendorf style possible. Stinnes had prospered as a coal and power supplier before 1918. But in the inflationary period that followed the war he used his assets to acquire foreign currency and build up the biggest industrial trust in Europe. Five years later the bubble burst, with disastrous consequences for Oskar and the family. But in the meantime the villa on Sophie-Charlotte Strasse was a safe haven, far away from the anarchy in Berlin.

Ellen Key, the Swedish reformer whose ideas on love and marriage Karen had admired earlier, would have approved of the Zehlendorf setting. Key had written in 1909 that marriage was unimportant, only an "accidental social form," and that the only immoral union is one that occasions "bad conditions for the development of . . . offspring."[5] A country setting was deemed ideal for the rearing of children. "Sport and play, gymnastics and pedestrianism, life in nature and in the open air," Ellen Key wrote, ". . . will be most excellent bases for the physical and psychical renewal of the new generation."[6]

Karen shared many of Key's child-rearing ideals. Like Key, she believed in fresh air and exercise, a minimum of control and direction, and allowing children's true nature to surface without the imposition of adult values. Like Key, she preferred progressive schools—coeducational, nonreligious, and nonpunitive. But Karen Horney differed from Ellen Key's ideal mother in one crucial way. Key insisted that the mother "should be entirely free from working to earn her living during the most critical years of the children's training."[7] This of course was not Karen's situation, nor would she have wished it to be.

And yet at times during the children's early years Karen seemed to be reaching for a domestic image of herself. In a family photograph, taken not long after the birth of Marianne, Karen and Oskar sit side by side, cozily, in wicker chairs. Oskar, with cigar in hand, looks into the distance with the smile of a proud papa. Brigitte, dressed in her country best, a dirndl with apron and white bonnet, leans her little arm on Oskar's knee and stares into the camera. Karen, in a demure braid-trimmed dress with a peasant flavor, has eyes only for baby Marianne, whom she holds in her arms. She looks young, wholesome, and entirely wedded to her maternal destiny. In another photo she sits between her two little girls at a tea party. In a third she is at the piano, with the two girls, nicely dressed up with huge bows in their hair, gathered around to sing. Dr. Horney is nowhere to be seen.

In the same spirit Karen entered progress reports on her daughters in a pretty little gold-embossed notebook. The soul-searching of earlier diaries is invisible in the small book. The notes, which she kept sporadically from 1912 to 1918, only report, without analyzing. They are the work of a woman who is trying her best to be more simple—to record and delight in the exploits of her children, as a good mother should. And, as in other endeavors, she suc-

ceeds. Her notes, though infrequent, provide vivid, lovingly rendered glimpses of all three little girls.

Renate, the Horneys' youngest daughter, was two by the time
the family moved to Zehlendorf. She had been a vigorous eight-
pound baby right at the start, and was already, as Karen wrote in
her little notebook, "crawling rather fast through the rooms." "If
she's not hungry or wet," Karen added, "she's very playful, and
jumps around in her carriage, uttering cries of joy, babbling understandably, plays with cooking spoons, the tops of pots...
Tobby [a teddy bear], the pyramid, and the keys."

The older girls, Marianne and Brigitte, were beginning to display their special strengths. "Biggi," as Brigitte was called in the
family, was seven, sang "very nicely and clearly," and showed
physical prowess on "the rings" at the playground and in the pool.
She was also an observer of people; she often commented on the
progress of wounded soldiers they saw in the street. As for Marianne ("Janne"), now five, she was "a chapter in itself. If you see
her together with other kids, for example in the kindergarten, it is
as if she has so much more desire to live and joy in living. They all
like her. She loves to visit in the neighborhood and is very trusting
with everybody who is friendly to her. Maybe a little more tender
with men, but not remarkably. She needs people, but she can, if
you give her something nice to play with, occupy herself for a
while."

In many ways Karen was a very modern mother—receptive,
nonjudgmental, and noninhibiting. She once said that her daughters had been given a "good psychoanalytic upbringing." While it
is not entirely clear what she meant by this, it is true that the
conceptual framework provided by psychoanalysis made her more
tolerant than her own mother might have been. For instance,
when Marianne at twenty-one months took to biting, she wrote of
sadism. "Marianne bit me in the arm today. Apparently it was
meant as a proof of love. She also has bitten Biggi a couple of
times, and hit her too. Apart from that she shows small sadistic
characteristics. For example...she is really amused when she
pinches me on the nose. But before she even touches me she acts
the way she expects I will react and says, with a very pitiful face
and moaning voice, 'ow!'"

When Brigitte at five made her doll utter obscenities, the behavior was understood and tolerated as projection. "Biggi is projecting all forbidden desires on her doll. The doll is wet, dirty, spits,

says 'Lord!' or 'bullshit' or 'what a crock.' She sticks her tongue out, she throws food on the floor, she breaks plates, in short is a plague of depravity. She does everything that has been forbidden to Biggi. But then also the doll has to be punished for it, has to go to bed, is beaten, is put in the corner, or doesn't get dessert. The doll also equals Marianne, and serves to help her identify with her mother."

There was discipline in the Horney family, as Brigitte's little pantomime with the doll suggests. Oskar sometimes resorted to the methods of his schoolteacher father. All the girls remember the time Marianne, rocking on her chair at Sunday dinner, pulled over the tablecloth with the china on it and got a strapping. Food, especially dessert, was sometimes withheld as punishment; in 1918 food was a precious commodity even in the Horney household.

Yet Karen's psychoanalytic training made her more than usually tolerant of the girls' curiosity, particularly their sexual curiosity. When, at various stages, they showed an interest in their bodily products or in seeing and being seen while urinating, Karen recorded it without judgment in the progress notes. And when Karen became pregnant with Renate, their curiosity was welcomed. "The children have been talking for a long time about 'little brother,'" Karen wrote shortly after Renate was born, "and it was natural for them that he was in Mama's belly and was growing. Biggi also knew from her questions that it would come out of the womb and once arranged, when I was close to giving birth...a game in this way—that I was the grandmother, she was the mother and Marianne the child." Then Brigitte gave her mother a doll, which was supposed to represent the father. Another doll she put "between her legs." Then she pulled the doll out, "showed her triumphantly to Marianne and said to her in a motherly, superior voice, 'Look, Janne, Mommy just had a little brother.'" In 1916 only a few parents would have approved of such a graphic enactment of the birth process.

The references to "little brother" in the girls' play suggest that the family was hoping for a boy the third time around. Yet femininity was not devalued—nor was it narrowly defined. Karen encouraged her girls in the active, independent behavior that more conventional mothers would have discouraged. When Brigitte was fearless in the water, her mother took note of it with pride. "Even when the waves were high it was difficult to get her out of the water." After the family moved to Zehlendorf, the girls spent hours up in the willow tree in the backyard. And all were encouraged to have opinions. After dinner, when she played the piano and they sang together, "each of them was allowed to choose a 'big' song and, alternating, one of them chose a small song.... They know exactly where each song is in the little children's song book, because there is a picture with each song."

It is probably not surprising, given the evidence in these early notes, that all three of Karen Horney's daughters grew up to be spirited, independent women. None of them would claim in retrospect, however, that she was an ideal mother. In varying degrees all felt the negative effects of another aspect of her "modern" mothering: she was very often unavailable. Marianne in particular felt that too much independence was expected of them too soon.

The most dramatic example of this occurred in 1918, the same year the family moved to Zehlendorf. The previous November, Brigitte, who had suffered on and off from a series of illnesses, contracted tuberculosis. TB was rampant in Berlin during the war years: in 1916, deaths from tuberculosis had risen to the epidemic levels of thirty years before. The Horney children were protected, by their class, from the malnourishment and poor living conditions that contributed in many cases to the illness. Still, a diagnosis of tuberculosis was not so surprising as it would be today. Nor was the doctor's prescription unusual: he recommended that Brigitte be sent to Zuoz, a treatment center high in the Swiss Alps where she could attend school and "take the cure" at the same time.

Brigitte was only six, but, according to her mother's notes, she had little trouble adjusting to the separation. "The farewell was easy for her. The first two–three days she missed me, but then she made herself at home and was happy with all the kids, the friendly teachers, and her sled. She was able to sled right away because she's not scared. She also skis and ice-skates. They all like her because she's very understanding and because she's able to be so intensely happy about little things." It seems surprising that a six-year-old would adjust so quickly to being away from home. But these were different times, and Brigitte was an unusual child; she had not found it easy to adjust to the arrival of siblings and may have welcomed the opportunity to be free of them for a while.

What seems more surprising is the decision Karen made (presumably with Oskar's approval) to send Marianne along to Zuoz some months later. Marianne was only five at the time and had no need of treatment for TB. The experience of being sent, quite unexpectedly, to live among strangers who spoke an unfamiliar

Swiss dialect, Marianne remembers, was terrifying. For a long time after she had returned she wouldn't let her mother leave her sight when they traveled together on the train. Many years later she concluded that her learning difficulties, which continued for several years after her return, were related to the trauma of being sent away at five.

Why would a mother do such a thing? Especially a mother who showed, in her progress notes and in her analytic writing, that she was capable of empathy with her children? Practical explanations fall short. Renate has suggested that food shortages in Berlin made her mother decide to send the children away. But even though there may have been fewer eggs than usual, Oskar's parents in Hessen kept the Horney household well provisioned from their garden. There was no reason to send Marianne to Switzerland for that purpose. What's more, Karen had plenty of help with the children; Marianne wasn't keeping her from her own pursuits. Perhaps her own explanation would have been that, as she noted in her little book, "Marianne misses Brigitte very much." And in 1918 separation from parents was not considered traumatic by the experts.

"When people are absent," Freud wrote in *The Interpretation of Dreams,* "children do not miss them with any great intensity; many mothers have learnt this to their sorrow when, after being away from home for some weeks on a summer holiday, they are met on their return by the news that the children have not once asked for their mummy. If their mother does actually [die], children seem at first to have forgotten her, and it is only later on that they began to call their dead mother to mind."[8] Only later did observation of young children lead psychologists to the conclusion that early separation could be traumatic.

There seems to have been a general denial, in progressive circles, of children's needs for mothering and nurturance. Children wouldn't behave so childishly, Ellen Key maintained in *The Century of the Child,* if we gave them more responsibility at an early age. "By treating the child every moment as one does an adult human being," Key maintained, "we free education from that brutal arbitrariness, from those over-indulgent protective rules, which have transformed him [the child]."[9]

It seems impossible to justify exposing Marianne to tuberculosis. But neither Freud nor Ellen Key would have claimed that Karen Horney's decision to send her five-year-old off to join her sister in Switzerland would leave emotional scars. Nor perhaps should we judge her: it is too easy in retrospect. But it is worth noting that the pattern of past relationships may have been repeated here. As in the past, closeness was followed by a need for distance. For all her cheery optimism about Brigitte's illness, Karen must have been scared by it. Even when Brigitte was very young, she described frightening fantasies of Brigitte becoming ill and dying. True to Freudian precepts, she interpreted these fantasies as wishes. But they were also fears, the wrenching fears endemic to motherhood. And now tuberculosis confronted her with the terrible possibility of losing a child.

At the same time Marianne must have been frightened by her sister's illness and sudden departure. Probably she made more demands on her mother. Two months after Brigitte's departure Karen wrote in her notebook that Marianne "depends very much on me" and "doesn't like to be dressed or undressed" by the nanny, says, "I want Mommy to undress me." As in the past, dependency—her own on her children and theirs on her—made Karen want to run away. But this time it was Marianne she sent away—even at some risk to the child's physical health.

Brigitte and Marianne returned from Zuoz sometime in 1918, both in good physical health. But their childhood memories of their mother from that time on are from special times—holidays, summer vacations, the cook's night off. For the most part what they remember about their mother is that she was deeply involved in her work. In the morning Renate would walk her mother to the horse-drawn bus that took her to the end of the streetcar line, and from there to her office in Kaiserallee in the city. In the afternoon the girls might see her briefly when she returned home to see patients. The patients, they remember, would arrive through the front door and wait their turn in the foyer at the foot of the staircase. During patient hours the children were not allowed to make noise in the house. And the doors to the front room, where the sessions took place, had a heavy curtain to keep the noise of the household out and ensure her patients' privacy.

Karen Horney's approach to child rearing in this period resembled her approach to gardening: both were something she supervised and others carried out. For a time after the family moved to Zehlendorf she had been an enthusiastic gardener, even joining a group of women who went out together to pick and arrange flowers from the meadow across the way. But before long she was hiring others to do the work. She planned vegetable and flower gardens, and she established two large compost heaps in the kitchen yard. In the fall she would oversee the canning activity, as fruits and vegetables were cooked, stored, and carried to the basement for the long winter months. But at this point no domestic pursuit was allowed to interfere with her work.

In a similar way she supervised the girls' progress. She took charge of hiring and firing nannies and governesses of varying degrees of competence (there was at least one, Molly Thomas, whom all the girls loved). And she seems to have made the decisions, without much consultation with her daughters, about their schooling. Predictably she gravitated toward "modern" schools that gave children a great deal of freedom. Marianne started out in public school but then was sent, with Renate, to a progressive school where children could choose what subjects they wanted to pursue, and could learn at their own pace. Later, quite arbitrarily, Marianne was sent away to a Quaker school on Lake Geneva, where the meals were vegetarian, the teachers were called by Indian names of respect, and part of each day was spent in meditation. Brigitte's schooling was also unconventional: once she had decided she wanted to be a dancer, she was sent right away to a professional school—bypassing a Gymnasium education.

Around 1925 Karen Horney decided that the girls' education should be supplemented with a course of psychoanalytic treatment with Melanie Klein. This seems like a preposterous idea in retrospect, since none of the children was asking in any obvious way for help. But it is a measure of the blind faith she and other early analysts had in the powers of psychoanalysis that they thought everyone could benefit from it. Perhaps she hoped the girls' treatment would be preventive. But if this was the intention, it backfired.

Child analysis was only about six years old when the Horney girls were sent for treatment. Melanie Klein, who had come to Berlin a few years before from Budapest, was one of its first practitioners. She had made the discovery that playing with toys could break the ice and help children to express their feelings. But judging from the Horney girls' experience, Klein hadn't yet refined her method of talking to children on a level they could comprehend. Brigitte, by then fourteen and strong-willed, probably made the wisest move: she refused to go for analysis at all. Marianne, twelve and more compliant, attended faithfully for two years but figured out a way to keep Melanie Klein's interpretations to a minimum. She would come in, lie down on the couch, and begin an account of her activities, starting with the time she had left the office after the previous visit and ending when she walked in the door for the current visit. She had perfected the timing so that Melanie Klein had about eight minutes to talk at the end. Klein's interpretations were given in the biological vocabulary of early Freudian theory: she talked about defecation, penises, and anuses. The whole thing was, as Marianne remembers it, "rather impersonal." At a time when Marianne could have used some help dealing with real-life difficulties with her sister and her parents, the Klein analysis was nothing but a dreaded obligation.

For Renate, who was only nine, it was even worse. She tried to cooperate in the first couple of sessions. "I had to tell Melanie what I did or thought and I would tell her about my trees and games and dolls and she would reply with explanations of penis envy, anus play, etc., etc." After listening once or twice, Renate made a conscious effort to arrive at the sessions as late as possible. When she got there, she would dive under the couch, put her fingers in her ears, and say absolutely nothing. She developed nightmares, and, with a friend, started dropping notes at neighbors' houses which would "tell them what I had learned in analysis." After several neighbors complained to the Horneys of finding notes in their mailboxes with "Greetings from your Fart" written on them in childish handwriting, the Horneys confronted Renate. She was to go to each neighbor's house and apologize. Renate went to one house and rang the bell. Fortunately the maid answered. The child quickly mumbled an apology and ran home to announce that she had made one call. Wasn't that enough? "My parents started laughing," Renate remembers, "and we all laughed until the tears came. I got a big hug and kiss and was excused." Fortunately Renate's mother also decided after the incident to put an end to the children's analysis with Melanie Klein. Years later Karen told Renate that the Klein analysis had been one of her worst mistakes.

The decisions about schools, analysis, and hiring and firing at home seem to have been made for the most part by Karen alone. But Oskar took more of an interest than she during the Zehlendorf years in the children's day-to-day experiences. Oskar's demands could sometimes be intimidating. Marianne remembers being terrified when he required her to recite aloud on special occasions. And with Oskar there was always the possibility of a spanking. Yet his sternness was a form of caring. And he was not always so grave. He was a great game player and engaged his daughters, particularly Marianne, in hours of chess, Mah-Jongg, and cards.

And he had perfected a little magic show, which he liked to perform at the girls' birthday parties.

Most of the time, though, Oskar was, like Karen, occupied elsewhere. And the children, left to their own devices, got along badly or not at all. There was incessant fighting between the older two, Brigitte and Marianne. Little Renate, often an onlooker, remembers one particularly wild day when Brigitte locked herself in Marianne's room in a rage, tore up everything in sight, and threw Marianne's sheets and mattress out the window onto the compost heap. This was, apparently, one day among many. The bitter rivalry between Brigitte and Marianne rarely abated.

Even if a parent had intervened more often, it is not clear how much it would have helped. Brigitte's jealousy of Marianne was so intense, right from the start, that there seemed to be no way to assuage it. The family explanation appears in Karen's progress notes from 1914, when Marianne was nearly two and Biggi nearly four. Brigitte's jealousy, she noted, was "probably intensified by the fact that Marianne with her sunny way, her blond curls, her incredibly blue eyes, and her roguish manner, usually stands out more than Biggi and usually others take more notice of her. Biggi then stands there with a sad face." In the end it was Brigitte who would become the great beauty and center of attention as a star of stage and screen—the ultimate revenge, one might add, for this childhood slight. But the jealousy she felt in childhood was deep and persistent; it was the most frequent subject of her mother's entries in the progress notes.

"At mealtimes Biggi eats slowly so that she will have some food left on her plate when Marianne is finished. During breakfast she occasionally asks Marianne with forced friendliness, 'Janne, do you still have some cocoa?' . . . Then she will wait for Marianne to finish the last drop . . . then . . . start to drink." Marianne's response to Brigitte's jealousy, which most often seems to center around food, is to show herself to be above it. Marianne, Karen notes, "often gives Biggi something if Biggi makes a fuss about it. For example, the other day there were a few cucumber pieces in the soup. Janne got one and Biggi didn't. Big fuss by Biggi. Janne took a piece on her spoon and handed it to Biggi and said, 'Here you go, Biggi-lein.' Biggi took it with a little shame and a little satisfaction. Biggi would never do something like that."

Karen seems to have tried conscientiously to be fair. While she might have been "more tender with Marianne" during her early months, she had tried since "to devote myself equally to both.

Now I don't have to make an effort to do that," she adds. "They have both grown equally dear to my heart." Later, when Biggi complains that her mother gets mad at her more quickly, Karen admits that "it is possible that there is some truth there because Biggi gets immediately disagreeable if she doesn't like something, whereas Marianne, even if she is stubborn, always keeps something nice or funny about her." Once again the sunny Marianne triumphs over the stormy Brigitte.

As every parent knows, however, children can imagine slights even when they are treated with scrupulous fairness. And siblings in many families quarrel endlessly, especially when they are so close in age. If there is any explanation for the unusual intensity and persistence of the Marianne-Brigitte rivalry, it is perhaps that there wasn't quite enough love and attention to go around.

When there was, the fighting abated. All three girls remember fondly their trips to the home of their paternal grandparents in Hessen. The woman the girls knew as "Grossmutti" was a much younger woman Oskar's father had married after his wife died. Her life was family, cooking, the garden. And when the three Horney girls came, Grossmutti, who was in fact younger than their own mother, gave them her undivided attention. She cooked *Pfannkuchen* for them; she trimmed their nails and mended their socks—details that tended to be neglected at home. At night, when they got into bed, they would discover that she had warmed the sheets in advance with a hot-water bottle.

With their own mother pleasures were on a grander and riskier scale. In the summer Karen and the children went to the seashore for vacation. Karen preferred island resorts in the North Sea which could be reached only with a small boat. Mornings would be spent on the beach, where the girls would establish territorial rights for the season by building a large sand castle. Afternoons were for exploration in the woods and along the cliffs. Renate remembers excursions with her mother into the sound at low tide to gather mussels, "always accompanied by a bit of fear, for the tides changed quickly and were very high." On one occasion Karen, Marianne, and Renate were caught in a gale on a trip to an island called Helgoland. Undeterred, they "decided to climb the cliffs to the upper island and walk all around it, as that was the thing to do." When walking became impossible, they crawled on all fours in order not to be blown off. "This seemed so silly that all three of us started to laugh and laugh, until our tummies hurt."

There were carefree times in Zehlendorf too. Sometimes Karen and Oskar gave parties, rolling up the rug in the living room for dancing. Christmas, which had always been a happy occasion in Karen's childhood, was made magical for her children as well. In German tradition, Karen and Oskar prepared the tree and gifts behind closed doors on Christmas Eve.

> Finally [as Renate remembers], a bell was rung and, dressed up and with beating hearts, we stood before the doors awaiting the great moment when Father would open them. What a sight! The tree lit in all its splendor with what seemed hundreds of . . . wax candles reflecting in the many silver spheres and bells and decorations. All tables around the room were loaded with gifts, one table for each one of us. Mother sat at the piano playing the carols which we sang as we entered, then Father read the Christmas story from the New Testament. Then more singing and reciting of poems by us children. When we could not bear it any longer, we were allowed to rush to our tables and see the many wonderful gifts.

Such a happy tableau—with father reading the Bible and mother playing carols—could have appeared in the weekly family magazine *Gartenlaube*. But it hardly captured the day-to-day atmosphere in the house at 15 Sophie-Charlotte Strasse. Although Karen and Oskar kept their troubles hidden most of the time, even the children were aware that they led very separate lives. They had different friends, except for a few left over from earlier days, different political sympathies (his were conservative, hers Socialist), and they spent little leisure time together. In the summer, when Karen and the girls went to the North Sea, Oskar joined them only occasionally. Still, Oskar and Karen might have gone on indefinitely, keeping up appearances in public and before the children while pursuing private gratifications outside the marriage, had it not been for the events of 1923. That year the disastrous effects of inflation reverberated at the Horney house in Zehlendorf. And the ties that bound the Horneys began to come undone.

10

Separation

World War I, historian Barbara Tuchman has observed, "lies like a band of scorched earth dividing that time from ours." By "destroying beliefs, changing ideas, and leaving incurable wounds of disillusion, it created a physical as well as psychological gulf between two epochs."[1] And what was true for Europe in general was particularly true for Berlin. Before the war Berlin had been stuffy and cautious. But after the November revolution of 1918 caution was replaced by wild abandon. There was almost nothing Berliners couldn't, and didn't, say and do in the interlude between the wars. Ironically, Berlin in defeat was more alive with art, with theater, with ideas than it has ever been—before or since.

The war experience fueled the creative surge. Erich Maria Remarque's *All Quiet on the Western Front* was the bitter fruit of the author's terrible days and nights in the trenches. George Grosz, another angry veteran, used his pen to scratch out venomous caricatures of arrogant generals and greedy capitalists for leftist periodicals. And Bertolt Brecht's experiences as a medical orderly inspired early songs and poetry, antecedents of the great works, including *The Threepenny Opera,* which appeared in Berlin as the twenties rolled on.

The war had brought disenchantment with old ideologies and a search for new ones. Some, like Brecht, saw Marxism, so recently established in the new Soviet Union, as the way of the future. Others formed a movement they called Dada, which rejected ideologies altogether. "We were against all ideology," as Dadaist Richard Huelsenbeck explained years later, "because the ideology based on Kant and Fichte and Hegel had become compatible with war. We were against culture because the culture of Goethe and Schiller had become compatible with war." Of course, Huelsenbeck acknowledged, Dada expressed itself in art, "even though we were against art."[2]

The members of Dada were not the only artists with a message. Sometimes the vision was hopeful and utopian: the architects of the Bauhaus group advocated simple functional design, made available to the common man. But more often the message was one of despair and alienation. Sometimes, as in the nightmare visions of Max Beckmann, it seemed to prophesy impending doom.

Berlin in the twenties was hardly a carefree place. Few would have characterized it as gay, like Paris, or *gemütlich,* like Vienna. But Berlin was where the action was. It was the home of Albert Einstein, whose theory of relativity was first proved in the field by a 1919 eclipse of the sun. It was a city, as one of its gifted conductors, Bruno Walter wrote, of "unparalleled mental alertness" and "a passionate general concentration upon cultural life."[3] There were forty-nine active theaters in Berlin in the twenties, three opera companies, and one hundred and twenty newspapers that devoted as much space to culture as to public affairs. Ives Hendrick, an American who came to study at the Berlin Psychoanalytic Institute in 1928, wrote home that Berlin was "a city whose personality is . . . as rushing, fatiguing, individual-crushing as New York's." The Berliners, he noted, are "quite as preoccupied in their own intensive lives, quite as indifferent to any of the swarms of friendless people who mingle with them, as are New Yorkers." But "as in New York, there is that vibrant, magnetic, urbanity which enables one to draw a certain satisfaction and vitality out of the very crowds in the streets, and in this way compensate considerably for the lack of personal contacts."[4] As playwright Carl Zuckmayer noted more succinctly, "Berlin tasted of the future, and that is why we gladly took the crap and the coldness."[5]

Berlin might have been cold, but it was not always serious. In fact, the astonishing amount and the variety of amusement available in Berlin in the twenties suggested a kind of "last whistle" [*letzte Pfiff*] desperation. There were variety productions and cabaret acts on every possible scale. At a small café on Behrenstrasse called the Weisse Maus one could watch Anita Berber undulate in the nude. ("She dances the coitus," a contemporary critic reported.)[6] Or one could seek less conventional thrills at the El Dorado, probably the first bar in the West where homosexuals and transvestites danced and mingled openly. As Stefan Zweig wrote later:

> Berlin transformed itself into the Babel of the world...the Germans brought to perversion all their vehemence and love of system. Made-up boys with artificial waistlines promenaded along the Kurfürstendamm...and in the darkened bars one could see high public officials and high financiers courting drunken sailors without shame. Even the Rome of Suetonius had not known orgies like the Berlin transvestite balls, where hundreds of men in women's clothes and women in men's clothes danced under the benevolent eyes of the police. Amid the general collapse of values, a kind of insanity took hold of precisely those middle-class circles which had hitherto been unshakable in their order. Young ladies proudly boasted that they were perverted; to be suspected of virginity at sixteen would have been considered a disgrace in every school in Berlin.[7]

It would be convenient if Karen Horney's life fitted neatly into this picture of the postwar years. But in fact she was out of step in many ways with her times. For the most part she was ahead of them. She had wanted to lose her virginity way back in 1903 as a Gymnasium student in Hamburg. And she and Oskar, as a young married couple in prewar Berlin, allowed each other a degree of sexual freedom that amounted to a "collapse of values." Had there been an El Dorado in prewar Berlin, Karen and her friends would have been among the first to drop by and have a look.

Nor did the war impose great hardships on Karen and her family. Karl Abraham, like other male analytic pioneers, had to put his psychoanalytic practice aside and leave his family to serve as a surgeon on the eastern front. But as a woman Karen was able to continue practicing and developing her psychoanalytic skills throughout the war years. Then too Oskar's job protected the Horneys. Because he was an executive in a war-related industry there was never any question of his serving in the army. And for a while at least the Horneys seemed impervious to the postwar inflation that, in the twenties, began to threaten rich and poor alike.

But the economic crisis of 1923 put an end to the Horneys' immunity. As the value of the German mark declined in the postwar period the German government had responded by printing more marks. In addition the government was operating with a huge deficit: the enormous reparations called for by the Treaty of Versailles imposed a heavy burden, one the government was reluctant to ease by the imposition of taxes. The result, in the first six months of 1923, was inflation on an absolutely preposterous scale. People were getting paid twice a day, leaving work after their first payment to stand in line at shops, knowing that everything would cost twice as much by the end of the day. In 1914 four German marks could buy what it took four *billion* German marks to buy at the end of 1923. You could be admiring a hare in the window of a butcher shop, George Grosz remembers, and "while you were just thinking . . . the prices went up. . . . You could almost hear it. . . . It wasn't funny. You decided in a flash and bought; while you were walking through the door, that hare could cost a million or two more."[8]

By 1924 the inflation had been brought under control. But there were many casualties. Unemployment soared. People of modest means lost their life savings, their businesses. Corporate high rollers, who had prospered in the initial years of inflation, lost everything almost overnight. The biggest loser among these was Oskar Horney's employer, Hugo Stinnes. Stinnes, a squat, swarthy man who affected workmen's clothes and heavy boots even after he had become a millionaire, got rich manipulating the foreign currency he accumulated from selling the coal of the Ruhr Valley. He had managed, in a few years' time, to buy up whole forests, iron and steel plants in Hungary, chemical and aluminum plants in Romania, newspapers and periodicals at home, until he owned in all some two thousand companies. Stinnes' appetite for acquisition was legendary. When he died, a cartoon in the satirical journal *Simplicissimus* pictured Saint Peter ringing a bell and shouting a warning: "Stinnes is coming! Wake up, children, or in a fortnight he'll own the whole works!"[9] But Hugo Stinnes would have had to start all over in heaven. When he died his shaky empire died too, a victim of the inflation that had made it possible in the first place.

The collapse of Stinnes in 1923 marked the beginning of a new and very difficult period in the life of Karen Horney. Oskar lost his job, and with it the income that had made the Zehlendorf life-style possible. And suddenly there were unexpected illnesses to deal with as well. That same year, without any warning, Karen's brother, Berndt, who was only forty-two, contracted pneumonia and died. The death of Berndt, the only surviving member of her immediate family, was a terrible blow. After her mother's death Karen's squabbles with her brother had abated; Berndt and his wife, Ollie, became frequent visitors to Zehlendorf. The children had loved his gaiety, and particularly his little tricks in games of croquet. And everyone loved his wife, who was, despite Berndt's earlier displays of anti–Semitism, half Jewish. Their son, also named Berndt, was just a little younger than Karen's youngest girl, Renate, and the two babies had been christened together. Berndt, as Karen wrote a friend, "belonged to those people who seem to burst with the joy of living." His death struck her as "something totally senseless."[10]

Sometime during that same year Oskar became very ill too. While traveling on business he contracted meningitis and had to be hospitalized in Cologne. He barely survived, and he may have suffered some brain damage. That at least is the family's (Karen's and her daughters') explanation for what happened next. Although he had apparently been a competent company man, after the collapse of Stinnes Oskar began to get involved in one losing business proposition after another. The first one, a movie company that was to rival the reigning UFA, had disastrous and far-reaching consequences. Not only did Oskar lose everything he had but he also lost his parents' savings, which they had invested at his suggestion. Other ventures, equally unsuccessful, followed.

By 1926 the Horneys were forced to sell the Zehlendorf house and move to an apartment in the city. But even then, out of pride or wishful thinking, they moved to a large, elegant apartment on a well-groomed green square, Steinplatz. It was an apartment on the grand Berlin scale, like the one English journalist Edward Edgeworth described, designed to impress visitors with "a drawing-room fit for a ball," and "a dining-room fit for a banquet," where "beds, twilight, cockroaches, and the smell of dinner lurk elsewhere."[11] Its special attraction was a tower room, up a winding staircase and above the hubbub of the house, where Karen could see her patients. Renate, who was ten at the time of the move to Steinplatz, remembers hanging crepe paper in anticipation of one grand party her parents gave there. But she also remembers that each piece of furniture in the grand rooms had a numbered sticker on the back. One day in school when a teacher was explaining bankruptcy she realized that the stickers meant that the furniture was being claimed by the authorities to pay off the family's debts.

It soon became impossible to keep up appearances. Oskar was bankrupt. And so was Karen and Oskar's marriage. Within a year

of the move to Steinplatz, Karen and Oskar decided to live apart.
With the three girls Karen moved to a smaller apartment nearby.
Karen and Oskar remained on friendly terms and didn't divorce
until years later. But they never lived together again.

The immediate reason for the split was financial. Oskar's bad
judgment threatened everyone's security. Karen, who continued to
earn a steady income from her practice, was understandably reluctant to see her earnings eaten away in bad investments and bankruptcy claims. But the financial crisis was merely the final wedge
dividing Karen and Oskar. For all their professions of tolerance,
the long-standing infidelities must have left scars. For some time
before the breakup Oskar had been spending his free time with his
secretary, Hanna. Hanna, whom he eventually married, was no
match for Karen in intellect, nor was she beautiful. But she was
devoted in a way that Karen could never be. Karen for her part
hadn't ever been monogamous for long. And there was little passion between her and Oskar to carry them through trying times.
Karen used to tell her daughters, laughingly, about the time Oskar
had complimented her on her new dress. "But Oskar," she had
replied, "I've been wearing this dress for two years!" It is a story
that explains, at least as much as Oskar's bankruptcy, why Karen
and Oskar were bound to part. Long before the financial crisis
they had stopped paying careful attention to each other.

Neither Karen nor Oskar spoke to their daughters about their
marital difficulties. Unlike Sonni, who had burdened her children
with her unhappiness for years, Karen kept whatever feelings she
was having to herself. Nor did she start a new diary, as she had at
other difficult times in her life. At age forty she turned instead to
her work, not only for consolation but also for understanding. The
energy that twenty years earlier had poured into her long diary
account of what had gone wrong with Rolf was channeled this
time around into professional writing. Over the next six years she
published a total of fourteen professional papers. Most were concerned, in one way or another, with issues of male and female
development and with relationships. Five papers addressed themselves specifically to marriage difficulties. And though she always
stressed in her discussions that she was searching for "common
denominators" rather than "individual factors,"[12] she drew often
on her own history.

When, in 1930, she wrote of the initial overvaluation of the
partner, she could have been describing the early, letter-writing
phase of her relationship with Oskar. At the outset "love stirs up

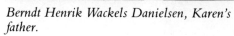

*Berndt Henrik Wackels Danielsen, Karen's
father.*

*Clothilde Marie "Sonni" Danielsen,
Karen's mother.*

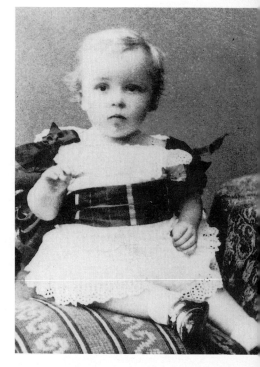

*Karen Clementina Theodora Danielsen,
around age two.*

Top: *The apartment house in Eilbek where Karen and her family lived in 1900–1901. The Danielsens' apartment occupied an entire wing of the third floor.*

Bottom: *The Setos, one of the ships Karen's father captained on his frequent voyages to South America. Captain Danielsen made eight trips on the Setos between 1883 and 1888. [Deutsches Schiffahrtsmuseum, Bremerhaven]*

A studio portrait of Karen and her brother, Berndt, about 1890.

Pastor Nikolai von Ruckteschell (seated), the much-admired preacher who conducted Karen's confirmation classes at the local Friedenskirche. Standing to the left is Karen's father, Wackels, one of the pastor's ardent followers.

Karen, age ten.

Karen (far left) with friends at the Gymnasium in Hamburg, about 1904. Ida "Idchen" Behrmann, standing second from left, would follow Karen to University in Freiburg and remain a lifelong friend. Standing third from left is Josine Ebsen (later Müller), who studied medicine with Karen and became, like her, a psychoanalyst in Berlin. The man in the picture is presumably a teacher.

Fräulein Doktor

38
Bruno Paul
The lady doctor
"You're mine at last!
I can hear your heart beating at my words! –
"You're wrong, dear, it's the abdominal artery."
Vol. 7, No. 49, 1903

A cartoon in the satirical periodical Simplicissimus *ridiculing "Fräulein Doktor."* [Goethe-Institut, Munich]

Karen Danielsen as a medical student in Freiburg, about 1907.

Top: Karen and friends hiking in the Black Forest near Freiburg, about 1907. From left: Louis "Losch" Grote, an unidentified male, Idchen and Karen.

Bottom: The hiking party, later that day.

Idchen in her Fasching costume.

Karen in Losch's lap, probably in the apartment on Sedanstrasse in Freiburg, 1907.

Karen, holding skull, poses with fellow students with dueling swords. Losch is at far left.

Inhabitants of Karen's "doll's house" in Freiburg. From left: Idchen, Sonni, Losch and Karen.

all of our secret expectations and longings for happiness, which slumber deep inside us." We invest the partner with "the glitter of sexual overestimation. We take the magnitude of such over-valuation for the measure of our love, while in reality it mere-ly expresses the magnitude of our expectations." Then too the ex-pectations may be contradictory. "The partner is supposed to be strong, and at the same time helpless, to dominate us and be domi-nated by us, to be ascetic and to be sensuous. He should rape us and be tender, have time for us exclusively and also be intensely involved in creative work." Disappointment is bound to follow. "The very nature of our claims makes their fulfillment impossi-ble."[13]

Long before her marriage to Oskar, Karen's conflicting feelings about commitment had dominated her relationships with men. With Rolf and with Losch her fear of rejection had caused her to pull away at the least imagined slight. When Rolf left Hamburg to study music, she left him for Ernst. When Losch started frequent-ing cafés, she declared she didn't love him anymore. After separat-ing from Oskar, she tried to understand the pattern. There is, she wrote in "The Distrust Between the Sexes," "a natural fear of los-ing ourselves in another person." Because we sense the possibility of "ecstasy," of "surrendering oneself, which means a leap into the unlimited and the boundless," we are "inclined to be reserved and ever ready to retreat. For like a good businessman, we are loath to put all our eggs in one basket."[14]

The comparison of love to investment also reflects Karen's own preoccupations. Not that she was particularly greedy or materialis-tic. But she did have a wish to be taken care of by a good provider. In the beginning Oskar's earning power had been one of his great attractions. When, early in her marriage, Losch paid a visit, she found herself thinking that "Losch would also have been a nice husband." But this thought, as she noted in her diary at the time, was followed immediately by another: "Losch has little chance to make a good living. That is strange. Losch has studied as long as Oskar—yet has slight pecuniary chances." She concluded that "my unconscious apparently sees my marriage as a money marriage. . . . Oskar's good prospects for a position and earnings attracted me, exactly the opposite of Losch and Rolf, and . . . I am now proud and happy that he has gotten so far."[15]

When she writes, in "Problems of Marriage," of the danger of choosing a partner "to fulfill an isolated condition," she could be writing of her "money marriage" to Oskar. "Some quality in the partner," she writes, "really corresponded to some of our expectations; something in him really promised to fulfill a longing in us; perhaps it actually did so in marriage. If, however, the rest of the self stands aside and has little in common with the partner, this strangeness will inevitably prove disturbing to a lasting relationship."[16]

Of course when Oskar ceased to be a good provider it deepened the disappointment. But, to be fair, Karen's and Oskar's was never *just* a money marriage. The early correspondence suggests it begin much more as a marriage of minds than of money. Nor was Karen a true gold digger. In fact, she didn't feel comfortable relying on anyone else, particularly financially. One of her biggest arguments with Rolf had been over his not allowing her to pay her share. And it may have been her ambivalence about dependency that led her to make what proved in the long run to be the wrong financial choice. Just two years after Oskar and Karen had married, Losch married Karen's friend Idchen and settled in Dresden, where he became the chief physician at a sanitarium. The piano remained a passionate avocation, but it never got in the way of Losch's medical career. Oskar's earning power, though more dazzling, proved less reliable in the long run than Losch's.

In leaving Oskar, Karen was taking the same step her mother had taken a quarter century before. But unlike Sonni, who spent the last years of her life in a state of worry over money, Karen had her own profession and her own income. And though there is evidence in her professional writing that the failure of her marriage troubled her, there is even more evidence that leaving Oskar was liberating. Free of Oskar's financial entanglements and of the need to pretend she was happily married, Karen began to do more of everything: not only more writing but also more teaching, more public speaking, more committee work at the institute, and more traveling. The years between 1926, when she left Oskar, and 1932, when she left Germany, were among the most productive of her life.

It wasn't easy at first. The new apartment was in a wonderful location, right in the heart of Berlin and so close to the Tiergarten park and zoo that you could hear the lions roar from the balcony. But even though it was a smaller, less expensive apartment than the one on Steinplatz, she had to take in a renter at first to make ends meet. There were still unpaid bills to worry about: Marianne's school wrote a letter insisting on payment. During the first winter, when there wasn't enough coal for the tile stoves in all the rooms, Karen's office was the only warm room in the place. Because there was only one maid now, new tasks fell to the children. When the pipes froze, Renate and Brigitte hauled up buckets of water from the hand pump on the street. Renate, who was twelve, was expected to shop twice a week at the open-air market and walk the long mile home with a heavy load of groceries.

Renate was generally unhappy as well. In her usual arbitrary way Karen had decided around that time that Renate needed a more structured education and had enrolled her in a small, elite private school. Renate hated it. And, as with the Melanie Klein analysis, she found a dramatic way to make her unhappiness known. She began climbing on rooftops in the neighborhood and throwing pebbles at the cars passing below. The police visited—twice. And the elite private school asked that Renate be withdrawn before she was expelled.

The complaints led to another educational about-face. Renate would be sent to the Salem School, a place in Switzerland with an international reputation for innovation. Renate remembers having an interview with the director one day in Berlin, then leaving for the school on a train the next day. Unlike many of Karen's impulsive educational choices, however, this one turned out well. For Renate, enrollment at the Salem School marked "the beginning of three of the happiest years of my life."[17] The school was set on a hill overlooking Lake Constance in the snow-capped Alps. Renate thrived there, academically and socially.

Meanwhile both of the older girls were becoming increasingly absorbed in their own pursuits in Berlin. Marianne had recently returned from a year at the Quaker school in Switzerland. Although she had learned a good deal of English there, she was badly in need of a program that would fill in the gaps in her education. Her mother enrolled her at a private school with a woman who provided a cram course that would enable her to pass the *Abitur* and go on to the university. Brigitte, whose plans to become a dancer were cut short by a knee injury, had begun training for a career in the theater. With Renate in boarding school, Karen could live what amounted to a single life. She began to go to the theater more often and to travel more outside of Germany. But for the most part her social and professional life revolved around the Berlin Psychoanalytic Institute.

It was an exciting time to be involved in psychoanalysis in Berlin. Like so many other Berlin institutions during the Weimar years, the Berlin Institute was becoming *the* center, more alive than

Vienna with new ideas, new faces, and with a sense of infinite possibility. It was in Berlin, not Vienna, that the future course of psychoanalytic training was being charted. Yet at the same time the Berlin Institute nurtured radicals and dreamers of every stripe. And as a founding member, a teacher, and a regular at meetings, Karen Horney was very much a part of it all.

There were a number of reasons for the Berlin Institute's liveliness. For one thing, it was easier to think independently of Freud in Berlin. In Vienna, as psychoanalyst Yela Lowenfeld has noted, they all felt themselves to be in the shadow of "the Giant."[18] Then too Berlin was a more cosmopolitan and tolerant city than Vienna, a city where a foreigner could feel at home. As a result the Berlin Institute acted as a magnet for a great array of people from all over the world. Young American doctors came from New York and Chicago and stayed the half year or year it took to complete an analysis. Often their analysts would be Franz Alexander or Sandor Rado, themselves transplanted Hungarians versatile enough to conduct analysis in English. Rado and Alexander were but two of a large analytic contingent that had fled Hungarian oppression and enriched the international mix at the Berlin Institute.

The institute reflected the Socialist-egalitarian sentiments widely held by Berlin intellectuals at the time. From its beginnings, in 1920, the institute polyclinic provided free analytic treatment, often to more than a hundred patients. And, beginning in 1927, the Berlin Institute provided inpatient treatment to about thirty more severely disturbed persons in a small renovated castle on the outskirts of the city. When Ernst Simmel, a Socialist analyst who succeeded Karl Abraham as institute president, looked back on the Institute's first ten years, he noted with pride that the polyclinic's free treatment did not differ in the least from that of patients paying high fees. "Here also, the doctor must occupy himself alone in a private room with his patient for the duration of an hour" and the patient is "entitled to as many weeks or months of analysis as his condition requires." In this way, Simmel concluded, the Institute was fulfilling social obligations incurred by society, which "makes its poor become neurotic and, because of its cultural demands, lets its neurotics stay poor, abandoning them to their misery."[19] Through analysis provided by clinics, Simmel predicted, men lost to drink, abandoned women on the verge of breakdown, and delinquent children would be helped to function again. Freud, in a tenth-anniversary tribute, hailed the Berlin Institute's effort "to make our therapy accessible to the great numbers of people who suffer no less than the rich from neurosis, but are not in a position to pay for treatment."[20]

In Berlin in the twenties there were those who believed that psychoanalysis could save the world. The *Kinderseminar* (children's seminar), an unofficial group of young, political psychoanalysts, met regularly to discuss politics and analysis. It included not only such dedicated Socialists as Simmel, Otto Fenichel, and Wilhelm Reich (who later became a Communist for a time) but also Edith Jacobson, whose activities in the anti-Fascist cause landed her in jail briefly in the Nazi era, and Erich Fromm. Edith Weigert, who attended some of the meetings as an institute candidate, remembers long conversations about "finding a bridge between Marx and Freud."

Even among less political analysts, such as Karen Horney, there was great excitement about psychoanalysis, as both a treatment and a method of research. At times analysts were known to pay their patients' carfare, just to continue the sessions. The faith in the curative powers of psychoanalysis is apparent in the 1930 Institute report: patients with all types of disorders, including schizophrenics and sufferers from facial tics and from organic nervous disease, were treated with psychoanalysis at the polyclinic. Of the 363 who completed analytic treatment, over 200 improved, some markedly, and 111 were declared, with an optimism few modern analysts would hazard, "cured."[21]

The members of the Berlin Institute, however, did not confine themselves to treatment. The *"Berliner energie"* Freud had admired in a letter to Abraham overflowed into evening meetings on a dazzling array of topics. There were clinical discussions of everything from transvestism to train phobia to the psychoanalytic treatment of a painter. And there were nonclinical evenings ranging over the whole of human activity. One night a guest spoke on the relationship of Chinese calligraphy to psychoanalytic concepts. Another night the topic was the writing of Oscar Wilde. A third night there was a discussion of the "latest press polemics on psychoanalysis in Berlin."[22] Sandor Rado, when he arrived from Budapest, concluded that the Hungarian group had been "not in the clouds but beyond the clouds somewhere" compared to the Berlin group. On the other hand, he noted, the Berlin group sometimes "suffered from overzealousness."[23]

According to the Berlin Institute news in *The International Journal of Psycho-Analysis,* Karen Horney was a typically enthusiastic member. The only woman among the six founding members in 1920 and the first woman to teach there, she had served at various times—beginning in 1914, when the group had met in Abraham's living room—as secretary and treasurer. But after her separation from Oskar her name began to appear more frequently in the *International Journal*. She attended nearly every lecture, offering comments, and gave papers on such clinical issues as the uncovering of a childhood dream and the particular problems of analyzing young girls. In addition to her case seminars Horney taught sexual biology to nonmedical candidates at the Institute and spoke frequently before non-analytic audiences—doctors, social workers, and the general public. One of her lectures, on the fate of women, drew an audience of two hundred. Another talk, on the "masculinity complex," got not only a lengthy write-up in a major Berlin newspaper but, according to the *International Journal,* a "very favorable and appreciative response" from the audience, a group of sexologists.[24]

Karen Horney's vacations, after she separated from Oskar, took a more adventurous turn. Instead of going north to the German coast, Karen traveled south with Renate—and sometimes Marianne and Brigitte as well—to Austria and Italian Switzerland. One year they went to Lugano, another year to Ascona on Lake Maggiore. Renate has a particularly vivid memory of one end-of-summer glacier hike her mother arranged in the Austrian Alps. At dawn one morning they all started out, tied together by ropes and led by a professional guide. "The weather was perfect, the sky was blue, and the sun plus its reflection transformed it all into a glaring, sparkling ocean of ice." The guide led them carefully across the glacier's deep crevices. "I remember looking down into their frightening depth, seeing little icy towers, bridges, a fairyland of formations."[25]

Tuti, Karen's old friend from elementary school, was invited along on several of these summer vacations. She and Karen were both single again—Tuti's much older husband had died—and had professional interests in common, since Tuti had become a social worker. Renate remembers that her mother called Tuti "the wise one." The two women often hung back, talking earnestly with each other on the trail.

On several vacations Karen's patients came along as well. This was not an unusual practice in the early days of psychoanalysis. "Institutes were still small and informal in the 1920's," psychoanalytic historian Nathan Hale, Jr., has written. "Analysands traipsed off to Menton or Dubrovnik on vacation with their analysts."[26]

One summer, when her patients were staying at some distance along Lake Maggiore, Renate was regularly dispatched to the pier to meet the steamer that brought them for their sessions. Seeing patients probably enhanced Karen Horney's enjoyment: she never liked to be idle all day, and she had the added satisfaction of paying for her vacation as she took it.

Back in Berlin, Karen's social life also revolved around her psychoanalytic interests. Her colleagues were her closest friends. There was Josine Ebsen, who had been a friend since Gymnasium and who had attended medical school with her at Freiburg. Josine was one of the first analysts to question Freud's ideas about female development.[27] She was married to Karl Müller-Braunschweig, another early analyst and close friend. Karl later divorced Josine and again married an analyst, Ada Schott. Karen remained friendly with all three—Karl and his new and former wives. Karen also got to know Hermine Hug-Hellmuth, the first analyst to attempt the treatment of children, when she came from Vienna to teach. Later the two women vacationed together.

It seems likely, however, that Karen Horney's deepest attachment during these years was to another member of the Berlin group, Hans Liebermann. Marianne remembers that Hans Liebermann often visited and that he and Karen had intimate talks. They were probably lovers. But eventually, to Karen's distress, Liebermann married a younger woman. Neither Karen nor his young wife, however, was able to alter Liebermann's tragic life course.

Liebermann had become addicted to cocaine after using it as a pain-killer during World War I. By the late twenties his addiction had gotten so bad that he fainted at least once during an Institute meeting. When he died in 1931, Max Eitingon eulogized him in the *International Journal* as a sensitive man, beloved by many patients, who might have been better suited to a life in art than in psychoanalysis. "In the last years," Eitingon wrote, "he struck me as a warrior who had chosen too heavy weapons, become ever more tired in battle, and finally broken under the weight of the assembled arsenal."[28] Like his colleagues, Liebermann had looked to psychoanalysis for insight into his own problem: as early as 1919 he had given a lecture at the Fifth International Congress entitled "Morphinismus."[29] But there was to be no psychoanalytic cure for Hans Liebermann.

Max Eitingon was another of Karen Horney's friends; her daughters called him "der Rosenmax" because he always brought roses when he visited. Such beneficence was characteristic of Eitingon. Although shy and afflicted with a stammer, Eitingon was a person of enormous importance in analytic circles. He had known Freud since 1907, when he traveled to Vienna from Bleuler's clinic in Switzerland to meet and learn from him. He was a member of the original "Committee," the circle of six analysts Freud chose in 1912 as "the small but select company in whose hands the future of psychoanalysis lies."[30] And he was a man of means, the heir to his Russian-Jewish family's fur fortune, who was singularly devoted to the cause. It was Eitingon who, in 1920, provided the first Institute quarters, on Potsdamerstrasse. And it was Eitingon, again, who underwrote the move some years later to bright and spacious new consulting, lecture, and meeting rooms, on Wichmannstrasse. When Karl Abraham died in 1925, Eitingon became president of the International Psychoanalytic Association.

Her friendships, her busy practice, and her active involvement in Institute affairs made Karen Horney a central figure in the early years of the Berlin Institute. "She was a very important factor in Berlin," remembers Marianne Kris, a candidate from 1925 to 1927. She was also "a very charming person."[31] Students liked Horney because she was down to earth and accessible. Fritz Perls, of Esalen fame, was in analysis with Wilhelm Reich in 1933 and seeing his own patients under the supervision of Otto Fenichel and Karen Horney. "From Fenichel I got confusion," he wrote many years later; "from Reich, brazenness; from Horney, human involvement without terminology."[32]

Gustav Hans Graber, who came from Switzerland to study at the institute in 1931, remembers how disappointed he was after he left Horney's lively case seminar for "schoolmasterly" Karl Müller-Braunschweig's.[33] And New York analyst Henry Lowenfeld, who attended an evening case seminar at her apartment on Lutzowüfer in 1928, "liked her very much because she had a certain talent for really understanding people much better than many other analysts. For instance, we had a case seminar with her and one with [Ernst] Simmel. Simmel had a very superior brain but did not have this talent for showing us what the patient was like. She did have this." She was also "rather nice to all of us. She had a Ping-Pong table in her apartment and played Ping-Pong with us. I don't think many teachers would have done that."[34]

Horney's most important contribution to the future of psychoanalysis grew out of her teaching role. She was a member of the education committee, the most important at the institute, from its inception and also on the education committee of the international society beginning in 1928. In the 1930 Berlin Institute report, Horney wrote a lucid and succinct entry entitled "The Establishment of a Training Program: On Its Organization." The guidelines set forth in this paper set the standard not only for Berlin but eventually for institutes everywhere. They are, with small modifications, the educational standards applied today in the United States.

Horney not only wrote the rules but also took steps to meet the standards more precisely herself. As laid out in the ten-year report, the preparation for becoming a psychoanalyst has three parts. First, the trainee must undergo a personal analysis, conducted by an analyst approved for that purpose; second, he or she must take the required institute courses; and third, the trainee must conduct several analyses under the supervision of institute-approved analysts. Of course Horney, as a founding member, had had no teachers or supervisors except Abraham to learn from. But sometime during the twenties she decided to supplement her first analysis, by now ancient history, with a second analysis—what Freud called an after-analysis (*Nachanalyse*). She chose for the purpose the Viennese-born Hanns Sachs, who was considered to be the Berlin Institute's senior "training analyst"—authorized by the institute to conduct the analysis of trainees. Karen Horney wrote nothing about this second analysis, and there is no way of knowing how it affected her. But from what others have said about the personality and methods of her second analyst, Hanns Sachs, it was certainly less than a perfect match.

Hanns Sachs was, like Eitingon, one of the original members of the "Committee." He was a lawyer by training and a great lover of literature whose psychoanalytic writings concentrated on cultural more than clinical issues. As his little book *Freud: Master and Friend** reveals, Sachs's relationship to Freud was one of worshiper to hero. In the small apartment where Sachs practiced in Berlin, a bust of Freud, placed on a high pedestal, was in the patient's direct line of vision when he or she lay down on the couch to begin free-associating. Sachs said very little during the analytic hour; if he did make an interpretation, he liked to put it, whenever possible, in the words of great literature.[35]

All of this, except possibly the literary quotations, could hardly have put Karen Horney at ease. By the time of the analysis with Sachs she was already beginning to question the infallibility of Sachs's hero. Further, she must have seen herself as Sachs's equal in

Freud: Master and Friend (Cambridge, MA: Harvard University Press, 1944).

experience and seniority. She was only three years his junior, had been involved in psychoanalysis almost as long as he, and had better credentials. Perhaps she hoped that Sachs could help her in ways that Abraham hadn't. After all, analysis had changed and so had she. But it seems more likely that she underwent the second analysis to prove her analytic legitimacy. For, despite her active and important role, Karen Horney was beginning to be viewed as troublesome.

When Max Eitingon died in 1943, Ernest Jones eulogized him as a man who "truly worshipped" Freud and made an important contribution to psychoanalysis, even though he didn't "add to the sacred texts."[36] Horney, however, never considered the texts sacred and didn't hesitate to add to them or criticize. Before she left Oskar she had begun to write a series of groundbreaking papers on female psychology. After 1926 she wrote a group of papers on marriage which testify to her new freedom from conventional restraints. She no longer had any need to justify marriage or to argue that psychoanalysis prolongs it. And her experience as an analyst and wife had carried her far beyond the naïve claim she made in 1917, in her maiden speech as a psychoanalyst, that "many a marriage" has "become healthy through analysis."[37]

In contrast, Horney's 1927 paper "The Problem of the Monogamous Ideal" is a litany of the ways in which marriage is bound to disappoint. We are driven into matrimony, she asserts, by "all the old desires arising out of the Oedipus situation in childhood—the desire to be a wife to the father, to have him as one's exclusive possession, and to bear him children." As a result, marriage is "fraught with a perilously heavy load of unconscious wishes." The old incest prohibition, which had forced the child to renounce his passion for the parent, is likely to revive and replace sexual desire with mere affection. The curtailing of passion in marriage can take a variety of forms. One partner may labor under an exaggerated sense of duty, resigning himself or herself to a life of sacrifice and overwork for the sake of the marriage. Or a woman may assume a wholly maternal role, resolving not to "play the part of wife and mistress, but only that of the mother." Whatever form the "limitation of love" takes, it is likely to lead husbands and wives to "seek for new love objects." That is why, Horney asserts, monogamy is problematic.

Monogamy is of course sanctioned by law, but there is a "deeply rooted instinctual basis" for monogamy that predates and underlies the law. The demand for monogamy is "a revival of the infantile wish to monopolize the father or mother." And since the early wish met with "frustration and disappointment" and "wounded our self-regard in its tenderest spot," we are all left with a "narcissistic scar." As a result, "our pride... later demands a monogamous relation and demands it with an imperiousness proportionate to the sensitiveness of the scar left by the early disappointment." But here the claim is "not made out of love; it is a question of prestige." When a partner obeys this demand for monogamy it is probably to assure the other's faithfulness. Monogamy is maintained as "an insurance against the torments of jealousy." And whatever the reasons for choosing monogamy, it is a choice that "imposes a restriction of instincts." The "essential condition of faithfulness," Horney asserts (echoing diary entries during her affair with Walther), is "genital inhibition."[38]

Time tempered Horney's rather harsh view of monogamy. Five years later, in "Problems of Marriage," she admitted to the possibility of a happy marriage, one that finds "an optimum between forgoing and granting, between restriction and freedom of drives." And she allowed, humbly, that "of all the difficulties that appear in marriage... the lion's share is introduced by ourselves as a result of our own development." But the paper ends with a call to "seriously review the absolute standard of monogamy by reexamining with an open mind its origin, its values, and its dangers."[39]

Horney's attacks on the institution of marriage could be dismissed as the self-serving pronouncements of a woman who has failed at it. On the other hand, one could argue that Horney's single state allows her the freedom to take a dispassionate look at marriage—something which, as she suggests, other psychoanalysts haven't dared to do. "For some time," she wrote in "The Problem of the Monogamous Ideal," "I have asked myself with growing astonishment why there has as yet been no thorough analytical exposition of the problems of marriage." Perhaps, she continues, "the conflicts... touch us too closely, lie too near to some of the deepest roots of our most intimate personal experience."[40] In other words, other analysts may have personal reasons for not submitting marriage to psychoanalytic scrutiny.

Horney's marriage papers might have shocked the more conventional elements of Berlin society. But they would not have gotten her in trouble within psychoanalysis, because they didn't question Freud's ideas, only applied them in a new way. Nonetheless the papers reflect the underlying difference in sensibility between Horney and Freud which set the stage for their theoretical clash over the psychology of women.

Unlike Horney, Freud rarely wrote about marriage. In "Civilized Sexual Morality," he discussed the ill effects of sexual abstinence on mental health at length, and he suggested that such suppression before marriage often led to permanent inhibitions after marriage.[41] But he stopped short of suggesting that monogamy itself could be unnatural or unhealthy. In general, Freud left "large-scale application of our therapy" to others willing to "alloy the pure gold of analysis," as he put it, with "the copper of direct suggestion."[42] Unlike Horney, he had no wish to defy convention in his own life or even to direct his relentlessly inquiring mind toward a question so sticky as matrimony.

Even though Horney was only one generation removed from Freud, and even though she grew up in a kindred culture, they lived in different worlds. In 1908 Freud wrote that "civilized women do not usually transgress the prohibition on sexual activity" before marriage.[43] Around that time Karen Horney was transgressing the prohibition. Freud hung onto the familiar in his day-to-day life; Horney was ever restless. Freud stayed married, lived and saw patients in the same house at 19 Berggasse for forty-seven years, and left Vienna only at the eleventh hour, barely escaping the Nazis. Horney had none of what the Germans call *Sitzfleisch*. The eight years in Zehlendorf were the most she had spent in any one place in her adult life. And in 1932, when Hitler was only menacing, she accepted the first invitation to leave Germany for the United States. Of course Horney's view of the world differed also because she was a woman. But there were many other women in psychoanalysis who did not react as Horney did to Freud's ideas about them. Only Karen Horney possessed the right history, and temperament, to take up the challenge.

11

Freud, Horney, and the Psychoanalytic View of Women

Sigmund Freud liked and encouraged the emancipated women among his followers. Lou Andreas-Salomé, who had been Rilke's lover and Nietzsche's companion, became an admired colleague. Helene Deutsch, who not only braved medical school but defied convention by carrying on a long-term affair before marriage, was one of the psychoanalytic theorists Freud valued most.[1] It is true of course that there were no women in Freud's inner circle of six, the "Committee" that ran the International Psychoanalytic Association in the early years. But there were very few women in professional life in general, let alone in psychoanalysis, before World War I. Once universities opened their doors, women quickly found psychoanalysis; not only Deutsch and Salomé, but also Sabina Spielrein, Marie Bonaparte, Ruth Mack Brunswick, and many others, were welcomed by Freud into the fold.

Freud's preference for strong, independent women was evident at home as well. From early on he shared his new ideas with Minna, his wife's lively unmarried sister, and once said she was one of only two people who believed in them.[2] And ultimately he chose a daughter, Anna, to speak for him in his ailing years and to carry on his work after his death. Of his six children, three of whom were sons, only Anna became a psychoanalyst; only Anna inherited the psychoanalytic authority of her father.

As a physician too Freud treated women with more than the usual respect. It was his attentiveness to hysterical women—dismissed by other physicians as malingerers or, worse, as genetically handicapped—that led him to his earliest discoveries about the unconscious roots of hysteria. Unlike other Victorians, who had assumed that sex was a burden for women, Freud insisted from the start that the wife's satisfaction was an important element of her mental health.[3] Nor did he accede to the commonplace arguments that neurasthenia, the disease that caused so many women to spend their days lying down in darkened rooms, was caused by too much strain on their delicate brains. "Intellectual work," he wrote in "Sexual Aetiology of the Neuroses," "is . . . a protection against falling ill of neurasthenia."[4]

Typically, the hysterical women who came to him were of unusual intelligence. Of Frau Emmy von N., Freud wrote in 1895 in *Studies on Hysteria* that "the woman we [he and Breuer] came to know was an admirable one. The moral seriousness with which she viewed her duties, her intelligence and energy, which were no less than a man's, and her high degree of education and love of truth impressed both of us greatly."[5] Another early patient, Frau Cäcilie M., astounded Freud with "the width and clarity of her intellect." She was such a good chess player that she "enjoyed playing two games at a time"—a fact that Freud made use of to argue against Janet's explanation of hysteria as a failure in "mental synthesis."[6]

And yet, as much as he was attracted to smart, independent women, Freud's deeply conventional attitudes prevailed when he came to write about ideals of feminine and masculine behavior. In his writing, ambition in women was likely to be viewed as a neurotic symptom, grounded in penis envy. "Behind this envy for the penis," he wrote in "The Taboo of Virginity," "there comes to light the woman's hostile bitterness against the man, which never completely disappears in the relations between the sexes, and which is clearly indicated in the strivings and in the literary productions of the 'emancipated' woman."[7] Women with "energetic traits" were perforce "masculine women."[8] And the equation of femininity with passivity, masculinity with activity, repeats like a litany throughout his work.

A woman's life, as it emerges in Freud's writings, is almost always second best. As a child she becomes aware of the fact that, in comparison with boys, she has a "stunted" (a word he uses repeatedly) penis. Because the vagina is not seen or known, according to Freud, until after puberty, she concludes that the male organ is the norm, that she once had a penis but lost it through castration. Envy of the male takes hold and is likely to last a lifetime. If she bears children, they will be experienced as a compensation for this profound deprivation. The most a woman can hope for in life, for herself or her daughter, is to marry well.

"The child," Freud wrote in an essay on narcissism, "shall fulfil those wishful dreams of the parents which they never carried out —the boy shall become a great man and a hero in his father's place, and the girl shall marry a prince as a tardy compensation for her mother."[9] When a marriage is childless, the woman loses "one of the things which might be of most help to her in tolerating the resignation her own marriage demands of her."[10] And a woman without her sexual potential is even worse off than one who has it. "It is a well-known fact," Freud wrote in a 1913 essay on obsessional neurosis, "and one that has given much ground for complaint, that after women have lost their genital function their character often undergoes a peculiar alteration. They become quarrelsome, vexatious and overbearing, petty and stingy; that is to say, they exhibit typically sadistic and anal-erotic traits which they did not possess earlier, during their period of womanliness."[11]

Increasingly, as time goes on, Freud greatest offense against women is that he ignores them. After the early years, when all of Freud's patients were women with hysterical complaints, women were less prominent in his writing, if not in his practice. The classic cases—Little Hans, the Wolf Man, the Rat Man—all are male after 1905. So too in discussions of child development, of theory, of culture, there is a tendency to simply bypass the girl's or woman's point of view. The female sense of having been castrated, imputed to women by Freud, is visited on women *by* Freud in his own work. Women are cut out.

As early as 1895, when Freud attempted to explain anxiety as a result of a buildup of sexual tension, he admitted to bewilderment about female sexuality. "Where women are concerned," he writes, "we are not in a position to say what the process analogous to the relaxation of tension of the seminal vesicles [in men] may be."[12] By 1905, when he wrote the important "Three Essays on the Theory of Sexuality," Freud was ready to concede that the "erotic life [of men] alone has become accessible to research. That of women— partly owing to the stunting effect of civilized conditions and partly owing to their conventional secretiveness and insincerity— is still veiled in impenetrable obscurity."[13]

Most of the time, however, Freud's male-sidedness is not even acknowledged, or perhaps even conscious. In 1908, for instance, he wrote that children characteristically "attribute to everyone, including females, the possession of a penis, such as the boy knows from his own body."[14] As happened so often, Freud slid into generalizing from the boy child's point of view. The female child was invisible.

When girls were mentioned at all, the reference to them was nearly always brief and generally to the effect that the same is true for girls, only in reverse. "As you see," Freud wrote in the *Introductory Lectures* of 1917, "I have only described the relation of a *boy* to his father and mother. Things happen in just the same way with little girls, with the necessary changes: an affectionate attachment to her father, a need to get rid of her mother as superfluous and to take her place, a coquetry which already employs the methods of later womanhood—these offer a charming picture, especially in small girls, which makes us forget the possibly grave consequences lying behind this infantile situation."[15]

Such formulations create a pleasing symmetry. Males are active, females are passive. Boys love their mothers first, girls love their fathers. Freud himself, however, often cited the words of his teacher Charcot—"Theory's all very well, but it doesn't prevent things from existing [*La théorie c'est bon, mais ça n'empêche pas d'exister*]."[16] In fact, the reality of women's experience didn't lend itself to such neat parallelism. As Freud conceded in writings after 1925, the first attachment, for girls as well as boys, is to the mother. This is a psychological truth that should be obvious from even casual observation of girl children. The fact that Freud didn't take note of it until thirty years after he began his psychoanalytic researches is a reflection of how little time and attention he devoted to the psychological life of girls.

Not all of Freud's followers, however, neglected female psychology. Karl Abraham, in particular, made an early attempt to flesh out Freud's theory in a lengthy, ambitious paper. When it was presented at the Sixth International Psychoanalytic Congress in Holland in 1920, "Manifestations of the Female Castration Complex" was the only paper on the program that addressed itself specifically to "female" (*weibliche*) concerns. Certainly it was the most important paper, to that date, on female sexuality. And eleven years later, despite the intervening contributions of Horney, Deutsch, and Jones, Freud still considered the Abraham paper "unsurpassed."[17] A modern reader will find some of its propositions laughable. Yet it provides the best illustration, in detail, of the analytic approach to female psychology to which Karen Horney was exposed by her training and reading. It is also the paper that moved her to reply with one of her own.

The Abraham paper opens with the claim that "many women suffer temporarily or permanently . . . from the fact that they have been born female." With this as a premise, Abraham takes Freud's theory of penis envy and elaborates on it, using case examples in such a way as to explain female unhappiness. According to Freud, the little girl notices early on that she lacks a penis, and explains this "defect" by developing a theory of castration. She had a penis once, but it was taken away. The vagina is viewed as the "wound" left after castration. The little girl, unable to accept the fact that she may be, in Abraham's words, "permanently defective," dreams and fantasizes about having a penis. She envies little boys and tries to urinate standing up as they do. She imagines that a penis could grow in time or be received as a "gift," especially a gift from her father, who has one of his own.

In time, after the little girl gives up hope of receiving the penis, she begins to hope for a child from her father "as a substitute for the penis not granted her, again as a 'gift.'" "The hoped-for possession of a child is therefore destined," Abraham writes, "to compensate the woman for her physical defect." This is the Oedipus complex as manifested in girls. It is characterized by a strong attachment to the father and jealous, rivalrous feelings toward the mother, who has been the recipient of the father's gifts of children. It is followed by a period of quiescence, latency, in which the intense feelings go underground. And then, ideally, a young woman emerges in puberty whose libido is free to find a new male object. "The normal adult woman becomes reconciled to her own sexual role and to that of the man . . . she desires passive gratification and longs for a child." But even in healthy women reminders of the early castration theory abide. The blood of menstruation, of "defloration," and, finally, of childbirth all recall castration and result in "traces of the castration complex" in all females.

In some women, according to Abraham, the castration complex continues to dominate. Unable to adapt to the female role, they become homosexual. Or the "repressed wish to be male" is sublimated into "masculine interests of an intellectual and professional character." Such women "proclaim that these interests are just as much feminine as masculine ones. They consider it irrelevant to say that the performances of a human being, especially in the intellectual sphere, belong to the one or the other sex." Abraham notes that "this type of woman is well represented in the women's movement of today."

The bulk of Abraham's lengthy paper is taken up with cataloguing the many ways in which women express their castration complex through neurotic "wishful" or "vengeful" behavior. The wish may be expressed physically: bed-wetting or urinating during intercourse represent "the infantile desire to urinate in the male position." In some women the nose may become a "surrogate of the male genital," resulting in redness and swelling. In others the eyes may take on a similar role. In the unconscious, Abraham notes (after Freud), "a fixed stare is often equivalent to an erection." A woman's pleasure in "thrusting an umbrella into the ground," or in "using a hose for watering the garden" may be unconscious expressions of the childish wish for a penis. Vengeful behavior in women suffering from the castration complex may take the form of kleptomania, a way of taking "forcible possession of the 'gift' which has not been received." Or it may result in frigidity in varying degrees. A woman may avoid men "who have pronounced masculine characteristics." Such women "direct their love choice towards passive and effeminate men, and by living with them can daily renew the proof that their own activity is superior to the man's."

In extreme cases the woman retreats into depression, refusing to compete with men but rejecting the female role as well. In a less extreme case a woman may entertain fantasies of attracting men with her great beauty, then turn a cold shoulder to them. Or on a more mundane level, a married woman may exact payment for the "waiting attitude" she is forced to adopt in sexual matters by keeping her man waiting "on all occasions in daily life." Or she may endure sex only if it does not involve her own "genital organ," in which case a "displacement of libido to other erotogenic zones (mouth, anus) takes place."

Abraham ends with the caveat that the ill effects of the female castration complex are far-reaching. A mother may disparage female sexuality to her daughters or pass on her aversion to men. Or she may disparage her son's sexual organ or prohibit masturbation on the grounds that it is "disgusting for him to touch his genital organ." And because the mother has more influence on children in the early years of life than the father, her castration complex can be "a dangerous enemy" of their development. Thus, Abraham concludes, "if we succeed in freeing such a person from . . . the burdens of her castration complex, then we obviate the neuroses of children, to a great extent, and thus help the coming generation."[18]

Karen Horney undoubtedly heard Abraham present his paper when she attended the International Meetings in Holland in 1920. It must have had a familiar ring: she had heard many of these ideas in Abraham's seminars in Berlin. Besides, Abraham's approach was familiar to her from her own analysis with him a decade earlier. She may even have seen herself among the cases he included in the paper. She bore a striking resemblance, for instance, to Abraham's "immaculate conception" type, the woman who insists she can 'do it alone.' Was she, perhaps, the patient Abraham had in mind when he wrote of those who "wish . . . to find everything in the psycho-analysis alone, without the help of the physician"?[19]

Two years later, at the next international congress, Horney made her debut with a paper that was a direct reply to Abraham's. "On the Genesis of the Castration Complex in Women" was only a mild dissent. But presenting it was without doubt a repetition of her lifelong pattern of declaring her independence from authority figures in her life. Karl Abraham and Freud now joined the pantheon, alongside her father, her childhood minister, the Christian God, and various teachers whom she had idealized, then rebelled against. Her critics have claimed, in fact, that if she had resolved her anger with her father through the transference to Abraham in her analysis, she might never have ventured into the heresies that began with "Genesis" in 1922. But such *ad hominem* arguments obscure the importance of Horney's contribution. It may well be that her anger and disappointment in her analyst sparked the paper she delivered at the Seventh International Congress in Berlin. But the paper, once begun, transcended personal issues.

The ideas Horney set forth in "Genesis" initiated a debate that came to involve Freud, Helene Deutsch, Ernest Jones, and others and that impelled Horney toward a more and more forceful and lucid statement of her views. Ultimately she wrote a series of fourteen papers between 1922 and 1935 on the psychology of women. Taken together, they constitute an impressively full and persuasive counter to Freud's theory of female sexual development. Had she written nothing else these papers would have earned Horney a place of importance in the history of psychoanalysis. Even Freud, while he disagreed with Horney, acknowledged her importance, citing her in the two papers he wrote subsequently on female sexuality. Ernest Jones, Freud's biographer and one of the six members of the "Committee," used Horney's writings as the basis of his own ambitious paper on female sexuality. And it seems likely that Horney's objections, really the first to be raised by a respected Freudian and peer, are what forced Freud to think and write more extensively about female sexuality, beginning in 1925.

Horney's clear intention in all the papers is to develop a theory of female sexuality which is faithful both to Freud's psychoanalytic theory and to her clinical experience. There are frequent references throughout to the work of Freud and his most loyal adherents. And often, particularly in the early papers, there is evidence that she is making a conscious effort to be measured and politic. Nowhere is this more apparent than in the first paper, "On the Genesis of the Castration Complex in Women." There is one moment, however, in the second paragraph, when Horney allows her indignation to bubble up. "We have assumed as an axiomatic fact," she notes, "that females feel at a disadvantage because of their genital organs . . . possibly because to masculine narcissism this has seemed too self-evident to need explanation. Nevertheless," she continues, "the conclusion so far drawn from the investigations— amounting as it does to an assertion that one half of the human race is discontented with the sex assigned to it and can overcome this discontent only in favourable circumstances—is decidedly unsatisfying, not only to feminine narcissism but also to biological science."

Apart from this brief protest, a harbinger of things to come, Horney's paper was far from revolutionary. She wholeheartedly accepted Freud's and Abraham's contention that women suffer from a masculinity complex in which feelings of envy and rage are directed toward the male, and especially toward his penis. The "castration complex" has been "very marked," she notes, "in the course of a practice extending over many years, amongst patients, the great majority of whom were women." She provided case examples, both more vivid and more sympathetic than Abraham's, of women's powerful attachment to their fathers, including fantasies of having been seduced by fathers.

But what she chose to emphasize in her discussion of the Oedipal attachment was the *disappointment* the daughter experiences when the Oedipal wish cannot be fulfilled. From one patient she heard "innumerable remarks constituting a direct proof of how very real this love-relation with the father had seemed to her." Once, for instance, this patient "recollected how her father had sung a love song to her, and with the recollection there broke from

her a cry of disillusion and despair: 'And yet it was all a lie!'"
Another patient, who had witnessed her parents having sexual relations, revealed her disappointment through a mishearing. Once,
when Horney was speaking of a time *"nach der Enttäuschung"* (after
the disappointment), her patient understood her to say *"Nacht der
Enttäuschung"* (night of the disappointment) and "gave the association of Brangäne keeping vigil during Tristan and Isolde's love
night."

Horney suggested that, in women in whom the castration complex is marked, the profound disappointment they have experienced at the hands of the father results in a retreat from femininity.
Since the original wish cannot be fulfilled, the girl gives up her
desire for a child and returns with renewed intensity to the earlier
wish for a penis. In many instances the woman—since she cannot
have the father—chooses to become *like* him. This mechanism of
identification with the lost love-object had been suggested by
Freud in his 1917 paper "Mourning and Melancholia." Horney
gives the example of one female patient's "pretensions to manhood" as an attempt to "act her father's part. Thus she adopted the
same profession as her father, and after his death her attitude to her
mother was that of a husband who makes demands upon his wife
and issues orders." Horney concludes that early-childhood penis
envy alone does not necessarily result in the castration complex but
must be reinforced by later experience during the Oedipal period.

> I think we cannot fail to recognize that a specially powerful penis envy
> (whether it is constitutional or the result of personal experience) does
> help to prepare the way for the changeover by which the patient
> identifies with the father; nevertheless, the history of the cases I have
> described ... shows that ... a strong and wholly womanly love-rela-
> tion to the father had been formed, and that it was only when this love
> was disappointed that the feminine role was abandoned. This aban-
> donment and the consequent identification with the father then revives
> the penis envy, and only when it derives nourishment from such pow-
> erful sources as these can that feeling operate in its full strength.[20]

Freud presided over the meeting at which Horney presented
"On the Genesis of the Castration Complex in Women." Thus
there is no doubt that he heard the paper. It seems likely, in fact,
that he made use of it a year later in his paper "The Ego and the
Id," in which he first proposed a division of the psyche into three
parts, id, ego, and superego. "Analysis often shows," Freud wrote
in what sounds like a gloss on Horney, "that the little girl, after she

has had to relinquish her father as love-object, will bring her masculinity into prominence and identify herself with her father (that is, with the object which has been lost), instead of with her mother."[21] Two years later, in "Some Psychical Consequences of the Anatomical Distinction Between the Sexes," Freud reiterated this point of Horney's, noting that "when the girl's attachment to her father comes to grief later on and has to be abandoned it may give place to an identification with him and the girl may thus return to her masculinity complex and perhaps remain fixated in it."[22]

Except for this concession to Horney's paper, however, Freud showed no inclination to alter his views on female sexuality. There were even more frequent professions of ignorance than in the past. "Unfortunately," he wrote in 1923, "we can describe this state of things only as it affects the male child; the corresponding processes in little girls are not known to us."[23] And in 1924 in "The Dissolution of the Oedipus Complex": "Insight into these developmental processes in girls is unsatisfactory, incomplete and vague."[24] At the same time, references to women in his work seemed to grow more negative. Writing of the ego-ideal in "The Ego and the Id," he noted that "The male sex seems to have taken the lead in all . . . moral acquisitions; and they seem to have then been transmitted to women by cross-inheritance."[25] Further, Freud was growing more adamant in his insistence on "the primacy of the phallus" for both sexes in early childhood[26] and on sexual polarity in healthy adults. Maleness "combines subject, activity and possession of the penis. Femaleness takes over object and passivity. The vagina is . . . valued as a place of shelter for the penis."[27]

Horney, faced with Freud's increasingly incompatible view of women, began looking elsewhere for inspiration. One source was Georg Simmel, an unusual philosopher and sociologist whose lectures she attended in Berlin. Simmel maintained that there are innate differences between what he called "male culture" and "female culture" but that the culture in which we live is "thoroughly male." As a result, there may be an unexplored female "continent of culture" unlike the one in which we live, where "a different form of knowledge is based on a different mode of being."[28]

Around this time Horney also was attracted to ideas of an eccentric on the psychoanalytic fringe, a physician named Georg Groddeck. Groddeck was a unique figure in psychoanalysis of the time. He was a medical doctor first and foremost, presiding over a small sanitarium in Baden-Baden that provided a strict regimen of diet, baths, and exercise, supplemented with massage and verbal dressing-downs by the imperious Dr. Groddeck in person. Even before he read Freud, Groddeck had begun to suspect that a physical symptom could be a symbol, a representative of an emotional illness.

Despite the kinship of his ideas with Freud's, Groddeck didn't write to Freud until 1917. Even then, he confessed that he couldn't finish reading all Freud's books because he was bothered by the way in which Freud had refined ideas *he* had stumbled upon independently. Nonetheless Groddeck professed a great admiration for Freud and his movement and asked if he might become a member of the Berlin Psychoanalytic. Freud's reply, like all his subsequent treatment of Groddeck, was gracious: "I must lay claim to you," he wrote "and must state that you are a splendid psychoanalyst."[29] Subsequently Freud's Psychoanalytic Publishing House issued two of Groddeck's books, including one, *The Book of the It* [*Das Buch von Es*], that had important consequences.

The Book of the It, published in 1923, was an exposition, in the form of letters to a young woman, of Groddeck's view that a powerful unknown force, the *Es,* or It, directs our actions. "The Affirmation 'I live,'" Groddeck wrote, "is only conditionally correct, it expresses only a small and superficial part of the fundamental principle, 'Man is lived by the It [*das Es*].' From his treatment of disease at Baden-Baden, Groddeck had become convinced that bodily illness in particular is linked to the *Es*. "For the *Es*," he maintains, "there is no distinction between organic and mental, and consequently ... even organic diseases can, and in certain circumstances must, be treated psychoanalytically."[30]

Groddeck's theories led him to some pretty extreme statements —the claim, for instance, that cancer of the breast or uterus is caused by sexual conflict or that "he alone will die who wishes to die, to whom life is intolerable."[31] Yet his insistence on the importance of the mind-body connection anticipated the whole field of psychosomatic medicine. He also provided the word that Freud began to use, with a narrower, less mystical meaning, to describe the unconscious, libidinal forces in the psyche. What we know in English as the id is *das Es* in German. It appeared in Freud's work for the first time in "The Ego and the Id" (in German *Das Ich und Das Es)* in 1923, with an acknowledgment of its origins in the work of Georg Groddeck.[32]

It is easy to guess why Horney was attracted to Groddeck. Like her, he was a rebel, and one who made her rebellion look tame. At the International Meetings in Holland in 1920 Groddeck got up and announced, "I am a wild analyst" (thus identifying himself with the "wild analysis" practiced by unqualified opportunists which Freud had inveighed against) and proceeded to free-associate without the use of notes.[33] Like Horney too, Groddeck bristled when confronted with psychoanalytic jargon. Once when a young colleague went on at great length about "anal erotism," Groddeck finally asked in exasperation, "Young man, you speak of anal erotism. Tell me, have you ever seen an anus?"[34]

But what must have been particularly endearing to Horney were Groddeck's views on the roles of the sexes, views we would now call feminist. He disapproved of the "enforced role" of ignorance, particularly about sex, which women played in society: "Thinks the poor anxious creature whom we call a young lady," he wrote in *The Book of the It,* "why should I not behave as if I really had nothing between my head and my feet, since my mother certainly desires it, my father regards it as self-evident, and my lover adores my purity."[35] And he admitted to feeling "envy that I am not myself a woman and cannot be a mother." This was true "not of me alone, but of all men, even of those who seem most manly." The masculine tendency in women, he pointed out, has its counterpart in men. "It is an indubitable scientific fact that man is formed by both man and woman, although in thought and argument we ignore this as we do many another simple truth . . . that a man should think of child-bearing is nothing strange, but only that this should be so obstinately denied."[36]

In her correspondence with Georg Groddeck, which seems to have begun around 1923, Horney dwelt a great deal on female psychology. It was Groddeck who first pointed out to Horney, sometime in 1923, that little girls' first attachment is to the mother. "I gave a lot of thought to the concept mentioned in your letter," she wrote Groddeck, "namely, that in fact *both* sexes have this primary female object." It annoyed Horney that the psychoanalytic writers tended to assume women were just the opposite of men, and that theory could simply be flipped over to apply to them. It was "one-sided," she complained to Groddeck, to present the picture from the male point of view and then "in a footnote" explain that the same applies, in reverse, for women. In fact, given the primary attachment of both sexes to the mother, the same does not necessarily apply. "Some fundamental differences between man and woman must be attributed to that fact," Horney told Groddeck.[37]

These were prophetic words indeed. The whole question of how females negotiate the extra step they must take, from primary attachment to a female to attachment to male objects, has been a preoccupation of psychology since Groddeck, Horney, and then Freud drew attention to it in the early twenties.

Even though Horney was the first woman to present a paper on female psychology at an international meeting, and even though she was one of the first to understand the importance of the girl's primary attachment to her mother, she was, like Groddeck, too independent in thinking and temperament to assume the insider role to which her early prominence would seem to have entitled her. Another woman was destined to play the insider. She was Helene Deutsch, a bright and articulate young psychiatrist who was analyzed by Freud in 1918 in Vienna and who delivered her first paper at the international meeting in 1924, just two years after Horney gave hers and set the debate in motion.

On a superficial level Helene Deutsch and Karen Horney had a great deal in common. Deutsch was born just one year before Horney. Like Horney, she was an early female medical student, a graduate of the University of Vienna who studied Kraepelinian psychiatry in Munich. Although she first was analyzed by Freud, she came to Berlin in 1923 for a second course of treatment with Horney's analyst, Karl Abraham. Like Horney, she took particular interest in psychoanalytic training, heading the Vienna training program from 1924 to 1935. And like Horney, she emigrated to the United States during the Nazi era.

But beneath the surface similarities were differences that proved far more consequential. Helene Deutsch had adored her father and despised her mother. There was always a powerful man at the center of her life: first her father, a prominent Jewish lawyer in the Polish town where she grew up, then her married lover, a leading Polish Socialist and criminal lawyer named Herman Lieberman, and then Freud; her husband, Felix, also a Freudian, played a less dominant role. Deutsch's loyalty to Freud, and to his theories, was absolute, at least in public.[38] In her writing she fully embraced the view that the emancipated woman is masculinized.

This idea led to rather sad consequences in her own case. She may have been describing herself, for instance, when, in her first major paper at The Hague, she spoke of "a highly ambitious and

intellectual" woman who "since the beginning of her marriage...
had lived in a constant state of conflict between her strong
masculine aspirations and the feminine role she had assumed as
housewife and mother." After the paper was received favorably,
she went alone to a park and sat on a bench crying, feeling she had
abandoned her motherly duties.[39]

Freud is said to have asked once why Karen Horney never came
to see him in Vienna, as other followers did. From what we know
of Horney, it is not surprising that she refused to pay tribute in
such a way. But given the price Deutsch paid for her tie to Freud,
Horney may have made the better choice. Certainly there are few
more striking examples of Freud's intrusiveness than the story of
his intervention in Deutsch's treatment with Abraham. Early in
the analysis Abraham received a letter from Freud informing him
that Helene Deutsch's marriage to Felix should not be disrupted by
the treatment. Abraham showed Helene Deutsch the letter. Later
she remarked, mildly, that the letter from Freud set a limit on what
she could hope to accomplish with Abraham in Berlin.[40]

The paper Helene Deutsch gave at the Salzburg meetings in 1924
and the paper Horney gave in Berlin in 1922 reflect their very
different sensibilities. Horney's work had been organized through
argument: first she brought up Abraham's view, then she presented her counter to it. Deutsch, whose paper was entitled "The
Psychology of Women in Relation to the Functions of Reproduction," eschewed controversy. When she cited others, it was only to
agree with them. Horney's paper was filled with clinical anecdotes
from her practice. Deutsch's paper, in contrast, was almost purely
abstract. References to patients remained vague, as when she explained, "I arrived at this identification-series... as a result of all
the experience which I have had of cases of frigidity and sterility."
Finally, and perhaps most significant, there was an undercurrent of
degradation in Deutsch that rarely appeared in Horney, even in her
"Freudian" period.

The man, Deutsch maintained in her talk at the Salzburg International, "attains his final stage of development when he discovers
the vagina in the world outside himself and possesses himself of it
sadistically." The woman has to discover a new sexual organ, the
vagina, through the process of "being masochistically subjugated
by the penis." In Deutsch's formulation great stress is laid on both
the girl's early attachment to the clitoris and its inadequacy in comparison with the boy's penis. The clitoris is "in reality so inadequate a substitute for the penis"; the clitoris "lacks the abundant

energy of the penis; even in the most intense masturbatory activity it cannot arrogate to itself such a measure of libido as does the latter organ." And yet the woman has to give up even this miniature member: "giving up the claim of the clitoris" in favor of the vagina may be "the hardest task in the libidinal development of the woman."

What was admirable in Deutsch's paper and subsequent book was the attempt to develop a theoretical framework in which to understand female experience through all its stages, from birth through menopause. Deutsch was trying to understand the larger scheme of things. Some of her equations, as for instance that between nipple/mouth in infancy and penis/vagina in adult sexuality, were useful. But this same love of schematization led her to some absurd conclusions, including the suggestion that women reach true orgasm only at the moment of birth. According to Deutsch's theory, the sexual act is completed for men through the emission of semen at the time of orgasm. Women, who don't discharge a comparable emission during coitus, can reach the "acme of sexual pleasure" only at the time of childbirth, the logical counterpart to male emission.[41]

It was this particular claim that provoked Karen Horney's strongest reaction when she reviewed Deutsch's book in the *International Psychoanalytic Journal* in 1926. Horney wrote:

> We must give expression, from a sober clinical point of view, to some criticisms of the extraordinary view that the actual orgasm of the woman takes place during childbirth, and so corresponds, as in the man, to the separation of soma and germ-plasm. It can hardly be disputed that the normal woman gains real terminal pleasure in the sexual act, that is, that there is complete discharge of sexual tensions, and thus coitus can claim the same "economic" importance for her as for the man. In the face of this fact, what practical and metapsychological meaning attaches to the assertion that the climax of female sexual pleasure lies in the act of childbirth, which occurs so incomparably less often?

Besides, Horney added, "intense pain greatly predominates [in childbirth] over the masochistic pleasure that accompanies it."

Horney's long review of the Deutsch book is more measured than this excerpt suggests. Only occasionally does the realist Horney square off against the theorist Deutsch. There is praise for Deutsch's effort to synthesize and for the richness of the content: "This review," Horney writes, "cannot do justice to the real wealth of observation and thought that this work contains." But Horney warns, echoing her complaint to Groddeck, we must "be careful in accepting any ideas based on a far-reaching parallelism between man and woman." Looking for similarities between men and woman "leads to much that is of value," but the business of further clinical investigations will be the reverse of this, and teach us to know and understand . . . differences."[42]

Horney's disagreement with Abraham in her first paper and mild criticisms in her review of Deutsch were the closest the discussion of female sexuality had come to confrontation. Indeed, Horney seems to have been the only one who *wanted* to debate. Deutsch, Abraham, Freud, and others might have preferred to go along forever without arguments, tolerating Horney's disagreements as mild static. Freud in his 1925 paper on the subject took the uncharacteristic step of praising "the valuable and comprehensive studies on the masculinity and castration complexes in women by Abraham (1921), Horney (1923) and Helene Deutsch (1925)."[43] Perhaps he hoped, by conferring equal approval on all three, to placate the one real dissident, Karen Horney.

But in 1926 Karen Horney's "The Flight from Womanhood" ("Die Flucht aus der Weiblichkeit") appeared, in German and English, in *The International Journal of Psycho-Analysis*. It was Horney's most ambitious and outspoken work to date, and one that demanded a response. Horney knew, as she revealed when she sent a copy to Groddeck before publication, that "The Flight from Womanhood" would create a stir. "You showed such a friendly interest in my earlier work on the female castration complex," she wrote Groddeck, "that I hope you will also enjoy reading my new and more elaborate work on the same topic. Especially since I discuss issues which you were the first one to raise. I have, however, deviated from theory accepted heretofore. Still your own thinking is so original that you will have complete understanding for similar ideas of others, even if they represent a blow to male narcissism." She goes on to explain that she had written it "more aggressively" at first but had decided, since the paper was to be published in a *Festschrift* in honor of Freud's seventieth birthday, to soften her argument.[44]

Her phrase in German was *"meine Steine etwas in Watte gewickelt,"* which means literally "wrapped my stone in a little cotton-wool" —an apt description of her method in "The Flight from Womanhood." The stone she throws is hard and well aimed, but several pages go by before the reader knows just what has hit him. In the first place, the title "The Flight from Womanhood" makes it sound as though this will be yet another affirmation of the old masculinity complex in women we've heard so much about already. And the essay begins with three paragraphs of citations of the very latest work by psychoanalytic authorities—first Freud, whom she calls "a male genius," then Abraham, then Freud again, and then Helene Deutsch. The first doubts are expressed then, but only briefly and with Freud's permission: "The question now arises," she writes, "as to whether these hypotheses have helped to make our insight into feminine development (insight that Freud himself has stated to be unsatisfactory and incomplete) more satisfactory and clear."

"Science," she continues neutrally, "has often found it fruitful to look at long-familiar facts from a fresh point of view. Otherwise there is a danger that we shall involuntarily continue to classify all new observations among the same clearly defined groups of ideas."

Having ventured out on her own momentarily, she takes refuge in another authority, the philosopher Georg Simmel, who introduces the central idea of her essay: namely, that modern society is dominated in every aspect by the male point of view. The standards by which mankind has judged male and female nature are, to quote Simmel, "essentially masculine." There is a "naive identification of the concept 'human being' and the concept 'man,' which in many languages even causes the same word to be used for the two concepts." As a result, "in the most varying fields, inadequate achievements are contemptuously called 'feminine,' while distinguished achievements on the part of women are called 'masculine' as an expression of praise." Women too, Horney adds, have "adapted" to this point of view and "unconsciously yielded to the suggestion of masculine thought." This has resulted in a psychology of women that "has hitherto been considered only from the point of view of men." And so "the psychology of women hitherto actually represents a deposit of the desires and disappointments of men."

Now we have reached the heart of Horney's argument. "How far," she asks, "has the evolution of women, as depicted to us today by analysis, been measured by masculine standards and how far therefore does this picture fail to present quite accurately the real nature of women?" She proceeds, through the use of a chart, to demonstrate that the ideas that have been imputed to girls about their bodies correspond strikingly to the ideas that *little boys* are likely to entertain about girls' bodies. Boys assume that little girls have a penis like theirs; girls are thought to believe that only the penis matters. Boys are troubled when they discover that girls have no penis; girls are thought to be troubled. Boys decide girls must have been castrated and that the castration was a punishment; girls are said to believe the same. Boys view girls as inferior because they lack a penis; girls are thought to see themselves as inferior and envy the boy his penis. Boys can't imagine how a girl could recover; girls are said never to recover. The boy dreads the girl's envy; the girl is said to desire "throughout life to avenge herself on the man for possessing something which she lacks."

Perhaps, Horney grants, this exact correspondence means nothing. But it bears asking "whether the remarkable parallelism I have indicated may not perhaps be the expression of a one-sidedness in our observations, due to their being made from the man's point of view." Even though "analytical research" is based on experience, there is room for subjectivity in the interpretations we draw from the material of "free associations, dreams and symptoms." And "if we try to free our minds from [the] masculine mode of thought, nearly all the problems of feminine psychology take on a different appearance."

The bulk of Horney's essay is a protest, presented with the same careful reasonableness, against the joyless picture of female experience that psychoanalysis has painted. To a certain extent the protest may have grown out of Horney's experience with patients. But one senses that her own experience—of masturbation, of sex, and of motherhood—has moved her to speak.

There is, first of all, the view put forth by Ferenczi, one of Freud's inner circle, that the true motive for coitus is the male wish to return to the mother's womb. From this he concludes that the woman "has to 'content herself' with substitutes in the nature of fantasy and above all with harboring the child." Like Deutsch, Ferenczi suggests that only the act of birth provides "potentialities of pleasure denied to the man."

Here Horney asks, "And what about motherhood," and proceeds to catalogue its pleasures—the "bliss" of bearing a new life, the "ineffable happiness" of expectation, the "joy" of the baby's arrival, the "deep pleasurable feeling" of nursing and caring for a new baby. While motherhood "*may* be a handicap," viewed "from the standpoint of the social struggle," it was not necessarily so "in times when human beings were closer to nature."

In fact, Horney continues, turning the usual arguments upside down, motherhood gives women "a quite indisputable and by no means negligible physiological superiority." There is reason, in fact, for men to envy women! "When one begins, as I did, to analyze men only after a fairly long experience of analyzing women, one receives a most surprising impression of the intensity of this envy of pregnancy, childbirth, and motherhood, as well as of breasts and of the act of suckling." Might not the depreciation of motherhood be a case of male sour grapes? "This depreciation would run as follows: in reality women do simply desire the penis; when all is said and done motherhood is only a burden... and men may be glad that they have not to bear it." She continues, following this logic: "Is not the tremendous strength in man of the impulse to creative work in every field precisely due to their feeling of playing a relatively small part in the creation of living beings, which constantly impels them to an overcompensation in achievement?"

Having introduced the possibility of "womb envy," Horney turns to its counterpart in women, the much-discussed penis envy. She begins by conceding that penis envy is readily observable in girl children, adding (in a gloss on her earlier paper "Genesis of the Castration Complex") that there are a number of real reasons for it. Not only is there the "narcissistic mortification of possessing less than the boy" but there are also the "manifest privileges" of having a penis: the boy can see his genital better, and he has it more readily at hand, to touch and play with in urination and masturbation. The result is a "primary" penis envy, based on anatomical differences and occurring before the little girl knows of her childbearing capacities. But there is a "secondary" penis envy, seen in adult female patients, which has very little to do with the first but rather "embodies all that has miscarried in the development toward womanhood." It has to do with the different way in which boys and girls negotiate the Oedipus complex. "In boys the mother as a sexual object is renounced owing to the fear of castration, but the male role itself is not only affirmed in further development but is actually overemphasized in the reaction to the fear of castration.... Girls, on the other hand, not only renounce the father as a sexual object but simultaneously recoil from the feminine role altogether." This is the "flight from womanhood" of Horney's title.

Why do girls flee womanhood? "Here again the situation is much clearer in boys," Horney notes, "or perhaps we simply know more about it. Are these facts so mysterious to us in girls only because we have always looked at them through the eyes of men?" To begin at the beginning, there is the question of masturbation. Little boys are thought to fear castration as a punishment for masturbation. But what of little girls, to whom "we do not even concede... a specific form of onanism [masturbation] but without more ado describe their autoerotic activities as male." Even if little girls have castration fears, there must be a difference "in the case of anxiety about onanism between a castration threatened and castration that has actually taken place!"

Horney goes on to suggest that the pleasures, and fears, of girls about masturbation may be quite different from those of boys. "My analytical experience makes it most decidedly possible that little girls have a specific feminine form of onanism (which incidentally differs in technique from that of boys), even if we assume that the little girl practices exclusively clitoral masturbation, an assumption that seems to me by no means certain." And here Horney adds a sharp defense of the much-maligned clitoris. "And I do not see why, in spite of its past evolution, it should not be conceded that the clitoris legitimately belongs to and forms an integral part of the female genital apparatus." Furthermore, Horney believes it "very probable" that little girls experience "vaginal" as well as clitoral sensations.

This suspicion is reinforced by the childhood fantasies adult women bring to analysis—fantasies "that an excessively large penis is effecting forcible penetration, producing pain and hemorrhage, and threatening to destroy something." These fantasies, Horney contends, show that "the little girl bases her Oedipus fantasies most realistically (in accordance with the plastic concrete thinking of childhood) on the disproportion in size between father and child." They demonstrate that "the vagina as well as the clitoris must be assumed to play a part in the early infantile genital organization of women."

Out of these alterations Horney comes to a different conclusion about the little girl's Oedipus complex. Freud and others have maintained that the little girl's very first attachment to the father grows out of penis envy. Horney suggests that the desire for a penis is mixed with a "libidinal interest of the little girl" in the penis. As evidence of this possibility she notes that "in the associations of female patients the narcissistic desire to possess the penis and the... libidinal longing for it are often so interwoven that one hesitates as to the sense in which the words 'desire to have' [haben *wollen*] are meant." As in adult life, "admiring envy" is particularly likely "to lead to an attitude of love."

From this revised view of female development Horney comes to the conclusion that the principal reason for the "flight from womanhood" is not the desire to possess a penis but "the desire to avoid the realization of libidinal wishes and fantasies in connection with the father," fantasies about which the girl feels both anxious and guilty.

Finally, and only very near the end of the paper, Horney points out that there are social reasons for women to take on a masculine role. Social explanations were generally discounted in psychoanalysis. Abraham dismissed them in the third paragraph of his 1920 paper: "Certain arguments," he noted, "are again and again brought forward," attributing women's envy to men's greater freedom in their professional and private lives. "Psycho-analysis . . . shows that conscious arguments of this sort are of limited value, and are the result of rationalisation—a process which veils the motives lying deeper."

But Horney insists that deeper personal motives for flight from womanhood "are reinforced and supported by the actual disadvantage under which women labor in social life. . . . We must not forget that this disadvantage is actually a piece of reality and that it is immensely greater than most women are aware of." The girl, she claims, "is exposed from birth onward to the suggestion—inevitable, whether conveyed brutally or delicately—of her inferiority, an experience that constantly stimulates her masculinity complex." Nor have women been able to sublimate their drives as easily as men, since "all the ordinary professions have been filled by men." "It seems to me," she concludes, "impossible to judge to how great a degree the unconscious motives for the flight from womanhood are reinforced by the actual social subordination of women."[45]

Horney's paper made a particularly strong impression on Ernest Jones, who cited her in the opening sentence of his long paper on female sexuality. "There is a healthy suspicion growing," he wrote, "that men analysts have been led to adopt an unduly phallo-centric view of the problems in question, the importance of the female organs being correspondingly underestimated."[46] Freud, however, would have none of it. "Karen Horney is of the opinion," he wrote in "Female Sexuality" in 1931, "that we greatly over-estimate the girl's primary penis-envy. . . . This does not tally with my impressions." Instead he insisted on the unique intensity

of the "first libidinal impulses" and their long-lasting consequences.[47] "To an incredibly late age," Freud insisted, the little girl
"clings to the hope of getting a penis some time. That hope becomes her life's aim, and the phantasy of being a man often persists
as a formative factor over long periods."[48]

It seems quite possible, since it was essentially a reiteration of his
1925 paper "Some Psychical Consequences of the Anatomical Distinctions Between the Sexes," that Freud's 1931 paper was provoked by the forceful dissenting papers Horney and Jones had
written in the interim. His annoyance with these revisionists becomes obvious in a testy footnote. "It is to be anticipated," he
writes, "that men analysts with feminist views, as well as our
women analysts, will disagree with what I have said here." They
"will hardly fail to object that such notions spring from the 'masculinity complex' of the male and are designed to justify on theoretical grounds his innate inclination to disparage and suppress
women. But this sort of psycho-analytic argumentation reminds
us ... of Dostoevsky's famous 'knife that cuts both ways.'" Those
on the other side (Freud, presumably, among them) "think it quite
natural that the female sex should refuse to accept a view which
appears to contradict their eagerly coveted equality with men."[49]
Freud ended his paper with praise for the faithful—Abraham,
Jeanne Lampl de Groot,[50] and Helene Deutsch—and criticism of
the doubters—Horney and Jones.

Of course Karen Horney read Freud's paper, and especially his
comments on her work, with great eagerness. Freud's opinion was
a matter of momentous importance in her circle. But his disapproval seems to have spurred her on. In the next six years she
produced some of her most important writing on female psychology. And by the time she left Germany in 1932 she had taken the
cotton off the stone. What she had merely suggested in "The
Flight from Womanhood," she asserted in later papers: sexual development, from an early age, is ruled not by phallic awareness
alone but by a consciousness of the female genital, the vagina. The
consequences of this view for Freudian psychology are, as Horney
noted, far-reaching. If, as Freud insists, the vagina remains "undiscovered" until puberty, then that argues for a "biologically determined, primary penis envy in little girls. . . . For if no vaginal
sensations or cravings existed, but the whole libido were concentrated on the clitoris, phallically conceived of, then and then only
could we understand how little girls, for want of any specific
source of pleasure of their own . . . must be driven to concentrate

their whole attention on the clitoris, to compare it with the boy's penis, and then, since they are in fact at a disadvantage in this comparison, to feel themselves definitely slighted." But if a girl experiences "vaginal sensations and corresponding impulses, she must from the outset have a lively sense of this specific character of her own sexual role, and a primary penis envy of the strength postulated by Freud would be hard to account for."[51]

In the five papers that followed "The Flight from Womanhood" in fairly rapid succession one can trace the circuitous route by which Horney arrived at her belief in vaginal awareness in childhood. First she went through a period in which she dwelt primarily on external influences—the real world—on development. Horney had always stressed *reality* in her work. On more than one occasion she had pointed out that psychoanalytic theory was based on a skewed sample; there was a need to study "healthy women," not just "neurotic women... from the intellectual upper strata of society."[52] It was she who first pointed out that the boy "as an actual fact" has an advantage over the girl anatomically when it comes to masturbation, since he can more easily look at and touch his organ. "Unless we are quite clear about the *reality* of this disadvantage compared with boys" she had written in 1922, "we shall not understand that penis envy is an almost inevitable phenomenon in the life of female children."[53] Also, real-life experiences "can cause the girl to shrink back from her female role." Gross favoritism toward a brother, for instance, or "accidental impressions, like real brutality on the part of the father and sickness of the mother, may increase in the child the notion that the woman's position is precarious and one of danger."[54]

But what preoccupied her now in the wake of "The Flight from Womanhood" was not individual but *social* reality. Discussing frigidity in women before a group of sexologists, she concluded that its frequency could not be explained "by analytic means alone.... It seems to me that the explanation for this frequency has... to do with supra-individual, cultural factors. Our culture, as is well known, is a male culture, and therefore by and large not favorable to the unfolding of woman and her individuality." A woman may be "treasured as a mother or as a lover," but "it is always the male who will be considered more valuable on human and spiritual grounds." The little girl "grows up under this general impression. If we realize that from her first years of childhood, the girl carries with her a reason for envy of the male, then we can easily grasp how much this social impression must contribute to justify her masculinity wishes on a conscious level, and how much it impedes an inner affirmation of her female role."

As for frigidity itself, it can be explained in part by the tendency in "educated men" to split their love life "into sensual and romantic components." Men tend to view their wives as spiritual partners and look for sexual excitement in extramarital relationships with prostitutes or others whom they don't respect. This attitude "must also result in frigidity. Since in women the emotional life is, as a rule, much more closely and uniformly connected with sexuality, she cannot give herself completely when she does not love or is not loved." Since man, in his "dominant" position can satisfy his needs, and since "custom and education" promote "female inhibitions," there are "powerful forces... at work to restrict woman in the free unfolding of her femininity."[55]

Returning to concepts of her 1915 dissertation, Horney concluded: the "*exogenous* or *endogenous* factors will be different in each individual case," but a "more accurate insight" into the "mode of their acting together" might lead to a "real understanding of the frequency of feminine inhibitions."

Wary, no doubt, that she would be accused of penis envy, Horney had long kept her anger toward male attitudes in check. But in 1930 she pointed out to members of the Berlin-Brandenburg branch of the German Women's Medical Association that women's diffidence served the dominant male culture. "At any given time," she observed, "the more powerful side will create an ideology... to help maintain its position and to make this position acceptable to the weaker one. In this ideology the differentness of the weaker one will be interpreted as inferiority, and it will be proven that these differences are unchangeable, basic, or God's will. It is the function of such an ideology to deny or conceal the existence of a struggle." That is one reason "why we have so little awareness of the fact that there is a struggle between the sexes. It is in the interest of men to obscure this fact; and the emphasis they place on their ideologies has caused women, also, to adopt these theories."

"The Distrust Between the Sexes," the paper Horney proceeded to present, is Horney's only real diatribe. As she notes:

[Woman] is said to be deeply rooted in the personal and emotional spheres, which is wonderful; but unfortunately, this makes her incapable of exercising justice and objectivity, therefore disqualifying her for positions in law and government and in the spiritual community. She is said to be at home only in the realm of eros. Spiritual matters are alien to her innermost being, and she is at odds with cultural trends. She therefore is, as Asians frankly state, a second-rate being. Woman may be industrious and useful but is, alas, incapable of productive and independent work. She is, indeed, prevented from real accomplishment by the deplorable, bloody tragedies of menstruation and childbirth. And so every man silently thanks his God, just as the pious Jew does in his prayers, that he was not created a woman.[56]

Speaking before an audience of women doctors, Horney allowed herself to let off steam. But then, having proclaimed to the public and to herself that sexism pervades the world, Horney took the next step and tried to understand why. This question led her inexorably back from social to individual psychology. Why do men and women do as they do? The result was two papers, the last two written in Germany, on the origins of sexism in individual psychology. The first and more substantial of the two, "The Dread of Women," asks a question she had pondered ten years earlier in a letter to Groddeck. "Why does man emphasize his superiority so much?" she had asked. And then, reaching toward an answer: "I have the impression men are more easily hurt, and more vulnerable in their feelings of superiority."[57] Her more extensive answer was laid out in "The Dread of Women: Observations on a Specific Difference in the Dread Felt by Men and by Women Respectively for the Opposite Sex."

Males in many cultures and in all ages, Horney pointed out, have feared women. To illustrate, she provided a long list of examples from literature and tradition: "The goddess Kali dances on the corpses of slain men. Samson, whom no man could conquer, is robbed of his strength by Delilah. Judith beheads Holofernes after giving herself to him. . . . Witches are burnt because male priests fear the work of the devil in them."

"The series of such instances," Horney notes, "is infinite." And "always, everywhere, the man strives to rid himself of his dread of woman by objectifying it. 'It is not,' he says, 'that I dread her; it is that she herself is malignant, capable of any crime, a beast of prey, a vampire, a witch, insatiable in her desires. She is the very personification of what is sinister.' "[58]

Freud's explanation of this dread of females was based on his castration theory. Woman's genitals are terrifying to the male because they embody castration. Thus woman in Greek myth is "a being who frightens and repels because she is castrated."[59] But Horney argues that castration anxiety is an inadequate explanation for the male dread of "a being to whom this punishment [castration] has already happened." There is, she argues, a dread of the vagina *per se*, which is reflected in myth and in the fantasies of male patients. Woman is seen as devouring; man is drawn to her but fears at the same time he may be undone by her. Woman is symbolized in Schiller by "the whirlpool" that "cleaves through the ocean /A path that seems winding in darkness to hell." Women are the watery enchantresses: the sirens in Ulysses, Lorelei in native song and story, who lure man into a deep unknown. Horney suggests that "the masculine dread of the woman (the mother) or of the female genital is more deep-seated, weighs more heavily, and is usually more energetically repressed than the dread of the man (father), and that the endeavor to find the penis in women represents first and foremost a convulsive attempt to deny the existence of the sinister female genital."

But whence comes this deep-seated anxiety about the engulfing female genital? Here Horney argues against Freud's theory that the vagina is "undiscovered" in childhood. "Surely the essence of the phallic impulses proper, starting as they do with organic sensations, is a desire to *penetrate*." These impulses "manifest themselves ... plainly in children's games and in the analysis of little children." "On the one hand, a boy will automatically conclude that everyone else is made like himself; but on the other hand his phallic impulses surely bid him instinctively to search for the appropriate opening in the female body. ... If we seriously accept Freud's dictum that the sexual theories formed by children are modeled on their own sexual constitution, it must surely mean in the present connection that the boy, urged on by his impulses to penetrate, pictures in fantasy a complementary female organ."

Herein lies the deepest source of men's dread of women. The boy, who "feels or instinctively judges that his penis is much too small for his mother's genital," reacts "with the dread of his own inadequacy of being rejected and derided." Thus his original dread of women "is not castration anxiety at all, but a reaction to the menace to his self-respect." Freud, she notes, has already mentioned the "narcissistic scar left by the little boy's relation with his mother." Freud notes that the little boy "behaves as if he had a dim idea that his member might be and should be larger." Horney adds that this behavior does not end in the phallic phase. "On the contrary, it is displayed naively throughout boyhood and persists later as a deeply hidden anxiety about the size of the subject's penis or his potency, or else as a less concealed pride about them."

What had begun as a protest, in "On the Genesis of the Castration Complex," ten years earlier, ends here in empathy. "One of the exigencies of the biological differences between the sexes is this: that the man is actually obliged to go on proving his manhood to the woman. There is no analogous necessity for her. Even if she is frigid, she can engage in sexual intercourse and conceive and bear a child. She performs her part by merely *being*, without any *doing*—a fact that has always filled men with admiration and resentment." In men love can be "overshadowed by their overwhelming inner compulsion to prove their manhood again and again to themselves and others. A man of this type in its more extreme form has therefore one interest only: to conquer." Other men choose women who are unlikely to challenge them. "From a prostitute or woman of easy virtue one need fear no rejection, and no demands in the sexual, ethical, or intellectual sphere. One can feel oneself the superior." The "most important and ominous way" in which man's dread of women displays itself is in "diminishing the self-respect of the woman." Men, from "Aristotle to Moebius, have expended an astonishing amount of energy and intellectual capacity in proving the superiority of the masculine principle." And the "ever-precarious self-respect of the 'average man'" has led him to favor "a feminine type that is infantile, nonmaternal, and hysterical, and by so doing to expose each new generation to the influence of such women."[60]

"The Denial of the Vagina," the second of these two complementary papers, steers clear of any discussion of social questions and concentrates on the individual girl's development. Here, once again, Horney argues that the vagina is known. While girls use the clitoris for masturbation, "spontaneous genital sensations resulting from general sexual excitation are more frequently located in the vagina." This instinctive knowledge leads to anxieties that have a "specific character" in little girls—anxieties about penetration and injury from a too-large penis, which are then reinforced by the observation of menstruation in female adults, in which the girl "sees demonstrated for the first time the vulnerability of the female body." Finally, she is likely to have anxieties about masturbation, particularly since, unlike boys, she cannot easily examine her genital. All of this anxiety leads to varying degrees of repression. "Often everything connected with the vagina—the knowledge of its existence, vaginal sensations, and instinctual impulses—succumbs to a relentless repression; in short, the fiction is conceived and long maintained that the vagina does not exist, a fiction that at the same time determines the little girl's preference for the masculine sexual role."[61]

The two last papers Horney wrote in Germany were carefully argued, clearly with the hope of winning over others within psychoanalysis to her point of view. But she did not succeed. Published one after the other in 1932 and 1933, they would be the last to appear in the *International Journal,* the principal journal of psychoanalysis, published in both German and English. While there is no way of proving it, her disappearance from the *International Journal* after 1933 probably represents an editorial decision that Horney was no longer quite orthodox enough.

In 1933 Freud addressed female psychology one last time, in a talk entitled "Femininity," which was part of a third version of his *Introductory Lectures.* It is an oddly inconsistent paper. In the beginning one has the fleeting suspicion that Freud is about to revise his thinking in response to the Horney/Jones critique. He begins by echoing a point made by Horney the year before: "masculine" cannot always be equated with "active," "feminine" with "passive." After all, he notes, "a mother is active in every sense toward her child." When he goes on to say that "we have begun to learn a little about" female development from "women colleagues in analysis," a shift or new insight seems imminent. But the female colleagues he cites are Helene Deutsch, Ruth Mack Brunswick, and Jeanne Lampl de Groot. And their work has to do with the ways in which the little girl's disappointment in the mother, who lacks a penis, ends in rage toward the mother and desire for the father, who has one. "The discovery that she is castrated is a turning-point in a girl's growth," Freud asserts. "Her self-love is mortified by the comparison with the boy's far superior equipment and in consequence she repudiates her love for her mother and at the same time not infrequently represses a good part of her sexual trends in general." While Freud tells his audience that these conclusions are "a product of the very last years," they resemble his previous ideas in their phallocentricity. Everything leads back, ultimately, to penis envy.

The final section of the paper makes Freud's impartiality on the subject of women more suspect than ever. It is a compendium of what he calls the "psychical peculiarities of mature femininity, as we come across them in analytic observation." Women are more narcissistic than men, "since they are bound to value their charms more highly as a compensation for their original sexual inferiority." Women have "made few contributions to the discoveries and inventions in the history of civilization." Women's strong preference for sons over daughters shows that "the old factor of lack of a penis has...not lost its strength." Women have "little sense of justice" because of "the predominance of envy in their mental life." They are "weaker in social interests" and have "less capacity for sublimating their instincts than men." As evidence for this Freud cites his observation that "a man of about thirty strikes us as a youthful, somewhat unformed individual," whereas a woman of the same age "often frightens us by her psychical rigidity and unchangeability."[62]

These were Freud's last published remarks on what he called "the riddle of femininity."[63] His last known mention of Karen Horney came in 1935 in a letter to Karl Müller-Braunschweig concerning a paper he had written that was sympathetic to her point of view. "Your work," Freud wrote, "fits into that of authors such as Horney, Jones, Rado, etc., who do not come to grips with the bisexuality of women and who, in particular, object to the phallic stage." Freud conceded that "the frequency of such writings seems in itself proof that something is missing, undiscovered or unsaid at this point." He promised to provide "a new answer." But even if his health had permitted him to write more on the subject, he would not have been likely to come around to the views of Horney and her handful of like-minded analysts. "We deal only with one libido," Freud insisted to Müller-Braunschweig, "which behaves in a male way."[64]

Horney continued, after she came to the United States, to develop her ideas about the psychology of women. But the official Freudian position was represented increasingly by Helene Deutsch. Deutsch's two-volume *The Psychology of Women* became the standard Freudian text on female psychology. Karen Horney's contribution was virtually forgotten. It wasn't until 1967, when her colleague and friend Harold Kelman translated and compiled her early works under the title *Female Psychology*, that contemporary feminists began to recognize her as an early champion of their point of view. Within psychoanalysis, as Zenia Odes Fliegel noted in a 1972 article in the *Psychoanalytic Quarterly*, Horney's continued "heresies" caused her early ideas to be ignored. "It became an increasing trend in the subsequent literature," Fliegel notes, "that ideas originating with Horney and supported by Jones were credited to Jones." The debate itself tended to be ignored as well: in Jones's three-volume biography of Freud no mention is made of it, even though Jones himself was intimately involved. And yet, as Fliegel notes, "in those early papers she [Horney] originated many ideas and observations which reappear in later writings on the subject—but in the fragmented and incomplete manner of the return of the repressed."[65]

In 1974, in an essay written in response to her 1925 paper "The Flight from Womanhood," the psychologist Robert Coles described Karen Horney as "a prophet" who "dared look with some distance and detachment at her own profession, and... anticipated . . . a future historical moment."

> For years [Coles noted] I have heard various psychoanalysts dismiss her ideas out of hand, or scorn them as of little value or interest. As one goes through this article and others like it, one wonders why the rejection, why the contempt or derision, why the condescension. She herself wrote tentatively, considerately; she does not come across as a shrill rebel or edgy critic or driven troublemaker or dissident. She merely wants her colleagues to stop and think for a while: as bourgeois men of the first half of the twentieth century, do they have blind spots about themselves as men and about women, and if so, what are they, and how do they affect their thinking?

It is a request, Coles concludes, "in keeping with the essential spirit of psychoanalysis."[66]

In the summer of 1923, writing to Georg Groddeck from the "idyllic tranquillity" of the North Sea, Karen Horney described her "ambivalent" feelings about "living within an analytic circle." "We are no less hypocritical than elsewhere, only a little different." Like religious Christians who go around saying "We are all sinners" but become very uncomfortable when a sin of their own is pointed out to them, analysts go around insisting that neurotics have "all these embarrassing complexes" without acknowledging any of their own.[67] Probably it was the narrow-mindedness of her peers that most annoyed her, just as it had in her father and Pastor von Ruckteschell when she was growing up.

This time, however, she was not a powerless child but a grown woman with a forum. And, unlike many others, she dared to use it. Horney stood up for Melanie Klein, even though her methods of child analysis hadn't helped Marianne and Renate, and even though she and Klein's ideas were in many ways in complete opposition. Klein, whose work eventually found a welcome in England, stressed the biological determinants of childhood development, while Horney increasingly stressed the social. They did agree, however, that girls were probably aware of their vaginas at an earlier age than Freud maintained. And they undoubtedly admired each other's independence. At one meeting of the Berlin Psychoanalytic at which Klein presented her views, Horney and her friend Josine Müller were the only ones to rise in her defense.[68] And Horney persisted in citing Klein repeatedly in her writings on female sexuality, noting that "insufficient attention has been paid" to Klein's work.[69]

Horney's commitment to heterodoxy is evident too in the role she played in the establishment, in 1928, of an organization called the General Medical Society for Psychotherapy (Allgemeine Artzliche Gesellschaft für Psychotherapie). The society, which sought to promote the use of psychotherapy in medical practice, was regarded with suspicion by the more orthodox Freudians because it included not only "wild analysts" but those who had earlier broken ranks with Freud, including Jung and Alfred Adler.[70] Even though there were also some Freudians in the mix, including Ernst Simmel and Felix Deutsch, it was not an organization in which a politic Freudian would choose to be highly visible. Horney, however, became the official reporter to the *International Journal* from the General Medical Society. She was also a featured speaker at society meetings in Baden-Baden in 1930.

There were other members of the Berlin group who resented the rigidity of the Freudians but lacked the courage to speak up for fear of alienating Freud. Sandor Rado, for instance, said later that psychoanalysis had the "completely isolated spirit of a cult," noting that "no paper ever written by Adler after his departure was even mentioned in the psychoanalytic journals. . . . I have never seen anything like that in any science." Rado, who was an editor of the *International Journal,* said he "couldn't get anybody to write up an Adlerian contribution from the psychoanalytic point of view. Very occasionally, on Freud's instigation, [Sandor] Ferenczi wrote disapproving criticism of one or another publication of Jung." But for the most part "these people were dead."[71]

Yet, when the opportunity arose to express disagreement with Freud, Rado passed it up. The issue was one of the most hotly debated and long-lived in the history of psychoanalysis: lay analysis. Should nondoctors be allowed to practice analysis? The question acquired new urgency in 1926 when proceedings were begun in Vienna against Theodor Reik, one of the "Committee," by the Austrian government. Reik, who was not a physician, was charged with breach of an old Austrian law against quackery. Freud came energetically to his defense and published a pamphlet called "The Question of Lay Analysis," which argued that analytic work need not be the exclusive preserve of doctors. The charges against Reik were eventually dropped, but the debate over lay analysis continued. The following year, a series of twenty-eight statements by analysts from all over the world were solicited and published in both the German and English editions of the *International Journal*.

Sandor Rado strongly disagreed with Freud and believed that psychoanalysis should be practiced only by the medical profession, but decided not to contribute, because "I couldn't oppose Freud."[72] Similarly, the contribution of Ernst Simmel, who was by then president of the Berlin Institute, is so cleverly balanced in its weighing of pros and cons that it is impossible to know in the end whether he is for or against lay analysis. Karen Horney had no such reservations about stating her point of view. She disagreed with Freud, along with most of the Americans and some others in the Berlin group, and, as usual, she didn't mince words about it.

At first glance it seems rather surprising that Horney would oppose lay analysis. After all, she had tried to open the institute to greater diversity. Might this be an instance of opposing Freud for opposition's sake? But her arguments in favor of medical training turn out to be grounded in her practicality. The *"sine qua non"* for analytic training is, Horney insists, "personal suitability." But when one goes beyond that to questions of background, a medical training is preferable. A training in the humanities—in history, anthropology, or literature—"gives a bias towards theoretical thinking." While this is valuable, "one cannot ward off an impression that we analysts fall victims to too much theorizing and not too little." Moreover, while the specific knowledge gained in medical school may be useless to the analyst, medical training engenders a "general attitude" that is valuable. It teaches the student to "observe the human being accurately." It "gives an education in dealing with sick people and a feeling of responsibility towards them, and above all a will to heal." Even here Horney's eclectic tendencies surface. A training in psychiatry, she writes, gives one the advantage of learning "other psycho-therapeutic methods, not only in order to mix them on occasion with the 'pure gold of analysis,' but to be able to judge what other possibilities there are for any special case." Despite her opposition to lay analysis Horney leaves the door open for limited lay practice. "In Berlin at least there had never been any difference of opinion on the point that an anthropologist or jurist who wishes for an analytical training . . . must have the possibility of gaining a personal impression of psychic mechanisms through conducting analyses himself."[73]

Several years later, when Horney gave a paper at a history symposium in Leipzig on Freud's recently published *Civilization and Its Discontents*, she expressed some doubts about the plausibility of the death instinct. Then she added, "From my remarks you will no doubt see that psychoanalysis is not a cult requiring that its adherents display blind allegiance to Freud's every word, although we have often been accused of this."[74] But the truth is that Horney's independence had cost her the goodwill of at least some of the analytic establishment. Her public lectures, which once earned her praise at the institute, seem to have inspired a discussion, in early 1932, of "how far controversy promotes our aims, whether conducted outside or inside the society."[75] Even a young trainee, Edith Weigert, noted "great tensions" between Horney and others around the institute when she studied there in the late twenties.[76]

Perhaps the most telling indication we have that Karen Horney was in trouble with the establishment is found in the diary of an American who underwent a brief treatment with Sigmund Freud in 1935. The diarist/patient is an M.D. named Smiley Blanton, and he quotes Freud's opinion of Karen Horney: "She is able but malicious—mean."[77] When Freud disapproved, word traveled fast. Everyone at the Berlin Institute, including Horney, probably knew he didn't like her.

Karen Horney's difficulties at the Berlin Institute were undoubtedly one cause of her decision to leave Berlin for Chicago in 1932. But institute politics were only part of the story. The politics of the real world presented an even more compelling reason for leaving Germany. In October of 1929 the last effective Weimar president, Gustav Stresemann, died. Three weeks later Wall Street crashed and Germany went into an economic tailspin. The next year unemployment in Germany reached five million. Adolf Hitler's Nazi party and the Communists made big gains in the Reichstag at the expense of the moderates. The diarist Count Harry Kessler, walking the streets of Berlin in October of 1930, watched "great Nazi masses" smash the windows of the department stores of Wertheim, Grünfeld, and others and listened to their chants of *"Deutschland erwache! Juda verrecke!"* (Germany awake! Destroy the Jews!)[78] Germans had "missed the sharp voice of command," George Grosz wrote in his autobiography. "Everyone had his own political opinion, a mixture of fear, envy, and hope, but what use was that without leadership?... The grumbling became increasingly threatening, finally dangerous. As no one felt himself guilty —a whole people never does—everyone looked for a scapegoat, and harmless old ditties about Jews suddenly had the odor of a pogrom."[79] For the new year of 1932 Grosz designed a greeting card on which a skeletal hand tosses the dice onto a card table where three cards are turned up: one shows the flag of Weimar, another a hammer and sickle, and a third a swastika. Above them hovers a large question mark with "1932" written on it.[80]

Things *were* very much up in the air in 1932. Especially in Berlin, where the Nazis got few votes, Hitler was thought to be an absurdity that couldn't last. Many agreed with the philosopher Ernst Cassirer that "this Hitler is an error of history; he does not belong in German history at all. And therefore he will perish."[81] It would be several years before German Jews would start to emigrate in large numbers and before many thousands of others, less fortunate, would be carried off and murdered in concentration camps. A few people, including George Grosz, Arthur Koestler, and Albert Einstein, left as early as 1932 because they were convinced the worst was coming. Others left early because they expected the worst and because they were running toward something as well as away from the threat of a Nazi Germany.

Among these was Karen Horney. As a non-Jew without dangerous political commitments Horney would not have had to leave Germany at all. But the Nazis threatened to destroy her world. And America offered the opportunity to escape the infighting of European psychoanalysis. As associate director of the newly formed Institute for Psychoanalysis in Chicago she would have a chance to exert her influence in ways not possible in Berlin.

The Chicago Institute owed its life to another member of the Berlin Institute, Franz Alexander. Alexander was six years younger than Karen Horney, and had come to analysis ten years later than she had. But after he enrolled, in 1919, as the Berlin Institute's first student, he quickly earned others' respect. Alexander traveled to the United States for a conference in 1931, and in 1932, after teaching in Boston and Chicago, he convinced Alfred K. Stern, a wealthy Chicagoan whom he had treated for stomach complaints, to provide backing for a psychoanalytic institute. When they decided to seek an experienced woman to be second in command Alexander thought of Horney, whom he had liked and admired in Berlin. Sometime during the early months of 1932, as

Karen Horney sat at her desk in her office on Lützowufer, the telephone rang. It was Franz Alexander calling from Chicago—an astonishment in itself—and asking her to join him there. Horney accepted.

Brigitte's and Marianne's situations made 1932 a good year for Karen Horney to think about leaving Germany. Marianne had entered medical school that year and was thus launched on her own career. And Brigitte had scored a theatrical triumph that virtually assured her future as an actress. That year Brigitte, who had been studying with the well-known actress Ilka Grüning, won the Reinhardt prize for acting. The prize, which was awarded as the result of a competition with forty-four young actors and actresses, brought not only fifteen hundred marks but also the promise of work and public attention. Soon after, Brigitte made her first movie—a film called *Abschied* (Farewell), directed by the promising young Robert Siodmak—and was described in print as "a newly emerging star in the film heavens." Brigitte, even more than Marianne, was at a stage where she could get along without her mother. Of her three daughters only Renate, at fifteen, was too young to be left behind to pursue her own life. Poor Renate, who had finally found a second home at her school in Switzerland, would have to be uprooted once again.

In September of 1932, following the International Psychoanalytic Congress in Wiesbaden,[82] Karen and Renate would board a ship bound for the United States. Marianne would follow a year later, after she had finished her medical course work. Brigitte would stay in Germany to pursue her film career.

At the International Congress that year President Max Eitingon spoke of the way in which political and economic events overshadowed interest in psychological questions. "We have . . . had to give up a large number of our most valued German colleagues to the American society," Eitingon noted. "First Alexander and Rado, and now Frau Horney and Sachs." But even with "reduced forces," Eitingon told the Congress, those left behind were determined to hold their own against the critics of psychoanalysis. "We will hope," Eitingon said, that the crisis "is a phase which will soon pass."[83]

But Eitingon was overly optimistic. That January, Hitler became chancellor. Christopher Isherwood wrote in his *Berlin Stories* that there was nothing in the newspapers but "new rules, new punishments, and lists of people who have been 'kept in.' This morning, Göring has invented three fresh varieties of high treason."[84] In February the Reichstag went up in flames. And in March the first concentration camp was opened at Dachau, outside Munich. That same year Eitingon decided to leave Germany before it was too late.

In 1929, when the international congress was held in Oxford, England, a Hungarian-born analyst named Sandor Lorand had brought along a movie camera. The home movie he made is a collection of nonevents: clusters of analysts waving gaily at the camera, one analyst lighting the other's cigar, analyst pairs strolling arm in arm toward the camera at Dr. Lorand's request, crowds of analysts assembling outside the congress hall for an official photograph. But the film, which is now in the Library of Congress, provides one of the last, vivid records of a gathering of psychoanalysts before their days were darkened by the menace of Adolf Hitler. Within five years after the Oxford congress the Berlin Institute had ceased to exist and most of its members had fled their homeland in fear of their lives.

Thus history has given the film a special poignancy. One knows, for instance, that Max Eitingon, a small, impeccably tailored man in a gracefully curving fedora, will be leaving Berlin within the next four years and starting over in Israel. Franz Alexander, the dark Hungarian whose stocky wrestler's build makes his suit look uncomfortable, will be leaving too, to found a new institute in Chicago. And it will be the destiny of Marie Bonaparte, the chic woman in the bucket hat whose face is surrounded with fur, to use her wealth and influence as a princess of Greece to effect Freud's last-minute escape to London, where he will live out the final years of his life, missing home and fatally ill with cancer.

At one point the camera catches Karen Horney unawares. There is a fleeting look of alarm when she sees the camera, then the American analyst next to her says something that, for a second, makes her break into a broad grin. The girlish mother of the Zehlendorf photos has grown matronly. At forty-seven her hair is a wispy white around her face, and her waist is thicker. Yet at the same time there is a grace in Horney's bearing that still photos did not capture. She wears a silk dress with flowing sleeves, the *de rigueur* dropped waist, and a long string of pearls. When she sits in a chair, preparing for the group photo, she turns slightly to one side, graceful hands folded and slender legs scissored. Her bearing is dignified, yet it contains in it the wish to be attractive to men. At the same time there is some sort of unease in her eyes and slight smile. She seems to be taking everything in, yet holding herself in reserve.

That summer, as the analysts gathered in Oxford, the greatest threat to the future health of psychoanalysis was thought to be the internal rift over lay analysis. Freud, who was too sick to attend the meeting, had warned in a letter to Sandor Ferenczi that spring that the opposition to lay analysis was "the last mask of resistance against psychoanalysis, and the most dangerous of all."[85]

But very soon there would be a different sort of enemy to deal with. The Nazis had been attacking psychoanalysis right from the start, labeling it "the Jewish science" and criticizing its ideas, particularly the frank discussion of sexuality. By May of 1933 Freud's books were being burned in a public square in Berlin. By 1934 over half the membership of the Berlin Psychoanalytic Institute had left. Four members were imprisoned and killed by the Nazis. The rest managed to reestablish themselves in other countries, most frequently the United States.[86] There was a pathetic attempt to salvage something of the Berlin Institute in 1933, when all the Jewish members resigned voluntarily so that the non-Jews could limp along until Hitler faded away.[87] But Hitler survived and prospered, and true psychoanalytic inquiry became an impossibility. The golden years of the Berlin Institute, and of Berlin, were over.

PART FOUR

Chicago
1932–34

12

Psychoanalysis in the New World

Karen Horney and her fifteen-year-old daughter Renate sailed into New York Harbor, on board the *Reliance,* on September 22, 1932.[1] The Great Depression had hit hard in America by then. President Hoover, who had been so slow to acknowledge the crisis, was warning that "millions of men and women approach the winter with fear in their hearts."[2] But Karen and Renate, although they had brought only a thousand dollars, were shielded from uncertainties by friends in the analytic world. Renate remembers being greeted at dockside by Sandor Rado, Karen's colleague from the Berlin Institute, and taken in a taxi to a luxurious hotel, with chandeliers even more ornate than any she had seen in Europe, then riding up to an elegant suite on a high floor with a "dizzying"[3] view of Manhattan. After Berlin the skyscrapers of New York came as a surprise.

In Chicago, where they went soon after, the buildings were not quite so tall. And there were even some ways in which the city resembled Berlin. Mark Twain, in fact, had once dubbed Berlin "the European Chicago"[4]—both were fast-growing cities rising out of the plain, cities of new buildings and broad boulevards. But Chicago, unlike Berlin, was a city built around water—a lake much larger than any in Europe. In many ways Chicago was a city more like Hamburg than Berlin, a city on the water and a city of commerce.

Chicagoans were proud of their city's commercial preeminence. Chicago was first in lumber markets, first in hide and leather markets, and its Merchandise Mart was the largest man-made structure in the world. When a visiting reporter asked a Chicagoan in 1932 why it mattered that the city was so big and prosperous, the reply was indignant. "Why, man! That's progress. You're interested in progress, aren't you?"[5] To a Berliner, midwestern high spirits could be refreshing. As Henry Pachter, a political scientist who emigrated from Berlin, noted: "We loved America for its promises, its youthfulness, its strength."[6] All of these qualities were evident in Chicago in 1933, when, despite the deepening depression, an extravagant World's Fair entitled "Century of Progress" opened to the public. As one critic noted, the futuristic buildings of the fair, lit up at night and painted in rainbow colors, were a testimonial to "Chicago's invincible optimism."[7]

Karen Horney's early love affair with the Karl May books had left her favorably disposed toward the New World. Thanks in part to Karl May, the picture she and other Europeans had of America tended toward the fantastic. "Whenever you read anything unbelievable, where did it happen?" asked George Grosz. "Always in America, the land of unlimited opportunities. . . . The wildest tales came from America."[8] America may not have been wild in Karl May fashion. But it was bizarre to a Berliner nonetheless. In 1932 Prohibition was still in effect in America; drinking alcohol, which was so much a part of life in Europe, was a crime. Stranger still than Prohibition was the underworld of bootleggers and gangs that Prohibition had spawned. Gang wars had led, as G. K. Chesterton noted after a visit to Chicago in 1931, to "an entirely new development . . . the organized use of machine guns by the ordinary criminal classes."[9]

Karen and Renate were welcomed into this land of Al Capone with appropriate fanfare. They had just checked into the Windermere Hotel, near the University of Chicago, when a great ruckus suddenly started up in the lobby. A robbery was in progress. Before it was over the thieves had made off with the cashier's drawer and several shots had been fired. It was but the first of several shocks and thrills Chicago had in store for them. Soon after, a well-meaning Chicagoan took them on a tour of the stockyards, Chicago's pride and joy. Long afterward Renate remembered "the pigs squeaking and jerking while coming down a funnel in which they were shorn...on their way to getting quartered and sausaged" and the elevator that "released one steer at a time" to be "greeted with a blow of a sledge hammer on his head."[10] According to Renate, it was a long time after that before either she or her mother could eat meat.

The tour was a vivid illustration of the cultural gap between Europe and America. Undoubtedly there were stockyards in Berlin as well as in Chicago, but what European would consider them a tourist attraction? As émigré Henry Pachter noted, America was a business culture "unadulterated by aristocratic or intellectual impurities."[11]

Once they had determined that Renate would attend a progressive school on the North Side, Karen and Renate chose an apartment on Lincoln Park West, with a view of Lake Michigan, that was convenient to both the school and the brand new Chicago Institute, on Ohio Street. For Renate, the American school was a shock: different in almost every way from her beloved Salem School in Switzerland. Karen's situation was easier in some ways. Because psychoanalytic training was entirely new and because she had been part of the bellwether training program at the Berlin Psychoanalytic, she commanded a great deal of respect in this midwestern outpost. She was bringing a European tradition to America, rather than adjusting to an American one.

Freud's ideas had been noticed in America as early as 1894, when William James discussed Breuer's and Freud's theories of trauma and catharsis.[12] But broader interest dates from 1909, when Freud was invited by the psychologist G. Stanley Hall to give a series of lectures at Clark University in Worcester, Massachusetts. The five Clark lectures, which Freud delivered without notes and with very little preparation, were subsequently published, and continue to be one of the best elementary introductions to his thinking. "They give an excellent idea," as translator James Strachey has noted, "of the ease and clarity of style and the unconstrained sense of form which made Freud such a remarkable expository lecturer."[13]

Not everyone, however, was favorably impressed by Freud's "Five Lectures on Psychoanalysis." A dean at the University of Toronto wrote that Freud seemed to be "advocat[ing] free love, removal of all restraints, and a relapse into savagery."[14] William James wrote a Swiss colleague that Freud's theories "can't fail to throw light on human nature, but I confess that he made on me personally the impression of a man obsessed with fixed ideas."[15] On the other hand, James Jackson Putnam, one of the nation's foremost neurologists and a professor at Harvard, became a staunch supporter after hearing Freud lecture.

After his appearance at Clark, Freud's work began to appear in English for the first time. Most of the early translations were the work of A. A. Brill, who had emigrated to the United States from Austria-Hungary in 1887 but had returned to Europe as a young doctor and learned about psychoanalysis at Bleuler's clinic in Switzerland. Eitingon described Brill—a short, rotund man with a Vandyke beard—as "the indefatigable protagonist and guardian of psychoanalysis in the United States."[16] Unfortunately Brill was a better advocate than translator, with the result that Americans read diminished English versions of *The Interpretation of Dreams* (in 1913) and *Three Essays on Sexuality* (in 1918).

Even in poor translation, however, Freud's ideas stimulated the popular press, mostly to disapproval or misappropriation. The *Nation* wrote of the tendency "to over-emphasize the potency of erotic influence in all of experience... leading to improbable and revolting explanations."[17] Max Eastman wrote a more sympathetic but greatly watered-down explanation of Freud's ideas in a two-part article in *Everybody's Magazine,* using cases to illustrate the "magic" of psychoanalysis.[18]

Eastman was one of the Greenwich Village cognoscenti for whom psychoanalysis quickly became *the* topic of conversation around this time. Another was the young writer Walter Lippmann, whose 1914 *A Preface to Politics* is informed by psychoanalysis. "When I compare his [Freud's] work with the psychology that I studied in college," Lippmann wrote in the *New Republic* at the time, "... I cannot help feeling that for his illumination, for this steadiness and brilliancy of mind, he may rank among the greatest who have contributed to thought."[19] Another Greenwich Village enthusiast recalls that "there must have been half a dozen or more people in the Liberal club who knew a good deal about psychoanalysis, and a score or so more who were familiar enough with the terms to use them in badinage.... Everybody at that time who knew about psychoanalysis was a sort of missionary on the subject, and nobody could be around Greenwich Village without hearing a lot about it."[20] By 1926, when Sandor Ferenczi came to New York to deliver a series of lectures at the New School for Social Research, psychoanalysis had acquired an uptown following: outside the doors of the New School a fleet of limousines stood waiting for the rich and powerful who had come to hear Freud's disciple.[21]

Knowledge and practice of psychoanalysis in depth, however, was slower to take hold in the United States. In the 1920s a few American psychiatrists began traveling to Vienna and Berlin for psychoanalysis with Freud and his followers. But systematic training didn't become available on this side of the Atlantic until European psychoanalysts began to seek asylum in America from the persecution of the Nazis.

The groundwork for the coming of the Europeans was laid in the spring of 1930, when the organizers of the first International Congress of Mental Hygiene decided to invite analysts from Europe to Washington, D.C., to participate. The invitations, issued to Otto Rank, Helene Deutsch, Sandor Rado, and Franz Alexander among others, offered to pay all expenses, a fact that caused Rado to toss his invitation out in disbelief. But Franz Alexander, who had analyzed and done research with Americans, was better schooled in their reckless ways. He convinced Rado that the invitation was genuine, and as a result, Rado and Alexander made their first trip to America.

Rado went back to Europe after the conference but soon returned at the invitation of the New York Society, a group of psychiatrists, some of them trained in Europe, who met on a regular basis at the apartment of A. A. Brill or in the Oliver Cromwell Hotel to talk over analytic ideas. The society asked Rado to come to New York and oversee the formation of the first training program in psychoanalysis in the United States; Rado agreed to come and establish an institute on the Berlin model.[22] Alexander, meanwhile, had stayed on in America, teaching for a time in Boston, then accepting an invitation from Robert Hutchins, the dynamic president of the University of Chicago, to join the medical faculty there.

In 1925, according to Ernest Jones, there was only one psychoanalyst west of New York,[23] a Chicago-trained neurologist/psychiatrist named Lionel Blitzsten, who had traveled to Vienna for analysis in 1921, when he was probably analyzed by Otto Rank, then six years later to Berlin for a partial analysis with Franz Alexander. When Blitzsten returned to Chicago and joined the faculty of Northwestern Medical School, word spread among the students that there was "quite a brilliant person"[24] who might be willing to talk, after-hours in his living room, about the new subject of psychoanalysis. The Blitzsten Monday-night seminars were the result.

The seminars were freewheeling and informal—often continuing into the small hours. And because Blitzsten talked interestingly about music, books, and travel as well as psychoanalysis, young medical students were dazzled. Karl Menninger, who came to Chicago from the family's Menninger Clinic in Topeka to study, remembers that Blitzsten "endeared himself to his students . . . by the evident delight he took in their conversation and company. Wherever he was, he kept open house, a kind of salon which was often distinguished by wit and brilliant discussions in which he was always at the center. . . . One was flattered to be included in this circle where one was sure to meet interesting people from various professions and arts, to hear good music and conversation, and to eat and drink well."[25]

Blitzsten's living room was one of the few places in Chicago that were hospitable to psychoanalysis. In 1930, when Franz Alexander was invited to join the University of Chicago faculty as professor of psychoanalysis, he discovered that most psychiatrists there had little use for it. A handful of nonmedical scholars, including sociologists Harold Lasswell and John Dollard, were keenly interested and met regularly with Alexander. But when Alexander delivered his first lecture to the medical faculty, a doctor in the audience got up and demanded to know if psychoanalysis was an experimental science. Alexander answered that it was not but was based on "clinical observation." With that the doctor declared that psychoanalysis was not a science and was therefore of no interest to him. He got up and left the room, taking part of the audience with him.

Freud, who was monitoring the experiment in academic psychoanalysis from Vienna, advised Alexander to ask his audience at the next lecture whether they considered astronomy and paleontology real sciences, since one cannot experiment with the stars or with fossils. Freud had a special interest in Alexander's effort in Chicago: he had always believed psychoanalysis should be a discipline within the university rather than isolated in autonomous "institutes." But Freud's advice from afar couldn't sway the doctors. After a year of continuing hostility, the university did the politic thing and discontinued Alexander's professorial appointment.[26]

Nonetheless, when Alexander left Chicago for Boston in 1931, he left many supporters and enthusiasts behind. One of them was Alfred Stern, a wealthy businessman who had traveled all over the United States seeking a medical remedy for a stomach ulcer and who had finally found it through a few months of analytic treatment with Alexander.[27] Stern, who was married to Marion Rosenwald, heir to the Sears fortune, brought together a board of wealthy Chicagoans, who raised enough money to found an independent Chicago institute. And in the spring of 1932 Stern and his group asked Alexander to return as its director. Soon after, at Alexander's suggestion, Karen Horney was asked to come to Chicago as associate director.

Alexander and Horney had gotten along well in Berlin. Alexander, the son of an illustrious Hungarian professor, had fled Budapest as a young doctor in 1919 during Béla Kun's short-lived Communist regime. He arrived in Berlin at just the right time to become the first psychoanalytic candidate at the Berlin Institute, where he was analyzed—like nearly everybody else—by Hanns Sachs and undoubtedly took classes with Karen Horney. Unlike Horney, Alexander paid several visits to Freud in Vienna and got to know him fairly well. Freud, for his part, viewed Alexander as a promising young disciple, awarding him a prize for the best clinical essay of the year, "Castration Complex and Character," in 1921.

Alexander, however, was not cut out to be an unquestioning follower. An imposing man, with the huge shoulders and short neck of a football tackle, he was widely read, fluent in several languages, and an electric presence in any room he entered, a fact that, according to Helene Deutsch, made him particularly effective in America. "Immediate . . . success really only fell to Alexander," she wrote home during her visit to the 1930 conference in Washington. He "is esteemed *much* higher in America than Freud, and in spite of the bad lectures that he gave, he had a magic power that made all homosexual men in highest places his slaves . . . one must have been in America to understand such a thing."[28] Alexander also worked his charms on women, although Helene Deutsch was clearly not among them.

In later years Alexander, like Horney, would quarrel bitterly with the analytic establishment. Even in Berlin he shared Horney's pragmatic bent—and her distrust of untested theory. "I sensed," he wrote later, "that our field was beginning to lose the proper balance between theoretical superstructure and observational foundation."[29] Alexander, like Horney, was interested in social realities. Working with an American colleague, Hugo Staub, he had written the first major psychoanalytic study of criminality* while still in Berlin. And, like Horney's mentor Georg Groddeck, he had devel-

---

The Criminal, the Judge and the Public (New York: Macmillan, 1931).

oped an abiding interest in psychosomatic medicine.

All of this should have made Karen Horney and Franz Alexander natural allies. And in Berlin it did. But in Chicago they were suddenly thrust into entirely different roles. Alexander was no longer junior, and Horney was no longer an outsider. They were the establishment, the voice of psychoanalysis. And perhaps more important, Alexander was now Horney's boss. This undoubtedly suited Alexander: anyone who could write a semiautobiographical book entitled *The Western Mind in Transition* clearly possessed a powerful sense of his own importance. But Horney was not equally well suited to her supportive role. Being associate director to a man six years her junior who had been her student in Berlin must have stung. And around the Chicago Institute, where everyone thought in Oedipal terms, she was cast unofficially in the role of mother figure and helpmeet to Alexander—roles about which she was, as we have already seen, deeply conflicted. All in all, it is not entirely surprising that Horney's sojourn as associate director in Chicago lasted only two years.

And yet for much of her time in Chicago Horney was an enthusiastic and effective partner to Alexander in pursuit of an improbable goal: transplanting a psychoanalytic institute, essentially a German institution, to the virgin soil of the American Midwest. The first brochure, issued in October of 1932, reflected both the high hopes and the enormity of the task ahead. The Institute for Psychoanalysis, the title page declared, was "Dedicated to Increasing the Knowledge of the Psychic Processes of Man." Inside, Alexander explained that "psychoanalysis, being a young science, has not yet found its permanent place in the official centers of teaching and research—the universities." This "conservative attitude," he went on to insist, is "no longer justified," since "psychoanalysis has secured its place in our present civilization." Indeed, Alexander continued, "for the intelligent public today, it is becoming as natural to consult a psychoanalyst concerning a psychosis or neurosis as it is to go to an ophthalmologist in the case of eye trouble."[30]

This of course was wishful thinking. The reality was that Alexander and Horney, described in the pamphlet as "two of the foremost psychoanalysts,"[31] had a lot of educating and persuading to do. Obviously the first step was to plan an educational program that would attract students to the institute for psychoanalytic training. But since analysts require patients, they would also need to excite the general public about the potential benefits of psychoanalytic treatment. And, in addition, there was the hostile attitude of the medical establishment to overcome. Medical students would never seek out analytic training if their teachers disdained it. And unsympathetic doctors would never recommend analytic treatment to their patients.

American doctors, like many of their European counterparts, suspected that psychoanalysis was quackery, on the level of spiritualism and other mind cures that had long been popular in America. Like the doctor who spoke up at Alexander's lecture, they wanted tangible proof that it was a "science," as Freud claimed it to be. The obvious way to win them over, Alexander reasoned, was through research that proved the connections between physical illness and psychological difficulties and demonstrated the effectiveness of analytic intervention. Right at the start the institute announced plans to do research on "psychobiological problems," particularly psychological factors in gastrointestinal disorders. The subject had already brought Alexander good fortune—his successful treatment of Stern's stomach ulcer had made the institute possible. The great hope, as the first brochure noted, was that further research would "contribute to the assimilation of psychoanalysis in the system of sciences to an unprecedented degree." To further promote the cause Alexander gave a series of lectures for physicians entitled "Psychoanalysis in Medicine."[32]

Karen Horney too put her shoulder to the wheel. In addition to helping to plan the analytic training program (a task to which she, as a former member of the Berlin and international committees on training, brought a particular expertise), she taught a course in psychoanalytic technique to staff and candidates and shared the teaching in a case seminar with Alexander. For five hours of each day she saw patients in analysis. Theoretically these patients were carefully selected to meet certain research criteria of the institute. But the reality in the beginning, as Alfred Stern revealed in a letter to another board member, was that several of her patients were taken on "where there was . . . a financial justification in the institute taking them." All analytic cases treated at the Institute were charged an average of five dollars a session. In addition, however, "a donation above the maximum charge was made in the beginning" when the patient's "financial ability" made it possible.[33]

Although Stern never missed an opportunity to raise money, he also didn't hesitate to spend it. The institute suite of offices, located on the ninth floor of a small, elegant building at 43 East

Ohio Street in downtown Chicago, had been planned by one of Chicago's leading designers in a sleek thirties modern style—pastel colors, chairs upholstered in rough, textured fabrics, a sizable library, and a Ping-Pong room for relaxation.

Horney had a large corner office, made bright by windows on two sides. The furnishings were minimal—a comfortable chair at the end of the analytic couch, a desk, a humidifier to combat the dry heat of Chicago winters—and the dominant color was apple green.[34] Unlike the Berlin Institute, where most of the members had seen their patients in private offices, everyone involved in the Chicago Institute conducted his or her practice on the premises. So it was here that Horney spent her full days, seeing patients and supervising students as well.

Horney quickly gained a reputation among the handful of young doctors who were beginning training as a skilled supervisor. Franz Alexander, as Lucia Tower, an early candidate recalled, was "too darn busy" to concentrate on supervision. "He was very glad when you didn't call him for a supervisory hour." Lionel Blitzsten, the lone analyst west of New York before Alexander's arrival, turned out to be erratic and unpredictable—a brilliant lecturer who quickly became involved in a rivalry with Alexander, about which he didn't hesitate to rant during supervision. Horney, although she too became embroiled in politics, kept them out of her supervisory hours. "She was very friendly with me," Tower remembers, "and I found her a very fine supervisor."[35] Leon Saul, who had Horney as his supervisor in the treatment of his first analytic case, found her "marvelous as a clinician." Horney's supervision was particularly helpful because Saul was "not a natural intuitive analyst at all." Whereas other supervisors would say, "Tell me about the case," Horney would ask him to tell her "what happened word for word during the hour."[36]

Educating analysts, however, was only part of Horney's job. To a great extent the future of the institute lay in the hands of non-analysts. And both she and Alexander devoted a large portion of their time to lecturing the laymen about the new science of psychoanalysis. They teamed up to teach a series of eight classes to social workers and teachers, beginning with a lecture by Alexander entitled "The Empirical Basis of Psychoanalysis" and ending with one by Horney titled "Practical Application to Social and Educational Work." In addition, Horney gave popular lectures on subjects calculated to draw an audience—"The Mother's Conflicts as

Expressed Toward the Child" and "Abuses of Psychoanalysis in Everyday Life."[37]

The most remarkable fact about all of this activity is not in the records: every bit of teaching, of analysis, and of supervision had to be done in English. Horney had had years of English in school and had even had at least one American in psychoanalysis while still in Europe. But in the beginning her accent was so thick it embarrassed Renate. And when it came time to draw up reading lists for courses, she had to enlist the help of American colleagues in finding books in English. To "lose the language of one's dreams," in the words of one German immigrant,[38] is to lose complexities and subtleties on which pychoanalysis in particular depends. And yet Horney managed the transition with remarkable alacrity.

The most dramatic evidence of this is a paper entitled "Psychogenic Factors in Functional Female Disorders," which Horney delivered before the Chicago Gynecological Society on November 18, 1932, less than thirty days after she had arrived in the United States. The paper is full of odd, unidiomatic turns of phrase. Yet it is both clear and persuasive in much the same way as her very first psychoanalytic paper, delivered in German fifteen years before. Both are briefs for psychoanalysis. But while the first, "The Technique of Psychoanalytic Psychotherapy," was given to sexologists in Berlin and explained the psychoanalytic method, this one tried to show gynecologists how psychoanalysis might help them deal with the complaints they heard in their offices day in and day out.

Horney focused on the "female disorders" every gynecologist would know well: menstrual pain, frigidity, infertility, complications in pregnancy. And knowing the skepticism of her audience, she approached the mind–body question with great care. First she made a bold assertion: in her own practice, women patients came into treatment for a variety of reasons—"states of anxiety of all sorts, compulsion neuroses, depressions, inhibitions in work and in contact with people, character difficulties." Yet, despite the variety of complaints, she had "not one case without some functional disturbance of their genital system: frigidity in all degrees, vaginismus [painful spasm of the vagina], all sorts of menstruation disorders, pruritus [an itching dermatitis], pains and discharges which had no organic basis and which disappeared after uncovering certain unconscious conflicts, all sorts of hypochondriacal fears [such] as fears of cancer or of not being normal, and some disturbances in pregnancy and childbirth which at least seemed suspicious of a psychogenic origin."

Having compiled this sweeping list of ailments that she suspects are psychogenic, Horney quickly returns to the experimental and biological territory where the gynecologists feel comfortable. She tells them scientific studies are needed. "Even a busy analyst sees only comparatively few cases." Only gynecologists who see larger numbers of women can test "the validity of our findings." Of course, she adds, such an investigation "would require from their side time and psychological training."

Much of what Horney says is meant to educate, as when she suggests that "with women you will find, on the average, a closer unity between their sex feelings and their whole emotional life" than with men. Or when she tells them that "children are already born with sexual feelings and can feel very passionately, very likely much more so than we grown-ups with all our inhibitions." But at the same time the paper is a prelude to new work. The outlines of a later, more ambitious paper for a psychoanalytic audience, entitled "The Overvaluation of Love," are visible in her discussion of women's "vague but deep fear of not being normal" and of the importance of women's childhood feelings toward other women, particularly mothers and sisters.

She ends with an appeal for empathy. "If only some time and attention would be given to the patients, at least some of them would reveal their conflicts very easily." Even though one must be careful not to "stir up emotions with which one is not able to cope," such an approach "might even have some direct therapeutic value."[39]

Horney's reception at the various meetings where she spoke seems to have been enthusiastic. The course she and Alexander taught at the institute for teachers and social workers attracted an average of seventy to each lecture. And Alfred Stern was soon writing to Max Eitingon in Berlin: "Dr. Horney is making an excellent impression in every quarter. I am more than ever convinced that we made the most logical and satisfactory choice of a colleague for Dr. Alexander that is possible." Citing conferences near and far where Alexander and Horney would be speaking, he concluded that "they are both beginning to receive the kind of professional recognition they deserve and the trustees and advisory board members can be duly proud of this."[40] If there was any complaint, it was, as Stern wrote, that they had to spend their time in rudimentary education about psychoanalysis and had little left for research.

Fortunately Horney, Alexander, and their small staff did not live for research alone. Despite the serious tone of the institute brochure, the atmosphere around the institute was lively and informal. There were only seven staff members, and of those only four had any real psychoanalytic background, so that distinctions between staff and students were often moot. Psychiatrist Helen McLean remembers: "I was on the staff at the same time I was trying to learn something."[41] Leon Saul, who had begun analysis with Alexander as a psychiatric resident in Boston and had followed him to Chicago to undertake psychoanalytic training, "didn't feel at all like a humble student." Saul was included from the start in all the conferences and research meetings and was on a first-name basis with everybody. "We were all a family, there was no great hierarchy."[42]

Contributing to the camaraderie was the decision, made early on, to convert the institute's laboratory into a kitchen. The first brochure promised that "the Institute's laboratory is equipped for adequate physical examinations," to be made by an internist as "related to research and to the patient's needs." It was soon equipped instead with a Scandinavian cook, who turned out sumptuous lunches for frequent staff meetings, where business and research progress was reported. There was a lot of socializing after hours as well. The gregarious Alexander frequently gave parties at his apartment. At other times the group gathered at the Gypsy Camp, a Hungarian restaurant not far from the institute, where Alexander and his compatriots were often moved to tears by heartfelt folk refrains played on the violin and cembalo. Prohibition, still in effect that first year, only added to the fun. Renate remembers being sent to the corner drugstore with a prescription for high-proof alcohol—to spike the punch at a party her mother gave. The punch, she remembers, tasted awful, but the guests drank it anyway.

It comes as a surprise, given all this evidence of hard work and good fellowship, to learn that Karen Horney was sometimes desperately unhappy. But, according to Renate, she and her mother both suffered during that first long winter in Chicago. "I was miserable, I was lost," Renate recalls. "And she was."[43] With her mother working long days, Renate filled her afternoons and evenings with movies. "I saw many," she remembers, "each one leaving me cold and empty." Renate's unhappiness was compounded at school, where she had to struggle with English and American mores all at the same time. She was surprised to learn that it was impossible for boys and girls to be "just friends" and hold hands in friendship. And she was disturbed by the preoccupation of the girls with necking "without there being any real feeling or friendship involved, more as a sort of status. . . . I just hurt all over," she remembers.[44]

To make matters worse, neither mother nor daughter talked about their unhappiness. "Instead of us getting together and talking it out and making it a joint effort, we were each sort of harboring our own misery." It is ironic that Karen Horney, who spent her days listening to patients talk about their troubles, was unable to talk about her own. But, as in the past, she chose to suffer in silence.

Renate vividly recalls one night when the silence was momentarily broken. Karen was in her bed and Renate was sitting on the edge of it when Karen suddenly blurted out, "If I don't live, what are you going to do?" To the sixteen-year-old Renate, who was feeling so lost herself, her mother's question must have been mysterious and terrifying. Was her mother dying of some disease? Or was she contemplating suicide? Years later Renate surmised that her mother's morbid thoughts were related to her preparations for taking the state medical exams. Every night, Renate recalls, her mother would go to bed with several thick volumes in English on anatomy or pathology. She was extremely anxious about the exams and sure she would fail them. Sometime during her studies she probably became convinced that she had one of the fatal illnesses she was reading about.[45]

But Karen Horney was, after all, a woman of forty-seven who had read much of this material before. The anxiety she felt could hardly derive just from rereading medical texts. There were indeed many other pressures. There was, for Horney as for all the other new arrivals, so much to take in all at once. One had to relearn some things—such as basic medicine—unlearn others, and learn many, many things for the first time. The refugee, as Anthony Heilbut observed in *Exiled in America,* "needed the sophistication of maturity and the buoyancy of youth in order to relearn almost everything—from spatial directions to verbal idioms to social customs to political temperament—quickly enough so that he wouldn't forfeit his few opportunities for advancement."[46]

Horney and other new arrivals also had to cope with a powerful assault on their identity. Right at the start they had a decision to make about how they would describe themselves: were they refugees, exiles, émigrés, or immigrants? Each word carried different connotations, none of which might seem quite right. There was a natural temptation, when thrown into this unfamiliar new environment, to hark back to the good old days. Emigrants who talked endlessly about the way "we" did things back home—*bei Uns*—were labeled *bei Unsers* and looked upon disapprovingly by more savvy new arrivals.

George Grosz was one of those who disapproved of the *bei Unsers*. "Their vague and pseudo-sophisticated talk of European culture and American nonculture seemed exaggerated, merely proof that these people neither wanted to, nor could, fit in." Grosz went to the opposite extreme and tried to obliterate his past. "I wanted to discard my 'German' personality along with my citizenship, the way one would discard a worn-out suit. . . . I was severe with myself . . . I repressed everything in me that seemed too Grosz-like, too original, too Teutonic."[47]

Karen Horney had more in common with the Americans than did most of her compatriots. She had always been pragmatic, impatient with theoretical excesses and interested in results. She hated the self-important Prussian style of some of her colleagues; she used to tell Brigitte that she had left Germany to get away from "finger-pointing Germans."[48] And yet, even though she wasn't nearly as "German" as some others, she was still, in the eyes of the Americans, a refugee—a "ref," in the parlance of Chicago circles at the time.[49]

When Horney smoked, as she often did, she held on to her cigarette with a metal clip. This was a ladylike measure for keeping her fingers free of tobacco stains. But it must have given her a commanding and distinctly foreign air. Dorothy Blitsten, the American-born wife of Lionel Blitzsten,* remembers that Horney, like the other new arrivals who began appearing in increasing numbers at the Blitzsten evenings, had "the 'ref' look." There was a difference, Blitsten maintains, in the way the women carried themselves. They were taught "the ladylike way to walk" was with the knees slightly bent, toes pointed out, which results in the head being held forward, the shoulders sloping. "It isn't our style. And anything one puts on doesn't have the flair." Horney, she re-

*She has since simplified the spelling of her name.

members, "was well dressed and it was good quality, but you'd know right away she was a ref. Refs had a style—handwoven materials, *handgemacht*—not necessarily that they were, but that's the way they looked. Chic they weren't. Always terrible shoes. I remember Horney had clunky shoes."[50] Horney's shoes were corrective ones, designed to ease a chronic bunion problem. But the reason for the shoes is irrelevant. The fact remains that Horney and her clunky shoes were seen as foreign in Chicago.

The Americans, by the same token, seemed foreign to Horney. The same things that bothered other Europeans bothered her. When she and Renate first arrived in New York she came back from a cocktail party in a rage. "How dare they all address me as Karen!" she fumed. Later, at the Chicago Institute, she was shocked once again by her colleagues' lack of decorum. She reported indignantly to Renate that on the first day they had asked her questions about how much money she had earned in Germany.[51] But these were superficial differences, which couldn't begin to explain the sense of loss Europeans felt. Heinz Kohut, an analyst whom came to Chicago from Austria as a young man, speaks of "the feeling of a crumbling universe. . . . I was passionately involved with German and Austrian culture, this was the peak of humanity to me—Goethe and the great German philosophers and writers and the German musicians and the whole refined Viennese culture. . . . It was the end of a world, it was the end of an era. And I had the feeling it was the end of my life . . . in terms of the continuity of my cultural existence."[52] The *bei Unsers* had a point after all: there was a level of education, of refinement, of sophistication in Vienna and Berlin that it was impossible to replicate in Chicago. What was sadder still was that new American friends couldn't imagine the other life one had led back in Berlin. Two lines of a Bertolt Brecht quatrain capture both the yearning and hopelessness of the émigré's situation: "I'm like the man who carried the brick with him/To show the world what his house had been like."[53]

What was most needed to make the shift to the new country was a certain flexibility. Women seem to have had a somewhat easier time than men getting acclimatized.[54] They often picked up the language more easily, and they found jobs more quickly than men, albeit lowly ones. Karen Horney, because she had a profession, had an even greater advantage than others of her sex and was able to join the social class she had left in Europe. And despite her anxiety about it, she passed the medical exams in English, the first time through, with flying colors. Horney was better off than later arrivals: as the numbers increased and native doctors felt economically threatened, the exams got more difficult and the requirements for practice stiffened. Many had to take the exams over and over before they passed, often because of language difficulties. The Viennese analyst Paul Federn never succeeded in passing, though he tried many times. It is said that he finally got so exasperated that he took to answering the questions with "See previous exam."[55]

Compared with Federn, and indeed with most others, Horney negotiated the external, practical requirements of changing countries with remarkable ease. Given her history, this is not surprising: she had long been adept at switching roles. "Adjusting," an American concept unfamiliar to many Germans, had been her way of life. "I automatically give myself differently to different people," she had told Oskar years before.[56]

But Horney's talent for being different things to different people had come at a price. Feelings of inner "chaos," of loneliness, and, on several occasions, thoughts of suicide—a "longing for sleep— even death"[57]—had been a recurring theme in her diary, particularly when she felt pressured or isolated. It was during the period of preparation for the medical exams in Germany, for instance, that her depression had led her to seek treatment with Karl Abraham in 1909. Even earlier, when she was studying for the *Abitur,* she had written in her diary, "If I don't pass the exam—! Then I'm finished. Then I can't go on living."[58] Taking the exams in Chicago must have reawakened some of those old feelings. And the new and unfamiliar surroundings must have evoked "the deep disconsolate feeling of being forsaken"[59] she had experienced as a newly arrived medical student in Freiburg many years before.

There is one story suggesting that not only the old feelings but also some of the old impulsive behavior returned during her stay in Chicago. Karen Horney probably had several sexual liaisons during her two years in Chicago. This in itself would be unremarkable—except perhaps as evidence that she was enjoying life. The story that implies desperation concerns her having an affair with a candidate she was supervising at the Chicago Institute —an American sixteen years her junior who was in analysis with Alexander. Other candidates heard at the time that Horney "seduced" this young man at her apartment and gave him such a fright that he was afraid to go to evening meetings for weeks afterward.[60]

If Horney did have an affair, no matter how brief, with a candidate at the institute, one has to ask, in some amazement, *why*? Even though things were informal in Chicago, there were limits. Supervising analysts aren't supposed to sleep with their supervisees. Furthermore, this supervisee was in analysis with Alexander, her boss; Alexander was sure to hear about the whole affair from the couch. In an analytic community her behavior was bound to be seen as "acting out"—perhaps a means of competing with Alexander through the patient, in the way that quarreling parents battle for the affections of the child. Given the repercussions, it seems likely that she "seduced" the candidate—if she did—in a moment of desperation.

The "seduced" candidate was Dr. Leon Saul, who has said only that he "always felt very warm and affectionate towards Karen, and I think she did towards me." He was, he said, "in the middle of my Oedipus" in analysis, and "so all I needed around was a mother figure to complement him [Alexander] as a father figure." One day when he told Horney he wasn't sure what to believe in psychoanalysis, she suggested he come over in the evening and work on a paper with her. He remembers that "we worked a number of evenings at her house" and that he got to know Renate, and Marianne, who joined them during the second year. "Karen would be very sociable and in the middle of the winter . . . serve Bolla, a wine mulled with strawberries and all kinds of things. And we would discuss what about all this analytic stuff can you really believe."

Alexander, Saul remembers, told him his visits to Horney's apartment were "ridiculous," since he "hadn't even begun to learn the field yet." Asked about Horney's looks, Saul said, "The main striking thing was that Karen had no sex appeal whatsoever. She was a one hundred percent maternal type, and not at all sexual." Her build was "sort of mediumish to largeish," and she "didn't stand very straight, but wasn't stooped." She had "a sort of pursed expression around her mouth" and "often had a manner of great benignity." Saul estimated her age at the time as "about sixty-five." She was in fact forty-seven.[61]

Leon Saul died before there was an opportunity to ask him about the seduction story. But of course his insistence on Horney's nonsexual quality can be read in two different ways. Indeed, everything about the incident can be read in several different ways. Another female candidate at the time remembers that Saul himself was quite flirtatious during those years.

Whether Horney seduced Leon Saul, merely flirted with him, or just had him over for the evening because she was lonely and liked his company will probably never be known. The two major papers she wrote in Chicago, however, suggest that her relationship to men was on her mind. Both papers concern the conflicts experienced by women who have a consuming need for a man or for one man after another. The first, "Maternal Conflicts," was the principal address at the annual meeting of the American Orthopsychiatric Association in Boston in February of 1933. The second, "A Frequent Disturbance in Female Love Life," was read in April of 1933 before the Baltimore-Washington Psychoanalytic Society and published later, with the new title "The Overvaluation of Love," in the *Psychoanalytic Quarterly*.

The woman patient whom Horney focuses on in "Maternal Conflicts" is a thirty-five-year-old married teacher, "endowed with intellect and capacity, a striking personality," who was troubled by the fact that certain of her students seemed to have "more than tender feelings for her—in fact, there was evidence that certain boys had fallen passionately in love with her." What emerged in time was "the sexual nature of her own feelings" and, indeed, a very real conflict over whether or not to act on them. One of her students, a boy of about twenty, actually followed the teacher into the city where she was being analyzed, "and she actually fell in love with this young boy." It was, Horney writes, "rather striking to see this poised and restrained woman fighting with herself and with me, fighting against the urge to have a love relationship with a comparatively immature boy."

The similarities between the teacher, contemplating an affair with her twenty-year-old student, and Karen Horney, similarly inclined (perhaps) toward her young supervisee, are striking. And even though the teacher differs from Horney in important ways—Horney concludes that the teacher's attraction to the student is a carry-over from her excessive involvement with her son—one suspects that Horney chose this particular case, consciously or unconsciously, because it resonated with her own concerns at the time.[62]

The second paper focuses on a different conflict but one also related to the seduction story. "The Overvaluation of Love" concerns a series of women patients whom she describes at one point as "boy crazy" and who show their preoccupation in a variety of ways. They may be "extremely inhibited in making any advances in establishing relationships with men, though craving for them to the exclusion of any other wish" or they may be "women of a veritable Don Juan type."

In one important way the thirteen women she groups together in "The Overvaluation of Love" are not like her. In all the cases there is "an inhibition in the sphere of work and accomplishment and a more or less well-marked impoverishment of interests." This hardly applies to Horney. But even though she doesn't fit the "type" she constructs, she shares some of the torments. For these women, she writes, "their relation to men was of great importance to them," yet "they had never succeeded in establishing a satisfactory relationship of any duration. Either attempts to form a relationship had failed outright, or there had been a series of merely evanescent relationships, broken off by either the man in question or the patient—relationships that moreover often showed a certain lack of selectivity." These women were "as though possessed by a single thought, 'I must have a man,'" so that "by comparison all the rest of life seemed stale, flat, and unprofitable."

When she writes of some women's need to "prove their feminine potency to themselves," we recognize the Karen Horney of the diaries. Such women's "interest in a man, such as may even amount to an illusion of being tremendously in love with him, vanishes as a rule as soon as he is 'conquered'—that is, as soon as he has become emotionally dependent on them." And this "tendency to make a person dependent through love" grows out of their "desire to be invulnerable" and, underneath, a profound "fear of the disappointments and humiliations that they expect to result from falling in love."

At other times one can only suspect that Horney is writing of herself as well as of her patients, as when she describes women "assuring themselves sexual intercourse, that is, of not being in the position of being suddenly cut off from the possibility of intercourse." Such efforts can take the form of "prostitution fantasies, the desire to marry, and the wish to be a man. Prostitution fantasies and marriage signify on this basis that there will always be a man available. The wish to be a man, or resentment against the male, derives in this connection from the idea that a man can always have sexual intercourse when he wants it."

Whatever "The Overvaluation of Love" may reveal about Horney's intimate life in Chicago, it marks a significant turning point in her oeuvre. Before "Overvaluation" her papers were either educational (written for non-analysts) or polemical. Her views were presented as counters or modifications or amplifications of the views of other psychoanalysts. But here we see evidence that she no longer feels the need to carefully place her ideas inside the framework of previous psychoanalytic writing. Despite the paper's length, there is only one reference to Freud, in a footnote. And of the three other analysts she cites—Melanie Klein, Wilhelm Reich, and Ernest Jones—two are mavericks.

Horney's thesis when she attempts to generalize about these patients is a variation on Freud and on her earlier emphasis on the little girl's disappointment. She contends that the underlying source of these women's difficulties is a particularly intense Oedipal disappointment in childhood at the hands of another woman, either an older sister or a particularly powerful mother. Though "defeat in relation to the father is . . . the typical fate of the little girl in the family situation," it results in these cases in "specific and typical consequences because of the intensification of the rivalry brought about by the presence of a mother or a sister who absolutely dominates the situation erotically or by the awakening of specific illusions on the part of the father or brother." Because of their childhood defeats these women suffer from deep feelings of inadequacy, feelings that they aren't normal either sexually or in other ways. They also harbor a sometimes murderous feeling of rage toward other women, whom they see as rivals to be brought low. As a result of their feelings of inadequacy and guilt (over their rage), they are unable to succeed in either love or work, where the same conflicts come into play. As these women age, life "seems increasingly to lack meaning, and gradually bitterness develops because these persons necessarily lose themselves more and more in their twofold self-deception. They think that they can be happy only through love, whereas, constituted as they are, they can never be, while on the other hand they have an ever-diminishing faith in the worth of their abilities."

Horney's generalizations about these thirteen women patients often seem forced. One suspects they have been grouped together as part of a "series," despite their differences, in order to satisfy the Chicago Institute's research goals. And yet, even though she has lumped the patients together, she writes descriptively of them in a way that allows us to hear their separate voices and to identify with them. The long-standing and deep "anxiety as to whether they are 'normal,'" she writes, often takes conscious form as "the conviction that the patient is ugly and therefore cannot possibly be attractive to men." The conviction is "quite independent of whatever the actual facts may be; it may be found, for example, even in girls who are unusually pretty. The feeling is referred to some real or imaginary defect—straight hair, large hands or feet, too stout a figure, too large or small a stature, their age, or poor complexion. These self-criticisms are invariably associated with a deep feeling of shame." One patient, for instance, "fasted for weeks because her brother had remarked that her arms were too fat." Often in such cases dress plays an important role, "yet without any permanent success, since doubts invade this sphere as well and make it a perpetual affliction. It becomes unendurable not to have articles of dress match perfectly, and the same if a dress makes the wearer look stout, or if it seems too long or too short, too plain or too elegant, too conspicuous, too youthful, or not modern enough. Granting that the matter of clothes is of importance to a woman, there can be no question but that quite inappropriate affects here come into play—affects of shame, insecurity, and even anger."

Here, more than in previous papers, Horney displays the quality that would make her such an enormously popular writer and speaker in America: her knack for describing the experience of others in a way that is instantly recognizable to them, in a way that makes them feel, "She's talking about me." Sometimes, as in the passage above, she was drawing on her own experience.

According to her daughters, Horney was self-conscious about her looks. She felt she wasn't pretty and disliked having her picture taken for that reason. Once when she was vacationing with Renate in Italy she became so ashamed of her corrective shoes that she didn't want to go into a luxury hotel to ask for a room. At other times, however, Horney demonstrates her ability to empathize with patients whose experience differs from her own, as when she writes of these women that "they expect, without being aware of it, to achieve distinction from the very outset—to master the piano, for example, without practice, or to paint brilliantly without technique, to achieve scientific success without hard labor, or to diagnose correctly heart murmurs and pulmonary sounds without training. Their inevitable failure they do not ascribe to their unreal and excessive expectations, but regard it as due to their general lack of ability." Such passages show Horney taking time and space merely to observe and describe, without binding her observations so tightly as before to theoretical argument.[63]

In many ways "The Overvaluation of Love" might be said to be Horney's first American paper. It is the longest paper—by far—

that she ever wrote. In part this may have been because it was written for a new American journal, the *Psychoanalytic Quarterly,* which fostered longer articles. But whatever the reason, the greater length allows for greater elaboration. Her discussion of women's deeply buried fears about masturbation, for instance, grows here from the brief allusions of previous papers to seven paragraphs of richly textured clinical exploration. Her writing has a new expansiveness, as though the wide-open spaces of America had allowed her to breathe more freely and range more widely. And it reflects America's pragmatic bias, placing greater emphasis on what is observed and less on theory to explain it. It refers less to precedent than do previous papers, in a country where precedent is valued less. All in all, "The Overvaluation of Love" suggests that Horney was starting to feel the effects of her new surroundings.

At the same time, events in Germany were making it increasingly clear that the "home" she had known there was disappearing forever. In June of 1933 the American journalist Dorothy Thompson described the movement toward *Gleichschaltung* (bringing everything into line) which had taken over in Germany during the first three months of National Socialism. She wrote in the *Saturday Evening Post:*

> The wave rolls forward, bringing everyone into line. Teachers are wanted for the new Spartan state. Out with everyone who believes in "humanitarianism." Whipping is reintroduced into the schools; dueling is restored in the universities, not to the position it had before the war, when it was tolerated but not legalized, but to the position it enjoyed centuries ago, and at venerable Heidelberg the students can boast that a duel was attended by the rector and municipal authorities for the first time in 500 years! German children must learn how to stand punishment; the new order is for those who can command and who can obey.[64]

Under the circumstances America was an attractive alternative. In January of 1933, in the Federal District Court in Chicago, Karen Horney filed a "Declaration of Intention" to become an American citizen. And in the fall of 1933, after a vacation in Switzerland with all three of her daughters, she returned not only with Renate but also with Marianne, who had just completed her classroom medical studies and planned to do her clinical work at the University of Chicago. Only Brigitte, deeply involved in her acting career, stayed behind.

The second year in Chicago was much happier than the first.

The first year's apartment, according to Renate, had been expensive and had had a "cold, impersonal, pseudo-elegance."[65] Karen and her daughters found a nicer apartment this time, on Lake Shore Drive and so close to the water that on some days the spray of waves reached their windows on the second floor. Marianne and Renate, who had always loved the water, often swam from the rocks out in front of their building. Even though Marianne quickly became absorbed in her medical studies at the university, her presence made Renate's life less lonely. "With the three of us and a nice German housekeeper," Renate recalls, "we had, again, a real home, a family life with fun and warmth. It now felt good to come home, for someone would be there. We had many guests, good, witty conversational dinners."[66] At the same time Renate began to find a place for herself at school; the actress Celeste Holm became her best friend, and the two of them triumphed in a school production of *Cradle Song*.

Before long Karen and her daughters felt ready to sample some typically American luxuries. They bought a car, a secondhand Chrysler with wire-spoke wheels, so they could get out to the dunes on weekends. Marianne and Renate learned to drive it and got their licenses. Karen managed to get her license too, but her daughters insist it was only because she played psychiatrist during the driver's test and helped the examiner with his problems. Despite her adaptability in other areas, Karen Horney somehow never caught on to the rules of the road. Years later, according to Brigitte, she still hadn't learned to use the rear-view mirror.

Karen also invested in stocks that year, on the advice of friends. She bought a small number of shares of Wrigley's chewing gum, since all America seemed to be chewing it, and of a cookie company called National Biscuit. Renate, who knew where to look in the paper, followed the stocks and reported on their progress to her mother. The chewing gum turned out to be a good investment, as expected, but National Biscuit kept going down. Finally one day Karen asked Renate to go to the corner store and buy some of National Biscuit's cookies. The very next day, magically, the stock went up. "So we decided all one had to do was eat the stuff."

With a maid in the house and the exams behind her, Karen had more time for entertaining. Dorothy Blitsten remembers her as a "generous hostess" who "set a good table."[67] After December of 1933, when Prohibition was repealed, it was even possible to serve wine, which would have added to Horney's enjoyment, since she enjoyed drinking. And since Chicago was becoming a mecca for midwesterners and European refugees interested in psychoanalysis, there were plenty of interesting people to spend evenings with. A number of psychiatrists from other American cities came on weekends to study at the institute. Karl and William Menninger both came regularly from their family's clinic in Topeka, another psychiatrist came from Denver, another from Baltimore. Through the Blitzstens, Horney met Harry Stack Sullivan, who had done original work on an "interpersonal" theory of psychiatry.

The new friends who were most stimulating to Horney's thinking during this period came not from psychiatry but from other fields, especially the social sciences. The importance of the social milieu had been a theme in Horney's writing beginning with her earliest papers on women. But in the Chicago period the papers began to reflect her new appreciation of sociology and anthropology as disciplines. "The Overvaluation of Love" begins and ends with a discussion of "sociological" (a word she uses repeatedly and for the first time) factors. She notes, for instance, that from the "sociological standpoint" women who try to develop their abilities must struggle against not only "external opposition" but also "resistances within themselves" created by the traditional idea of woman as "exclusively sexual."[68]

Even during her first, difficult year in Chicago, Horney showed an increased interest in social factors. That first fall she led a series of discussions at the Institute on group phenomena, which included lectures on culture patterns, delinquency, and the psychology of dress. The sociologist Harold Lasswell, who gave a lecture, "Historical Materialism from the Psychoanalytic Point of View,"[69] became a friend.[70] Horney also met and talked with Margaret Mead.[71] But the person who had the most important influence on her work during this period, and for years afterward, was Erich Fromm. Fromm had come to psychoanalysis from philosophy, but his writing and thinking were always grounded in social and historical realities.

Karen Horney had known Erich Fromm and his wife, Frieda Fromm-Reichmann, in Berlin, where all three had studied psychoanalysis. Fromm had been analyzed by Hanns Sachs (it sometimes seems impossible that Hanns Sachs was only one person) and had practiced analysis in Berlin, beginning in 1930. In 1933, when he visited Chicago as a guest lecturer, his friendship with Horney, who was fifteen years older than he was, intensified. Over the next decade it is impossible to sort out Fromm's influences on Horney from her influences on him in the writing they each produced. But a small example illustrates their closeness. The two papers Fromm published in 1933 concerned a three-volume work of scholarship by an anthropologist named Robert Briffault.* That same year Horney cited Briffault's work, which focused on matriarchal societies, in the opening paragraphs of "The Overvaluation of Love." Obviously she and Fromm were sharing reading, as she and Oskar had many years before. It was during the Chicago years that Fromm and Horney's intellectual relationship deepened into a romantic one.

It may have been the company of Fromm and other social scientists that inspired Horney to deliver "The Problem of Feminine Masochism" at the midyear meeting of the American Psychoanalytic Association, in December of 1933, in Washington, D.C. The paper, written in her old polemical style, was a forceful critique of psychoanalytic methods of deduction, particularly as applied to women. She addressed herself primarily to two papers on female masochism: a 1929 paper by Helene Deutsch entitled "The Significance of Masochism in the Mental Life of Women" and a 1932 paper by Sandor Rado, "Fear of Castration in Women." Deutsch argues in her paper that "turning in the direction of masochism is part of the woman's anatomical destiny." Deutsch dates this inevitable turn toward masochism from the time of the little girl's realization that her clitoris doesn't measure up to boys' penises. "In place of the active urge of the phallic tendencies, there arises the masochistic phantasy: 'I want to be castrated,' and this forms the erotogenic masochistic basis of the feminine libido."[72] Rado, in a much longer paper, placed greater emphasis on the particular moment when the little girl "catches sight of a penis." "From her emotional chaos," Rado writes, "emerges the strident desire: 'I want it!' which is followed immediately in fantasy by, 'I have it.' Then comes the humiliating reflection, 'But I haven't';—this knowledge produces severe psychic pain, and terminates in something like a paralysis of feeling." The bulk of Rado's long paper is a catalogue of forms of "genital masochism" which result from this traumatic realization.[73]

In her paper at the Washington meeting Horney took issue not with the description of masochistic phenomena, which she conceded may occur, but with Deutsch's and Rado's claims of univer-

---

The Mothers: A Study of the Origins of Sentiments and Institutions (New York: Macmillan, 1927).

sality. "When it is claimed . . . that the desire for masculinity is not only a dynamic factor of primary order in neurotic females, but in every human female, independent of individual or cultural conditions, one cannot but remark that there are no data to substantiate this claim. Unfortunately little or nothing is known of psychically healthy women, or of women under different cultural conditions, due to limitation of historical and ethnological knowledge."

Horney continues to hammer away at the methodology: "As there are no data about frequency, conditioning, and weight of the observed reactions of the little girl to the discovery of the penis, the assumption that this is a turning point in female development is stimulating, but can scarcely be used in a chain of proof." Deutsch's claim that masochism is "psychobiologically necessary in all women" is "unconvincing." And Rado's theory that the little girl's sight of the penis is so humiliating that she forswears the pleasure of clitoral masturbation doesn't square with everyday experience. "It would imply, for instance, that a man who thought Greta Garbo more attractive than other women, but had no chance of meeting her, would as a result of the 'discovery' of her superior charms lose all pleasure in having relations with other women available. . . . The principle applied by Rado is certainly not the pleasure-principle, but might better be called the greediness-principle." In sum, Rado and Deutsch have both been guilty of "unwarranted generalization from limited data." If generalizations are to be made, they must be made from research that takes "social conditioning" into account. Woman is stereotyped as "weak, emotional"; she "enjoys dependence, is limited in capacities for independent work and autonomous thinking." And these qualities are rewarded by men, who prefer such women. In short, "In our culture it is hard to see how any woman may escape becoming masochistic to some degree, from the effects of the culture alone." She ends with the assertion that "the importance of anatomical-psychological-psychic factors has been greatly overestimated by some writers on this subject."[74]

Despite the merits of Horney's arguments, they do not seem to have been weighed judiciously at the Washington meetings, largely because Sandor Rado was in attendance. Rado was, by many accounts, a man with a sharp tongue and a quick temper, and he apparently reacted angrily to Horney's criticism of his paper. His clash with Horney created what A. A. Brill, the aging founder of the New York Society, described as a "disagreeable spectacle." The argument fanned the flames of a factional battle that was already under way in American psychoanalysis.

On one side were the defenders of orthodoxy, led by Sandor Rado and the New York Psychoanalytic. On the other side was the eclectic group, led by William Alanson White and the Baltimore-Washington Institute and cheered on by Harry Stack Sullivan, formerly with the Baltimore-Washington group but by then in New York. Horney was undoubtedly moving toward the eclectic camp —where her sympathies would naturally lie—even before the Washington meeting. After the Washington meeting the lines hardened. As A. A. Brill reported to Ernest Jones in London, Rado was determined to block official recognition of the Baltimore-Washington group, while "the 'Americans' of the Baltimore-Washington and some of our own group are talking seriously of taking steps to have Rado deported. I am not taking them very seriously, but the feeling is very high against him."[75]

Ernest Jones, then president of the International Psychoanalytic Association, was having some difficulty grasping the ins and outs of what he called the "American Analytical Civil War" from across the Atlantic. He asked Brill, who stood somewhat above the fray, to try to explain. "You would help if you would let me know anything about the source of this extraordinary hostility to Washington," Jones wrote Brill. "What are the personal foci?"[76]

Brill replied with a long letter in which he dated the hostility from the 1933 midyear meeting, at which "Rado noticed that Horney was very friendly with the B-W [Baltimore-Washington] group, or to be more precise with Sullivan, Hadley [a prominent member of the Baltimore-Washington group], and with Blitzsten of the Chicago group." Apparently "during a committee meeting Rado and Horney clashed, and Blitzsten, Sullivan and the other members of the Chicago and [Baltimore-Washington] groups voted against Rado. Rado then ran away from the meeting... and since then he is morbidly antagonistic to Horney and her friends."[77]

The fighting in the American Psychoanalytic Association had repercussions in Chicago, where tensions had already developed between Alexander and Horney. Lionel Blitzsten had been antagonistic to Alexander almost from the start, even though he had been in analysis with him for a time in Berlin. Increasingly, as time went on, Horney sided with Blitzsten against Alexander. Dorothy Blitsten remembers her coming over in the evening to rant and rave about Alexander. Hovering in the wings was Harry Stack

Sullivan, whom Horney liked and who wrote encouraging Blitz-sten in his fight against those who "feel that the somewhat bovine Franz [Alexander] should sit on the throne of America." Sullivan disliked the pretensions of the Europeans, who "are principally occupied in the spinning of a dense scholastic web that will give them the position of illuminati by isolating them as a foreign-language group from the eroding influences of fair criticism on the level of the common psychiatrical herd."[78]

Early in 1934 Horney decided, for a number of reasons, to leave Chicago for New York. The murmuring about Horney's seduc-tion of a candidate had probably created some discomfort. Further, the politics of the "American Analytical Civil War" contributed to her decision—although going to New York was walking into the mouth of the lion. Indeed, Sandor Rado enlisted Brill in an effort to keep her from coming. But the most important reason for her leaving was undoubtedly the anger that had grown up between her and Franz Alexander.

Alexander provided an official-sounding explanation of the breakup in an account of the early years of the Institute in *The Western Mind in Transition:*

> The only major strife developed in relationship to Dr. Karen Horney, whom I had invited from Berlin to become my associate in the direc-tion of the Institute. I knew her abilities from Berlin and admired her independent thinking. I did not know, however, the deeply rooted resentment she harbored against Freud.... Horney's resentment against Freud expressed itself in her attempts to discredit some of his most fundamental contributions, with the ambitious goal of revising the whole psychoanalytic doctrine, a task for which she was not fully prepared. She had excellent critical faculties but did not succeed in supplying anything substantially new and valid for what she tried to destroy.[79]

This dismissal from on high, however, can hardly be the whole story. According to Leon Saul, Alexander was angry at Horney for more personal reasons. For instance, she rarely spoke up at the lunch meetings when is research on gastrointestinal disorders was discussed, but word got back to him that she was making critical remarks about it to people outside the institute. Saul's theory was that she wouldn't have clashed with Alexander if she had worked through her angry feelings toward her father in her analysis with Abraham. But since she hadn't, she was bound to gravitate to "men who were hostile to strong men, like Lionel Blitzsten."[80]

According to Dr. Lucia Tower, who went to a farewell party at Horney's apartment just before she left town, Horney felt deeply sympathetic to Lionel Blitzsten and indeed told Tower that she felt "guilty" about leaving him behind to fight the battle with Alexander on his own.[81] And according to Dorothy Blitsten, Horney and Lionel Blitzsten had legitimate reasons for their anger at Alexander: his research was careless, and he allowed wealthy lay people without training too much of an inside role in the Institute. But, Dorothy Blitsten added, "I think she probably would have left anyway because, if you want to know what I think of Karen Horney, I think that in no way could she ever remain second in command anywhere."[82]

New York

1934–52

13

New York Energy

Soon after she arrived in New York, in the spring of 1934, Karen Horney filled out the application for membership in the New York Psychoanalytic Institute. Conscientiously, in carefully printed letters, she listed the German universities where she had studied, the Berlin hospitals where she had worked, the licensure exams she had passed, the analyses she had undergone. Only when the form asked for the names of her supervisors did she show impatience. "As long as the institution of supervised analyses exists—since 1920—I have *done* supervising work," she wrote. To the request for a list of training courses "in detail," she responded: "As long as psychoanalytic training courses exist, I have *given* courses, such as lectures on technique, case-seminars, lectures on feminine psychology, etc."[1] Horney's brusque reply was understandable: she had more experience than any one of the analysts who had devised the application form. Why should she have to recite the details of her analytic education for their benefit? Besides, as her response makes clear, the first teachers, herself among them, could have no teachers.

At the same time this very first encounter between Karen Horney and the official New York Psychoanalytic is a portent of the tug-of-war to come. On one side we have Karen Horney, impatient with formalities, temperamentally opposed to proving herself

277

by providing a long list of credentials. They should *know* who she is without having to be told. On the other side we have the education committee of the New York Psychoanalytic, guardians of Freudian orthodoxy against interlopers of every stripe. Some of its members have direct ties to Freud from days in Vienna. All of them see the New York Institute, the first to be established in the United States, as the standard bearer for all others on their side of the Atlantic. As increasing numbers of Europeans arrive seeking membership, the committee has increased its vigilance, excluding non-M.D.'s from practice and casting a skeptical eye on anyone, even of Horney's stature, who has a reputation as a nonconformist. There are reasons for the rules, as the committee sees it, and the rules—as well as the committee—are owed respect. As Horney sees it, the committee owes *her* respect, and the devil take the rules.

Aside from this undercurrent of tension in her application there was little about Karen Horney's arrival in New York to suggest trouble to come. On the contrary, the New York years promised to be some of the happiest of her life. In the first place, there was a man in Horney's life, Erich Fromm, who was both expressive and intellectually exciting. Fromm came to New York the same year Horney did, and joined the faculty of the International Institute of Social Research, which had been transplanted from Frankfurt to Columbia University. It is possible that Horney chose to move to New York and brave the orthodox psychoanalytic climate because of Fromm. But this can be only a conjecture, since no correspondence between Fromm and Horney has survived. Friends from the early New York days, however, remember them as constant weekend companions. The psychologists Ernest and Anna Schachtel, who arrived in New York a year later, spent many weekends with Fromm and Horney and traveled with them to Lake Tahoe, to Monhegan Island, and later to Horney's country house in Croton.[2] And Karen Horney's first two books, written during the early New York years, are laden with references to Fromm's works, published and unpublished. Some whispered that Horney was getting all her ideas from Fromm. The exchange, however, was anything but one-sided.[3] The two were intertwined, emotionally and intellectually, in a relationship that must have fulfilled, perhaps for the first time in Horney's life, the dream of a marriage of minds, which she had envisioned in her letters to Oskar thirty years before.

And then there was New York itself, a city almost as lively and cosmopolitan as Berlin. Right away, with the help of Renate, who came along to get her settled, Karen managed to find an apartment in the Essex House, overlooking Central Park, which nearly replicated the location of her last apartment in Berlin, at the edge of the Tiergarten. New York, in fact, was becoming more like Berlin all the time, as more and more Jews, along with some non-Jews, fled Germany. Beginning in 1934, New York had its own German-language newspaper, the *Aufbau*. The Upper West Side was filling up with Viennese coffeehouses, and across town on the Upper East Side, in Yorkville, it was possible to choose among several German-language movie houses, to buy German books and Christmas ornaments, and to read German papers over a slice of Sacher torte at the Café Geiger. Increasingly, as Hitler's threats became policies, the intellectuals of Weimar Germany and Austria were arriving in New York. They were "a group of immigrants," as a *New Republic* writer observed at the time, "unlike any the world has seen before—individuals of such distinction that never, under ordinary circumstances, would they dream of transplanting themselves."[4]

In Chicago most of Karen's social life had been contained within the small psychoanalytic community. In New York, with Fromm at her side, she found non-analyst friends in the newly arrived German intelligentsia. Among them was the theologian Paul Tillich, a non-Jew who couldn't stomach Hitler and who had come to New York, with his wife, Hannah, at the invitation of the Union Theological Seminary. The Tillichs often got together with Karen for dinner at her apartment, since her analytic practice afforded her more luxury than they had. There was always very good wine, from a wine seller Karen had discovered on her corner, and carefully selected cheeses. They would talk about films and books and ideas, all in German of course. Karen, as Hannah Tillich remembers, was particularly interested in Paul Tillich's philosophical ideas: the two of them would argue at times, with Karen occasionally teasing "Paulus," as his friends called him, about his feelings of "ominipotence." More often, however, "she was the one who listened and drew out the other people."

The evenings were hardly so solemn as this suggests, however. One night, at the apartment of Paul and Marga Kempner, the socializing took a farcical turn. The Kempners, who had been wealthy in Berlin, were making the best of their greatly reduced circumstances in Manhattan. Marga Kempner, who was a descendant of the composer Felix Mendelssohn, told Hannah Tillich that she loved small houses "because she had only lived in large ones." Nonetheless, even in the Kempners' small apartment there were, as Hannah remembers, "a lot of Monets and Manets on the walls." Marga Kempner "had one thing she made—a chicken fricassee I think it was. She was not used to cooking, but she cooked this one thing very well."

On this particular evening the fricassee was supplemented by wine tasting, and the guests included not only Karen Horney and the Tillichs but the author of *All Quiet on the Western Front,* Erich Maria Remarque. All, but particularly Karen and Paulus, were getting quite drunk. Somehow or other the conversation came around to Salvador Dali, whom Remarque knew to be staying in New York at the time. When Hannah Tillich said she admired Dali and would like to meet him, Remarque insisted that they seek him out. So they all took a cab to a luxurious hotel and summoned Dali, who appeared looking very stiff and formal—and quite sober—in white tie. By that time Karen and Paulus were so thoroughly drunk they couldn't talk—every time they looked at each other, they went into paroxysms of giggling. Remarque and Hannah Tillich desperately tried to ignore them and make polite conversation. But Dali, understandably nonplussed, soon left their company. At that point Remarque shepherded the drunken party out of the hotel and hailed a police car to take them home. But the policeman must have found them insufferable too: he drove them only around the corner, where they all fell into a taxi.[5]

Paul Tillich, as this story suggests, was a new kind of theologian, and he and Hannah tended to shock their more staid colleagues at the Union Theological Seminary. They loved to wander in red light districts, spend evenings in Harlem honky-tonks, and, in general, break all the bounds of conventional morality. Hannah Tillich, in her memoir *From Time to Time,* writes of fulfilling her "dream" in the United States of bringing together four people (not including her husband) for sex.[6] Paul, for his part, was almost always having an affair or looking for one. Hannah Tillich is sure that he and Hannah Arendt were lovers and would not be surprised if he and Karen Horney were too on occasion.

And yet, although she suffered terrible jealousy with some of her husband's liaisons, Hannah Tillich never felt resentful toward Horney. "She took me as a friend," Hannah recalls, and listened with "beautiful, but invisible, attention." Even when she was "gay with men, she'd never forget the woman." Since Hannah was very shy, "she would bring me out, get me to participate in the conversation."[7] Once Hannah showed her some of her poems, and Karen singled out one she particularly liked, a poem about a woman enclosed in a crystal so that her lover can never see her whole but only refracted through the cut-glass surfaces.[8]

Karen had endeared herself to Hannah early on at a party the Tillichs gave on the roof garden of the Union Theological Seminary. The Tillichs' idea was to "reproduce the gay atmosphere of Frankfurt"[9] by turning the roof into a European café. "Paulus" had written a poem for every single guest, and he and Hannah had arranged paintings of them on the gray walls. But to Hannah's dismay, the "stiff and stuffy atmosphere" of Union, where "nobody smelled of anything,"[10] prevailed. Karen Horney, however, arrived wearing a Japanese kimono and a coolie hat, with a bottle of wine tucked under each arm. "It was a wonderful festive European style," Hannah remembers. "I loved her for that."[11]

Though it may not have been evident at the party, the Europeans were beginning to have an effect in New York intellectual circles. Uptown, the Institute of Social Research was providing a haven for such leftist thinkers as Max Horkheimer, who influenced Horney's work, Walter Benjamin, and Theodor W. Adorno, as well as Erich Fromm. But the locus of émigré activity which was to play a central role in Horney's New York development was a unique downtown institution called the New School for Social Research.

The New School had been conceived as a community of scholars, but by the twenties it had become, out of economic necessity, an unusually exciting center of adult education. Among the part-time lecturers were critic Lewis Mumford and behavioral psychologist John Watson, and, during a brief sojourn in the United States, Freud disciple Sandor Ferenczi. In 1933 the New School took on a new and vital mission. Using Rockefeller Foundation and other funds, New School president Alvin Johnson established what he called the University in Exile at the New School and recruited endangered European scholars to join its faculty.

From 1933 to 1944 between 1000 and 2000 European intellectuals settled in the United States. Of these the New School appointed 178—more than any other institution—to its faculty. Many of the appointees were social scientists who had had particular difficulty gaining entry to the U.S., partly because they tended to be, as the Rockefeller Foundation representative noted, "Jews or Social Democrats or worse."[12] Some, such as Hans Staudinger, had been high officials in the Weimar Social Democratic government before its collapse. A few, such as the German dramatist Erwin Piscator, were Marxists. Many others, including Gestalt psychologist Max Wertheimer and philosopher Hannah Arendt, were too original to be classified. Before and after the birth of the University in Exile (later called the Graduate Faculty), the New School was, according to faculty member Henry Pachter, "a place of constant experimentation and of complete freedom for teachers and students. We always had a house Communist . . . but we also had a house reactionary, a house mystic . . . and several other oddballs." The New School was so full of Europeans, Pachter remembers, "you had the impression that a correct English pronunciation would be conspicuous or improper." And yet it seemed likely to him that "a place so European is possible 'only in America'; it was endowed with the best of Europe without any of the drawbacks."[13]

The New School building, like its faculty, was a unique blend of American pluralism and European energy. Designed by Joseph Urban, a Viennese architect who worked in the international style, its flat, pale brick and glass façade shouted modernity, in startling contrast to the delicacy of the nineteenth-century row houses along Twelfth Street, in Greenwich Village. Inside the visitor encountered the powerful visions of Mexican muralist Jośe Clemente Orozco, who celebrated popular revolution, and American Thomas Hart Benton, whose murals documented life in America in the twenties.

It is hard to imagine an institution better suited to Karen Horney's temperament than the New School. And indeed the New School was to be her one unbroken affiliation. She began to teach there during her second year in New York at the invitation of board member (later dean) Clara Mayer and continued to give at least one course a year until her death. For the most part she gave evening lectures in the New School's adult-education program, but on at least two occasions she joined members of the Graduate Faculty for an interdisciplinary seminar that placed her in challenging company. The other participants were Hans Speier, a sociologist with literary interests, Kurt Riezler, a philosopher and diplomat who had been the architect of German foreign policy during World War I, and Max Wertheimer, the leading Gestalt psychologist and a critic of psychoanalysis. The seminar was supposed to address the relationship of psychology to sociology, but in fact it merely provided a forum for all four to present their ideas. It was, Hans Speier remembers, "quite an event. People came from as far away as Boston, very distinguished people." Some came "because they thought there would be fireworks," and indeed Horney and Wertheimer "did clash in a friendly way."

Speier remembers that Horney "held her own against Wertheimer, which wasn't easy," since he tended to be "intellectually aggressive." She would "consider what he said and translate it into her language. To what extent is it true in view of what I have experienced with my patients? That seemed to be her approach. There was a firmness about her which impressed me," and "a sort of down-to-earth quality which I personally liked."[14]

Had Karen Horney stayed in Germany, her "down-to-earth quality," her ability to put complex ideas into simple language, might never have attracted much attention. There, for the most part, specialists talked to other specialists, in their own shared vocabulary. But in the U.S. there was a great thirst among laymen for knowledge of how to cope, how to succeed, or perhaps more often, how to survive the pressures of the rat race. As psychologist Marie Jahoda has observed, the ambitious young working-class man in Europe "knew that class structure was holding him back. . . . Society was at fault, not he. His counterpart in the States . . . believed in his heart that he had nobody to blame but himself. . . . Such a society, geared in times of good fortune and bad to individual self-appraisal, to the search for understanding of one's own fate, and no longer fully supported by the faith of its Puritan forefathers, is ready for any system of thought that explains man to himself."[15]

For people curious about psychoanalysis but overwhelmed by the unnecessarily technical language of many analysts, Horney's jargon-free delivery was refreshing. "Glory be to God," as one auditor wrote in his notes at the time, "I understand!"[16] Horney's daughter Marianne, who attended some of the New School lectures, recalls how carefully organized they were, "so that at the end of the lecture, she had completed a perfect circle, coming right back to her initial point."[17] Alexander Reid Martin, a psychoanalytic candidate, remembers that "her delivery was hard to follow until you got used to it," but that he was soon impressed by her "beautiful organization of material. I could take notes very logically and very easily."[18] Most important, Horney had a sort of genius for touching people. Listeners might come away from a lecture by Franz Alexander, for instance, feeling they had encountered a brilliant European. They came away from Horney lectures feeling they had encountered themselves.

Horney derived the power to touch people from empiricism. Just as, with Wertheimer, she had gone back to her patients for understanding, she continually used her clinical and personal experience as a touchstone, employing the particular as a road to the universal.

This had always been true of Horney's work, of course. Her experience as a woman had been the source of her first critical psychoanalytic paper. But after she came to the United States, she dwelt more and more on the descriptive. The tendency had been evident in "The Overvaluation of Love," the long paper about women's dependence she wrote in Chicago. In the New School lectures, and in the books that grew out of the lectures, she worked harder than ever at capturing the various attitudes and syndromes she had observed in herself and others. And as this brief passage from Horney's first book, *The Neurotic Personality of Our Time,* suggests, she was very good at it.

> If the outside world is felt to be hostile, if one feels helpless toward it, then taking any risk of annoying people seems sheer recklessness. For the neurotic the danger appears all the greater, and the more his feeling of safety is based on the affection of others the more he is afraid of losing that affection. Since his own relations to others are thin and fragile he cannot believe that others' relations toward him are any better. Hence he feels that annoying them involves the danger of a final break. . . . His extreme fear of making or even feeling accusations puts him in a special dilemma because, as we have seen, he is filled with pent-up resentment. In fact, as everyone knows who is acquainted with neurotic behavior, plenty of accusations do find expression, sometimes in veiled, sometimes in open and most aggressive forms.[19]

Observations such as this, grounded in experience, had an immediacy that engaged Horney's audiences. Of all the responses to Horney's lectures and subsequent books, the most frequent by far is self-recognition. "At times I felt she was looking directly at me, into me," as one listener put it. "She was describing *my* feelings and conflicts."[20] Or, "When I read her books, I recognized myself." Or quite frequently, "Reading Karen Horney got me through a terrible time in my life." Her ability to touch people made her enormously popular. Whenever she taught, even when her classes were held in the egg-shaped interior of the six-hundred-seat New School auditorium, the room was filled to overflowing.

Horney had quite a lot of white in her flyaway hair by that time, and her stocky five-foot-three frame couldn't have raised her much above the lectern. She smoked incessantly, sometimes puffing so frequently that it interfered with her speech. And yet those who heard her found her enormously attractive. "You know, she was not a beautiful woman," her friend Katie Kelman recalls, "but she was a *beautiful* woman. She was a little coy, she had a little of the actress in her. Her expression was so lively . . . her face was shining and she had wonderful hands, wonderful movements. . . . And everybody was just *hanging* on what she had to say. And standing applause. It was not just an *ordinary* talk, it was a very moving experience."[21]

There is something irresistible about her delivery, even as it is preserved on tape. What one notices first is the voice itself—a deep, round sound that resembles the middle range of a French horn. Her accent is obvious, but so is her care in getting the pronunciations right. For the most part she succeeds. Still, the inflection remains purely German, going up where English goes down. The overall effect is of a conscientious schoolgirl giving a class presentation, but in confident, womanly tones.

Charming as Horney's delivery was, however, the subsequent popularity of her books proves that her ideas had their own powerful attraction. *The Neurotic Personality of Our Time,* which came out in 1937, went through thirteen printings in a decade, and her next three books were equally popular. Paperback editions of her books, which began appearing in the 1960s, have sold over half a million copies.[22]

Horney's popularity with laymen seems to have come naturally to her—explaining psychoanalysis to the outside world had been one of her talents even in the early Berlin days. What was more difficult, for Karen Horney, was staying in the good graces of her psychoanalytic peers. And in that regard her peers at the New York Psychoanalytic Institute presented her with her most formidable challenge to date.

In many ways the New York Institute was the antithesis of the New School. The New School was full of Europeans operating in an atmosphere of American liberalism under the leadership of a midwesterner, Alvin Johnson. The Institute, in contrast, was controlled by Americans who were the first products of systematic European psychoanalytic training and who, as historian of psychoanalysis Nathan Hale has written, "burned with the gemlike flame of truth and discipline. The young American elite accepted the insistence on exclusively medical and psychiatric backgrounds, which of course had been their own. There were no laymen among them and, by comparison with Europe, few influences from the humanities or the social sciences."[23] As the Institute grew, the leadership became more formal and more hierarchical and the loyalty to Freud more fierce. Paradoxically, the New York Institute, under European-trained Americans, became more stereotypically German than the Berlin or Vienna institutes had ever been.

There were plenty of reasons for such an institute to regard Karen Horney with suspicion. In the first place, she was known to be involved with Fromm, a nonphysician who was practicing psychoanalysis. In addition, Horney had made a teaching arrangement with the Baltimore-Washington Society, whose eclecticism had caused the New York group to try to exclude it from the International Psychoanalytic Association. During her first two years in New York, Horney gave two series of lectures on technique at the Baltimore-Washington Society. What was more, after she came to New York Horney began to meet regularly for drinks or dinner with three former leaders of the Baltimore-Washington group— Harry Stack Sullivan, Clara Thompson, and William V. Silverberg—who had since settled in New York. Some of this group had begun meeting in speakeasies on Monday nights several years before Horney arrived in New York. On a whim of Sullivan's the group took to calling itself the "Zodiac," and members picked animal names. Sullivan was a horse, Silverberg a gazelle, Thompson, because of her love of cats, a puma, and Horney a water buffalo. Horney's association with the Zodiac group, insofar as it was known at the New York Psychoanalytic, was further proof of her nonconformist ways.

Perhaps the least controversial Zodiac member was William V. Silverberg, a New York–trained psychiatrist who had studied at the Berlin Psychoanalytic from 1928 to 1930 and had been analyzed there by Franz Alexander. Back in the States, he had been director of research at Sheppard and Enoch Pratt, a venerable psychiatric hospital in Baltimore, and a founding member of the Baltimore-Washington Institute before coming to New York.

Clara Thompson, the other woman in the group, was to be Karen Horney's partner in the struggle ahead at the New York Psychoanalytic. Thompson, eight years younger than Horney, had grown up outside of Providence, Rhode Island, the child of a self-made businessman and his devout Baptist wife. By the time she graduated from college she was resolving "to succeed in my fads and overcome my virtues"[24]—hardly a recipe for a conventional future. As a medical student at Johns Hopkins she was impressed by her encounter with one of the very earliest American-born women to take an interest in psychoanalysis, the psychologist Lucile Dooley. Later, a paper she delivered at Johns Hopkins led to a meeting with the man who was to influence her most profoundly, Harry Stack Sullivan.[25]

At Sullivan's suggestion, Clara Thompson traveled to Europe to undergo analysis with Ferenczi in the summers of 1928 and 1929 and again for longer periods from 1931 up until the time of Ferenczi's sudden death in 1933. Since Ferenczi was one of Freud's original circle, Thompson's analysis with him would once have ensured the respect of the Freudians in America. But in the last years of his life Ferenczi began to experiment with what he called "active technique," which involved showing affection to the patient, sometimes in physical ways, and which made a Ferenczi analysis a credential of dubious value in orthodox circles.

By far the most controversial of the Zodiac foursome was Harry Stack Sullivan. An Irish-American, Sullivan had not been analyzed in Europe—and may not have been analyzed at all in the strictest sense.[26] Although Sullivan considered himself to be a psychoanalyst, he had his own original and sometimes highly successful approach, particularly in the treatment of schizophrenics. William Silverberg remembers asking Sullivan to see a twenty-one-year-old schizophrenic patient of his one day at Sheppard Pratt. "Within five minutes that boy and Sullivan were talking sense. It was amazing. He had a sort of uncanny ability. I could have talked to this patient for months and got no further than we were on the first day."[27] Sullivan's "interpersonal" theory and method had an important influence on psychotherapy as well.

Despite his gifts, Sullivan's was an unpredictable personality. He had a biting wit and a sometimes violent temper, especially after a few drinks. His difficulties in handling money had on one occasion led him into bankruptcy. And his housemate for much of his life was a man considerably younger, whom he adopted, informally, after he managed to lead him out of a schizophrenic state. Karen Horney liked Sullivan's eccentricities. She was in the audience once when he confided to his listeners, "I am a schizophrenic." Afterward, according to another member of the audience, Horney spoke of how courageous Sullivan had been to say that.[28] But Sullivan was obviously the sort of person the New York Psychoanalytic, in its quest for respectability, preferred to keep at a safe distance.

If Horney's friends put her at a disadvantage in New York, so did her enemies, or, to be more precise, her enemy Sandor Rado. At this point the issues become secondary to personalities. Theoretically Karen Horney and Sandor Rado had every reason to be allies within the New York Psychoanalytic: both were unhappy with the Institute's strict orthodoxy, and both ultimately criticized classical analytic technique for similar reasons. But Rado had apparently never gotten over Horney's attack on his paper on female castration anxiety at the meeting of the American Psychoanalytic in 1933. He was so opposed to her coming to New York that he had asked A. A. Brill, the *éminence grise* at the New York Psychoanalytic, to try to prevent it.[29] Horney expected not just to belong but also to teach at the New York Institute. And since Rado was officially director of education there, his opposition mattered.

Of all the active members of the Institute, Sandor Rado was the only one who could claim roots almost as deep as Karen Horney's in the development of psychoanalytic education. Born in Hungary in 1890, Rado as a student in Budapest had first learned of Freud through a pamphlet by his fellow Hungarian Ferenczi. After he graduated from medical school he traveled to Berlin in 1922, where he underwent a year-long analysis with Karl Abraham. He soon joined Horney on the Institute faculty and was involved with her in drawing up standards for psychoanalytic training. Then in 1931 he was invited to New York by A. A. Brill, with the understanding that he would set up a New York Institute on the Berlin model.

By his own account Rado seems to have incurred envy and resentment wherever he went. When Freud invited him to edit the *International Journal,* he describes being envied by the Viennese. "On the one hand," he told an interviewer years later, "they kowtowed because that was the decision of Freud. On the other hand, they wanted to murder me. . . . The jealousy and envy of the Viennese increased as the significance of Berlin, as a center of psychoanalysis . . . increased. The lion's share fell on my head." When Rado decided to leave for the United States in 1931 and encouraged others to follow, he incurred the resentment of Freud, who "did not want to believe" that the Nazi threat was real.[30]

In Berlin and New York, Rado impressed many candidates as a lucid teacher of psychoanalytic theory. Alix Strachey, who worked with her husband, James, on translating Freud's works into English, found him an excellent teacher when she studied at the Berlin Psychoanalytic. "I think he's got a better grasp of the subject than Alexander, whose penchant for theory makes his views too schematic," she wrote home to her husband. "Rado manages to be theoretical & solid at the same time. And I think he's got a really inventive mind."[31] But Rado's tactlessness and short temper also earned him numerous detractors. One member of the education committee in New York, for instance, deplored his technique of "sticking a dagger into a topic and turning it in order to cause as much pain as possible."[32] Alexander, writing in *Psychoanalytic Pioneers,* described Rado as "terse, to the point, logical to the utmost, and often devastating. Although this did not contribute to universal popularity, even his enemies respected his brilliant cognitive abilities."[33]

Alexander knew whereof he spoke, since Rado had quarreled with him too. New York analyst Harmon Ephron remembers attending one Alexander-Rado debate that turned into comic opera. Rado—very short, balding, and feisty—delivered his paper and then ran for the door to catch a train. Alexander—bigger, broader, and smoother—rose to respond and quickly made a statement that infuriated Rado, by then halfway out the door. Rado ran back to the platform, refuted Alexander, and ran for the door again. Then Alexander made another provocative statement, and Rado ran back to the platform to rebut him once again. "Rado made about ten trips back and forth," Ephron remembers.[34]

By 1936, when Karen Horney wrote to the education committee announcing that she would like to teach, Rado was beginning to lose favor, both because of his aggressive style and because of his increasingly unorthodox ideas. Later on, this would have a complicated effect on Horney's position in the Institute. But in the beginning Rado's opposition might not have worked entirely to her disadvantage. However, the education committee had also had an opportunity by that time to hear Karen Horney speak for herself. Beginning early in 1936, Horney's name begins to appear regularly in the minutes of meetings, held monthly at the house on West 86th Street that served as the New York Society headquarters. She was listed among the discussants of papers by others, including Rado, and another important teacher, Herman Nunberg. And in the fall of 1936 she herself gave a paper entitled "The Problem of the Negative Therapeutic Reaction."

"The Problem of the Negative Therapeutic Reaction" was really a continuation of another paper, written two years before in Chicago, "Conceptions and Misconceptions of the Analytical Method." Taken together, these two papers on technique represent a major turning point in Horney's thinking. Indeed, they are the warning shots that signal her turning away from orthodox psychoanalysis in the last fifteen years of her life.

There were two major themes in Horney's dissent. The first was that orthodox psychoanalysis claimed to be universal when in fact it was culture-bound. This theme had been reinforced by her exposure to sociology after she arrived in the United States, but it had roots in her earliest papers on the psychology of women, in which she pointed out that Freud's ideas about female sexuality had less to do with anatomy than with the cultural dominance of males. The second theme, which emerges for the first time in a cohesive way in these papers, is that what are sometimes called "deep interpretations" (or "vertical interpretations," as she would call them in her second book, *New Ways in Psychoanalysis*), which connect the patient's present behavior with his childhood experiences, don't work. Here once again Horney's clinical and empirical orientation guides her. If psychoanalysis is primarily an intellectual pursuit, then these connections between early-childhood experiences and their adult transformations are the pot of gold. But if psychoanalysis is primarily a treatment, as Horney always believed it to be, then the connections are important only if they help the patient to change. Although the idea had been in the beginning that the patient's insight into his past led to change, Horney was finding that analysis was a far more complicated process, a process in which it was often more productive to address the present than the past.

As before, when she first voiced her dissent regarding female sexuality, Horney chose to "wrap her stone in cotton-wool" in the first of these two papers. She began by presenting a thumbnail sketch of the practice of psychoanalysis, as non-analysts were wont to see it:

> The psychoanalytic procedure is based on the free-association of the patient. The analyst is dependent on what the patient chooses to tell him. The analyst usually veils himself in silence ... and only now and then makes some wisecracks which he calls interpretations. These interpretations chiefly concern connections which the analyst constructs between present actions, attitudes and symptoms of the patient, and childhood experiences mainly of a sexual nature and supposedly radiating from the so-called Oedipus complex. The interpretations are of an arbitrary character both in content and sequence. There is no assurance of correctness and relevance and no guarantee against the analyst's power of suggesting thoughts alien to the patient. The analysis takes a

long time, the outcome is difficult to estimate, and there remains a secret or expressed doubt whether or not the benevolent interest of an understanding physician for the same length of time might not have led to the same result. Testing the procedure is only possible after having submitted to the same process oneself as in an initiation rite.

Slyly Horney goes on to say that while this might be an accurate description of early psychoanalysis, it is no longer the case. The truth is, however, that her sketch *does* describe the way many analysts continued to conduct psychoanalysis, as numerous patients of the period have attested. Her real quarrel is with this older style, and specifically with the "arbitrary.... content and sequence" of interpretations.

Horney postpones her most controversial point, however, until late in the paper, interjecting first a discussion of the efforts of others[35] to turn psychoanalysis into a "describable and teachable method." She stresses, with them, that the verbal material provided by free association is but one source of information in the analysis. Just as important, and less subject to distortion, is the analyst's direct observation of the way the patient relates to the analyst and responds to events in the analysis itself. Few of Horney's peers would have objected to the paper thus far. But then Horney introduces her own opinion that the analyst should stay for a very long while with the patient's attitudes in the present rather than try to relate them to events in childhood. "Interpretations which connect the present difficulties immediately with influences in childhood are scientifically only half truths and practically useless." To rush too early to connections between a patient's impersonal attitude toward the analyst, for instance, and angry feelings toward his mother is a mistake "for the simple reason that I do not know enough about implications of his relation to his mother."

Furthermore, such connections are simplistic. "It is useless for a patient who wants to have nothing to do with women to get the idea that this is because he was disappointed by his mother or intimidated by his father. It may be true but it would mean giving him the first and the last link in a chain with all intermediate links missing." And finally, such "deep interpretations" may "serve as an impediment to further understanding." In the case of a female patient, for instance, who was acting alternately seductive and hostile to the male analyst, Horney suggested that it was necessary first to understand what had led to her behavior in relation to the *analyst.* Only then could the analyst successfully explore the patient's past with her. "If one constantly proceeds this way, always analyzing only the immediate motives for the observable attitudes of the patient, one traces gradually the emotional causal chains which lead from the present symptoms to the earliest shaping influences in infancy."[36]

In "The Problem of the Negative Therapeutic Reaction," the first paper she presented before the New York Society, Horney arrived at the same conclusion but by a roundabout route. This time she took as her starting point a concept introduced by Freud, the "negative therapeutic reaction." This, as Horney explained, was not just any therapeutic failure but a particular paradox Freud had observed in certain treatments—"the fact that the patient may show an increase in symptoms, become discouraged, or wish to break off treatment immediately following an encouragement or a real elucidation of some problem, at a time, that is to say, when one might reasonably expect him to feel relief." At this point Horney took some pains to acknowledge (no doubt with her New York colleagues in mind) "the keenness and importance of Freud's observation." But whereas Freud took the "negative therapeutic reaction" as a poor prognosis for treatment, Horney saw it as a point of departure. What one must do, once again, was to stay with the reaction itself, and learn from it.

What made Horney's presentation different from most that would have been heard at the New York Society in 1936 was her emphasis on the surface reactions rather than on underlying structural or theoretical issues. Freud in his discussion of the negative therapeutic reaction ascribed it to an overdeveloped, punitive superego—an excessive sense of guilt that led the patient to impede his own progress. Horney didn't dispute Freud's conclusion. She just didn't deal with the question on that level. She didn't once use the words "ego" and "superego" in her paper, except in reference to the work of others.

When the analyst "either states clearly a problem of the patient's current difficulties or offers a partial solution of it, or throws light on hitherto incomprehensible peculiarities of the patient," the patient reacts first with relief and then in one of several negative ways. Patients may react competitively, seeking to belittle the analyst, for instance. Or they may take the interpretation as a great narcissistic blow, because their "self-esteem . . . rests on the shaky ground of (unconscious) grandiose illusions about their own uniqueness and therefore collapses like a card house at a light touch." Or they may react with anxiety or feel the interpretation as an accusation or a rejection.

Having discussed with some care the array of feelings underlying these reactions, Horney returns to the point she made in her Chicago paper: stay with the present.

> As long as the negative reaction persists I select out of the material offered by the patient those parts which I can relate to his reaction to the analyst, and interpret those only.... I refrain from making any construction of the past nor do I make direct use of one offered by the patient. The reason lies in the fact that *the attitudes we see in the adult patient are not direct repetitions or revivals of infantile attitudes, but have been changed in quality and quantity by the consequences which have developed out of the early experiences.*

This last assertion, which Horney chose to put in italics in the printed version of the paper, is clearly the one she felt most strongly about. She also knew, however, that it was controversial, since she hastened to add that "this procedure does not mean that I attribute less importance to childhood experiences than any other analyst."[37]

Horney's assurances notwithstanding, the suspicion lingered that Horney *did* attribute less importance to the Oedipus complex, if not to childhood in general, than her colleagues. There was something else in Horney's presentation too which must have made the society audience uneasy. Horney seemed to be ignoring Freud's theory of transference—that the patient transferred feelings onto the analyst that had first been experienced in relation to parents. If she didn't make these connections—that is, "You're feeling toward me the way you always felt toward your mother"—did that mean that she didn't believe in transference in the classical sense? And furthermore, why didn't she make use of psychoanalytic language? Why didn't she say "transference" once in the whole paper?

Eight years after Horney's presentation at the New York Society, the psychologist David Rapaport wrote in one of his penetrating essays on psychoanalysis that Karen Horney's discussion of the defenses had anticipated Anna Freud's influential book *The Ego and the Mechanisms of Defence*.[38] "Horney really was the one who, possibly somewhat earlier than Anna Freud, pushed the investigation of defense mechanisms to the fore," he wrote, "justifiably so, because the psychoanalytic method... obliges the analyst to investigate both the unconscious material the patient prevents himself from communicating and the defense mechanisms by which he chooses to prevent . . . such communication."[39] In 1936, however, Horney's heresies were more apparent to many of her colleagues than her vision.

14

"*The Neurotic Personality of Our Time*"

A few months after she gave the paper on the negative therapeutic reaction, Horney wrote to the chairman of the education committee announcing that she would like to give a series of lectures in the fall, "Changes in Analytical Technic [*sic*] and Their Theoretical Implications"—a five-hour course for advanced students and practicing psychoanalysts. She added, "I should also like to give a case seminar within the next year."[1] She was fifty years old when she wrote the letter, and she had been making the long train ride to Baltimore and Washington for two years to give similar courses. Even though the atmosphere was more congenial there, it must have been tiring and couldn't, at a charge of fifteen dollars per student, have paid her much of anything.[2] It may have been this, as well as her natural desire to be accepted, that made her want to teach in New York.

She followed up her request with a course outline and had a long telephone conversation with Rado about the course's contents. Nevertheless, when the education committee chairman, Adolph Stern, took her out to dinner, it was to inform her that her course was unacceptable. Horney took the rejection quietly at first. But in March of 1937, when she discovered that Rado was to teach a course entitled "Recent Developments in the Study of the Neuroses," she wrote Stern an irate letter.

She was "amazed," she wrote, to see an announcement of such a course by Sandor Rado. "As you will remember, I had announced a series of lectures on technique in the Fall," which was not accepted for the reason that "students should first get acquainted with Freud's views. Now, Dr. Rado gives a course, which from what I gather . . . from the critical views Dr. Rado has presented in his lectures this year, is very similar to what I had in mind. . . . It seems to me to be a strange kind of procedure, to refuse this course at the beginning of the year and to accept a similar course which is offered much later." She concluded: "I should be glad to have you explain this procedure to me."[3]

Stern responded with a telephoned apology, which only partly satisfied her. "As far as personal implications," she wrote a few weeks later, "I consider the matter to be straightened out by your having told me you had forgotten my having announced a course on technical questions and that you felt sorry about it." But, she continued, she had discussed the course with others on the committee as well. "As an analyst, I must ask for reasons for such a collective amnesia." She ended by asking Stern to bring both her letters to the attention of the entire education committee and "to ask them to take an open stand as to the question of my giving lectures at the Institute. If there are reasons why my lectures are not considered desirable these should be stated frankly and I should accept them though I should be sorry as I feel, as do some of the students that I have something constructive to offer. If, as I hope, the attitude of the Committee is a positive one, I should be glad to consider the difficulties as misunderstandings, liable to happen in any organization and to co-operate."[4]

Horney's reference to her popularity with students may well have been calculated. In the late thirties the institute suddenly found itself inundated with young psychiatrists seeking analytic training. In 1937 there were seventy candidates in training at the New York Institute. Four years later there were a hundred and ten. The institute had changed within a few years from a small coterie of followers to a sizable training institution. It had been possible in the early years to rely almost entirely on the talents of Sandor Rado. But even if Rado had continued to adhere to classical ideas, he couldn't effectively teach such large numbers. Horney was well aware that other members—some with far less than her ability— had begun filling in.

At the time of her protest to the education committee Horney was already supervising eight students once a week and had two other students in training analysis. These students, as Horney noted in her letter, were impressed. And in a place as insular and given to talk as the Institute, word gets around. It couldn't have escaped the committee's notice that Horney was a talented clinician and a better teacher than most on the faculty. As for credentials, she had a background in psychoanalysis second to none. Two months after her protest the education committee responded by giving her a rather condescending pat on the back. The education committee, Stern wrote, "regrets the annoyance resulting from the misunderstandings" and wishes to "assure you that at no time was there in the minds of any of the Committee any question of the value of your scientific achievements."[5] The next fall they relented further and invited her to teach. The subject was "Narcissistic Phenomena," less sweeping than her proposed subject, "Changes in Analytic Technique." The following spring, however, she was invited to teach a clinical course in which she would have a chance to discuss her somewhat unorthodox ideas on technique as well. Horney had won the day.

While Horney's popularity with students may not have been the only consideration, it was an important weapon and one she continued to use in her struggles with the education committee. The committee would complain that Horney's students too often became devotees, that, in the words of one classical analyst, "she never made it possible for them to work out the negative aspects of their transference relationships to her."[6] But what the committee failed to acknowledge, and what some of these candidates still testify to many years later, is that Horney owed much of her popularity to others' rigidities. Alexander Wolf, one of Horney's supervisees during these years, remembers feeling her "interest in my development as well as the patient's.[7] She worked continually, warmly and empathically with my counter-transference to a patient I was treating."[8] One time, when the young Dr. Wolf blushed during supervision, "she went into it in a kindly way."[9] Although he later returned to a more orthodox point of view, Wolf continues to believe that "in many ways she was more helpful to me than my own personal psychoanalyst.[10] She helped me in supervising my own candidates."[11] Another supervisee, Judd Marmor, remembers that he was "studiously silent" with patients, following "the model of Sigmund Freud," before his work with Karen Horney. She taught him that "analysis required more" than merely collecting information from the patient. "The way we react is an important part." Horney "gave me freedom to be warm without being seductive. . . . I feel deeply indebted to [her] for opening my eyes to this."[12]

For candidates who had been in treatment with very silent analysts Horney's method was often a great relief. Dr. Alexander Reid Martin, who had been in analysis briefly with Paul Schilder in Washington before coming to New York to undergo training analysis with Horney, remembered that "in analysis, she said very little," but that was still more than Schilder had said. "I saw him seven days a week, an hour each day, for three months. Schilder said . . . about five words the whole three months." In an Oral History Colloquium of the American Academy of Psychoanalysis some years ago Dr. Martin provided the best picture we have of Horney's analytic style. "She really listened," Martin remembers. "This was her cardinal characteristic. You knew she listened, and you knew she wanted to hear. And you felt you had something worth listening to." After Martin had been lying on the couch in Horney's office for "two or three months" he "dared to look around to see her. And there she was, very intent."

Early in the analysis, he remembers, he had a question about which courses to take at the institute.

> There was a brief pause, and she said quite thoughtfully, "You are asking for something. And it might be helpful first of all for you to find out how you have felt about asking for anything." This brought up many memories and fears about asking, and how jittery and concerned I had felt in the past, and more immediately in asking for her advice. I realized that I had deliberated for days, and I became aware of the great effort involved in making the request, wondering how to phrase it, was I presumptuous, etc., etc. Through these experiences and without the terms ever being mentioned I came to know and acquire a feeling for what was meant by manifest and latent content.

Even though "she never gave explicit reassurance," she would behave in a way that was "implicitly reassuring." Once Martin was "deeply and outwardly moved in vividly recalling a memory of being mocked and teased by my older cousins, when I was around seven or eight years old. After listening intently to my sobbing distress, she said, 'That was very hard on a little boy.' I thought of the effect of this afterward, and it seemed to me that the fact that she expressed this sympathy not for me in the present, but for me as a 'little boy,' kept the sympathy appropriately localized and therefore acceptable."

Sometimes when Martin would "report some elaborate, complex, intricate, involved experience," Horney would "point to something simple and obvious that I had overlooked. This happened again and again." Horney was good at stripping events of their disguises—"'embroidery' was her word"—and "getting down to what she so many times said, 'down to the bottom.'" Horney never told Martin what to do. But

> she kept reminding me, usually by way of questions, and she had a phenomenal memory. She would remind me that I was developing some theme or pattern by saying, "Isn't this something the same as you were talking about yesterday, or last week?" She would keep me working on the same theme in the present and would point to something similar from my past history, and I would make the connection. She had a feel for the variations on a theme.... And when I caught on, and began to realize what I was in the habit of doing, she would grunt —sometimes quite emphatically. For me, it was an indication that she was sharing my satisfaction and excitement and enthusiasm ... these grunts were reassuring.[13]

Had Horney confined her innovations to supervision and analysis, she might never have come into conflict with the education committee. Many analysts, Freud among them, were known to be much freer in their analytic work than they claimed to be in public. But as Horney's letter of protest to the education committee attests, she had changed since she arrived in the United States, and particularly since she had come to New York. In the past she would have been just as angered by such a slight, but she might not have confronted the authorities about it. Rather she would have grumbled and sniped ineffectually, as she had in her letters to Groddeck about the hypocrisy at the Berlin Institute. But Karen Horney was no longer content with the minor role she had played in her first fifteen years in psychoanalysis. She had discovered that there was little room in psychoanalysis for what could be called the loyal opposition. Her attempts to be a critic from within, taking Freud to task for his views on female sexuality, had been written off by Freud and forgotten by nearly everyone else. Nor was she content to be called, as she so often was, "a good clinician." Everyone knew this was a subtle put-down, often applied to females with "good instincts" but no intellectual rigor.

Karen had always had great dreams for herself, even in her days
at the Convent School. But New York, and the events in her life
after she arrived there, had begun to make her feel that more was
possible. She felt loved, she felt successful, and this in turn made
her feel expansive and brave. In her lectures at the New School she
had already begun to lay the foundation for her own alternative
psychoanalytic system. Although she might have denied it, by the
time she began teaching classes at the Institute she was also starting
to do what Freud had done thirty years earlier. Through her dis-
course with younger analysts and candidates she was beginning to
build a following.

In some ways Horney was her own best argument for the important effects of culture on personality. It had been America's
passion for self-improvement that made her such a popular lecturer at the New School. In America, she had discovered, it was
possible to be famous without being considered a charlatan (except
perhaps at the New York Psychoanalytic).

Popularity had also brought financial rewards. Horney had
never given much thought to money. In fact her secretaries over
the years despaired over her carelessness. But as a result of the
New School lectures and the books that followed, people of means
were seeking out Horney for treatment. She found herself able to
afford things that hadn't been possible since the Zehlendorf days.
She could buy good wine, which she loved. She could afford a
housekeeper and a secretary. She could afford to travel. And, perhaps most important of all to her way of thinking, she could afford
real estate.

She had long had a passion for owning houses, particularly ones
with spectacular views. Before she left Berlin she had bought a
house high on a hill near Locarno, in Switzerland. There is disagreement among her daughters on just when and why she made
this purchase. Brigitte remembers spending time at the house
while the family was still living in Zehlendorf. Renate is sure that
it was a last-minute purchase that made no sense at all and used up
all her mother's available funds just before she left for the United
States. In any case, it was a very beautiful, run-down Italian farm-
house, surrounded by vineyards, with a spectacular view of the
valley. The house did provide a haven for Oskar Horney for a
time, after his business failures had left him in a bad way. But since
it was located up a steep road, a good distance from town, it had
never been a very practical investment for a woman without a car.

Sometime after Karen came to the United States the house was sold.

In New York, Karen began to think again not just about owning but about building. She asked the architect Albert Mayer, brother of New School dean Clara Mayer, to draw up plans for an ambitious remodeling project involving two apartments on the twenty-sixth floor of 240 Central Park South, just a few doors down the street from her apartment in the Essex House. Combining the two apartments would allow her to have her office and home in the same place. (Until then she had been seeing patients at an office on East 76th Street.) She and Mayer devised a plan that would allow patients to come in by one door, which brought them into her dining room, and leave by another, without seeing each other. And of course from that height there would be long views out over Central Park.

Karen hadn't yet moved into her new apartment when she began planning another project with Mayer: a small country house, about thirty miles north of the city along the Hudson River, in Croton. Renate, who spent Christmas with her at the Essex House in 1938, remembers how excited she was about both these undertakings. Not long after that she moved into the remodeled apartment. And in the summer of 1940 she spent her vacation at her new house in Croton. The house sat high on a hill on a large plot that stretched down almost to the river. One wall was taken up with a huge fireplace, and there was a picture window with a spectacular view of the Hudson River Valley. With the declaration of war in 1941 and the gas rationing that followed, however, it grew more and more difficult to make the trip to the Croton house. Eventually she decided to sell it. But there was never a time, for the rest of her life, when Karen wasn't in the process of buying, selling, or enjoying the ownership of a place in the country.

Some years earlier, in 1935, Karen had addressed the National Federation of Business and Professional Women's clubs on the subject "Women's Fear of Actions." We women are too concerned, she told the group, with "what is feminine and what is not. . . . We have to realize that we demand something as human beings— demands for independence, development of potentialities do not concern womanhood, but human personality."[14] There is perhaps no more potent symbol of triumph over conventional restraints on women than the ownership of property. In the Germany of Karen

Horney's childhood the vote was denied to all women except a few who had inherited property. In America, then and even now, a woman who owns property without a partner has achieved an unusual measure of financial and psychological independence. Buying houses was one more manifestation of Karen Horney's newly optimistic and ambitious frame of mind.

Another gratifying development during the New York years was the professional flowering of her two older daughters, Marianne and Brigitte. Marianne completed medical school in Chicago in 1935 and stayed on there for an internship in medicine. Then, surprisingly, and, she says, quite by accident, she got involved in psychiatry courses and ultimately in a psychiatric residency at the Payne Whitney Clinic, at New York Hospital–Cornell Medical Center. Ruth Moulton, who was in medical school with Marianne in Chicago, remembers her as "rather shy and gentle, but extremely bright." She "knew what she was doing" and as a result was often asked to teach others.[15] As a psychiatrist she proved to be similarly talented. Some years later her supervisor in analytic training described her as "the most gifted student I have ever controlled, very intelligent, intuitive and sensitive," with "an unusual grasp of the total situation."[16] Marianne doubts that her mother cared much one way or the other about her choice of a career in psychiatry. But it is hard to imagine that Karen didn't have some feelings about it—perhaps there was a measure of rivalry, but also a feeling of pride that her daughter was following in her footsteps.

Certainly Karen had had ambivalent feelings about the success of Brigitte in the movies in Germany. To be an actress had of course been Karen's childhood dream. When Brigitte announced, at fifteen, that she wanted to go into the theater, Karen's first response was disbelief. "When I was your age," she told Brigitte, "I could recite the classics by heart."[17] This was followed by a demonstration. Once over this first outburst of rivalry, however, Karen supported Brigitte's ambition by seeking out good teachers. The first was someone known to the family. But the second, Ilka Grüning, was a leading Berlin actress and, according to Brigitte, a wise and gifted teacher as well. Physically Brigitte was her mother's opposite in almost every way. She was a striking beauty —tall, slender, and dark, with a very long face, the high cheekbones of Dietrich but more sultry eyes, and a fuller mouth, which allowed her to play Mediterranean types. Her voice may have been the one physical attribute she inherited from her mother—it was big and very deep.

She also inherited something of her mother's temperament. When she auditioned for the Reinhardt prize in 1930 she noticed that the committee of judges occupied only the first eight or ten rows of the theater and thought to herself, Why be loud? But she wasn't far into her first piece, a sort of interior monologue from Grillparzer, when she heard the great Max Reinhardt call up from the front row, "Miss Horney, would you kindly speak a little louder?" Brigitte was momentarily startled. But she collected herself and looked down toward the judges. "Wait," she said firmly, "that will be later" and went on in exactly the same voice. "Then in the second thing I had to show them, I opened up." The judges must have been impressed: Brigitte won the Reinhardt prize that year and embarked on a career in theater and film that continues even now.[18]

By the time Karen arrived in New York, Brigitte's movies were appearing regularly at the German-language cinemas in Yorkville and being reviewed, briefly, in the *New York Times.* The *Times* reviewer (identified only by the initials HTS) fastened on the word "allure" to describe Brigitte and stuck with it. She had a "rather indefinable allure" in a 1938 film, *Verklungene Melodie* (Dead Melody),[19] was a "sadly alluring brunette" in *Wintersturme* (Winter Storm) later that year,[20] had "peculiar allure" in *Aufruhr in Damascus* (Tumult in Damascus) in 1939,[21] and was as "alluring as ever" in another 1939 production, *Ziel in den Wolken* (Destination in the Clouds).[22] On a few occasions HTS did have praise for Brigitte's acting as well as her looks, noting that she managed to "run the full gamut of emotions but never overdo it" in the 1938 film *Katzensteg* (Cat's Bridge)[23] and did "excellent work" in *Aufruhr.*[24] Despite her reputation for clowning off camera, Brigitte tended to be cast in the role of the beautiful young heroine caught in some grave dilemma. In *Cat's Bridge,* for instance, she was a humble village maid forced to betray her Prussian countrymen by an agent of Napoleon's troops. More than once she found herself in a familiar role for German womanhood: struggling in vain to keep her brave lover from risking his life in combat.

It is natural to assume that films made in the Nazi era must have been dull and unimaginative, if not downright offensive. But this is not quite the case. In the first place, in the Weimar period the German film industry had become enormously prolific and successful, producing more films than all the other European countries combined. Its success had earned the industry a fair amount of autonomy, even after it was bought out by right-wing companies after the great inflation. Under Hitler, film makers continued to operate with profit more than propaganda in mind. There were anti-Semitic films made in this era, the most vicious of which was *Jud Süss* (Jew Süss; 1940), but according to historian Walter Laqueur, there was "not a single . . . openly Nazi" one.[25]

Nationalistic films, however, abounded. Brigitte starred in 1934 in a film called *Ein Mann will nach Deutschland* (A Man Wants to Get to Germany), which dramatized the struggle of a patriotic young German working in South America in 1914 who braves great danger in an effort to return to his homeland. When *A Man Wants to Get to Germany*, appeared in New York, some refugees claimed that the theater was doing great business because everybody wanted to find out who would be crazy enough to want to go toward Germany rather than away from it. There was a proliferation of films set in the Napoleonic era, which drew an implicit parallel between the Prussian struggle against Napoleon and the German suffering at the hands of French enforcers of the Treaty of Versailles after World War I. The film *Katzensteg,* in which Brigitte starred, was one of this genre and ended with the Prussian hero riding away at the head of his company, presumably to defeat Napoleon at Waterloo.

Perhaps the closest thing to a propaganda film Brigitte made was *Der Gouverneur,* which appeared in 1939 and which *The New York Times* called "a glorification of militarism."[26] In it Brigitte played the beautiful wife of a young general who dissolves the parliament in an unidentified country in order to deal with civil and border unrest—all of which could be a code for a story of Hitler as hero. However, the plot turns out to be more akin to soap opera than Nazi propaganda, revolving around complications that occur because the general's wife is having an affair with a young lieutenant in the general's own regiment.

At the same time serious and artfully produced films continued to appear from time to time. One in which Brigitte appeared was *Tumult in Damascus,* which the *Times* reviewer considered "one of the best-made and most objective films based on the First World War . . . ever turned out by any . . . German producer." Set in Syria in 1918, it portrayed the efforts of the Turks and the German allies to hold out against the British and their allies. The filming was done on location in the desert near Tripoli and was "directed . . . so skillfully that the spectator's interest is held to the end. The fact that there can be no really 'happy ending' from the Teuton standpoint, as Damascus was occupied by British cavalry on October 1 and 29 days later Turkey sued for peace, is offset by the heroism of the German company in its battle with burning sands and human enemies."[27]

The fact that Brigitte Horney continued to make films throughout much of the Nazi era prompted speculation among Karen Horney's friends in New York that she had connections in the Nazi regime. It was said that she was part of Goebbels' inner circle and even that Karen sat in Goebbels' box once when she returned to Germany in the mid-thirties to visit Brigitte. There is no evidence to support these claims. Marianne, who was deeply disturbed by the Nazi rise to power, insists that no one in her family, except Oskar, had any sympathy for fascism. Brigitte says that she hated the Nazis and that her only contact with Goebbels was at a reception, following a performance, where she was required to meet him and where she managed to get around using his formal title by greeting him in English with "Hello."[28] Apparently Brigitte did provide vital assistance to her Aunt Ollie, who had been married to Karen's brother Berndt and who was half Jewish. That could mean that she did have some connections. But if so, she at least put them to good use in this instance.

It is certainly not the case, as some tend to assume, that everyone who worked in motion pictures in the Nazi period was sympathetic to the regime. Brigitte didn't need to rely on political connections for work. She was a skillful actress, attractive, nonpolitical, and not Jewish. Altogether Brigitte made an astonishing twenty-seven films between 1930 and 1943 and became a star in the process. Any German old enough to have gone to the movies in the thirties is likely to remember Brigitte Horney. She has continued to work in films, on the stage, and recently in television. But she has never worked at the feverish pace of those early years, when she was glamorous *and* young.

While Brigitte and Marianne were pursuing their careers, Renate, Karen's youngest daughter, had chosen to become a wife and mother. In 1935, after a carefree year in Chicago with Marianne, Renate returned to Germany and married her high school sweetheart, Fredy Crevenna. In May of 1936 Renate gave birth to a daughter. Karen immediately sent packages to Germany "filled with everything she felt her granddaughter needed." That the little girl was named Kaya, Karen's childhood nickname, must have pleased and flattered the new grandmother.

She managed several trips to Germany as well, first within a month of the birth and then at Christmastime for two years in a row. Her second Christmas visit, in December of 1937, was preceded by a telegram from mid-ocean requesting that Renate buy lots of *Kieler Sprotten,* a special kind of sardines from the Baltic Sea, in preparation for her arrival. This attempt to get something delicious for herself may have been linked, in a childish way, with the fact that she was bringing something delicious to Renate and her family. When Karen's train pulled into the station in Berlin she ceremoniously handed two very heavy bags out the window "with a happy excited glow on her face. It felt," Renate recalls, "like rocks." At the apartment Karen stowed her gift in the snow on the balcony until Christmas Eve, when it appeared at last under the tree: ten pints of whipping cream and several pounds of butter. The gift was her response to Renate's letters about how difficult it was, even for a nursing mother, to get dairy products. "Never in my life," Renate recalls, "did I taste whipped cream as good as that." One final rendezvous occurred in Switzerland the following summer, where they spent much of their time trying to figure out how Renate and her family could get out of Germany.

Fredy Crevenna, Renate's husband, was the son of *haut bourgeois* parents who wanted him to take over the successful family business and stay in Berlin. But Fredy wanted to become a movie director instead. Nor did he and Renate want to stay on in Nazi Germany. "It had become obvious to our spying neighbors," Renate wrote later, "that I was evading every summons to citizen's duty and contribution to the cause. My arm became paralyzed when I was supposed to raise it for a Heil Hitler . . . my husband would always walk slightly behind me to give my arm a sufficient kick to simulate a salute. It was high time we packed up and got out before it was too late."

Somehow Renate's husband managed to convince the authorities that he should be given a tourist visa to visit the United States in order to compare the quality of Agfa and Kodak color photography. The officer who gave permission for a "short stay overseas" added a surprising bit of advice. "When you get across the water," he said, "stay there. Heil Hitler!" The Crevennas had every intention of doing just that. But by the end of 1938 emigration to the United States was out of the question: quotas were filled for years to come. According to Renate, Karen tried every possible connection but to no avail. The only alternative was Mexico, where a school friend had settled.

Karen had already visited Mexico and loved it. Early in 1939 Renate and her family found a home in Mexico City. "We took to

Mexico," Renate remembers, "like ducks to water, in spite of not knowing a word of Spanish and having no money and a question mark as a future. But I felt that I had come home at last, that this would be the country of my children, that this would be the place where I would feel free again and all my fears would vanish in the clear thin mountain air." Before long the young couple had found a nice apartment and Fredy had found a job. Not long after that a second child was on the way.

For Karen, Renate's progress was a source of both pleasure and concern, for Renate was increasingly unhappy in her marriage. By the time the family had arrived in New York on their visit in 1938, Renate recalls, "I had become a bundle of nerves and fears." While her husband made a trial visit to Mexico that Christmas, Karen and Renate talked, for the first time in Renate's memory, about their feelings. They went out to Montauk Point, on the tip of Long Island, on Christmas Day, walked together, letting "the fresh, invigorating air blow the fears and accumulated poisons out of us far to the open sea. We talked a great deal. She knew only too well what I was up against; she had been with us several times and saw the whole picture. She saw also a repetition of some of her own fears and struggles. . . . I had become a frightened female who had lost the right to have her own opinion or further her own inner development. If I dared have [an opinion] that differed from my husband's, poisoned darts would fly, and so to protect myself and my child, I became a 'nothing.' "[29]

Karen continued over the years to try to help Renate with her marital difficulties, even traveling alone with her son-in-law to the Mayan ruins during one of her many visits to Mexico, and making what was probably an ill-advised attempt to be both mother-in-law and counselor. But while she may have sympathized with Renate's insecurities, they were no longer Karen's own. Even her looks reflected Karen's growing confidence during these early New York years. Margaret Mead, who knew her first in Chicago, remembered that in those days she "never paid any attention to her appearance and I remember people saying that she looked like a typical Viennese intellectual." Later, in New York, "she used to dress very elegantly and rather ostentatiously."[30]

Mead dated the change in Horney's style from the early forties. But a series of photographs taken in 1938 suggests the transformation started earlier. In these she is wearing a silk dress, gathered to a ruff around the neck, and a long, luxuriant fox boa is draped over her shoulders. Her gray-white hair is permanented and rolled at the nape of her neck, and she holds a cigarette daintily in her familiar clip. She is smiling, a little self-consciously, at being photographed repeatedly from a variety of angles. But the slightly alarmed look she often showed the camera on earlier occasions has been replaced by an air of benign, almost regal, patience. Four years later a photograph from this series would appear in a reference book entitled *Notable New Yorkers,* a group to which, thanks to her books and lectures, Karen Horney had come to belong.

At the time the photographs were taken Horney was at work on her first book. Although it was essentially a compilation of her lectures to New School lay audiences, she wrote her editor, W. W. Norton, from Mexico in the summer of 1936 that the book was addressed "in the first place to psychiatrists, psychoanalysts, psychosociologists, social workers. As far as sociologists and ethnologists are concerned, I think they will welcome it because it gives them psychological data to work with. This was at any rate the response I got from Ruth Benedict, Margaret Mead, John Dollard, Harold Lasswell." At the same time, she pointed out, "it is written in such a simple—though bad!—language, that interested and educated laypersons can read it, and—I feel pretty sure—will read it, because it concerns their own problems." (The reference to "bad" language had to do with Horney's difficulties with English —difficulties that were, judging from her letters, less severe than she supposed and that were made almost to disappear in the editing process.) "As far as I see," she told Norton, "it contains quite a few *new* contributions to the subject of neurosis."[31]

The heart of the book was a description of the "neurotic personality" of the title, a person who is guided in most life situations by a neurotic need for love, or perhaps more precisely, a need to *be* loved—"an indiscriminate hunger," in her words, "for appreciation or affection."[32] The need is grounded not in attraction to or desire for the other person but rather in a feeling of profound insecurity that makes him or her seek constant reassurance. Underlying the need is a deep feeling of anxiety—what Horney called "basic anxiety"—that originated in childhood and has continued into adult life as a result of the conflict the person feels between angry—or even assertive—impulses and the need to hang onto the affection of others. Horney sees this particular neurotic configuration as especially widespread in modern America, a culture in which outward success is so often viewed as a measure of one's worth. The effect of such a fiercely competitive environment is to make the individual feel "emotionally isolated. Emotional isolation is hard for anyone to endure; it becomes a calamity, however, if it coincides with apprehensions and uncertainties about one's self."[33]

As the book unfolds it becomes clear that "the neurotic" is in fact not one but many neurotics who share the same "basic anxiety" but whose strategies for dealing with it are very different indeed. Some seek power and success, others withdraw or devote their energies to making themselves lovable. Whatever their strategy, it is ultimately one that merely compounds and escalates the problem in what Horney calls a "vicious circle." In the case of the neurotic who recoils from competition, for instance, the discrepancy between "high flown ambitions and the comparatively poor reality" may become "so unbearable that it demands a remedy. . . . More and more the neurotic substitutes grandiose ideas for attainable goals. The value they have for him is obvious: they cover up his unendurable feelings of nothingness; they allow him to feel important without incurring the risk of failure or success; they allow him to build up a fiction of grandeur far beyond any attainable goal."[34] But these grandiose ideas are not a solution, since the neurotic—unlike the psychotic—is in touch with reality and therefore "cannot help registering with painful accuracy all the thousand little incidents of real life which do not fit in with his conscious illusion. Consequently he wavers in his self-valuation between feeling great and feeling worthless."[35] This is the "vicious circle" at work: the grandiose ideas provide some reassurance, but they also reinforce the neurotic's tendency to withdraw from competition and lead to feelings of rage and anxiety when he is reminded of the discrepancy between his fantasy and the reality.

Such passages as this one, in which Horney displayed her ability to make sense of complicated behaviors, were universally praised by reviewers of *The Neurotic Personality of Our Time.* Franz Alexander, despite his falling-out with Horney in Chicago, praised her in the lead review in the *Psychoanalytic Quarterly,* noting Horney's "independent, scrutinizing attitude, uninfluenced by accepted abstractions. . . . She studies the material with her own clinically trained eyes and is never satisfied with 'mechanisms' but only with well understood psychological connections. Here lies her strength and her contribution toward counteracting a current trend to substitute theoretical abstractions for psychological understanding."[36] Or, as sociologist John Dollard wrote in the *Psychoanalytic Review,* "Dr. Horney is at her best in the stubborn thinking-through and literal realistic expression of the actual present-day character structure of her patients."[37]

Dollard and other sociologists were particularly pleased, as she had predicted they would be, with Horney's emphasis on the role of culture in neurosis. Margaret Mead wrote to congratulate her on her "creative hypothesis," which she predicted would "inevitably lead to more and better thinking, like a road that leads out from a confined little walled town on to an open plain, where there are many paths."[38]

Horney's argument that, as she put it in her opening chapter, "there is no such thing as a normal psychology that holds for all mankind"[39] was one she had made before but that she fleshed out in the book with illustrations drawn from anthropological observations. "One can diagnose a broken leg without knowing the cultural background of the patient," she noted, "but one would run a great risk in calling an Indian boy psychotic because he told us that he had visions in which he believed. In the particular culture of these Indians the experience of visions and hallucinations is regarded as a special gift, a blessing from the spirits."[40] A reviewer in the journal *Social Forces* praised her for seeking "to do justice to the cultural relativity of all neurotic disturbances, surely a significant insight that has been neglected by the great psychiatric chieftains who have tried to build a strategy of psychiatry without much regard to the changing social circumstances that have no small part in determining the battlefield where human impulses clash at any time and place."[41] Another, writing in the *American Journal of Sociology,* congratulated her for her independence from "the *echt* Freudians," who "continue to find the main motivations for adult behavior in instincts or in impulses which they contend unfold in every culture in more or less the same form."[42]

Not surprisingly, the strongest criticism of *The Neurotic Personality of Our Time* came from those very same *echt* Freudians. For them Horney's most controversial assertions had to do with the question of childhood sexuality, and particularly with the question of the centrality of the Oedipus complex. Horney contended that the Oedipus complex was not universal, even in our culture, but was "generated through the atmosphere in which a child grows up" and was itself "a neurotic formation."[43] She maintained that neurosis did not result from the frustration of biological drives but rather grew out of some "lack of genuine warmth and affection" in parenting. Horney suggested that isolated traumas, which played such an important role in Freud's thinking, could be overstressed. "A child can stand a great deal of what is often regarded as traumatic—such as sudden weaning, occasional beating, sex experiences—as long as inwardly he feels wanted and loved. Needless to say, a child feels keenly whether love is genuine, and cannot be fooled by any faked demonstrations."[44]

These ideas, introduced almost casually and without much fanfare in *The Neurotic Personality of Our Time,* were far more radical than any of Horney's previous departures. They went to the heart of the libido theory, and they provoked indignation in Freudian quarters. "What really recedes into the background," Ernest Jones wrote in the *International Journal of Psychoanalysis,* "is infantile sexuality." Horney's contention that "a great part of what appears as sexuality has in reality very little to do with it, but is an expression of the desire for re-assurance" is, to Jones's way of thinking, "a dangerous half-truth. The fact that the motivation of sexual impulses may be over-determined by anxiety and other factors does not make the acts in question any the less sexual; what it does is to show the enormous importance of sexuality both for itself and for extrinsic purposes like re-assurance. To draw a contrary inference is equivalent to emptying the baby with the bath."[45]

What angered Horney's peers even more than her theoretical departures was the offhand way in which she presented Freud's work. Psychiatrist Robert Knight complained that "by appearing to treat disdainfully the established facts of infantile psycho-sexual development and the theories of biologically founded instinctual drives, she gives the false impression that her excellent analysis of ego defenses and attitudes is all of psychoanalysis that is important, to the neglect of the great body of psychoanalytic knowledge of the unconscious tediously built up by Freud and other analysts as well as by her own previous contributions."[46] Another critic from the analytic camp, writing in the *Nation,* thought he detected Horney's own repressed anger toward the founding father. "Since so much of Dr. Horney's work is concerned with hostility, it is interesting to note the ill-concealed hostility toward Freud and other analysts through this section of the work."[47]

Such *ad hominem* arguments, in which criticism was equated with personal hostility, are, as Clara Thompson has observed, an "insidious custom"[48] in psychoanalysis. But in 1937 there were particular, historic reasons to personalize the issues. Psychoanalysis was seen, as one analyst wrote years later, as "young and delicate."[49] And the delicacy of the theory was linked in many minds with the precarious situation of Freud himself. As everyone in the field was painfully aware, Freud was still in Vienna, bravely enduring the pain of a fatal cancer and the threat of the Nazis. The following year, when Freud was obliged, at eighty-two, to leave his home for exile in London, protective feelings toward him were further intensified. The timing of Karen Horney's critique could not have been worse.

15

"New Ways in Psychoanalysis"

Although the publication of *The Neurotic Personality of Our Time* passed without comment at the interval meetings of the New York Psychoanalytic, Horney was encouraging a debate in smaller forums—in her classes at the institute and in informal meetings held at her apartment in the Essex House. Harmon ("Saul") Ephron, an analytic candidate who attended some of the meetings, remembers walking in Central Park afterward and passionately defending Horney's point of view against other candidates who, just as passionately, took the opposite side. "We were intolerant," Ephron recalls, "and they were intolerant...none of us knew what we were talking about." Ephron was the survivor of a very silent and unproductive analysis who became an admirer of Horney's after he began going to her for supervision. "Horney would have something to say," Ephron remembers, "that's what I liked about her." Besides, he was young and politically radical at the time: allying himself with Horney seemed a natural extension of his generally rebellious feelings. "It was an interesting thing for a young person, to be in the midst of a battle."[1]

By that time many candidates were beginning to sense that sides were being taken. There was a feeling among Horney's supervisees, for instance, that she expected them to be loyal. Judd Marmor remembers feeling that Horney "was a little hurt when I terminated my supervision with her after I had had the requisite number of hours. But I wanted to have a varied learning experience. I'm not somebody who becomes a disciple."[2] By the same token, there came to be a tacit understanding that certain members of the faculty were out of favor with the Institute hierarchy. Sandor Rado, although still no friend to Horney, had come to be grouped with the outsiders because of his quarrels with Freud's instinct theory. So had Abram Kardiner, closely tied to Rado and having a particular interest in sociological applications of psychoanalysis. The other two were Karen Horney and Clara Thompson, the only other member of the Zodiac group who belonged to the Institute and Horney's only real kindred spirit on the faculty. The outsiders tended to sit together at meetings, to vote together, and to refer their students to each other for analysis and supervision.

Had it not been for the confluence of two events in 1939, however, the existence of a small dissident faction within the Institute might have been tolerated indefinitely. There were quite a few Institute members, including the 1938–39 president, Bertram Lewin, who felt strongly that the organization could and should make room for a variety of viewpoints. But early in 1939 Karen Horney's second book, *New Ways in Psychoanalysis,* more directly critical of Freud than the first, appeared. Not long after that an ambitious and energetic young analyst, Lawrence Kubie, ascended to the presidency of the New York Psychoanalytic Society and Institute. Although Kubie started out by extending an olive branch to Horney, he proved in the end to be her most zealous opponent. His actions, along with the indignation touched off by *New Ways in Psychoanalysis,* made a confrontation between the orthodox group and what came to be called the "deviationists" inevitable.

New Ways in Psychoanalysis is a more carefully reasoned book than *The Neurotic Personality of Our Time,* directed at a more knowledgeable audience. Responding perhaps to the accusations that she had trivialized Freud in her first book, Horney began by acknowledging that "nothing of importance in the field of psychology and psychotherapy has been done since Freud's fundamental findings without those findings being used as a directive for observation and thinking; when they have been discarded the value of new findings has been decreased."[3] To lend weight to this general statement Horney went on to discuss what she considered to be the "elementary principles" of psychoanalysis that were indisputable.

First and foremost was Freud's discovery "that actions and feelings may be determined by unconscious motivations."[4] Second, Freud's hypothesis "that psychic processes are as strictly determined as physical processes" made it possible to begin to understand "psychic manifestations which had hitherto been regarded as incidental, meaningless or mysterious, such as dreams, fantasies, errors of everyday life."[5] The third principle was "the dynamic concept of personality"—the idea that conflicting "emotional drives" are characteristic of psychic life and result in a great array of strategies that Freud and others have learned to recognize in treatment—displacements, projections, repressions, rationalizations, slips of the tongue.[6] Fourth was Freud's discovery that dreams are, in essence, wish fulfillments and can provide access to the unconscious. There was, in addition, Freud's finding "that character and neuroses are molded by early experiences to an extent hitherto unthought of." And last, there were the "tools for therapy" that Freud had devised, particularly "those relating to transference, to resistance and to the method of free association."[7]

The second chapter of Horney's book was, predictably, a discussion of her differences with Freud. Entitled "Some General Premises of Freud's Thinking," it is only nine pages long. Yet within those pages Chapter Two displays the same prescience, in identifying vulnerable points in psychoanalytic theory, as Horney's 1926 critique of Freud's female psychology, "The Flight from Womanhood." Even the language is reminiscent of that article. There she had argued that psychoanalysis was "the creation of a male genius" and therefore tended to overlook the female experience. In Chapter Two Horney noted that "no one, not even a genius, can entirely step out of his time" and that "despite his keenness of vision his thinking is in many ways bound to be influenced by the mentality of his time."[8]

Horney goes on to summarize the ways in which she believes Freud was influenced by the scientific values of the nineteenth century. She suggests that such values produced Freud's biological orientation, which leads him, for instance, "to explain psychic differences between the two sexes as the result of anatomical differences,"[9] to view development as proceeding through oral, anal, phallic, and genital stages, and most important, to place instincts at the center of his theory. Further, Freud's tendency to "view psychic factors as pairs of opposites" was a sort of "dualistic thinking ... deeply ingrained in the philosophical mentality of the nineteenth century." It results, in Freud's theory, in "the dualism he finds between instincts and the 'ego,'" which he "regards as the basis of neurotic conflicts and neurotic anxiety." It also results in his "conception of 'femininity' and 'masculinity' as opposite poles."[10] A final limitation is caused by what Horney calls Freud's "mechanistic-evolutionistic thinking," the idea that "present manifestations not only are conditioned by the past, but contain nothing but the past."[11]

The next fourteen chapters elaborate on the limitations Horney believes are imposed by this orientation. Each chapter bears the name of some Freudian concept: "Libido Theory," "The Oedipus Complex," "The Concept of Narcissisim," and so on, and each begins with Freud's view and ends with Horney's. It is not—as critics were to point out—a modest approach. But it does make very clear just why and how Horney differs. As Horney stresses at the outset, the central difference has to do with the question of the role of biology in psychic life. Freud operated with the conviction that the drives—or instincts—and their gratification or frustration were the source of psychic conflict; Horney was proposing that neurotic behavior had its origins not in the frustration of drives but in "basic anxiety," a "deep feeling of helplessness toward a world conceived as potentially hostile."[12] This meant that many behaviors that Freud explained in terms of frustration or gratification of drives were explained by Horney in terms of the need for security, for reassurance, for affirmation.

Thus such qualities as greediness or possessiveness, which "in the psychoanalytical literature are described as 'oral' or 'anal,'" should be viewed, Horney believes, as "a response to the sum total of experiences in the early environment."[13] Similarly, a "woman's wish to be a man" is "seen as a result of penis-envy" when it should be viewed as resulting from "the totality of her life circumstances, particularly in childhood."[14] The libido theory, she suggests, "constitutes a temptation to understand a whole machine out of one wheel."[15] The theory of the Oedipus complex, for instance, "has helped to make parents conscious of the lasting harm inflicted on children by exciting them sexually and also by being overindulgent, overprotective and too prohibitive in sexual matters. On the negative side, it has fostered the illusion that it is enough to enlighten children sexually and to refrain from forbidding masturbation, from whipping them, from letting them witness parental intercourse and from attaching them too strongly to parents."[16] This overlooks the importance of "such parental attitudes as having real interest in a child, real respect for it, giving it real warmth, and of such qualities as reliability and sincerity.[17] The emphasis should be not on the isolated traumas of early childhood but on the quality of parenting over time.

Horney's view of Freud's death instinct is consistent with her critique of libido theory. To Freud's pessimistic contention that destructive impulses are inborn, and in conflict with the libidinous forces, she counters that hostility and destructiveness are defensive. Once again, they are activated by anxiety. "If we want to injure or kill, we do so because we are or feel endangered, humiliated, abused."[18]

The most controversial chapter of the book, from the point of view of her analytic peers, was probably the one entitled "The Ego and the Id." Horney must have been aware of its potential to make waves: she worried over it and changed it right up to the last minute—actually asking her editor to call up the printer and tell him to hold off on printing it until she got a revision to him. "I am sorry to bother you," she wrote Norton's assistant, "but the chapter is not good as it is."[19] Horney's principal point was to become an enormously important one for psychoanalysis in succeeding decades. It had to do with the parasitic role of the ego in Freud's scheme of mental functioning. Although Freud had ascribed a far more complex role to the ego and added the superego as his ideas developed over his lifetime, the grounding of psychoanalysis in instinct theory made the id the source of energy and the ego a borrower of it. "In his concept of the 'ego' Freud denies —and on the basis of the libido theory must deny—that there are any judgments or feelings that are not dissolvable into more elemental 'instinctual' units. . . . It means that theoretically there is no liking or disliking of people, no sympathy, no generosity, no feeling of justice, no devotion to a cause, which is not in the last analysis essentially determined by libidinal or destructive drives."[20] Horney argues that there can be genuine responses that have their origins not in the instincts but in the self in some larger, undivided sense. "As long as the 'ego' is considered to be by its very nature merely a servant and a supervisor of the 'id,' it cannot be itself an object of therapy. . . . If, however, this 'ego,' in its weakness, is regarded as an essential part of the neurosis, then changing it must become a task of therapy. The analyst then must deliberately work toward the ultimate goal of having the patient retrieve his spontaneity and his faculty of judgment, or in James' term, his 'spiritual self.' "[21]

In 1939, when *New Ways in Psychoanalysis* was published, there was a growing consensus within psychoanalysis that the role of the ego had to be reexamined and attention to ego functions increased. Anna Freud's *The Ego and the Mechanisms of Defense,* published three years earlier, launched a new era of exploration of what is now generally referred to as "ego psychology." Interestingly, members of the New York Psychoanalytic Institute, most notably Heinz Hartmann, Ernst Kris, and Rudolph Loewenstein, were to be major contributors to ego psychology only a few years after *New Ways* appeared. But Horney was not inclined to cast her lot with renovators of Freud's structure. "It is often regretted in psychoanalytical literature," she wrote, "that we know little about the 'ego' in comparison with our extensive knowledge concerning the 'id.' This deficiency is attributed to the historical development of psychoanalysis, which led first to an elaborate study of the 'id.' The hope is expressed that just as elaborate a knowledge of the 'ego' will follow in time, but this hope is likely to be disappointed." The reason, Horney contended, was that Freud's feet were still stuck in the mud of biology, of instincts, which "leaves no more scope, no more life to the 'ego' than is indicated above. Only by abandoning the theory of instincts can we learn something about the 'ego.' "[22]

There is a puzzling contradiction running through *New Ways in Psychoanalysis.* On one hand, Horney seems to have had a genuine desire to play the role of critic from within the Freudian fold. Writing to W. W. Norton about the title of the book, she told him she liked "New Ways" because "it would say implicitly that it concerns a critical evaluation of psychoanalysis, it would also imply that the book contains contributions of my own, and finally it would imply that I do not want to found a new school but build on the foundations Freud has laid."[23] This same intention was reiterated in the book's introduction, where she wrote: "I suppose there are many analysts and psychiatrists who have experienced my uncertainties as to the validity of many theoretical contentions. I do not expect them to accept my formulations in their entirety, for these are neither complete nor final. Nor are they meant to be the beginning of a new psychoanalytical 'school.' "[24]

But the modest and conciliatory tone of such statements competes with criticisms so sweeping that it is hard not to believe Horney *is* founding a new school. Not only does she call for "abandoning the theory of instincts" but she also insists that "psychoanalysis has to rid itself of the heritage of the past if its great potentialities are to develop"[25] and that "the libido theory in all its contentions is unsubstantiated."[26] Or, writing of Freud's ideas, she asserts that "underlying observations of great keenness and depth are robbed of their constructive value because of their integration into an unconstructive theoretical system."[27] Furthermore, the structure of *New Ways* suggests that Horney saw herself as an alternative to Freud. Rather than taking on one aspect of Freud's work—his view of the ego, for instance—she attempted to take on the whole oeuvre, piece by piece. She even proposed abandoning Freud's ego, superego, and id in favor of her own "neurotic trends." On some pages she seemed to be building on Freud's foundation as promised. But whether she admitted it to herself or not, her two books did represent a radical departure.

Horney was proposing abandonment of the cornerstone of Freud's system, the conflict between underlying libidinal and aggressive drives and the adaptive and moderating forces of the ego. The ego psychologists, like Horney, wanted to give a lot more attention and credit to the ego. But they continued to believe, with Freud, that biologically based drives played a critical role in individual history. In the opinion of psychologist David Rapaport, Horney's denial of the role of drives resulted in a "lopsided"[28] theory that ignored the "seething cauldron" of early passions. "Horney and others tried to get away from . . . the seething cauldron."[29]

Horney herself certainly struggled with her impulses. But her struggle was set in a different arena. And her books, like all her previous writing, were an attempt to find a theory that fitted with her experience. *New Ways in Psychoanalysis* is among other things a synthesis of all the ways in which psychoanalysis, as Horney experienced it, had failed her. Horney first suggested to her editor, W. W. Norton, that the book be called "Personal Outlook in Psychoanalysis," because, as she explained to him, "All we can say about anything, and all that is worth saying, is after all something personal. Versus eternal truths."[30] Although the title was dropped, the underlying principle remained operative.

When she writes, for instance, of the importance of "reliability" and "sincerity" in child rearing, she might be referring to the stormy and unpredictable atmosphere of her own childhood. And when she criticizes the one-sided libidinal preoccupations of parents influenced by psychoanalysis, she might be thinking of her own self-avowed mistake in sending Marianne and Renate to Melanie Klein for child analysis. She may well have been thinking of herself too when she wrote: "The fact that a person can function well sexually and yet have neurotic disturbances shows the fundamental error of the libido theory."[31] For Horney had never been bound by the constraints and inhibitions of Freud's world, yet she suffered from neurotic conflicts of sometimes debilitating force. For Horney it made better sense to regard neuroses as "the ultimate outcome of disturbances in human relationships . . . sexual or non-sexual."

The word that best describes the group of disturbances Karen Horney experienced and wrote about, beginning with *The Neurotic Personality of Our Time,* is "narcissistic." The term "narcissism," which Freud borrowed from the sexologist Havelock Ellis, has become so weighted down with competing meanings as to be confusing. However, as Arnold Cooper has pointed out in a recent essay, the elements of the clinical meaning of the word are contained in the myth of Narcissus itself. Narcissus was a physically perfect young man, the object of love among the nymphs, whom he ignored. One nymph, Echo, who loved him deeply, approached him one day and was rejected. Afterward, in her grief and humiliation, she pined away and died, leaving behind only the echo of her voice. The gods, acceding to the nymphs' wish for revenge, arranged for Narcissus to experience a similarly painful, unrequited love. One day he spied his own image in the water and fell in love with it, thinking it a beautiful water spirit. He was unable to tear himself away, yet every time he tried to embrace the reflection it disappeared. He too eventually pined away and died. When the nymphs came to bury him, even his body had disappeared, leaving behind a flower.

The features of narcissism as a neurotic disturbance are suggested in the myth: arrogance, self-centeredness, grandiosity, lack of sympathy or empathy, uncertain body image, poorly differentiated self and object boundaries, absence of enduring relationships, and a lack of psychological substance, an inner emptiness.[32] They are also, to a large extent, the qualities that Karen Horney laid out in her description of *The Neurotic Personality of Our Time,* and elaborated on in the four books that followed. In *New Ways,* for instance, she discusses perfectionistic patients, whom Freud was inclined to see as overburdened by guilt feelings, as driven by "a need to maintain the *appearance* of perfection." Such a person is "ostensibly comparatively independent of people. It is this impression that gave rise to Freud's belief that the 'super-ego,' though originally arising from infantile love, hatred and fear, eventually

Oskar Horney, age twenty-four.

The Horneys and the Grotes trading partners for the camera. Losch is on his knees, with his hand on Karen's shoulder. Karen has her eye on Idchen, who has fallen into a swoon on Oskar's shoulder.

A studio shot of Karen and Oskar with friends around 1910 in Berlin. Standing, from the right, are Oskar, Karen and Walter Honroth, who became her lover. Seated to the left is Rita Honroth.

Karen expecting. This photo probably dates from 1910, when Karen was undergoing psychoanalysis to combat her depression.

Karen holding her first child, Brigitte, who was born in 1911.

Karen and Oskar with Brigitte (standing) and the baby,
Marianne, born in 1913.

The three Horney daughters, outside the house in Zehlendorf, about 1919. From left,
Marianne, Brigitte, and Renate.

Karl Abraham.

Georg Groddeck.

Karen Horney as a young doctor in Berlin, around 1915.

A section of the group photograph taken at the International Psycho-Analytical Congress in Oxford, 1929. Bottom row, third from left, Otto Fenichel, sixth from left, Hanns Sachs, seventh from left, Rudolf Loewenstein, third from right, Herman Nunberg, far right, James Strachey. Second row, far left, Sandor Ferenczi, second from left, A. A. Brill, fourth from left, Karen Horney, fifth from left, Marie Bonaparte, sixth from left, Max Eitingon, seventh from left, Anna Freud. Seventh from right, Ernest Jones, sixth from right, Helene Deutsch, second from right, Ernst Simmel. Third row, sixth from left, Sandor Rado, seventh from left, Ruth Mack Brunswick. Top row, far left, Franz Alexander, second from left, Gregory Zilboorg, ninth from left, Bertram Lewin, third from right, Alix (Mrs. James) Strachey.

Karen Horney with daughters Marianne (left) and Renate (right) in Chicago, 1933–34.

Brigitte as she appeared in the film Liebe, Tod und Teufel *(Love, Death and the Devil) in 1934.*

Erich Fromm.

Gertrude Lederer-Eckardt, in 1949.

Karen working on Our Inner Conflicts *during a stay in*
Cuernavaca, 1944.

Members of the Japan traveling group. Clockwise from bottom left:
Cornelius Crane, Daisetz Suzuki, Karen Horney, Richard DeMartino.

Karen in Switzerland in the late 1940s.

became an autonomous intrapsychic representation of moral prohibitions." But, Horney maintains, such a person's independence is "born of defiance rather than of inner strength, and for this very reason it is largely spurious. Actually they are extremely dependent on others—in their own specific way. Their feelings, thoughts and actions are determined by what they feel is expected of them, whether they react to such expectations with compliance or defiance."[33]

Of course this portrait hardly resembles Karen Horney, any more than Freud resembled the Wolf Man. But the point is that the "narcissistic" constellation of issues and themes was her own, more than the libidinal ones. If there is a single explanation for the popularity of her books over the years, it is that these issues also had relevance for many others. In the last decade Christopher Lasch (*The Culture of Narcissism*) and other social critics have begun to suggest that narcissism is *the* malady of our time. In psychoanalysis too narcissistic issues have come to the fore, particularly in the work of Otto Kernberg and Heinz Kohut. And here and there, as psychoanalytic writers review the history of these ideas, Karen Horney has begun to reemerge as one of the earliest contributors.[34]

Such recognition, however, has been a long time in coming. When *New Ways in Psychoanalysis* appeared in 1939 it was greeted by psychoanalytic colleagues with nearly unrelieved hostility. Paradoxically, it was probably because *New Ways* was a better book than *Neurotic Personality* that it drew more fire. *Neurotic Personality* had seemed to many analysts to be essentially a piece of pop psychology for the layman—the sort of thing other institute members had indulged in. But *New Ways* couldn't be dismissed as a pop book. For one thing, it had the word "psychoanalysis" right in the title; for another, it took on Freud in a way that couldn't be ignored. What was more, the non-analytic press viewed Horney as an insider, a spokeswoman for the Freudians. And finally, perhaps most distressing of all, non-analyst reviewers all liked the book.

"Dr. Horney," wrote George A. Lundberg in the *American Sociological Review,* "is a psychoanalyst who consistently practiced the Freudian system for fifteen years and came to see its inadequacies. . . . For years to come, [*New Ways in Psychoanalysis*] will probably serve as a standard guide to the newer, more sociological, more realistic Freudianism."[35] Leonard S. Cottrell, Jr., hailed the book in the *American Journal of Sociology* as "an excellent constructive critique of Freudian theory" and "a pioneering work in bringing sociologists and clinical psychologists into a more fruitful relation."[36] Livingston Welch of *The New York Times* had, oddly, assumed in his review of *The Neurotic Personality of Our Time* that Karen Horney was a man. But in his review of the second book he got her sex right and concluded that "Dr. Horney's pruning is not only constructive but something that psychoanalysis has been in need of."[37]

Inside the field, however, the reaction was quite different. Perhaps the most indignant response was registered by Otto Fenichel in the *Psychoanalytic Quarterly.* "Anyone who knows psychoanalysis realizes that what Dr. Horney wants to abolish is the essence of psychoanalysis. If all that is to be stripped off what psychoanalysis remains will be similar to Lichtenberg's 'knife without a blade that had no handle.'" The most Fenichel is willing to concede is that "because the conceptions of Dr. Horney have little to do with psychoanalysis, that is not to say that they are all false." Horney is right that "psychoanalysis has long neglected character problems" and has paid too little attention to cultural factors. But "the value of psychoanalysis ... is rooted in its being an instinctivistic and a genetic psychology."[38]

A great deal of the opprobrium centered around what was perceived as Horney's arrogance. Karl Menninger, writing in the *New Republic,* suggests:

> If she had been content to advance her point of view in a modest and well documented way without setting herself up as a champion of "New Ways," her book might have been a major and timely contribution. But Miss Horney starts out by saying that *she* has been dissatisfied with the therapeutic results of psychoanalysis, that *she* found in every patient problems which psychoanalysis couldn't solve. She used to attribute this to her lack of experience or some other fault of her own, but finally came to realize that something was essentially wrong with Freud's concepts. These she proposes to correct ... Any attempt to refute or criticize Miss Horney gives rise to the cry that she is being made a martyr to the bigoted orthodoxy of the majority. I am fully aware that this review may be construed as further evidence of such inhospitable and ungallant behavior.

The sexism in Menninger's review deserves comment. Whereas male psychiatrists in the same review are referred to as "Dr.," Menninger, who knew Horney in Chicago, persists in referring to her, entirely inaccurately, as "Miss." It also seems unlikely that he would choose the phrase "ungallant behavior" if he were writing about a male.

Once again analytic reviewers complained that Horney distorted Freud. Menninger protested that "her book deliberately makes its appeal to an audience unprepared to recognize its many inaccuracies, distortions and misstatements."[39] Fenichel asserted that "Dr. Horney seems simply to have misunderstood Freud." He cites as an example her claim that "the essential characteristic of the 'ego' is weakness."[40] This is an illuminating example, since it points up both Horney's faults and those of her critics. Because Horney was writing for a general audience, she was obliged to present the broad outlines of Freud's theory before expressing her differences with it. The difficulty in this undertaking, however, is that the ideas defy easy summary: no one can present Freud's ideas as persuasively as Freud himself. The scope of Horney's book was also daunting: she was taking on twenty-three volumes of Freud in one three-hundred-page book. The result was that she wound up both overstating and flattening out rich material. (Here too the difficulties of writing in a second language contribute.) And yet Fenichel's indignation was unjustified. In the spirit if not in the letter, Horney's point about the weakness of the ego in Freud's theory was accurate. Although Freud began to move toward the idea of "inborn ego roots, independent of instinctual functions," in 1937,[41] the concept of an independent ("autonomous") ego was really developed fully not in Freud's writing but by others who followed.

Some of the greatest indignation was reserved for Horney's discussion of psychoanalytic technique in the final chapter of *New Ways*. She called for an attitude of "constructive friendliness" on the part of the analyst.[42] The patient must lead the way and "there will be many hours in which the analyst does nothing but interpret." But "as soon as I believe that the patient is running into a blind alley, I would not hesitate to interfere most actively and to suggest another way, though of course I would analyze why he prefers to proceed along a certain line, and would present the reasons why I prefer that he try to search in another direction."[43] This was seen by J. F. Brown, writing in the *Nation,* as further proof that what Horney was doing was not analysis. "We have known for many years," Brown wrote, "that there are easier ways than psychoanalysis to help some neurotics. Suggestive psychotherapy, hypnosis, Christian Science, Couéism and even events in real life, like inheriting a fortune or losing one, all these effect 'cures.' The demonstrable trouble with these cures is that they are pretty short-lived. I am afraid that many of Horney's cures with the 'new' method may turn out to be short-lived too."[44]

In September of 1939, just a few months after *New Ways* appeared, Sigmund Freud died in London. A memorial service was held at the New York Psychoanalytic, and many felt genuinely grieved by the loss and the sadness of his final years. Horney, however, had seen no need to stifle her dissent. Indeed, despite her praise for Freud in *New Ways*, her old anger toward him still erupted from time to time, particularly regarding his views on women. "As far as the alleged given inferiority of woman is concerned, Freud has, to be sure, made a remark which it is quite a relief to hear from him: 'You must not forget, however, that we have only described women in so far as their natures are determined by their sexual function... *an individual woman may be a human being apart from this.*'... I am convinced that he really means it, but one would like to have this opinion of his assume a broader place in his theoretical system."[45] The italics are Horney's, as is the bitterness. And yet, despite the fact that Freud had little tolerance for dissenting views and was fatally ill besides, Horney seems to have held on to some hope for a response. In a postscript to a letter to W. W. Norton, shortly after publication of *New Ways*, she queried, "Should we send a copy to Prof. Sigmund Freud?"[46]

In addition to the appearance of *New Ways* at a time when Freud was so sick, there were other reasons for colleagues to resent Karen Horney in 1939. She was an early arrival and was established and prospering by the time refugees started coming in large numbers in 1938. Later arrivals had a harder time getting started—partly because the medical establishment created more stringent requirements out of fear of competition and partly because their numbers made competition stiffer. Furthermore, Horney was a non-Jewish German, which meant she was a member of a tiny minority in psychoanalysis. Martin Grotjahn, another analyst in the same situation, recalls that his "Jewish friends never completely forgave my Prussian background; I had the impression that they would have respected me more had I done what Freud suggested to the non-Jewish analysts in Germany: to fight the German brethren on the home front." Grotjahn's situation was further complicated by the fact that he had a brother who was an officer in the German army.[47] While Horney had no officers in the family, she did have Brigitte, a highly visible success during the Nazi regime. Jewish colleagues tended to regard the prominence of Horney's daughter with resentment and suspicion.

Nor did she always respond sympathetically, on a personal level, to the individual plights of victims. Dr. Antonia Wenkart, who escaped Vienna with her husband and two young children in 1939 after living for six months in fear of death, recalls telling Horney of her experience and hearing her respond, "This would have never happened to me."[48] Edith Jacobson was met with a similarly unempathic greeting when she went to visit Horney shortly after her escape from Nazi Germany.

Jacobson, who had been a student at the Berlin Institute, was arrested by the Nazis in 1936 for her anti-Fascist activities and put in prison. When she became ill and was temporarily freed so she could recover, analytic friends managed to smuggle her across the Czech border to freedom. When she arrived in New York she "had the feeling that I had to see the German analysts, and she [Horney] was one—I was strange in New York. I came five minutes late— not that I'm the most punctual person, anybody knows that, including my patients. But it was at that time very understandable because . . . I didn't quite know about how long it would take me in a taxi. . . . And she, instead of saying I am glad to see you and you escaped and so on and welcome to New York . . . said, 'Why are you late?'"

Jacobson replied indignantly. "Listen, Dr. Horney, I thought you would welcome me. I didn't come for a session. If you don't have the time . . . I wanted to say hello to you, my old teacher from our Berlin Institute." After that, Jacobson recalls, she was "very, very nervous, and . . . a bit irritated because I was so frank. . . . I was flabbergasted." Jacobson adds a telling afterthought to this anecdote: "Maybe she did know that I had never liked her so very much."[49] Given Horney's sensitivity to rejection, she may well have sensed that Jacobson was visiting her out of duty rather than affection.

Horney did do things to help refugees. She wrote, and got others to write, to members of the House and Senate in support of a bill to admit ten thousand refugee children, half Jewish and half Gentile, to the United States in 1939 and 1940. She joined an organization (which was to cause her endless trouble during the McCarthy era) called the American Committee for the Protection of the Foreign-Born. She was also on a volunteer panel of the Jewish Family Service and National Refugee Service, and provided psychiatric advice in her office on call. The director of social work considered her "approachable and understanding and helpful to both our social workers and the patients."[50] When the daughter of her Berlin friends the Honroths needed to come to the United States with her husband, Horney provided the necessary affidavit and supported the couple financially until they were able to find jobs.[51]

At the same time Horney seems to have been somewhat naïve, or merely opportunistic, in her attitude toward the institution that took over power from the Berlin Institute and other groups under Nazi rule. She had been a founding member in 1926 of an organization called the General Medical Society for Psychotherapy—a group genuinely committed to heterodoxy in the field and with no significant political bias. In 1936 a member of this group named Matthias Heinrich Göring, who was a Nazi party member and cousin of Hermann Göring, established a Nazi-sanctioned German Institute for Psychological Research and Psychotherapy in Berlin. The German Institute was an outgrowth of the General Medical Society but also embraced what was left of the crippled Berlin Psychoanalytic Institute. The psychoanalytic segment of the Göring Institute, as it came to be called, was named the German Pyschoanalytic Society and included in its membership Horney's old friend Karl Müller-Braunschweig.[52] In 1936, when she went back to Germany to visit Renate and Brigitte, Karen Horney gave a paper before the German Psychoanalytic Society on the neurotic need for love. Afterward, in correspondence with Norton, she urged him to send a copy of The Neurotic Personality of Our Time to M. H. Göring, noting, "He is the most influential man as to a German edition!"[53]

Of course America wasn't in the war yet, and many Americans were complacent about Germany. But Horney, who had been back and seen the effects of the regime and who was surrounded by colleagues who had suffered from them, seems to have been particularly apathetic. Typically, she must have become aware of this quality in herself somewhere along the way, because in 1939 she wrote a brief paper, "Can You Take a Stand?," for the Journal of Adult Education. She concluded that people who are afraid to take a stand are constrained by "a deep feeling of insecurity . . . their feelings and thoughts are largely determined by others. As a result, they are easily swayed, now this way, now that. . . . It is people with these traits who succumb most easily to Fascist propaganda. Fascist ideology promises to fulfill all their needs. . . . Decisions and judgments of values are made for [the individual] and he has merely to follow. He can forget about his own weakness by adoring the leader." Educators, she concluded, must try to help each student understand that "he, as an individual, matters. . . . Show them how imperative it is to take a stand upon all important questions.... In a word, try both by precept and by example to give each of them the courage to be himself."[54] Perhaps Horney was thinking when she wrote the article not just of international politics but also of psychoanalytic politics. Because in 1939 it began to look as though her own courage to be herself was going to be tested as it had never been before.

16

The Split

When Lawrence Kubie assumed the presidency of the New York Society and Institute in the fall of 1939, American psychoanalysis was in a standard-setting mood. As a report from the Boston Institute's education committee had warned two years earlier, "The increased number of candidates are bringing to the Institute and Society a number of problems. . . . There is a danger, particularly in American psychoanalysis, of a dilution and rejection of some of the most fundamental aspects of analysis under various guises, such as progress, eclecticism, 'scientific' work, and other illusions. It is the function of any training group to see to it that those under its guidance and jurisdiction shall be properly equipped to represent psychoanalysis in its most fundamental and scientific form."[1] Particularly in 1938 and after, an influx of European refugee analysts, some of whom were laymen or supporters of lay analysis, posed another sort of threat to American standards.

No one was better qualified to deal with threats to "fundamental and scientific" psychoanalysis from both these quarters than Lawrence Kubie. Although he was only forty-three when he became president, he had already made a name for himself in national psychoanalytic politics as a setter of standards. In 1937 he had been named chairman of a special subcommittee of the American Psychoanalytic Association assigned "to formulate standards for professional training applicable to all of the American societies."[2] Around the same time he took charge of the Emergency Committee on Relief and Immigration, which provided information and assistance to refugees from Nazi Germany.[3]

The Emergency Committee was justly praised for its humanitarian work: it provided émigrés with vital information and affidavits and raised tens of thousands of dollars to finance the passage and settlement of European analysts in the U.S. What was rarely noted was that, under Kubie's leadership, the committee also played a policing role, issuing stern warnings to nonphysicians about the dangers of attempting to practice psychoanalysis in the United States. The committee sent out a memo, for instance, to "Psychoanalysts Who Desire to Emigrate," which warned that while it was acceptable for lay analysts to teach and while it might be possible in some instances for them to treat children, "the practice of psychoanalysis on adults without a medical license and a medical degree is a violation of the law for which severe penalties have sometimes been imposed."[4] This statement seems to have been wishful thinking on the part of the committee, since in fact such non-M.D.'s as Erich Fromm and Otto Rank practiced with impunity after coming to the United States. The Viennese who read the memo, in any case, found its pronouncements on the lay issue "tactless and rude."[5] Kubie played a similar role on a subcommittee of the National Committee for Resettlement of Foreign Physicians—a group in charge of evaluating the credentials of foreign doctors. Most, but not all, were deemed qualified to practice in the United States.[6] Thus Kubie was a champion of the refugee doctors' cause, but only if their credentials were in order.

In all of his leadership positions, including the presidency of the New York Institute, Kubie played this same part—that of a caring but stern and controlling father. He always insisted to his critics that he was not a rigidly orthodox Freudian, that he was in fact a believer in heterodoxy. His point was only that candidates should not be exposed to unorthodox ideas too early, before they were grounded in Freud. It was the need to protect candidates—as it was the need to protect refugees—which made the rules necessary.

What made both Sandor Rado and Karen Horney anathema to Kubie was their tendency to resist all attempts at control and regulation. In a letter to a colleague early in his presidency Kubie complained that although "I value Rado and his teaching highly . . . for the last three or four years I have been pleading with him both by word of mouth and by letter, to be less emotional about it;

and I have gone repeatedly to a few sessions of his courses each year, only to be thrown off each time by the atmosphere of bitterness which crept insidiously into his teaching."[7] With Horney the issue was not teaching style so much as content—and particularly her habit of holding what he viewed as "secret" evening meetings at her apartment and turning out "proselytes."[8]

Nothing like these accusations was ever voiced to Horney or Rado, however. Indeed, Kubie is remembered by all who knew him as suave and well mannered, hardly capable of such venom. New York–born and Johns Hopkins–trained, Kubie had bypassed the usual journey to Vienna or Berlin for analytic work and had spent two years at the London Institute instead. It was there perhaps that he acquired a hint of an English accent to go with his worldly style. Sam Atkin, in a tribute after his death, praised Kubie's "gracious manner, his elegance, his wide connections, and his felicity of thought and expression."[9] Saul Ephron remembered him as "a polished gentleman. He was *more* than refined, he was re*faned*."[10] Kubie had an office on 81st Street, just off Fifth Avenue, and what was widely believed to be "the fanciest practice in New York." Rather incongruously, as Judd Marmor recalls, Kubie also became "an aggressive spokesman" for the European classical analysts, many of whom were "almost inarticulate" in English but who were seen as emissaries of Freud himself.[11]

It was perhaps some intimation of the meaning of the Kubie presidency that caused the students of the New York Institute to organize in June of 1939, around the time of his election. At two student meetings that month, attended by about half the eligible candidates, a consensus was formed that certain things about the Institute training program had to change. Some of the requests were astonishingly humble: the students wanted library privileges at the Institute, some form of catalogue of courses so that they could plan, and some means of informing the patients they were treating, under supervision, that they had been approved by the Institute to do analytic work. In addition, the students wanted fewer requirements and greater variety in the curriculum. In addition to a course in Freudian principles, they requested a course in more severe disturbances ("narcissistic neuroses, psychoneuroses, and psychoses") to be taught, perhaps, by Harry Stack Sullivan, as well as a lecture course by Karen Horney, and case seminars taught from different points of view. It was also suggested, tentatively, that student reactions to courses should be given "from a constructive point of view."

Kubie responded to the student initiative in the gracious manner that was to become the trademark of his presidency. In fact there was almost nothing to his liking among the student requests and a great deal that irked him. He once said—to take just one example—that Harry Stack Sullivan was one of only three people in the world he truly hated. Nor did he feel much friendlier toward Karen Horney. Nonetheless he began by welcoming the students' input, inviting the students' seven representatives to an evening meeting at his luxurious apartment in the East Nineties, where he was joined by the three other new officers of the institute. There he listened to their proposals and presented his own "tentative ideas" on the curriculum.

The next fall, without any further consultation with the students, Kubie presented a new curriculum to the members of the society which was absolutely unresponsive to student demands. There was to be no lecture course by Horney, let alone Sullivan, and Clara Thompson had been assigned the job of teaching Freud's early writings—perhaps on the grounds that the subject matter would keep her on the straight and narrow. As the students pointed out, they had asked for fewer required courses, but "instead we have this year a greater number of required courses spreading over three years and a more rigid curriculum.... According to the new curriculum, the lecture and clinical courses which are given credit toward required hours are almost entirely those which are presented from the classical point of view. This places undue restriction on the student in his selection of courses. The students feel that such an attitude is not progressive nor scientific when considered in the light of other branches of medicine where divergent attitudes are encouraged and stimulated." By the time the students wrote this letter of complaint, however, it was too late. The new curriculum was a *fait accompli,* approved at a September meeting of the membership.

The curriculum had not been approved without protest. Karen Horney, for one, had argued for greater diversity. "Dr. Horney felt," the secretary, George Daniels, wrote in the minutes, "that a democratic organization should balance one group against another, and felt that the decision lay between a rigid teaching institution or a progressive one." Horney of course would be expected to object, since the proposed curriculum ignored her work.[12] A more disinterested objection came from a member of the education committee named David Levy. Levy, a child psychiatrist, wrote to the chairman of the committee: "I do not agree with the recommendations of the Educational Committee for the teaching of psycho-analysis, and will take the privilege of expressing my opposition, if need be, from the floor. I believe the recommendations do not represent in any sense the combined efforts of the members of the Committee. They represent the imposition of certain ideas upon them by Dr. Kubie."[13]

Over the next year and a half Levy was to play a unique role in the quarrel between the Kubie forces and the nonconforming group. Only he corresponded with both sides in the escalating battle, and only he seems to have been committed, above all, to trying to do the right thing. Levy had first met Horney when she was in Chicago and had corresponded with her on occasion about the clinical data he had collected on such subjects as masturbation in girls. Horney admired Levy's work, once writing him that his "investigation on thumb sucking puts the whole problem of the oral organization on a better clinical basis."[14] She shared Levy's commitment to empiricism, confiding at one point, "It is more and more amazing to see with what supreme disregard facts are treated in psychoanalysis."[15] Levy, for his part, respected Horney's clinical observations—he once called her a "capable connoisseur of human attitutdes"[16] —but he didn't always agree with her and didn't consider himself a follower. Because he was independent and respected in psychoanalysis and in the wider world, Levy became Karen Horney's most important ally.

David Levy was once described by a colleague as "curious and tender," useful qualities in a man whose work with children some-times made it necessary to conduct psychiatric interviews under the desk. Educated at Harvard and the University of Chicago Medical School, the American-born Levy learned the fundamen-tals of Rorschach testing during a sojourn in Switzerland and was one of the first to introduce the Rorschach test to American clini-cians. In his work with children he used free play with dolls and toys as the instruments for exploration. He had a strong empirical bent, reflected in his studies of sucking in babies and puppies, for instance, or in his study of babies' memories of inoculation. He was a man who appeared, according to the same colleague, "dis-armingly simple," with an "outward composure" that "was some-times mistaken for absent-mindedness."[17]

Despite his quiet exterior, however, Levy's opposition was not a thing to be borne lightly. He was, for one thing, a man of wealth, the husband of Adele Rosenwald, a Sears heiress (the sister of the

Chicago Institute benefactor Marion Rosenwald Stern) and major contributor to worthy causes around town. Mrs. Levy was the first to offer support, for instance, to the University in Exile at the New School.[18] At another point David Levy bailed out the chronically overextended Harry Stack Sullivan. Levy was also active and popular in national psychoanalytic politics and was elected president of the American Psychoanalytic in 1940—during the period of his confrontation with Kubie in New York. It was perhaps Levy's experience in psychoanalytic politics on the national level that made him suspect, as he wrote early in 1939, that "despite all Kubie's protests about liberalism and the teaching program, a reactionary movement lurks behind it."[19]

Kubie's method of dealing with the opposition was always to try first to melt it away with a magnanimous gesture. He met with the student group, for instance, before instituting a curriculum they were bound to object to. Similarly, in the fall of 1939, just as they were about to announce the curriculum, the education committee (of which Kubie was an *ex officio* and dominant member) invited Karen Horney to take one or even two interval meetings of the society to present her ideas and "in particular their variance with Freud's teachings."[20] It was an invitation that accomplished two things at once. First, it flattered Horney and gave the impression of liberalism that Kubie wanted to promote. But at the same time, since candidates were not invited to interval meetings, it limited student exposure to Horney's seemingly infectious ideas.

Horney readily accepted the invitation, suggesting her talk be called "The Emphasis on Genesis in Freud's Teaching" and that participants read four chapters from her book *New Ways in Psychoanalysis*. She proposed Abram Kardiner and Clara Thompson as discussants but added that she was "more interested in hearing opposing points of view of colleagues who are sufficiently open-minded as to deviating viewpoints." One such open-minded member, she suggested, was Lawrence Kubie. As an afterthought she wrote at the bottom of the page that "if there is sufficient interest to extend the discussion over another evening, I am very willing to do so."[21] Horney's attitude, as the education committee secretary observed at the time, was "certainly a very friendly and cooperative one."[22]

There was to be nothing friendly or cooperative, however, about the atmosphere in the smoke-filled hall of the New York Institute on October 17 when Horney addressed the membership.

Some observed later that Horney presented her ideas differently—
so as to make them less controversial—from the way she had
stated them in her book. But the ideas were still troublesome
enough to provoke angry outbursts and to cause one member to
make an appeal for "greater interest in scientific work and less
political hostility in the Society."[23] Afterward Sam Atkin, a
younger officer of the institute and Kubie ally, challenged Horney:
"You say that neurosis can be formed without there being an unre-
solved Oedipus. Why don't you, when you get up there and talk,
give one example of your claim? That would be of much greater
value than all the theoretical discussion." Horney apparently told
him, in a manner that struck him as both "haughty" and "arrogant," that she was writing a book about it.[24]

Seven days after the talk Kardiner wrote a blistering letter to
Kubie accusing him of being "eager . . . to create the impression of
fairness rather than to be fair." He continued:

> The last meeting . . . created no good feeling, and for this failure in part
> I blame you. You permitted the tone of discussion to go unchallenged;
> you tolerated criticism of an empirical scientific procedure by the stan-
> dards of religious sectionalisms; you permitted one member to call
> another a liar on a matter which you—as chairman—should have been
> able to settle or verify; you permitted scientific slander to take the
> place of criticism; you permitted unlimited use of the term "ortho-
> doxy," and allowed unchallenged the political device of analyzing the
> speaker and discussions by slips of the tongue—and allowed it to stand
> as a criticism that Dr. H[orney] had a "sense of guilt" to the libido
> theory and that Thompson and I were ambivalent, thereby drawing a
> big red herring over the entire scientific issue. This is an all time low
> —and yet you have the illusion that it created the impression of fair-
> ness.[25]

Kubie, smarting perhaps from Kardiner's accusations, wrote
David Levy a month after the evening in question deploring
the "impugning of dishonesty to those we disagree with. This
has been the besetting sin of the Society on all sides." Kubie conceded that "there have been serious and painful accusations. . . .
Everybody has sinned, and . . . we can only clean up the mess in
the Society by abandoning those tactics entirely. I think that you
know that I am working to this end; and in turn I have confidence
in your driving towards the same goal, namely, that we can disagree and yet respect one another."[26]

Kubie's appeal for rationality seems to have created a temporary lull in which he and Levy were able, briefly, to exchange substantive opinions on the issue of psychoanalytic education. Kubie insisted that he had only one basic educational purpose:

> to see that every student in the Institute will have to be exposed fully to every single viewpoint that is represented by an intelligent and matured teacher in the Institute. The only thing I am dead against is that one group of students shall hear nothing but Horney, another group nothing but orthodoxy, and a third group little but Rado, etc. I doubt that you are aware how much this was the case in the past; and in fact the Horney group have told me quite frankly that the main thing they have against the new regime is that "their" students will have to be exposed to teachings other than their own.[27]

Levy's response was surely one of the most thoughtful among dozens of letters and statements that were to fly back and forth as the debate continued. He wrote Kubie:

> I agree with you that students should not start their training under the influence of a teacher or a group of teachers whose mission is to extol their own particular doctrine in preference to that of Freud. I recognize also that where several such contending schools of thought compete in persuading the student, confusion may well result. I have learned to disagree with you, however, on a basic point. . . . Your attitude, it seems to me, may be put to the student in these words, "First learn the truth, which is Freud, then you will be protected from the adversaries." . . .
>
> I see one objective clearly, the selection of as good teachers as we can get, who will teach the courses as they wish, critically from the start. After all, the students are not such naive things that they will adhere to the opinions of anyone just because he states them with conviction. Otherwise, I think the whole method of teaching is a type of scholasticism. I do not mean that anyone giving an elementary course discounts all Freud's ideas for his own, I mean simply that in teaching from the basic writings of Freud, he is free to use his own critical judgment.
>
> The old-timers from Vienna are a good example of the danger of starting with holy writ. You get it so readily at our meetings. It is as though when they hear a paper they never ask themselves the question, "What is the truth?" They ask, rather, "Does he agree with Freud?" implying "There is no truth but Freud." And that is also why the discussions are so little grounded in empiricism, so thoroughly dialectic.[28]

Not surprisingly, Kubie defended the "old-timers" in his reply.

> It is partly their loyalty to Freud in this case, and partly the temporary state of mind of the refugee who doesn't want to feel that everything that he has had and everything he knows has been swept away and superseded by something better. That's very natural and human, and if it is handled with tact I think we will find that after a short period of adjustment, all of the younger ones will react to our American attitude of criticism with great eagerness, provided only that the criticism is couched in friendly and non-provocative terms.

As for the educational program, Kubie insisted he was committed to diversity. "But I don't think you realize that we literally had four cliques growing up in our student body, as in the Society itself,—each more or less hermetically sealed from the other . . . It was this situation which was threatening to wreck the Society completely." Nor, Kubie insists, is the danger over. "Rado still sulks like Achilles in his tent. Abe [Kardiner] still explodes with sudden paranoid flourishes. . . . Horney still says one thing to the Society and to mature analysts, and a very different thing in her books and to students. All of which has obvious seeds of danger in it for us and for analysis itself." Kubie closes his letter by proposing that Levy work with him, "because I think that together we can do a lot to remove some of these unnecessary sources of friction."[29]

Nothing came of this proposal from Kubie, however. On the contrary, within two months Kubie called a meeting of a "special subcommittee" of the education committee, minus David Levy, and proceeded to draft "recommendations" that amounted to an ultimatum to the unorthodox factions. The subcommittee proposed that "all basic changes in viewpoint on matters of theory . . . will first be presented fully and repeatedly at closed meetings of the Society for full and frank discussion," that society members with differing views will be called before the education committee to discuss "at what point in the student's training the new points of view can most profitably be introduced into the curriculum." Finally—and most important—training analysts would henceforward be assigned by the education committee rather than chosen by students.[30] This last proposal was intended of course to break up the "cliques" of students and analysts that Kubie claimed were wrecking the society. There could be no hope, after such subterfuge, of cooperation, or even dialogue, between Kubie and Levy.

Not long after the subcommittee meeting a new figure took center stage, for a brief time, in the controversy. Fritz Wittels, who had arrived in the United States even before Horney, had been one of the earliest members of the Vienna Psychoanalytic and had taught a course in psychoanalytic principles at the New School. In 1924 he had written a biographical study of Freud.* Although the work was clearly an act of devotion, Freud greeted it with decidedly mixed feelings. While he conceded in a letter to Wittels that the book "is by no means hostile," Freud also noted that "there are positive distortions," which grow out of "a preconceived notion of yours. You think that a great man must have such and such merits and defects, and must display certain extreme characteristics; and you hold that I belong to the category of great men. That is why you ascribe to me all sorts of qualities many of which are mutually conflicting."[31]

Freud's cool reception does not seem to have dampened Wittels' zeal. He continued to publish both nonfiction books in the social-uplift category—addressing such topics as modern child rearing—and fiction that revealed an astonishingly lascivious fantasy life. A 1927 Wittels novel, entitled *The Jeweller of Bagdad,* amounts to a sort of high-toned pornography in an exotic Middle Eastern setting. The book recounts the love of Achmed the jeweler for the beautiful Enis, "his friend, his playmate, his property." When Achmed commanded, Enis carried out "impudent and shameless motions" in dance. But then Achmed "meditated what more he could do to cultivate this flower of his love." He suddenly asked her: "Shall I beat you?"

"She was lying with her head on his knees, gazing dreamily into emptiness. He bent over her and put the question. She closed her eyes and whispered: 'Yes, with a whip!'" The subjugation of Enis continues through chapter after chapter. Enis "lived in him and for him alone. . . . She said what he had taught her to say, and thought what he thought—not as he thought, but as he wished her to think. . . . Thus a man's will and spirit took possession of a woman's soul." By the end of the book Enis has danced nude for other men at Achmed's command and has finally murdered in order to preserve his honor.[32] It isn't difficult to imagine how the man who created Enis—the woman who thought on command—could work up to the furious attack on Karen Horney that Wittels sent out to society members in March of 1940.

Sigmund Freud: His Personality, His Teaching and His School (New York: Dodd, Mead, 1924).

Like his fiction, Wittels' long letter appears to have been written in the heat of passion:

I consider it my duty—as a man who has devoted his life to psycho-analysis—to survey in plain language what has happened so far [in the New York Society].

In the spring of 1939 Dr. Karen Horney has published a book writ-ten for the general public, in which with one sweeping gesture she refuted most of the fundamentals of psychoanalysis.... While she pre-tended to have retained the unconscious and some of its dynamics, all experts expressed their opinion that Dr. Horney's unconscious has nothing in common with Freud's concept of this psychic system and the laws ruling it. [Lay readers] are full of praise for any book which ...kills the contention that our sex life is of fundamental importance in the structure of human psychology. [As a result] forty years of pa-tient scientific work was thrown to the dogs.

Bewildered by Dr. Horney's book, which all experienced analysts, with the inexplicable exception of one or two, consider absurd in its essentials, we invited the author to discuss her viewpoints with us in the society. [As a result] we lost the better part of a session in discuss-ing what she presented. To our surprise Dr. Horney refrained from mentioning the bold assertions of her book and...emphasized [that] cultural difficulties, in whose midst the patient lives, should primarily be considered.... What she emphasized in her verbal discussion looked to some of us like old stuff....

Some of us got the impression that Dr. Horney was not sincere with us. Did she perhaps feel that the time had not yet come to smash Freud's psychoanalysis in his own stronghold [that is, the New York Institute]? The issue is Freud or no Freud. Is it in accord with scientific ethics to still call a theory and a practice psychoanalysis after having stripped it of its fundamentals?

Wittels' letter went on to chronicle the behavior of the Horney camp.

Dr. Horney has surrounded herself with a group of younger and youngest members of our psychoanalytic society whom she has either analyzed herself or supervised. Some of these adolescents in the field show clearly that their transference to their master is still in full bloom, openly confessing in our meetings their deep gratitude for help which they got from Dr. Horney. I have never heard that mine or anybody else's former training analysands have done anything of this kind and if it occurred we would consider it not only in bad taste but evidence of an incomplete analysis.

None of Horney's group, Wittels complains, shows "knowledge of Freud's works or even the wish to study them. Instead they study the by-laws of our society and are eager to show up in all our business meetings in order to scare into submission the majority of our society."

It is, Wittels suggests, an "astonishing fact" that "a number of the Freudians in our society seem to fall for this slogan of democracy," even though "the standard works of psychoanalysis should enjoy more credit than amendments to the constitution. . . ." He continued:

> Our students come to us because of Freud's invulnerable name expecting to be taught the result of forty years of patient psychoanalytic work. Instead, we are urgently asked to teach them a doctrine diametrically opposed to Freud's findings and rejected by probably ninety-nine percent of the experienced members of the International Psychoanalytic Association. The result is confusion of which the students rightly complain.

Winding down to a conclusion, Wittels proposes that Horney either return to Freud or teach her ideas "under a new name, e.g. 'Social Psychotherapy'" in another place.[33]

It is conceivable that society president Lawrence Kubie put Wittels up to writing this letter. Certainly it would have been a characteristic piece of Kubie stagecraft. Even if it wasn't staged, however, the letter came at the perfect time to serve Kubie's purposes. His reply was judicious and presidential. Yes, he regretted with Wittels that Dr. Horney presented her views first to the public, that her talks before the society didn't focus on her "more drastic . . . theoretical deviations." It was indeed unwise to allow any individual teacher to exert exclusive influence on students, and this had resulted in "one-sided and disastrous warping of the students' training."

All of this led up to the punch line: therefore the society must, *at the upcoming meeting five days hence*, approve the amendments giving the education committee control over student choice. He hoped that all groups, particularly this "small divergent minority," would understand that the amendments "have a protective as well as restrictive value . . . for them as much as for the rest of us."

In closing Kubie made a show of both fairness and toughness. He was against a purge, defending with Voltaire "the right to teach of those with whom I disagree profoundly provided only that they are experienced and gifted teachers, able to inspire students to think for themselves and able to move students to enthusiasm." As long as the members "accept in good faith the authority of their Educational Committee" no such drastic steps will be necessary. If, however, "a teacher should claim . . . the right to limit a group of students to any one set of ideas, and should therefore refuse to abide by the decisions of the Educational Committee as approved by the Society, then such a teacher would certainly have to be deprived of teaching functions. I am hopeful however, that no such situation will arise."[34]

Wittels' diatribe and Kubie's calculated response seem to have had the effect that Kubie hoped for. At the next interval meeting the education committee was granted its request for final say (really veto power) in student choice of training analysts. Horney rose at the meeting to request that Wittels' letter be discussed. But a member suggested she talk it over in private with the education committee instead.[35]

Horney did meet with the education committee and the board of directors of the Institute in April and, as a result, produced an outline of a course on "divergent theoretical issues." She had already outlined this course once before during Kubie's tenure. But she would never teach it.[36] In June, Fritz Wittels was elected to a three-year term on the education committee along with two other supporters of the anti-Horney point of view. Clara Thompson and Abram Kardiner, who also ran, were defeated; David Levy came to the end of his term. Kubie, who was ending his presidential term, would remain on the education committee, where he would exert great influence, particularly because the new president of the Society and Institute was Adolph Stern, an older and milder Hungarian-born analyst. A charismatic Russian-born analyst named Gregory Zilboorg was elected to a key role as chairman of the education committee. The defenders of what Wittels described as "Freud's stronghold" were dug in and ready to do battle.

During the fall, however, it looked as though there would be no further conflict. On September 12, 1940, shortly after the analysts got back from vacation, members and candidates heard honorary president A. A. Brill and the new officers exhort everyone to follow Freud and avoid other temptations. The students seemed to take the message to heart: their most controversial request that fall was that it might be possible for some non-M.D.'s to teach child analysis.[37] Karen Horney, having spent her summer vacation at her new house in Croton, seems to have come back in the fall determined to do her own work and stay away from the Institute. Although she had frequently been listed among those who rose to comment on papers at interval meetings in the past, her name disappeared from the minutes in the fall of 1940.

By December of that year things were so quiet that Lawrence Kubie decided the time was right for a controversial move: he proposed that the education committee depose Sandor Rado. Kubie had written a conciliatory letter to Rado the previous June expressing the hope that "whether in the future we agree or whether we differ on specific matters of education policy . . . we will never again hear those differences expressed in such bitter and distrustful terms as have been used this year" and adding that "we look forward to seeing you on the Cape."[38] Given Kubie's habit of seducing only to abandon, Rado should have sensed that the friendly letter meant his days as educational director were numbered.

In December, Kubie wrote Sam Atkin, his close ally on the education committee, that "the situation has cooled down a great deal" and that the time had come to "find a solution for the problem of the Educational Directorship." What Kubie proposed was a reorganization that would deprive Rado of power by getting rid of his position, thus avoiding any "ungracious" or "ungrateful" gesture.[39] Kubie prepared a lengthy memo to accomplish this end, concluding that "no one who has listened to Dr. Rado can doubt that he is among the most brilliant, gifted, and versatile of the critics of psychoanalytic theory." But, Kubie continued, it is "nonetheless justifiable to raise the question of whether Dr. Rado is temperamentally fitted for the role of director of educational policy" and whether "he himself is actually a good executive." The upshot of this long discussion of Rado's merits was that he should be asked to trade the job of educational director for that of "permanent consultant in research, a position in which his special gifts and powers would have the widest possible play."[40]

Rado was eventually deposed. But before the education committee had time to deal with Kubie's proposal, a new and potentially explosive issue was raised by the students. On January 9, 1941, in a letter to the education committee chairman, Gregory Zilboorg, they claimed that "students trained by certain faculty members who hold views not in accordance with the libido theory, or doing control work with these faculty members, or writing theses in accordance with the teachings of these faculty members are less likely to receive admission to the Society." The letter ended with a demand that ultimately backfired: "In all fairness to the student body, those training instructors whose students are not acceptable to the Educational Committee be dropped from the list of approved instructors."[41]

Once the issue of "student intimidation" was raised, things began to happen very quickly. Not long after the letter arrived, education committee chairman Zilboorg asked four student representatives to his office for a meeting with him and institute president Stern. Zilboorg, while insisting he was sympathetic to the student committee, spent most of the time trying to extract the names of students who had been intimidated. When the representatives, for obvious reasons, refused to give names, Zilboorg became (as the students reported) "livid with rage, used cajoling . . . verbosity, jokes, dramatics, and cleverness" to try to bring them around. In any case, the students had gone into the meeting with the feeling that Zilboorg was "the most vicious intimidator of all." A typical Zilboorg tactic in class, the students claimed, was to attack a student by telling him, "Your unanalyzed homosexuality is apparent. Who was your analyst?"[42]

What no one in the Institute knew then about Gregory Zilboorg was that, throughout his tenure as education committee chairman, he was carrying around a guilty secret about his *own* behavior which made his role as defender of the good name of psychoanalysis a joke.

Zilboorg, a flamboyant analyst and a dazzling intellect with connections to the White Russian movement, had already been accused of shady dealings in 1934 when he issued an "incomplete" report on the funds of the Institute bookshop.[43] Around the time that the student-intimidation issue surfaced, Franz Alexander received a telephone call from a former patient of Zilboorg's, a successful public relations executive who had sought treatment for a drinking problem and who had gotten a fleecing instead. Zilboorg, it seemed, soon discovered that this patient had access to all kinds of perks and was perfectly willing, in his vulnerable condition, to pass them on to his psychoanalyst. First there was the watch the patient was wearing (but with a different band, at Zilboorg's request), then there were tickets to the Joe Louis fight (first or second row, at Zilboorg's request), then a radio. Finally Zilboorg, who needed cash to pay taxes, offered to supplement his analysis of the patient with advice on business undertakings, since the patient—because of his drinking—needed all the help he could get. Zilboorg proposed that the patient pay him a fee of five thousand dollars, in advance and in cash, for his dual role as analyst and business consultant. At this point the patient, even in his dependent state, began to feel used. He paid Zilboorg the first thousand dollars in hundred-dollar bills but then left treatment.

Sometime after that, at the suggestion of a woman friend, the patient called Alexander in Chicago to get another opinion on Zilboorg's behavior. Alexander told the patient to write Zilboorg and get his money back, which he did. Alexander also took steps to prevent Zilboorg from practicing psychoanalysis. But many months passed before Zilboorg's unethical behavior was made known to the New York Society. During those months Zilboorg was chairman of the education committee and became particularly indignant at anyone who dared to criticize his—or his committee's—integrity.[44]

Writing to Karen Horney shortly after the students complained of intimidation, he assured her "that the Educational Committee will not tolerate diversions of any kind from the principle of impartial, scientific education."[45] On February 11, when a member raised a question about intimidation at a society meeting, Zilboorg "objected to any insinuations against the committee" and "called attention to the fact that it is the Society which has vested its trust in the Educational Committee, and that only facts and not rumors must be discussed."[46] Two weeks later, at another meeting of the society, Clara Thompson, Abram Kardiner, and Karen Horney rose to ask that the education committee report their findings on the issue of student intimidation. "Dr. Horney," according to the minutes, "made a remark about the [Education] Committee which appeared disparaging and Dr. Zilboorg moved that Dr. Horney be censured for drawing a comparison which was disparaging to the Committee as representative of the Society." (One wonders what she could have called the committee—"Fascist," perhaps?) Zilboorg moved that Horney either withdraw her remark or be "censured immediately." Horney withdrew her remark.[47]

Two months after the students registered their complaint with the education committee, Chairman Zilboorg finally issued an official response—a four-page letter insisting that the entire problem was of the students' making. "It is a matter of great regret to the Committee," Zilboorg wrote, "that despite the efforts of Dr. Stern and myself over a period of many hours to convince you that it would be best to cite us specific cases, you deemed it wise to withhold specific instances and names. Under the circumstances nothing is left but to answer your point in a general way." In the first place, Zilboorg began, the students were "under the misapprehension that training in the Institute... automatically confers membership in the New York Psychoanalytic Society. This is not so." Further, students "who are trained one-sidedly are naturally at a disadvantage." Nonetheless, Zilboorg insisted, there is no evidence that students of so-called "liberal" analysts have had more difficulty in getting approval than those who have worked with "orthodox" ones. The "real crux of the matter," Zilboorg maintained, is that the students want the society to teach "two types of psychoanalysis," while the society is committed in its constitution "to teach psychoanalysis as it was founded by Freud." The only student suggestion the committee agreed with was that it might be possible to have non-M.D.'s teach courses in child analysis, since even medical schools allow non-M.D.'s to teach. [48]

The imperious tone of Zilboorg's letter infuriated many of the students. In a series of "Resolutions" they submitted to the society in response, they began by quoting the most offensive part of the letter, Zilboorg's statement that "it is obvious that students— despite their intelligence and industry—are unable, before their training is complete, to take a definite stand on a matter of scientific controversy, since they are busy studying the fundamentals out of which the controversy has arisen." [49] This statement, the students claimed,

> masks a serious scientific fallacy, i.e., that what is historically early in the development of psychoanalysis is automatically fundamental, and must therefore be thoroughly inculcated in the student before permitting him to become acquainted with later development and trends. This is equivalent to insisting that a student in chemistry or physics be thoroughly indoctrinated with the early theories of the constitution of matter before permitting him any contact with the atomic theory.... The Educational Committee fails to make the elementary scientific distinction between the rich body of factual matter unearthed by Freud and the theories he propounded to explain these facts.... They have taken the profoundly unscientific position that nothing new has been or can be developed in psychoanalytic theory and practice beyond the original teachings of Freud.

Moreover, the education committee had misread the society's own constitution, which calls for teaching psychoanalysis not as it was "*founded* by Freud" but "as *developed* by Freud and his pupils."

The student response goes on to recommend fundamental changes in the curriculum and in the organization and operation of the education committee.[50]

The education committee took as hard a line toward Karen Horney and Clara Thompson—who were now singled out as the chief troublemakers—as it had toward the students. Thompson, after raising the issue of intimidation, had agreed to meet with the education committee early in March and present her complaints in detail. It is obvious from the official reports of this meeting, however, that the committee had no intention of taking Thompson's complaints seriously. Thompson was inexperienced in such wrangling, and her confusion made her an easy target for the education committee to shoot down at the general society meeting later that month. Zilboorg, reporting on the meeting with Thompson, asserted that "no facts were disclosed to substantiate the allegations that any intimidation has ever been exercised against students. Dr. Thompson ultimately concurred with the committee" and "agreed to communicate her satisfaction to others. But on leaving, she said she was 'dissatisfied.' "[51]

Kubie rose to add his "supplementary report":

> Libelous gossip is being circulated among the students by certain members of the Society against other members of the Society, against the Society itself, and against the Society's Educational Committee. Factual evidence of this is already in the hands of the committee and the committee is coming reluctantly to the conclusion that the "serious condition" which exists among the students and the "something rotten which is going on," referred to by Dr. Thompson, is due entirely to the fact that the minds of certain students are being poisoned by hostile and irresponsible members of the Society.[52]

By this time both Horney and Thompson had begun to suspect that a schism was inevitable. As early as January of 1941 Thompson told one candidate beginning analytic work with her that she might not belong to the New York Institute for very much longer.[53] Horney and Thompson began to talk of starting an alternative institute. Horney even held a meeting with Sandor Rado early in 1941 to plead with him to join her should she decide to walk out.[54] Perhaps the only unaligned person left, and the only person who was still trying to honestly address the issue of student intimidation, was David Levy.

Levy, who was president of the American Psychoanalytic at the time, had talked with Horney and with some students when the issue of intimidation was first raised. He then proposed to the education committee, of which he was no longer a member, that he conduct a survey of students, in an attempt to understand what was really going on. (Levy had already conducted surveys of student opinion on teachers, so he was the natural choice for the job.) When the education committee refused the offer, he decided to go ahead on his own. On February 14 he sent out a questionnaire to all the students, asking them (1) if they had been "intimidated" by any instructor or society member, (2) if they had ever been advised not to take a course because it might imperil their chances for membership, (3) if they had ever been advised to avoid a certain training analyst for the same reason, and (4) if, in the absence of specific warnings, they had been influenced in their selection of analysts by such considerations. The students were free to elaborate and to give or withhold their names.[55]

The fact that so many students chose not only to answer yes or no but to elaborate at length on their answers suggests just how troubling and pressing many of them felt the intimidation issue to be. In all, seventy-two of the one hundred and ten candidates answered the questionnaire. Twenty-three, or about a third, said yes to one or more of the questions about intimidation. But their elaborations were more telling than the statistics. A few who denied that there was intimidation wrote indignant defenses of the education committee and the orthodox point of view. "I firmly believe this questionnaire implies a distrust of the Educational Committee," one respondent wrote. Another complained of intimidation from the other side, "carried out by students who sit together at lectures and seminars to audibly deride the Freudian sense of the lecturer. They frequently egg each other on to deliver opposing points of view to the assembled group, and these points of view are always anti-Freudian."

The students who affirmed the presence of intimidation were more likely to have stories to tell. Several had had their final papers rejected for what they suspected were doctrinaire reasons. "I felt the reasons for the rejection were emotionally tinged," Janet Rioch wrote, "and were not direct, forthright criticism of the paper itself." Rioch was struggling with whether she wanted to "get into the Society 'at all costs,' or . . . stay out and remain one of the 'kibitzers.' Actually, I have a certain feeling that I would like to get in and make a more direct fight for openness and honesty, but I sure do hate to have to do any kowtowing in the process. . . . I have re-written my paper as closely to the party line as possible, without perjuring myself, but it gives one a bad taste in the mouth."[56]

Another student wrote:

I and many other students have attended scientific meetings of the Society in which Dr. Horney's views were presented and have witnessed scenes in which some of those who disagreed with these views have displayed such animus that no calm and decent consideration of the scientific issues was given. This sort of thing precipitated discussions among the students who were about to prepare papers for the consideration of the faculty and the question was freely aired: shall a student present work which indicates he has been helped by . . . those who open the way to critical discussion of Freud's work . . . or shall he suppress this aspect of his education at the Institute and show only a rote intellectualized grasp of the principles of classical Freudian psychoanalysis?

Undoubtedly the most dramatic evidence of intimidation was presented to Levy by a student named Herman Selinsky. Selinsky received a friendly letter from Zilboorg on March 20 informing him with "pleasure" that the education committee "has endorsed your training" and only awaits a final paper. Four days later Selinksy attended the student meeting where the "Resolutions" were drawn up condemning the education committee. The day after the meeting Zilboorg sent another letter to Selinsky informing him that the education committee had had second thoughts about him. "The consensus of opinion was that your clinical work is not entirely satisfactory and that there are many aspects of it which need to be improved considerably," and that therefore the thesis should be prepared with "particular care."[57]

A beginning student at the Institute confessed to his bewilderment. "From the talk going on among students it just isn't safe to choose any of the 'ego' analysts. Many of the students feel disgruntled and persecuted. . . . The whole business seems very silly to me, and I cannot understand how any group of men who are supposed to be psychoanalyzed themselves can establish themselves as a hierarchical body with the aim of directing the thought processes of adult students along a prescribed groove."

David Levy's conclusion, in a four-page letter to members dated April 14, was that the questionnnaires revealed "an appalling situation," and that "to deny that it exists is . . . pure sophistry." He asked that a special meeting of the society be called to "consider remedial measures."[58]

The education committee, however, had already made up its mind before they saw the results of Levy's survey of student opinion. On March 28, in one last attempt at conciliation, Kubie wrote Levy regarding Clara Thompson's "preposterous accusations and allegations."[59] Levy replied that "the matter goes far beyond [Thompson's] particular set-to with Dr. Zilboorg and her rather weak defense of her own position," adding, "I am just now summarizing the results of the investigation . . . and will, I hope, be able to send you a letter about it in a few days."[60] But Kubie and the education committee clearly didn't want to know what the questionnaire revealed. Shortly after Levy's letter, and a week before he sent the questionnaire results, the education committee met and voted unanimously "that Dr. Horney's status should be changed from that of instructor to lecturer."[61]

The decision was announced to the society three weeks later in a report read by Zilboorg. He began by citing the increase in enrollment and need for "a uniform plan of imparting the fundamental elements of psychoanalysis," adding that "anything that is apt to generate premature contentions and precocious exclusiveness becomes a disrupting factor injurious to the student and teacher alike." Then, moving on to the heart of the matter:

> A preparatory analysis may not and cannot proceed on the basis of preliminary indoctrination with theoretical and emotional orientations which are contrary to the fundamental principles of psychoanalytic education on which the Psychoanalytic Institute was founded. The published writings and contentions of Dr. Karen Horney present, in this respect, a case in point. The Educational Committee is fully in favor of free and unhampered discussion of all points of view existing in psychoanalysis. Such discussions are possible and most fruitful only if the preparatory analyses and preliminary, theoretical fundamentals are such as not to prejudice the student in advance to the basic principles of psychoanalysis. The Education Committee has therefore decided to change the status of Dr. Karen Horney from that of Instructor to that of Lecturer, effective at the end of this academic year."[62]

Dr. David Levy stood up twice after the statement was read and "questioned the wisdom of the course."[63] But the report was accepted by a vote of 24 to 7, with at least 10 abstentions. Immediately after the vote Karen Horney rose from her seat and headed for the door. Clara Thompson and three younger analysts, Har-

mon Ephron, Bernard Robbins, and Sarah Kelman, followed her
out.

Two days later the five analysts sent an official letter of resignation to the secretary of the New York Psychoanalytic Society:

Dear Dr. Lehrman:

For the last few years, it has become gradually more apparent that the scientific integrity of the New York Psychoanalytic Society has steadily deteriorated. Reverence for dogma has replaced free inquiry; academic freedom has been abrogated; students have been intimidated; scientific sessions have degenerated into political machinations.

When an instructor and training analyst is disqualified solely because of scientific convictions, any hopes we may have harbored for improvement in the policies of the society have been dispelled.

We are interested only in the scientific advancement of psychoanalysis in keeping with the courageous spirit of its founder, Sigmund Freud. This obviously cannot be achieved within the framework of the New York Psychoanalytic Society as it is now constituted.

Under the circumstances, we have no alternative but to resign.

The letter was signed by Harmon S. Ephron, Sarah B. Kelman, and Bernard S. Robbins, as well as Thompson and Horney.[64]

There was some speculation after the resignations that the education committee was hoping the demotion of Horney would induce an equally troublesome member, Sandor Rado, to walk out. But Rado, even though he did leave three years later, had never had any intention of joining forces with Karen Horney. Abram Kardiner seems to have toyed with the idea of following Horney, but in the end he stuck with Rado while encouraging his students to leave. This caused one of them to comment, sardonically, that Kardiner "wanted his students to have the courage of *his* convictions."[65] Ultimately fourteen students did leave the institute training, citing the "unscientific spirit and undemocratic attitude of the Educational Committee" in their letter of departure.[66]

Just one week after the meeting at which Horney was demoted, Franz Alexander and David Levy (to whom Alexander went because he was president of the American Psychoanalytic) confronted Gregory Zilboorg with his unethical behavior during the meetings of the American Psychoanalytic in Richmond, Virginia. Zilboorg was initially repentant and promised to give up practicing psychoanalysis if they kept the story to themselves. But his repentant mood soon wore off, and before long he was making plans to run for office and continue practicing as before. As a result, the matter was brought before officers of the New York Society, who held hearings and took testimony from the wronged patient, Zilboorg, Alexander, Levy, and others. The upshot was a recommendation by the board of directors that Zilboorg be reprimanded. On March 3, 1942, a little less than a year after Karen Horney's demotion, the New York Society met to decide the fate of Gregory Zilboorg. For a number of reasons, one of which was concern about the reputation the society was acquiring for squabbling, the majority of the society voted not to reprimand Zilboorg. He remained a member in good standing.[67]

Shortly after the vote was taken David Levy submitted his resignation to the New York Psychoanalytic Society. The immediate reason for his resignation, as he wrote, was that "I am unable to stomach the recent action of your Society in connection with the disciplinary proceedings against Dr. Zilboorg."[68] Levy was also enraged by attempts, before and after the Horney resignation, to ignore and discredit his report on intimidation. "In fact, there was a move in the Society to condemn any such investigation because the prestige of the Education Committee was involved; that prestige was considered to be more important than the welfare of the Society."[69]

17

A New Institute

There are two memories, seemingly contradictory, of events on the night in April 1941 when Karen Horney was stripped of her status as training analyst at the New York Psychoanalytic Institute. Another woman analyst at the meeting, Yela Lowenfeld,[1] remembers that when Horney, a striking figure with her red dress and white hair, turned to walk out, there were tears streaming down her face. But Clara Thompson, one of the five who followed Horney out in protest, claims that her mood was jubilant. Soon after they left the building someone in the rebel band started up a chorus of "Go Down Moses." With arms linked, the five defecting analysts marched down Fifth Avenue singing, "Tell old Pharaoh, to let my people go."[2]

There are reasons to doubt the literal truth of both these stories. The first, of Horney in tears, is remembered by only one, not very sympathetic, witness. The second, of walking down Fifth Avenue singing a spiritual of liberation, is doubted by Harmon Ephron, one of the five defectors. Ephron suspects that if he and the others sang at all, it was after they'd had a few drinks at a nearby bar. And yet both memories reflect and dramatize the powerful feelings that accompanied what turned out to be a resounding event, both in the life of Karen Horney and in the history of psychoanalysis. Whether she cried or not, there can be no doubt that Karen Horney was deeply hurt by the vote against her that night. For a woman who had devoted her entire adult life to teaching and practicing psychoanalysis such a demotion at the hands of her peers had to be devastating.

But Horney was never one to expose her hurt to the world. From Horney herself we have only one veiled reference to her feelings about the affair, an ironic one that stresses not tears but laughter. In January of 1942 Horney wrote a letter to southern Ohio author Charles Allen Smart praising his book *Wild Geese,* a collection of ruminations on "living as an art." The book, she tells him, "has given me something of great value in that it elicited the faculty to look at myself with a sense of humour—benevolent humour. And since I have some pretty exciting weeks behind me, it was simply grand to see the excruciatingly funny sides of so many situations. That is a help of another kind than analysing oneself, but curiously enough to the same effect."[3]

Aside from the tears, which may be apocryphal, the best measure of Horney's pain is the amount of energy she immediately poured into challenging those who had rejected her. Unlike Moses, who led his people out of the Pharaoh's land into freedom, Horney intended to compete with the New York Psychoanalytic on its own turf. Even before the vote to demote her, the Horney group had been talking about setting up an alternative organization to the New York Psychoanalytic. After the vote the futile struggles with Zilboorg and Kubie could be set aside in favor of a fresh and challenging enterprise: the creation of a new institute. "It's the most exciting thing that has happened to me in many years," Clara Thompson wrote a friend the September after the walkout. "Not only are the events exciting, but the necessity to have courage to take a dangerous step (one might have been ruined professionally) has made a new person of me."[4]

Horney and her group moved with impressive speed after the walkout. Within three weeks they had decided on a name for their organization: the Association for the Advancement of Psychoanalysis (AAP). Soon after, a slim first volume of the organization's journal, the *American Journal of Psychoanalysis,* appeared, listing fifteen "charter members" in New York and a handful in other cities. The journal announced a "tentative prospectus" of no fewer than thirteen courses for "students in training and interested physicians," as well as four courses to be taught at the New School for graduate students in psychology and other disciplines. There was no mention in the first issue of the journal of an institute that would provide training in psychoanalysis.[5] But plans for an institute, with Karen Horney as dean, solidified over the summer, and the second issue of the journal announced a curriculum "to train psychiatrists for the clinical practice of psychoanalysis." There were to be clinical conferences and case seminars, like those at the New York Psychoanalytic. But as the announcement made clear, the atmosphere at *this* institute was going to be different. "Students are acknowledged to be intelligent and responsible adults," the catalogue stated, "full-fledged physicians engaged in post-graduate training. . . . It is the hope of the Institute that it will continue to avoid conceptual rigidities, and to respond to ideas, whatever the source, in a spirit of scientific and academic democracy."[6]

In December of 1941, just as the new institute was getting started, the Japanese bombed Pearl Harbor and impelled the United States into World War II. Soon after, many of the institute's candidates would be drafted to serve overseas. Yet the ominous prospects of war could not dampen the enthusiasm of Karen Horney and her group for their new undertaking. "I've learned to fight," Clara Thompson reported triumphantly that spring, ". . . a thing I never really did before."[7] "They were glorious days," Harmon Ephron remembers. "The revolution was on."[8] There was a feeling of camaraderie between candidates and faculty during those early days that would have been unthinkable at the New York Psychoanalytic. At a party at Karen Horney's house in Croton one candidate delivered a lecture on a new psychoanalytic concept, "The Oy," and another sang, meaningfully, "It Ain't Necessarily So."[9]

Some of the enthusiasm for the new association took the form of admiration for Horney, its leading light. Walter Bonime, who was in the first institute class, remembers reading *The Neurotic Personality of Our Time* and thinking it was "like a swim on a hot day in a cold brook."[10] When his daughter was born he named her Karen. Ruth Moulton, another candidate, also gave birth, in 1942, to a daughter she named Karen. Karen Horney sent her flowers and "a very nice note saying she hoped I had thoroughly enjoyed the whole experience, which was much the way I felt about pregnancy and childbirth."[11]

Karen Horney, however, was not the only attraction of the association in those early years. In addition to Clara Thompson, who was a respected and independent teacher, Erich Fromm joined the association and taught courses there. Harry Stack Sullivan signed on. And William Silverberg, who had been part of the Zodiac group but never a member of the New York Psychoanalytic, served as the association's first president. During the winter of 1941–42 an impressive roster of speakers appeared by invitation at monthly meetings, including Margaret Mead, Franz Alexander, Abram Kardiner, Frieda Fromm-Reichmann, and Horney's defender at the New York Psychoanalytic, David Levy.[12] There was even, in the spring of 1942, an annual convention of the new association at the Copley Plaza in Boston. A formal banquet was held and recorded for posterity in an official photograph. In it, Karen Horney sits at the center of a vast U-shaped banquet table, her face partially obscured by a large flower arrangement, flanked to left and right by thirty members and spouses sporting tuxedos and corsages. The "annual dinner," as it was designated on the official photograph, bore witness to the determination of the new association to be taken seriously.

In truth, the photograph of the "annual dinner" implied a feeling of permanence that had not yet been achieved. The association didn't have a home of its own, and many classes were held in teachers' homes or offices. There *was* the promise of an affiliation with a medical school. During that first year three courses were offered—by Silverberg, Horney, and Thompson—at the Post-Graduate School of New York Medical College at Flower Fifth Avenue Hospital. And of course there were the New School classes and the analytic classes. Given the limited number of faculty members, it is difficult to see how all the promised classes could actually have taken place. And indeed a number of candidates who had been about to graduate from the New York Psychoanalytic at the time of the split were soon pressed into service as faculty members. But there was no denying that the association had managed to put a lively program in place in almost no time at all. Not only that, but the program had twice as many students as had resigned from the New York Psychoanalytic.

The program itself reflected the point of view articulated by William V. Silverberg in his presidential address that first fall. "Psychoanalysis was begun by Freud," Silverberg stated, "and, of all psychoanalysts, Freud has been the most diligent worker, the most original, the most fruitfully productive. But what Freud founded has already become greater than Freud. Freud opened our eyes to a vast new era of knowledge about human nature; psychoanalysis is not merely a therapeutic method; it is a psychology, and as such infiltrates into and illuminates every field in which an understanding of human nature is important." In addition to case seminars, basic readings in Freud, and courses on technique—all sounding very much like those offered at the New York Psychoanalytic—the association programs stressed social issues. Papers were given on "Problems of Group Behavior," for instance, and "Unconscious Motivations for the Loss of Employment."

In 1941 it was natural for a group that emphasized the effects of culture on personality to address itself to the war. The annual convention included a panel on the "sociological and psychological implications of destructiveness." There was also a "War Effort Committee," which published a series of papers in the journal, including one by Karen Horney, "Understanding of Individual Panic." Since the possibility of air raids or even invasion was on every American's mind in those days, panic was a timely subject.[13] As a result, Horney's article attracted media attention, which in turn incurred the indignation of her old nemesis Lawrence Kubie. Kubie sent Adolph Stern, who had succeeded him as president of the New York Psychoanalytic, three clippings—from the *New York Post,* from the newspaper *PM,* and from the *Journal of the American Medical Association*—"all glorifying," he noted with sarcasm, "that well known American girl, Karen Horney."[14]

Kubie couldn't have been pleased, either, by the appearance, of Karen Horney's third book, *Self-Analysis,* just a few weeks after all the publicity given the article. Lionel Trilling, an ally of the Freudian establishment, claimed that "in her latest book Dr. Horney carries her rejection of Freud's theories about as far as it can go. . . . She propounds the belief that by adapting the techniques of regular analysis a neurotic person can effectually analyze himself."[15]

The idea of self-analysis, however, was not so radical as Trilling seemed to think. Freud's *The Interpretation of Dreams* was largely the product of his analysis of himself. Moreover, the suggestion of the title is immediately tempered within the book. A person may undertake self-analysis, Horney suggests, "during the longer intervals that occur in most analyses: holidays, absences from the city. . ." Or someone who lives a great distance from cities where analysts . practice may undertake analysis between "occasional checkups." It may also be possible for "a person whose analysis has been prematurely ended to carry on by himself." And last, "and this with a question mark—self-analysis may be feasible without outside analytical help.["16] With all those qualifiers, *Self-Analysis* is hardly a call for a patient revolt against professional help.

Indeed, the book seems to have had the opposite effect, at least in Horney's case. Around the time *Self-Analysis* came out, Horney's books and lectures, coupled undoubtedly with talk on the New York grapevine about her break with orthodoxy, had created an enormous demand for her services. "Everyone," Harmon Ephron remembers, "wanted her as an analyst. I had so many referrals from her I kept five other analysts busy.["17] For the most part the patients weren't referred by M.D.'s, he remembers, but by other patients and social workers.

And yet, despite Horney's popularity with non-analysts and despite the relatively uncontroversial content of *Self-Analysis,* the book was either ignored or reviled by virtually every popular and psychoanalytic publication. The *New York Times* and *Herald Tribune* didn't review it at all. Trilling, writing in the *Nation,* complained that "in Dr. Horney's hands culture becomes as much an absolute as she claims biology is in Freud's"[18]—a criticism that could apply only to earlier books, since *Self-Analysis* has almost nothing to say about culture. The *Psychoanalytic Quarterly,* the only "orthodox" journal that took note of the book at all, characterized Horney as "unfriendly to psychoanalysis" and crippled by "an insistence on current situation which, like neighborhood gossip, comes close to being cultural illiteracy."[19] Bertram Lewin, a prominent member of the New York Psychoanalytic, conceded in the *Saturday Review of Literature* that the book is "very smoothly written in an exceptionally clear style" but complained, predictably, that it lacked "insight into infantile sexuality, especially the Oedipus and castration complexes, and into those unconscious things which are the quintessence of Freudian analysis."[20] J. F. Brown, who had been consistently critical in the *New Republic,* didn't like the book's promise to provide "the key to self-analysis for three dollars." He described Karen Horney as the "the stormy petrel of the controversies concerning theory and technic which have characterized American psychoanalysis in recent years."[21]

The critical reaction to Horney's *Self-Analysis,* more hostile by far than the reaction to either of the first two books, is undoubtedly a reflection of the power of the New York Psychoanalytic Society. Beginning in the fall of 1941, the society had undertaken a far-reaching campaign, spearheaded by Lawrence Kubie, to inform not only psychoanalytic colleagues but the wider world that the

defection of Karen Horney was nobody's fault but her own. Kubie
had sounded the alarm in October, six months after the walkout.
At a special meeting of the society he called for "prompt action . . .
with regard to the false accounts and rumors which are now current concerning the resignations which took place last spring."[22] A
special committee was drawn up and prepared a long statement,
which was not only published in the *Psychoanalytic Review* but dis-
tributed to the broadest possible audience: hospitals, foundations,
social-work agencies, editors of journals and magazines, medical
societies; even important individuals in Horney's sphere of influence, including Margaret Mead and W. W. Norton, received copies
of the statement. It had been drafted by Lawrence Kubie, and,
even after revisions in committee, it carried the slightly condescending tone of many of his pronouncements.

In most cases, the statement began, the public didn't need to
concern itself with the details of scientific disagreements. But in
this case the dissenting group had organized a new society and
training institute under names—the Association for the Advancement of Psychoanalysis and the American Institute for Psychoanalysis—that suggested "national scope and acceptance." Moreover,
the group's public statements implied that it was founded "as a
protest against scientific dogmatism entrenched behind political
power within the New York Psychoanalytic Society." Because of
these "unfounded allegations," as well as possible public confusion
about the new group, the society had decided to speak out.

The statement continues for two pages making claims for the
society's fair-mindedness. No "invidious distinctions" were made
among courses, and faculty members "who hold divergent theoretical convictions" continued to be tolerated (here presumably a
reference to Rado and Kardiner). Furthermore, "special opportunities" were provided to members with differing viewpoints to
present their theories at meetings (a reference to the two meetings
at which Horney spoke). "On every issue," the statement concludes, "the allegation that anyone was excluded from teaching for
reasons of theoretical 'unorthodoxy' falls to the ground." As for
student intimidation, "without claiming an impossible degree of
perfection," it can be "stated fairly" that it is "based on nothing
more substantial than the occasional momentary expression of individual fears and resentments."

Next the statement takes the offensive, describing the training
standards of the institute and implying (still without mentioning
any names) that the dissenters violated them by "injecting the stu-

dent into the midst of... heated controversy" and placing him "under the exclusive influence" of one point of view. New theories and modifications should be tried out "only by those who are already mature in experience." Because of "confusion" among "elementary students" and "an unscientific tendency to form cliques" and because some students were "encouraged to make radical technical departures" it became the "duty of the Institute" to act.

The action, which is finally revealed in the closing paragraphs, "did not deprive Dr. Horney of teaching privileges, but merely shifted the impact of her teaching from elementary... to intermediate and advanced... students. In this step there was no violation of academic freedom." In fact, it was not the society but *the dissident group* that "violated academic freedom by attempting to maintain an exclusive influence on the education of a small group of students."[23]

Not content with spreading the word in print, Kubie took to the road later that winter, traveling with fellow member Leonard Blumgart to the Philadelphia and Chicago institutes to present the story from the society's point of view. In Philadelphia, at least, the presentation seems to have had the desired effect. Dr. LeRoy Maeder wrote Kubie afterward that he and all members were "very much impressed and influenced by the presentation of facts by Dr. Blumgart and yourself and by the simple, direct, patient and fair attitude you and Doctor Blumgart maintained all through your handling of the situation and at our meeting. I know that the presentations did definitely modify the attitudes of several to whom I talked who were potentially sympathetic to Doctor Horney's point of view."[24]

Another member, O. Spurgeon English, wrote Kubie that he found himself "really hating to take sides against Clara [Thompson] and Bill [Silverberg]. I like them both so much and they both feel they are so right." But, nonetheless, after the visit he would cast his vote with the New York Psychoanalytic.[25] The reaction in Chicago appears to have been more restrained. From the Baltimore-Washington Society, the former home of Sullivan, Thompson, and Silverberg, Kubie received word he was welcome to come, "especially if you could accept with the understanding that Dr. Clara Thompson would also speak on this occasion." Baltimore-Washington Society secretary Ralph Crowley added drily that "a minority will consider the whole theme vastly irrelevant in wartime—if not actual evidence of internecine strife of a type that gives aid and comfort to the enemy."[26] Later, however, even this hedged invitation was rescinded; Crowley wrote that the society had decided against Kubie's visit "due to limitations of time."[27]

Kubie fired off a response that revealed just how troubling the Horney defection had become. "Suppose that a controversy had rent the Baltimore-Washington Society apart, and that members of some other group had joined one of these warring camps... without careful and scrupulous efforts to investigate both sides of the controversy." Since he hadn't been allowed to speak, Kubie announced, he was sending a letter stating his position to every member of the Baltimore-Washington Society.[28]

The Baltimore-Washington Society was not the only institution that proved resistant to Kubie's blitz. Four months after the New York Society issued its statement about the split, the senior attorney of the State Department of Education wrote to point out that the society's claim to be "the only organization for training in psychoanalysis chartered by the University of the State of New York"[29] was false. After the Horney group threatened a libel suit, the New York Psychoanalytic sent out a retraction, admitting that "so far as the University of the State of New York is concerned, the status of the New York Psychoanalytic Institute does not differ from that of the American Institute for Psychoanalysis."[30]

The retraction must have gratified the Horney group; concessions from the New York Psychoanalytic were hard to come by. Yet a dispassionate observer would have discerned that the Horney group had already lost the only credential fight that mattered: the battle for recognition by the national organization, the American Psychoanalytic Association.

In May of 1941, exactly one month after Horney had walked out of the New York Psychoanalytic, the American Psychoanalytic Association held its annual meeting at the Hotel Jefferson in Richmond, Virginia. The New York forces had not yet had time to consolidate their position, and there appears to have been a good deal of sympathy for the Horney group. Not only were the dissidents' ideas attractive but there was also plenty of resentment of the power of the New York Institute—the New York Yankees of psychoanalysis. The "orthodox" candidate for the presidency of the American Psychoanalytic Association was a midwesterner, however—Karl Menninger. The alternative candidate was the president of the Association for the Advancement of Psychoanalysis (AAP), William Silverberg. According to Saul Ephron, Silverberg came within one vote of overthrowing the old guard. If he had, he probably would have paved the way for the AAP's training program to be officially recognized. But after that first year a reaction set in.[31]

Karl Menninger, in his presidential address to the American Psychoanalytic the following year called for a "stronger central organization," with more authority over the constituent societies and over accreditation. He likened Freud's position in psychoanalysis to that of Galileo in astronomy and Newton in physics. "It is neither our duty nor our privilege to attempt to accomplish self-advancement in the name of intellectual freedom," he intoned, "by proclaiming criticisms of Freud or exploiting great discoveries of our differences with him." Although Horney was never mentioned by name in the speech, she was present in nearly every paragraph. "For the sake of dignity, unity, and prestige," Menninger insisted, "scientific differences of opinion must be confined to the halls of our meeting places rather than used to obtain popular support by appealing to the prejudices and so-called common sense of persons unfamiliar with the details and history of science."[32] The Menninger speech signaled that the American Psychoanalytic was closing ranks.

There would never be another real opportunity for the AAP to be recognized by the American Psychoanalytic Association; and the effects of this on the AAP can scarcely be overestimated. It would make it more difficult for the Horney institute to attract students, since their training wouldn't be recognized by the national organization. Horney group members wouldn't be able to publish in mainstream psychoanalytic journals. Nor would they be welcome at meetings of the American Psychoanalytic Association or even for that matter of the International Psychoanalytic Association (since the American insisted on holding the key to membership in the international organization). The most important result of this exclusion, by far, was the professional isolation that resulted. As Clara Thompson was to observe some years later, being part of the American Psychoanalytic would allow for exchange of ideas with "people who disagree with you" and counter the "cult-like attitude" that is likely to grow in groups isolated from the mainstream. There is a tendency to one-sidedness in such groups, Thompson noted. As the result of such polarization, many of her students, for instance, wrongly assumed that she didn't believe in the Oedipus complex or in the importance of the patient's sexual

history.[33] It should be said, conversely, that the American Psychoanalytic might have benefited as well from greater diversity.

For Karen Horney personally the exclusion from the American
had the tragic effect of leaving her without independent collegial
responses to her work. All of her books were reviewed in *Psychiatry,* the journal of the Baltimore-Washington Society. But the reviews were often written by admirers she suggested for the job. It
is a remarkable fact that after *Self-Analysis,* which received a hostile
review in the *Psychoanalytic Quarterly,* not a single one of the three
Horney books of the ensuing years was reviewed by a "classical"
journal. The *Psychoanalytic Quarterly* and the *International Journal of
Psychoanalysis* reviewed all kinds of books during these years, including trivial books, popular books, books only tangential to
psychoanalysis. But Horney's books *Are You Considering Psychoanalysis?, Our Inner Conflicts,* and *Neurosis and Human Growth* were
not mentioned once. It was as though she had died on the day she
left the New York Psychoanalytic.

This brutal and complete exclusion from the parent organization
of psychoanalysis was to haunt the Horney group for years to
come. At first it had been exhilarating to play David to the Goliath
of the New York Psychoanalytic. But before long some of the
defectors began to suspect that they had been imprudent and returned to the fold. Judd Marmor, one of those who returned, explains that he "could be more effective as a critic within the ranks
of the American Psychoanalytic than outlawed and discredited as a
non-analyst." He adds that "the only penance they made me perform was to have additional supervision with Larry Kubie."[34]
Over time, the New York Psychoanalytic's control of accreditation
put pressure on the Horney group to find alternative institutional
support. And this pressure exacerbated tensions that were already
heating up. As so often happens in excluded groups, quarrels
began to develop over who was getting more of the pie—more
classes to teach, more students, and so on. In 1943, just two years
after it had begun with such high hopes, the association split into
two groups. Within a year after that another walkout took place,
further dissipating talents and energies.[35]

Irving Bieber was a candidate at the AAP when he was drafted
into the army in 1942, and the AAP gave a party for him at Clara
Thompson's apartment. He remembers that there was a big flag
over the doorway, for patriotism, but that "everyone was interested in the organization." When he returned from the war four

years later the organization had divided into three organizations, all at odds with one another.[36] The intolerance which drove Horney and her followers out of the New York Psychoanalytic had come back to divide them.

18

Dissension Within

The worst wounds to the Association for the Advancement of Psychoanalysis were inflicted not by the New York Psychoanalytic or the American Psychoanalytic but by the AAP's leaders, who proved incapable of working out their differences. Factions seem to have developed almost from the start, with Thompson and Fromm angered that most of the new students were taken into analysis by Horney. Horney in turn (according to several students) appeared to resent Fromm's popularity with students. And in the spring of 1943, when students requested that Fromm teach a clinical course in the institute program (he had been teaching only at the New School until then), these rivalries erupted into an open disagreement over whether Fromm, who was not an M.D., should be allowed to teach such courses to candidates in analytic training. Horney took the position that allowing a nonphysician to teach clinical courses would make it more difficult for their institute to be accepted as a training program within New York Medical College. But Fromm and his supporters, most notably Clara Thompson and Harry Stack Sullivan, pointed out that in fact no one at New York Medical College had raised any objections to a lay teacher.

In April of 1943, when the question was put to a vote in the faculty council, Horney's position prevailed. Fromm, who had in fact been functioning as a training analyst in the privacy of his office, where he was analyzing and supervising students, was officially deprived of training status. As a result, he resigned, along with Clara Thompson, Harry Stack Sullivan, and Janet Rioch, one of the candidates who had left the New York Psychoanalytic at the time of the first split. Together, they immediately made plans to start an alternative institute.[1]

Ruth Moulton, who was head of the student group at the time, vividly recalls the meeting at which the announcement of Fromm's demotion was made. After a lecture by Dr. Viola Bernard on peptic ulcer, nonmembers of the association were asked to leave because "Dr. Horney had a special message for us." Horney came forward "with Dr. Robbins on one side and Dr. Silverberg on the other" to explain the circumstances surrounding Fromm's resignation. She explained that as a lay analyst he might jeopardize the association's affiliation with a medical school. Moulton tried to present a counterargument. "I pointed out that our group had given up prestige and status once for the right of free scientific discussion and that it seemed very odd that a liberal group should take this kind of stand only two years later. I suggested that the real issue seemed to be a political one and that we, the students, were not being given all the data." At that point Moulton was branded by the Horney faction as "a representative of the Fromm group."[2]

But another student, not composed enough to speak up at the meeting, congratulated Moulton afterward on her "hair-raising frankness." Ralph Rosenberg, writing to her a few days later, suggested that "we children should get together and spank our unruly parents for their childish behavior":

The *students* may hold the balance of power in the mess. Thompson expects to recruit enough students from our gang and other sources to start a third school. . . . If the students boycott the third school will we not force them to fold up? If we hold this threat, can we not gently but firmly urge them to heal their differences and rejoin the present group? Similarly, Horney was obviously scared at the violence of the students' reactions that night. She would probably go a long way to compromise with the third group to bring back and restore the students' undivided loyalty. The faculty has little to gain by the split and its accompanying mud slinging. The students lose the services of outstanding teachers. . . . We do not know the actual issues causing the split. . . . I therefore suggest that the students invite the Fromm and

Horney group to discuss their differences in the presence of the students.

At the end he adds a P.S.: "We should act promptly before they get too set in their incompatibility."[3]

It is a sad letter to contemplate in retrospect. Like a child in the midst of a divorce, Rosenberg overestimates the power of the students to bring the "grown-ups" to their senses and underestimates the grown-ups' intransigence. No such meeting with students was ever held, nor did the "actual issues" involved in the split ever become entirely clear to anyone. But what did become increasingly clear is that Fromm's being a lay analyst had very little to do with it. Horney's daughter Marianne, in a paper written thirty-five years later and entitled "Organizational Schisms in American Psychoanalysis," noted that "the arguments presented at the time by Horney, Robbins, and Silverberg fail to convince, even on rereading, that lay analysis was the sole issue."[4]

It is just possible that Karen Horney convinced herself that Fromm's nonmedical status would be a liability in wooing New York Medical College. Certainly, after being ostracized by the American, she had reason to worry about the AAP's status. Then too Horney had argued against lay analysis as early as 1926; in that way her position was consistent. And yet none of this comes close to explaining her insistence on ejecting Fromm from the faculty of her institute.

As Clara Thompson pointed out in a statement written at the time, other institutes, in Boston and Detroit, had made exceptions for unusually qualified laymen, including them on their faculties and yet continuing to be recognized as medical societies by the AMA (and, for that matter, by the American Psychoanalytic). She suggested that the lay issue was an "effective red herring." The true explanation was that "the group in power (the Horney group) feel themselves politically threatened by the increasing strength of another point of view. I think this has developed very clearly in the faculty council meetings this year, where it became increasingly apparent that any reference to Fromm met with the idea of insuperable difficulty although in the preceding year he had been accepted fully as a teacher. . . . The group in power finally showed its hand quite clearly in a final event, the reaction to the request of the students for a course with Fromm."[5]

Some version of Thompson's view was held by other observers

of the split. Ruth Moulton suggested in a talk many years later that the appearance of Fromm's first book in English, *Escape from Freedom,* in 1941 may have aroused Horney's jealousy, particularly since Fromm drew praise and attention from the same lay audience that admired Horney's work. Fromm was, in any case, the only teacher on the faculty who had Horney's kind of charisma. She remembers that once, introducing him, Horney slipped and called him "Dr. Freud" instead of "Dr. Fromm." Everyone laughed at the time, but it was only a few months later that Horney led the group that ousted him.[6]

A more Machiavellian version of the motives behind the split was suggested by Janet Rioch, in whose apartment the announcement was made. For some time Harry Stack Sullivan had been hoping to establish a branch of his Washington School of Psychiatry in New York. Rioch suspects that he subtly promoted the split because he wanted to draw off Thompson and Fromm to form the nucleus of a new group. Sullivan was present on the night the split was announced and was, she believes, "happy about the turn of events."[7] Very soon after, a New York branch was established and named after William Alanson White, the prominent American psychiatrist who headed Saint Elizabeth's Hospital in Washington for many years and was a bridge builder between psychoanalysis and the rest of psychiatry.

All of these explanations seem inadequate, however. Thompson came closer to the truth when she referred, rather mysteriously, to the possibility that the actions could only be taken "under emotional stress or when one has a personal axe to grind."[8] The truth is that the split with Fromm, although a public event, had deeply personal origins.

What Thompson and others surely knew but didn't say is that Karen Horney and Erich Fromm had had an intimate relationship for years, beginning around the time they both arrived in New York in 1934 and ending in the early forties. Their breakup, like the relationship itself, is veiled in mystery. But Horney's secretary, Marie Levy, remembers Horney confiding to her that it was over and that Fromm was a "Peer Gynt type."[9] Since Horney was writing about Peer Gynt in *Our Inner Conflicts* around the time of this comment, it is possible to elaborate a little on what she meant. The Peer Gynt maxim, according to Horney, is "To thyself be enough. . . . Provided emotional distance is sufficiently guaranteed, he may be able to preserve a considerable measure of enduring loyalty. He may be capable of having intense short-lived relationships, relationships in which he appears and vanishes. They are brittle, and any number of factors may hasten his withdrawal." As for sexual relations, "he will enjoy them if they are transitory and do not interfere with his life. They should be confined, as it were, to the compartment set aside for such affairs." Or, "He may have cultivated indifference to so great a degree that it permits of no trespassing."[10]

Horney's version of Peer Gynt/Erich Fromm suggests that the relationship with Fromm may have ended because she wanted more from him than he was willing to give. Might she have suggested marriage, for instance, and scared him off? On the other hand, however, Fromm couldn't have been entirely averse to marriage, since he married twice after his relationship with Horney ended. Perhaps, since both his subsequent marriages were to younger women, he was looking for a less powerful partner. Horney was fifteen years older than he, had published more books, and was better known at the time. Even though his first wife, Frieda Fromm-Reichmann, had been older and further along in her career as well, he may have wanted a different sort of second marriage. It is also true that Horney herself possessed many of the attributes of the Peer Gynt type. Could her typing of Fromm have been a projection? Was it she, not he, who backed off when the relationship reached a certain level of intimacy?

What is known is that Karen Horney was deeply hurt when the relationship ended. Ernst Schachtel, with whom Fromm and Horney had vacationed in Maine and the West, remembers her coming to him before the split in the association occurred and announcing that she didn't want to continue their friendship unless Schachtel stopped seeing Erich Fromm. "I was surprised she would make such a condition," he recalled later. "I continued to see him, because we were old friends. . . . I think she was deeply hurt by Erich Fromm."[11] Only a deep personal injury seems consistent with Horney's behavior in the association quarrel. She was capable, in other instances, of remaining socially pleasant to adversaries. She even remained on cordial social terms with Lawrence Kubie after the New York clash.[12]

There was another complicating dimension of Karen Horney's relationship with Fromm during these years. At Horney's suggestion her daughter Marianne had entered into psychoanalysis with Fromm, beginning in 1936 and ending in 1940. To be treated by a man so deeply involved with one's mother would seem to present insuperable difficulties. Even though Freud analyzed his daughter

Anna, and Marie Bonaparte's son was analyzed by her lover Rudolph Loewenstein, therapists generally don't try to treat people with whom they have such highly charged connections.

In a talk given years later Marianne confided that her analysis changed her life. Before analysis, she had been pleasant, conscientious, even-tempered, liked, but detached and without close friends. After two years of analysis, she experienced irritation, not only with her analyst, but also with the artificiality of her relationship with her mother. This was followed by a wish for closer relationships and resulted in new friendships and, a year after the analysis, meeting her future husband and embarking on a "rich, meaningful" life, including "two marvelous daughters." The analysis had not provided a "cure" but had "unblocked . . . the capacity for growth."

Marianne believes that Fromm was able to help her not only because he was "warm, kind, wise, and very generous" but also because he had been a good friend of her mother's for many years, and knew her "erratic relatedness or unrelatedness to people." As a result, he was able to "affirm a reality which I had never been able to grasp."[13]

For Karen Horney the success of Marianne's analytic work with Fromm was a mixed blessing, since it meant that for the first time Marianne expressed some of her unhappiness to her mother. Marianne remembers "one outburst" and another occasion on which she "criticized her openly."[14] But for the most part Marianne simply became more distant. Karen apparently blamed the changes in Marianne on Erich Fromm, whom she suspected of "projecting his antagonism to her onto me."[15] Although Marianne insists this was absolutely not the case, it is easy enough to see how Horney's hurt feelings about her breakup with Fromm might be compounded by Marianne's newly critical attitude.

Since Marianne was a student at the AAP's institute at the time of the split, she was faced with an extremely difficult choice between loyalty to her mother and to her analyst. Her solution was to choose neither. She withdrew over time from the AAP but never became a member of any other New York group. Others were free to express their indignation more openly. Two students, both of whom were Clara Thompson's analysands, resigned (five other Thompson analysands had left for the war by then). Ruth Moulton, one of those resigning, wrote Karen Horney that "until the time of the student meeting, I was honestly looking forward to controlling with you, and had saved material on one of my most interesting cases since January to bring to you. However, the presentation to the students seemed so unfair and one-sided that I feel it gave me ample genuine reason to be resentful."[16] In a letter of resignation Ralph Crowley wrote: "The A.A.P. . . . is founded basically on the idea that purge and punishment should be outlawed if done to Horney, while they are all right if done to someone else."[17] Others, who didn't resign, felt deeply disillusioned. "Many of those who remained with the Association," Judd Marmor recalls, "did so with considerable ambivalence and largely because they could not tolerate the thought of another split coming so soon after the first."[18]

The differences within the AAP didn't end with the Fromm matter, however. By the end of the year the association was embroiled in yet another divisive debate, this time over affiliation with the department of psychiatry of New York Medical College. Everyone in the AAP seems to have believed that some sort of affiliation was a good idea; everyone seems to have believed as well that the AAP should retain some autonomy. The differences were over how to strike a balance between the two goals. And, as usual, in practical terms they came down to questions of trust. There were those who trusted Stephen Jewett, the head of the department of psychiatry at New York Medical College's Flower Fifth Avenue Hospital and felt he was committed to fostering a psychoanalytic training program. There were others who were concerned that Jewett might swallow up the AAP, simply recruiting members to his staff without allowing the association to maintain a separate identity.

At a meeting in December of 1943 in Horney's apartment, faculty members lined up on one side or the other. Bernard Robbins, Silverberg, and Marmor were inclined to join Jewett at the medical college. They saw it as a great opportunity. Horney, along with two candidates who had left the New York Psychoanalytic with her, Harold Kelman and Muriel Ivimey, were more cautious. Horney pointed out that they had all put a lot of time and effort into the new institute, that it was going well, and that the medical college had everything to gain from the affiliation. What was in it for the institute?[19] There must have been a feeling by then that the issue could lead to another rupture; four days after the meeting in Horney's apartment Horney moderated an interval meeting called "Psychological Difficulties in Our Group" and described it as "an attempt to come to an understanding by frank discussion."[20]

But the attempt proved futile. The doubts raised at the December meeting were written up and forwarded to Jewett, who seems to have taken them as a sign that it was going to be difficult to work out a plan with the AAP. In the exchanges that followed, each party demanded clarification from the other, and neither provided any. On February 18, 1944, Jewett wrote the association secretary that "the difficulty seems to be in working out satisfactory arrangements with a group as a whole which is already organized into an Institute. Upon careful further reflection it seems wise that I . . . develop the plan independent of an already existing organization."[21] The following day six members of the association —Silverberg, Robbins, Marmor, Ephron, Frances Arkin, and Isabel Beaumont—resigned from the association and joined the effort to form a comprehensive training program in psychiatry at New York Medical College.

Karen Horney's position in this second split within the association seems a little more rational than in the first. After her experience at the New York Psychoanalytic, she had reason to be wary of any alliance that would erode her independence. And she *had* worked hard, along with her group, to build the association. Nor does Stephen Jewett seem to have been particularly forthcoming and cooperative in dealing with the association. On the other hand, Horney contradicted herself. If she had been so concerned about the affiliation with New York Medical College that she had sacrificed Erich Fromm, why did she become so suspicious and resistant to the idea less than a year later? Why didn't she try a little harder to make it work? The proposal to sponsor psychoanalytic training within a department of psychiatry, Judd Marmor wrote later,

> appeared to present a significant and historic opportunity to bring psychoanalysis into the framework of organized medical education. Not only would we be reaffirming the roots of psychoanalysis in medical practice, but also we would be bringing it into a university setting, where academic freedom was a long established and hallowed principle. . . . Horney's great reluctance seemed to confirm fears of some that what Horney wanted to do, consciously or unconsciously, was to perpetuate her own particular school of thought rather than sponsor an open system of psychoanalytic training. Although most of us admired her tremendously, we did not wish to be her disciples or anyone else's.[22]

The two splits had deprived the association of the best of its faculty. Of the group that had walked out of the New York Psychoanalytic, only two—Horney and Sarah Kelman—were left after February of 1944. Harmon Ephron and Clara Thompson were gone, as were Bernard Robbins, William Silverberg, and Judd Marmor. There could be little doubt at this point that Horney was preeminent; but it was also painfully obvious that a terrible price had been paid.

Not only had the association lost teaching strength, it had also lost the leaders who had played an essential role in creating a viable organization in the first place. Horney could attract people and inspire them, but right from the start she had relied on others to take charge of day-to-day administration of the organization. Thus, because the splits created a leadership vacuum that had to be filled, they profoundly influenced the future course of the association. Before the second split Robbins and Silverberg had been Horney's lieutenants. After they left she turned for a time to two women in the group, Muriel Ivimey and Elizabeth Kilpatrick. But increasingly, as the association struggled to recover from the two demoralizing ruptures, she turned to a more forceful ally, an ambitious young psychiatrist named Harold Kelman.

Horney once told Harold Kelman, "I'm not a good fighter."[23] Kelman, on the other hand, *was* a good fighter and not averse to making enemies. A handsome man with deep, dark eyes, he became president of the AAP in 1944 and continued to serve in that capacity or as president of the board of trustees for most of the next decade. Because he was a strong personality in a position of leadership, over the next twenty-five years Kelman had a pervasive influence on the direction, the philosophy, and the atmosphere of the AAP. This was a mixed blessing. Without Kelman the AAP might not have survived and certainly couldn't have thrived. But Kelman could be cold, arrogant, and dictatorial in his dealings with people. Inevitably, for many, these unfortunate qualities in Kelman came to be equated with the AAP itself.

Harold Kelman was born in Wallingford, Connecticut, in 1906. The youngest of eight children, he graduated from Yale University, where he played football, and from Harvard Medical School, and then trained in psychiatry and neurology at Columbia. In 1937 he began training at the New York Psychoanalytic Institute, where he was in analysis with Abram Kardiner. It was there that he first demonstrated his organizational abilities. In 1939, when students of the institute met for the first time, it was Kelman who chaired the meeting, presented a prospectus of issues to be addressed, and typed up the minutes afterward. And it was he, along with five others, who met with Lawrence Kubie on the students' behalf five months later. When the student demands forced a showdown in the New York Psychoanalytic, Harold Kelman, who would soon have graduated, was one of the fourteen who defected.

The progress of the AAP and its institute after 1944 was a testament in large part to Harold Kelman's organizational skills. After the second split, according to Kelman, Horney was "in despair"[24] and wanted to withdraw from all organizations. Yet within a year the AAP had its first home, at 135 East 63rd Street. Despite the drain on faculty caused by the ruptures, the training program continued and upheld rigorous standards for admission and graduation. The AAP's institute continued to require medical degrees as a prerequisite for analytic training, and the training requirements were as rigorous as those at the New York Psychoanalytic. (Four years of course work, a personal analysis, two supervised analytic cases, and a thesis were required for graduation.) The faculty, which tended to be recruited right out of graduating classes, must have suffered from lack of experience. And yet the institute continued to grow, especially after 1946, when a new generation of psychiatrists, back from the war and innocent of psychoanalytic quarrels, were attracted to the AAP program in increasing numbers. Kelman also contributed to the success of the Auxiliary Council, a group of supportive laymen who came in large numbers to hear lectures by Horney and others and who contributed significant financial support.

Although he was an effective administrator, however, Harold Kelman was less successful in the classroom and in the consulting room. Dr. Henry Holt, who was sent to Kelman for analysis when he entered training at the institute, describes his treatment as "long but unhappy. The man was to my mind very rigid and obsessive-compulsively involved with theoretical matters. And he had very little capacity for true warmth." Kelman had some of "the best students at the institute," and was "very bright and well-educated" and a "true lieutenant of Horney's," in fact taught "the gospel according to Horney."[25] But in class he could be unpredictable. He once blew up at a candidate and called him an SOB in front of the class because he had bought a book from a bookstore instead of, as Kelman thought proper, buying it through the association. When Esther Spitzer took a course on dreams with Harold Kelman, she

was warned not to ask questions. "He was so arrogant," she remembers; "he talked down to you."[26] Once, sitting in someone
else's lecture, Harold Kelman got up, announced he was wasting
his time, and walked out. Harmon Ephron, looking back on the
history of the association, believes that allowing Harold Kelman to
rise to power as a "colossal mistake."[27]

Horney's dependence on the much younger Harold Kelman,
however, was enormous, particularly during the first four or five
years after the splits in the AAP. She needed him, not only because
he was a forceful administrator but also, apparently, for personal
reasons. Kelman was bright, and Horney enjoyed sparring with
him intellectually, tossing ideas back and forth. But Kelman and
Horney were more than just intellectual companions. They behaved together with the easy familiarity of a couple. Janet Frey, an
AAP secretary, remembers seeing Harold Kelman go into Horney's pocketbook on one occasion without asking permission.[28]
Kelman and Horney also traveled to Guatemala together twice,
and once Kelman came down to Mexico to work with her on a
book.

People who knew Kelman doubt that his relationship with Horney was primarily sexual; many got the impression that Kelman,
who never married, was either asexual or homosexual. But he
seems to have provided something Horney hungered for, particularly in later years: unquestioning adoration. "She was seduced by
people who worshiped her," Judd Marmor claims. "That was very
important to her. And Kelman was a bachelor, he had no family,
and he devoted himself constantly to her, he was at her beck and
call. He was a strange man, a bright man, not without ability . . .
his personality was a little odd."[29] "Kelman played vassal," another
student remarked, "to Horney's queen. Each needed and used the
other."[30]

Kelman's devotion to Horney, however, seems to have been
genuine. After her death he described his "sheer pleasure" at seeing
her happy during the period from around 1944 to 1948, when
things were going well at the institute and "all was well with the
world." "It was like a child bursting into delight with themselves
and with life. . . . It happened rarely before and it happened rarely
after. But it was there."[31] When, sometime after that happy period,
Horney began to criticize Kelman, he was devastated. Morris
Isenberg, an AAP-trained analyst, remembers Horney taking Kelman to task in front of students, following a course on dreams,
telling him, "This is your own theory, not mine."[32] Afterward, in

the car driving home, Kelman was very shaken and confused and close to tears. Even though Horney criticized and quarreled with Kelman in her last years, he continued to be devoted to her ideas.[33] Ultimately, as Horney grew increasingly unhappy with Kelman's leadership, she enlisted the support of another lieutenant, a Berlin-born psychiatrist named Frederick Weiss, who had joined the AAP in 1943 and quickly demonstrated impressive breadth of learning and intellect. Weiss frequently challenged Kelman in public forums at the AAP. Although the quarreling didn't really do much to erode Kelman's power, it created a tense atmosphere at the AAP once again. Marianne Eckardt has noted that her mother had a way of promoting rivalries in the AAP, just as she had between Brigitte and Marianne at home.[34] It is also true that the quarreling and splitting that occurred at the AAP was a re-enactment on a larger scale of the quarreling of young Karen's parents throughout her childhood. Just as she had never found much peace at home, Karen was never able to create a tranquil, cooperative atmosphere in the organization she founded.

Wounded in love and disappointed by the AAP, Horney now turned to pleasures and passions over which she had more control. She continued to supervise candidates and teach at the institute, but she took longer and longer vacations in Mexico and Europe, where she devoted herself with characteristic intensity to her writing (in the morning) and her other pleasures (in the afternoon). Although she continued to have relationships with men, they tended to be of the Peer Gynt type. Her more lasting devotion was to a woman, Gertrude Lederer-Eckardt, who became a constant companion during the last years of her life, and to a cocker spaniel, Butschi, whom she indulged shamelessly and who, it was said, had to like you if you wanted to gain admission to the institute. In this comfortable and safe atmosphere Horney was able to make a brave new departure: to propound a psychological theory that was her own—not a reaction to Freud but an alternative.

19

Solo Flight

The candidates who saw Karen Horney for supervision in her later years often talk about how early in the morning she started work. One, Harry Gershman, used to listen to his wife complain because he had to be at Karen Horney's office on Central Park South at 7:30 A.M. He assured her, however, that when he went in, there was someone else coming out, who must have arrived at 6:30. And *that* person claimed that when he had arrived, there was another one leaving, whose hour began at 5:30 A.M. Besides the early hours, the candidates had to put up with Horney's passion for fresh air. Even in the winter, according to Gershman, the windows were "wide open." "I was really freezing and my teeth were chattering, and she said, 'Are you cold?' She was wrapped up in a shawl, and with my timidity I would say, 'Oh no, I'm just fine,' and we'd proceed. She was always business, dug right into the case presented."[1]

Despite the frigid air and the early hours, however, Horney's office was not an austere place. One entered the office through a waiting room, which was also the dining room. The principal magazine offered for patient perusal was *Gourmet*. The dining room table was usually covered with manuscripts, and Horney's office was, as candidate Norman Kelman (Harold Kelman's nephew) recalls, "cluttered with enormous quantities of books,

375

desk piled high, worse than my desk." Horney's cocker spaniel was always around, but sometimes in the middle of a session the housekeeper would knock on the office door and open it a crack, and Butschi would go bounding out for his walk.[2]

One gesture of Horney's made an indelible impression on the younger Kelman, who was in treatment with her. It was hot in Horney's office on that particular day, despite the open windows, and she had a glass of seltzer on her table which the maid had filled a little too full. To Kelman's amazement she picked up the glass and spilled some of it onto the rug. For somebody so careful about keeping things in order it was "a picture worth a thousand words." Another time Kelman dreamed that he was on a cruise with a lot of people who were "playing cards and deck games and dancing and drinking." Kelman, who had worked as a sailor on a cruise ship, knew the atmosphere. But in his dream he was with friends on vacation, feeling "very apart from the holiday. As I looked out over the water I saw in the distance a porpoise, gamboling, diving, leaping in the air, swimming on its back, singing at the top of his lungs, wonderful. I put my leg over the rail, ready to dive in the water to join that porpoise. And was immediately stricken with a panic. Woke up in a cold sweat." When Kelman told Horney the dream, she said, "A porpoise-less porpoise." From that brief comment Kelman was able to understand something of his "need to have everything sequential and linear and orderly" and his difficulty with "doing something simply for itself."

Horney hadn't lost her talent for enjoying the moment. And since the AAP was a small institute in which analysts and trainees were often thrown together, Kelman had other opportunities to see her in action. There was always, he recalls, at least one toast at the AAP's annual dinner to "luxurious and lecherous living." And when AAP members traveled to other cities, Horney was always ready to have fun. In Montreal and Detroit she sought out the best restaurants. When the meetings were in St. Louis she and her group had sauerbraten at a rathskeller, and she ordered a particular 1938 wine to go with it. In Cincinnati she heard that there was gambling across the river in Kentucky and immediately wanted everyone to come along and join the fun—everyone, that is, except Norman Kelman, who, she decided, in queenly and arbitrary fashion, should stay behind because it would interfere with his analysis to join her at the gaming table.[3]

It was, as Norman Kelman acknowledges in retrospect, an im-

possible way to conduct analysis. Even though she was "impeccably correct"[4] during the analytic hour, all of the extra-analytic
aspects of their relationship, not the least of which was Kelman's
ambition to rise in the institute, kept intruding. Kelman kept having dreams, for instance, about "putting her out to pasture,"
usually into retirement in Mexico. Actually, whatever hostile
wishes might have been implied, the Mexican retirement dream
also carried an element of reality. By 1946 Horney's schedule had
become, according to Kelman, "extraordinarily luxurious. She
saw patients usually three times a week, certainly that was when
she saw me. She took long vacations in the summer, usually leaving about the middle of June and coming back a week or two after
Labor Day."[5]

Even during her working months she lived more and more for
her time outside the office. Louis DeRosis remembers arriving at
her office for the first time for an interview and being greeted by a
woman in blue jeans with a garden trowel in her hand. Horney
explained, in her formal, accented speech, that she was going to
the country after their interview.[6] Horney was in her sixties by
then, but her appetite for life remained prodigious. Even though
she began the day at dawn, she would often call Frederick Weiss's
wife, Gertrude, in the evening and insist that they go to the
movies together. Horney particularly loved the films of Hans
Moser, an Austrian comic with a plastic, expressive face and a gift
for dialect. On one occasion Gertrude Weiss ran into her at a lecture and concert by the Indian musician Ravi Shankar.[7]

It wasn't just enthusiasm for life that sent Horney out at night;
she also didn't like being at home alone. And although she had
vowed to give men up after her relationship with Erich Fromm,
she was always in search of a man. She told her secretary, Marie
Levy, in the early forties that she was trying to decide whether to
get involved with Hans (a younger German man she had met) or
buy a dog.[8] That was when she acquired Butschi. But Butschi,
despite his rambunctious personality, was hardly an adequate substitute.

There was at least one more relationship with a man, and of all
her liaisons it was the one that showed the poorest judgment. The
partner was a young candidate at her institute who was in treatment with her. Few people knew about it, for obvious reasons.
Horney certainly knew such a relationship was highly unprofes-
sional. When asked in an interview around this time about socializing with patients, she responded, "As a rule, it is better not to

have social relationships with a patient, but I am not terribly rigid about it. Generally, I have none or a restricted relationship."[9] Certainly Horney would not condone another therapist's making love to a patient, thus transforming the relationship into something other than therapy and, often, leaving permanent scars. That she had such an affair suggests that her old impulsive ways survived into late middle age.

Even though this relationship with a younger man lasted until the end of her life,[10] as the forties progressed, she began to rely more and more on the companionship and support of a woman she had met through her daughter Marianne, Gertrude Lederer-Eckardt. In her native Germany Gertrude Lederer-Eckardt had already played a supporting role to two Heidelberg professors. Her second husband was Emil Lederer, an eminent economist who had left Hitler's Germany to become the first dean of the University in Exile, at the New School. Gertrude's own training was in physical therapy and exercise, and it was through an exercise class at the Payne Whitney Clinic at Cornell Medical Center that she first met Horney's daughter Marianne. When Gertrude, whose husband had died the previous year, invited her class to her apartment for tea one day, Marianne met Gertrude's son, Wolfgang von Eckardt, who "lightning quick fell head over heels in love with her." During Marianne and Wolfgang's courtship, Gertrude and Karen, two women alone, began to take a liking to each other.

Right from the start Gertrude, who was ten years younger, took care of Karen. Karen asked Gertrude if she would be willing to give her a massage for her aching back. Soon Gertrude came regularly, twice a week, not only to give her massage but to do exercises with her. Karen, for her part, recommended Gertrude to "quite a few of her patients, and colleagues, too, and my career started in earnest." When Karen's secretary left, Gertrude offered to help out. And increasingly, as Karen's relationship with Harold Kelman soured, Gertrude became her social companion as well. Gertrude always knew when Karen had had a quarrel with Kelman, because then *she* would be invited to come along to a concert or the theater.

Fortunately for Karen, Gertrude, or "Trübel," as she was nicknamed, seems to have been almost endlessly accommodating in such matters. In a vivid memoir written some years later she recalls going with Karen to a movie on a rainy Saturday evening in New York. It was a dark Danish film which Gertrude found silly and overdone, and she wasted no time in saying so when they emerged from the movie theater. Karen turned away from her in a rage, hailed a cab, and left her standing in the rain. Later Karen called to apologize but protested that Gertrude was always so quick in her judgment that she didn't have a chance to make up her own mind about the movie. In time Gertrude figured out that, even though Karen liked to talk things over with her, she sometimes resented her disagreeing. "When I noticed this, I suggested that she should tell me at the very beginning . . . whether I should play 'wall' [and just let her talk it out, without reply] or whether she wanted my opinion on it. This worked out wonderfully."

For Karen the relationship was a haven away from the strife of institute politics and the preoccupations of her practice. "I stood outside her professional life," Gertrude noted, "was no way mixed up with what went on within the institute, or the association, did not care one way or the other about her colleagues, but was seriously interested in *her* as a human being." Gertrude also had practical know-how that proved invaluable. It was she, for instance, who discovered that Karen had a housekeeper who was not only disagreeable but also probably dishonest and who insisted on telling Karen her personal problems. When confronted with the inadequacy of "Mrs. S." Karen confessed that she knew she was the wrong person but that it was so much trouble to find someone else. And besides, she confided, she was afraid of "Mrs. S." Gertrude took the matter in hand, fired the housekeeper, and found another one, named Sofie, who was to become beloved. Yet, though Gertrude sensed immediately from "a very brief, sudden smile" that Sofie was the right person, Karen wasn't sure, feeling that she was perhaps "a little sinister." When Gertrude assured her that Sofie would be perfect, Karen agreed to hire her.

Karen came to rely on Gertrude for more and more practical decisions, including financial ones. If she wanted to buy a dress, or even a car, she would ask, "Trübel, how much money do I have in the bank?" "She never kept track," Gertrude explains, "or wrote down the amounts she took from or deposited." She also had no idea of prices, often thinking something was expensive when it was reasonable, or worse, thinking it cheap when it was outrageously overpriced. It bothered Gertrude that Karen didn't even look at Sofie's grocery accounts or at her own. "I remember that I once said to her, 'Pretend at least to look at it.'" Her answer was, "Why should I?" When it came to buying and selling houses, Gertrude was once again put in charge. It was Karen who made the decisions—impulsively—but it was Gertrude who was left to carry them out.

The first such team effort involved a beautiful modern house right on the water on Fire Island which Karen fell in love with. When she and Gertrude started off for Fire Island that morning they had been planning to search for a "little shack," not necessarily on the water. But as they were walking along the beach with an agent Karen spotted this big house with a *For sale* sign and insisted that the real estate agent go back to his office and find the keys. It was a much grander place than she needed—eight rooms, four bathrooms—and it had been lived in only one summer before the owner went off to Hollywood. But once she had seen it, other, more practical, possibilities were forgotten. At 6:00 A.M. the morning after the trip to Fire Island, Gertrude got a call from Karen: she had fallen in love with the house and had to have it. It was the summer of 1941, only a few months after she had walked out of the New York Psychoanalytic. Perhaps she needed a big house that year for confidence. In any case, the Croton house, which had been designed for her and which she had loved, was turned over to an agent and never visited again. From then on it was to be Fire Island.

Not surprisingly, the house bought in such haste turned out to have drawbacks. Karen found she didn't like being surrounded by so many people she knew and who knew her from the city, and she couldn't get to the house in the late fall because the ferries stopped running. Within a couple of years she and Gertrude were house-shopping again. Karen had found an ad in the *Times* for a two-bedroom place on the south shore of Long Island in a section called Wildwood Hills. It turned out to be a shabby little bungalow with only a small garden, squeezed in between two other, similar houses and perched high on a bluff above the bay. To reach the ocean you walked down a hundred and thirty-two steps, where you encountered "a little bench and a half-broken maple tree." Karen immediately decided she wanted that house, despite the outrageous price (three times its real value, as Gertrude found out later). Her only condition was that she wanted to spend the *following* weekend in the place. Since it was late April, bitterly cold, and the house had no heating to speak of, such a condition must have puzzled the broker. Nonetheless Karen's will was done. She and Gertrude "dressed up like Eskimos, with heating pads and warm water bottles and plenty of blankets," and went down to

Wildwood Hills the next weekend to enjoy the new property. From that moment Karen never set foot again on Fire Island, leaving it up to Gertrude to sell the place and dispose of the furnishings.

The purchase of the Wildwood house set a happy weekend routine in motion, beginning midday every Friday. "Ten minutes before one o'clock," Gertrude Lederer-Eckardt writes, "I stood waiting for her [Karen] with the car before 240 Central Park South. Then, Sofie came down with a basket of food on one arm, and the reluctant Butschi being dragged on his leash, laundry, books, and what not balanced on the other arm. And right after her Karen appeared, already in slacks, mostly still munching on her luncheon sandwich, so not to miss one single minute of her precious free weekend."

Gertrude drove in town—a wise precaution given Karen's unpredictable style behind the wheel—but somewhere around the Triborough Bridge, Karen took over. Gertrude had no sense of direction when driving, so Karen would make a point of asking her, "Tell me, where do you think we should go, right or left?" When Gertrude said, "To the right," Karen promptly turned left. Gertrude admits that it was usually the right direction. Along the way they always stopped at the same vegetable stands, where the farmers knew them, and arrived at the house by four. In summer they hurried down to the beach for a swim. But when it was cold, they lighted a fire, unpacked, and sat down to a game of rummy or double solitaire. Karen was a notorious cheat at cards, a fact that Gertrude would point out indignantly when she caught her at it. Karen would laugh and say impudently, "You should have stopped me before."

Such playful humor graced their time together. Since Gertrude often brought along her Siamese cat, Mocha, there were dog-and-cat incidents to laugh over: Mocha always got carsick, and Butschi's loud snoring kept Gertrude awake, even from the next bedroom. Once, when the two animals had fought, their owners joined in, discovering that "Butschi and Mocha were just symbols of quite a few things we had to say to each other." But before long "we started to laugh, and the air was clear again." Before dinner, which Karen often cooked, the two would have an exercise session, then afterward a walk with Butschi along the beach in the starlight.

For the most part the Wildwood routine involved Gertrude's taking care of Karen. After lunch, for instance, Karen loved to have Gertrude bundle her up in a blanket on a deck chair in the sun. One September, when the two of them were alone in the country on Karen's birthday, it was Gertrude who called up friends of hers, the Lowenfelds, and asked if it would be all right to stop by with a cake to share Karen's birthday. Still, when Gertrude became seriously ill with hepatitis, Karen rose to the occasion and looked after her. "She insisted on the doctor, she ordered the nurse, she saw to it that I got to a hospital, and she came to see me every day." After the crisis was past, Karen gave up two weeks of a trip to Guatemala in order to spend it in Wildwood with Gertrude while she recuperated.

People who observed them together suspected that Gertrude was exploited by Karen. But each benefited from the relationship in her own way. As Gertrude acknowledged in her memoir, she liked to be needed. "I like to play mother-hen, and she loved to be a little spoiled and pampered." Nowhere was the mutual need more dramatically enacted than when Gertrude was seriously ill in the hospital, refusing to eat, despite the doctor's insistence. "Why doesn't he leave me alone?" she complained to Karen. "I have had a good life and when it's over, it's over." When Karen looked up, after a pause, "tears were slowly running down her face, and she said very slowly and softly: 'And when you die, what then shall *I* do?'" For Gertrude this was renewed reason for living. "Who am *I* that I *dare* to want to die, when there is Karen who needs me and wants me to live?" Self-centered as Karen's remark was, it had a therapeutic effect. From then on Gertrude made "a tremendous effort to get well."[11]

Both Karen and Gertrude understood, without it being spoken, that what Gertrude did for Karen allowed Karen to do her work. And since childhood, when she had written in her diary that school "is the only true thing after all," work had been Karen Horney's most consistent passion. By the 1940s her passion had shifted, to a large extent, away from psychoanalytic teaching and practice toward writing. She continued to do a great deal of supervision right up to the end of her life. And she was still treating patients, including several very troubled ones. According to analyst Morris Isenberg, one of Horney's patients committed suicide during the early forties. Karen was very upset and called another AAP colleague, Elizabeth Kilpatrick, afterward for help and reassurance.[12] At the opposite extreme was a woman named Barbara Westcott, who had been hospitalized for severe depression and who, after reading one of Horney's books in the hospital, sought her out for treatment. Six months after treatment began she wrote a long letter to Horney describing her new feeling of being truly alive for the first time. Spurred on by Horney's asking her, "What *do* you want, really?" she began to "see the significance of the self." Westcott's letter was published, anonymously, in the *American Journal of Psychoanalysis* in 1949 with a preface by Horney.[13] Many years later Barbara Westcott's husband wrote that he had "no doubt that Karen Horney saved my wife's life."[14]

Despite this evidence of continued work with patients, the truth was, as Norman Kelman learned firsthand in his own treatment, "at the time I knew her, she was less interested in doing analysis than in writing."[15] For all her enjoyment of weekends in the country and vacations in Mexico, time away was always structured around this most important activity. "In Wildwood," Gertrude remembers, "the morning until lunch was entirely given to her writing." She would be up to five to make herself breakfast and let the dog out, then go "back to bed with a second cup of coffee and a cigarette" to work, "surrounded by books and paper. When the weather was nice, she took her things out in the garden, otherwise she sat in her room, smoking cigarette after cigarette, looking out over the ocean, or, when no thoughts would come, playing a solitaire. She always had her cards near; it relaxed her and permitted her thoughts to work unforced."[16] Toward the end of a book project she became obsessed with it. "In the last six to nine months of the writing of a book she was a person seized by a creative passion," Harold Kelman writes in his book *Helping People*. "She was moody, restless, and, at times, intensely irritable."[17]

But far worse, according to Renate, were the times when her mother announced she'd been working entirely too hard and needed to take a complete break. Renate, who continued to live with her family in Mexico after 1939, was always horrified when her mother wrote and said she was coming for a complete rest. Karen was not the kind of grandmother who comes to help out; in fact, she was more like another child. "I had three kids and a complicated household and a very difficult husband. So when she said, 'Do nothing,' I knew it meant that she would keep me busy shopping, picnicking, touring, playing cards, you name it, but... something all the time. Everything had to be structured, she could not completely relax, ever."

Even in her free time Karen did everything with great concentration and intensity. She had begun to take painting lessons one summer at Fire Island, for instance, and when she visited Renate in Mexico she would often venture out in the afternoon with her canvas and easel. Renate remembers her in her apron and kerchief nestled against a high wall painting a colonial chapel she had chosen as her subject and so intensely involved in her task that she remained completely oblivious of the crowd of children who had gathered on top of the wall to watch her work.

Karen visited Renate and her family often, at their house near Mexico City at first, then in a rented house in Cuernavaca, and then—during two especially prized summers—in a primitive but spectacular setting in Ajijio, a little village on the shore of Lake Chapala, in the shadow of the mountains. There was an English-run hotel in the village, but Karen, Renate, and her husband and three children preferred the accommodations provided by a lanky German expatriate named, improbably, Pablo. Pablo's bungalows had no toilets, electricity, or running water, but they were right on the lake. His eggs (from hens roaming freely on the grounds), coffee, and native fruits were the freshest imaginable, and he fermented his own cognac on the roof of his house. Almost every night Pablo and his guests huddled together around an oval table singing to Pablo's guitar while thunderstorms raged outside. "The thunder," Renate recalls in her memoir, "bounced back and forth between the mountain ranges and echoed and re-echoed."

It is characteristic of Karen that she took to this experience with gusto. When Harold Kelman came down for a few days to work with her on a writing project, she checked in with him to a luxury hotel nearby. But the first night a bolt of lightning slithered through the hotel room, and the next morning the coffee at the restaurant was cold. Karen interpreted these events as sure signs she wasn't meant to be living in luxury. She packed up immediately and went back to Pablo's, with Kelman in tow.

Karen was enthusiastic about expeditions too, always studying the maps and wanting to see everything that promised to be interesting, on and off the road. Once, when her plane was postponed because of a hurricane, she insisted on driving through a virtual monsoon to seek out a buffet she'd read about in a magazine. According to Renate, the buffet, prepared by an Austrian chef at a restaurant in a tropical rain forest, lived up to expectations. But the drive was terrifying. Karen, however, thoroughly enjoyed the entire outing.[18]

Both Renate and Gertrude Lederer-Eckardt marveled at Karen's capacity to enjoy herself. She was, Renate remembers, "like a child in front of a Christmas tree, full of wonder, full of the joy of the moment." "I never knew anyone who could enjoy life so whole-heartedly," Gertrude recalled. "And it was absolutely irrelevant what it was that pleased her so much at the moment. It could be a flower, or Butschi having done something funny, or a plain fresh piece of bread or winning at a game. . . . She had the sweetest, most childlike smile you can imagine."[19] There were two photographs taken in Mexico that convey some of the deep pleasure she seems to have experienced, especially on her vacations. In one, taken at a party at Pablo's to celebrate the birth of a burro, she is leaning back from a table with a glass in one hand and a cigarette in the other and laughing. Her hair by this time is pure white and has receded, so that her face seems even larger. Wearing a big old sweater, with her flying hair, deep tan, and flashing smile, she looks like a hardy adventurer, perhaps even a female version of a Norwegian sea captain. In another photo there is a quieter feeling of contentment. She wears a simple dress, her hair is pulled back sedately into a bun, and she sits erect over the table, with fountain pen in hand. Although she is barely smiling, her face reflects the pleasure of deep immersion. It is morning in Cuernavaca, and she is working on a draft of *Our Inner Conflicts*.

Taken together, *Our Inner Conflicts,* which came out in 1945, and *Neurosis and Human Growth,* which appeared five years later, represent a new departure for Karen Horney. In her three previous books she had concentrated on making distinctions between her views and Freud's or on writing descriptively about various neurotic behaviors. In these, her last two books, she attempts to distill her observations into general principles. A great deal is familiar from her earlier writing: there is the same stress on "basic anxiety" as the cause of "neurotic trends," the same emphasis on the need for security as a motivator of behavior, the same insistence on the importance of the environment as opposed to inevitable, biologically determined conflicts. Even some of the characters are the same: the dependent personality of *Our Inner Conflicts,* for instance, bears a strong resemblance to Clare in *Self-Analysis,* who in turn resembles the patient described in the article "The Overvaluation of Love." Indeed, Horney's last two books can be read as an introduction to her ideas, since they review most of the territory of the first three. But while it was possible, after the first two books, to speak of Horney's theories, the last two made it possible to speak of a Horneyan—as of a Freudian or Jungian—psychology.

The outlines of the psychology, as sketched by Horney in her introduction to *Our Inner Conflicts,* concerned what she saw as the neurotic's solution to inner conflicts, conflicts that "originally concerned contradictory attitudes toward others" but came in time to concern "contradictory attitudes toward the self, contradictory qualities and contradictory sets of values."[20] There were, she postulated, four principal ways of trying to resolve these conflicts. One was to "eclipse part of the conflict." Here Horney was referring to her observation that many neurotics were either compulsively dependent (this was the "compliant type" of earlier articles, who dared not assert himself or herself for fear of losing love) or compulsively aggressive, needing to deny and bury all dependency needs. A second solution to the conflicts involved "moving away," "maintaining an emotional distance between the self and others" which "set the conflict out of operation."[21]

A third solution, and the one that preoccupied Horney increasingly in her last two books, was one in which the neurotic "instead of moving away from others... moved away from himself."[22] This solution involved creating an idealized image that explained away the conflicts. The problem was that it also involved living a lie—since there was always a big difference between the idealized version of oneself and the real version. Different neurotics live this lie in different ways. Sometimes the emphasis is on believing in the idealized image, in which case the neurotic has a great hunger for praise and admiration, all of which he believes he deserves. Sometimes the emphasis is on the "realistic self, which by comparison with the idealized image is highly despicable." In this case the neurotic is compulsively self-derogatory. Sometimes the emphasis is on the *discrepancy* between the idealized self and real self, and all the neurotic's energy is devoted to attempting to "whip himself into perfection."[23] Such a person lives under what Horney termed "the tyranny of the should."[24] He is "at bottom as convinced of his inherent perfection as the naively 'narcissistic' person, and betrays it by the belief that he actually could be perfect if only he were more strict with himself, more controlled, more alert, more circumspect."[25]

Horney's fourth solution to neurotic conflict, externalization, is an outgrowth of the third. It is, in her words, "the tendency to experience internal processes as if they occurred outside oneself and, as a rule, to hold these external factors responsible for one's difficulties."[26] It involves not only shifting responsibility onto other people and circumstances but also shifting feelings. Thus "a person who tends to externalize may be profoundly disturbed by the oppression of small countries, while unaware of how much he himself feels oppressed. He may not feel his own despair but will emotionally experience it in others."[27]

Our Inner Conflicts is a short but rich book. The first half is devoted to describing and illustrating these four "solutions" to conflict. The second half discusses the consequences of adhering rigidly, as neurotics do, to these solutions. Such unsatisfactory solutions result in living with many fears, particularly fears of ridicule and exposure, or in living a shallow life, cut off from deep and genuine feeling. Hopelessness, and sadism born of complete alienation, can result as well. The general goal of therapy is to make the neurotic aware of the conflicts and their neurotic solutions and to help him get in touch with his "real self." This "real self," Horney believes, has a will to grow once it has been given a little encouragement. An analysis "can be safely terminated if the patient has acquired this... capacity to learn from his experiences—that is, if he can examine his share in the difficulties that arise, understand it, and apply the insight to his life."[28]

Between writing *Our Inner Conflicts* and *Neurosis and Human Growth* Karen Horney made one attempt at writing with others, producing a book from a lecture series entitled *Are You Considering Psychoanalysis?* The book, which was published by Norton in 1946, consisted of nine essays, each answering a question about psychoanalysis for those who might be considering treatment. Horney and five other members of the AAP, Alexander Reid Martin, Valer Barbu, Muriel Ivimey, Harold Kelman, and Elizabeth Kilpatrick, contributed essays. Horney herself edited the book and wrote two essays, "What Does the Analyst Do?" and "How Do You Progress After Analysis?" As usual, she was practical and helpful, and many of the other contributors were too. Although the book was produced by the Horney group, it was admirably fair to other schools, including the Freudians.

But team efforts were not Horney's real forte. Furthermore, her editors at Norton preferred her own books to such collaborations. In October of 1946 Storer B. Lunt (her editor after the death of W. W. Norton the previous year) wrote asking her whether the lectures announced for the New School the next spring might be "the groundwork of another possible Karen Horney book. We'd love to see another solo flight from you... so do please consider it. I'm rather hoping you are again getting the itch to bring another book into being."[29] Within the week Horney wrote back, unidiomatic but enthusiastic: "As a matter of fact I *do* consider to write a book on the subject of self-condemning, self-belittling and self-frustrating. It is profoundly intriguing and of great therapeutic importance."[30]

Neurosis and Human Growth, as the book was ultimately titled, was to go through many drafts and take considerably longer than Storer Lunt had hoped. It appears to have been the most difficult book for Horney to write. Deadlines were agreed upon and broken, and there were numerous reports of hard labor dispatched by Horney to her editor from various parts of the world. "This is undiluted paradise," she wrote Lunt from Lake Maggiore in Switzerland in 1949. "With all that I am working hard. . . . Never again shall I write a book—but I have felt this way before."[31]

When it appeared, in 1950, *Neurosis and Human Growth* was greeted by Ashley Montagu in the *New York Herald Tribune* as "the author's most important book since *The Neurotic Personality of Our Time.*"[32] With the benefit of hindsight, however, *Our Inner Conflicts* strikes this reader as the better book. For one thing, *Neurosis and Human Growth* is long for a Horney book—perhaps because Lunt told her he wanted "a more substantial book than *Our Inner Conflicts,* which really was a little on the slight side."[33] The result is that Horney goes over familiar ground *too* thoroughly and takes a very long time to get to new ideas. Then too the early chapters have an irksome, preachy tone, as when she writes that "to work at ourselves becomes not only the prime moral obligation, but at the same time, in a very real sense, the prime moral *privilege.*"[34]

What has troubled many serious critics about Horney's shift away from biology is that it resulted, increasingly over the years, in her replacing Freud's tragic view of humanity with one that sometimes sounded falsely optimistic. In Freud's universe everyone compromises with early primitive drives in the service of the rules of civilization. Even in Berlin, Horney had begun to argue with this fatalism. In her 1931 paper "Aggression in Society: Some Thoughts and Objections to Freud's Death Instinct and Drive for Destruction" she had taken issue with Freud's thesis that there is "an unalterable, innate, constitutional, instinctual drive to destruction. . . . It is not the will to destroy that drives us, but the will-to-life that forces us to destroy."[35]

Of course, as Horney herself was to point out, just because a theory is optimistic doesn't mean that it's wrong. But there are times when Horney's anti-tragic view seems to limit her capacity to feel deeply. Writing about the Ranevsky family's fate in Chekhov's *The Cherry Orchard,* for instance, she suggests that the family is unable to build "small houses for rent on part of the estate" because of their "hidebound views." "If their mentor were a good analyst he would say: 'Of course the situation is difficult. But what makes it hopeless is your own attitude toward it. If you would consider changing your claims on life there would be no need to feel hopeless.'"[36] Such responses made the critic Lionel Trilling describe Horney as "one of the symptomatic minds of our time ... symptomatic of one of the great inadequacies of liberal thought, the need for optimism."[37]

The most unfortunate result of this insistence on optimism may have been that it allowed people to dismiss Horney as superficial. As Paul Wachtel, a more sympathetic critic, has observed, Horney's tendency to use "sentimental slogans" may be useful for "motivating patients" but is "debilitating to serious intellectual inquiry." In fact "Horney's vision, if examined in its entirety, is not really so sunny. . . . She differs from Freud not in her view of what men are capable of doing, but in her view of what the ultimate source of their behavior is."[38]

Of all her books, *Neurosis and Human Growth* is most encumbered by Horney's tendency to preach. But eventually she does get to new ideas and new ways of looking at old ones. Cautioning that humans defy "precise classification,"[39] she proposes three general types of solutions to conflict: the expansive solution, the self-effacing solution, and the resigned solution. Each of these solutions has its own reward. For the expansive group the reward is mastery, for the self-effacing group the reward is safety, and for the resigned group the reward is freedom. The point is not that any one of these solutions is all wrong but that each is too much of one thing. Because of the fear of being hurt, for instance, the resigned person is determinedly unambitious, whereas the expansive person may never be able to stop pushing himself. Each of these types is burdened with an image of himself that is rigidly adhered to and that grows out of what Horney now calls a "pride system." In this book for the first time she makes the sweeping statement that "in all neurotic developments the alienation from self is the nuclear problem."[40]

Interestingly, the theme of Horney's final book, *Neurosis and Human Growth,* harks back to the earliest preoccupations of her childhood diaries. Here she is dealing again with questions of authenticity—what is real and what is false—just as there she was concerned over the hypocrisy of her father and the Church and troubled by her own hypocrisy in pretending to believe. Even the moralistic tone seems to echo the atmosphere of her childhood. Further, Horney frequently finds examples for her points in the plays of Henrik Ibsen, a Norwegian like her father but one whose sensibility comes much closer to her own. Indeed, the characters of Ibsen would seem to lend themselves well to Horney's theory: Nora's story in *A Doll's House,* for instance, is about imprisonment within a "false self." And layers of deception of self and others permeate not only the characters she cites—John Gabriel Borkman, Peer Gynt, Hedda Gabler—but the plays themselves. Horney's concern with finding the real self speaks even more directly to the preoccupations of her late adolescence, when she wrote of not knowing which of her many selves was the real one. When she writes in *Neurosis and Human Growth* of how "the emphasis shifts from being to appearing,"[41] she is writing of some of her oldest and deepest concerns.

In other ways, however, Horney's last two books foreshadow an adventure yet to come. In discussing "impoverishment of personality" in *Our Inner Conflicts* she notes that "in Zen Buddhist writings sincerity is equated with wholeheartedness, pointing to the very conclusion we reach on the basis of clinical observation— namely, that nobody divided within himself can be wholly sincere."[42] She goes on to quote a conversation between a monk and a master, taken from a book by D. T. Suzuki called *Zen Buddhism and Its Influence on Japanese Culture.* It was natural for Horney, given her increasing emphasis on finding the real self, on authenticity, to be drawn to Zen Buddhism. It also happened that D. T. Suzuki, a respected Japanese interpreter of Zen to the West, was teaching at Columbia during those years, so that Horney had an opportunity to meet him, through a mutual friend, and to invite him to lecture at the AAP. Around the time that *Neurosis and Human Growth* appeared, she, Suzuki, and some of her friends began to plan a trip to Japan to experience Zen life firsthand. Two years later she made the journey. The trip to Japan with Suzuki was to be one of the happiest of Karen Horney's many adventures, not only because it was a journey of discovery but also because she was accompanied by her daughter Brigitte, from whom she had been separated for so many years.

Despite her success in movies in the late thirties, the war years had turned out to be very difficult ones for Brigitte. In 1940 she married a cameraman named Konstantin Irmen-Tschet, a Russian of aristocratic origins who had fled the revolution and had made an artistic imprint, along with other White Russians, on German film of the time. She and Konstantin were particularly close to an actor named Joachim Gottschalk, who had been her leading man in four films, and his wife, Meta. Joachim Gottschalk and Brigitte were together in Tripoli making *Aufruhr in Damascus* when they got news of *Kristallnacht*, the night of looting and terror against Jews in Germany. The news was particularly terrifying to Gottschalk: his wife was Jewish, and they had a young son.

Soon Gottschalk began to be penalized by the Nazis for his marriage to a Jewish woman. A popular actor in the past, he started getting small parts or none at all. Brigitte says that she tried to get him, his wife, and their son to leave, even made arrangements for them. But they couldn't, or didn't. Then one day, when Gottschalk had just finished a theater engagement, he got a draft notice from the army. Knowing Meta and the boy would be in mortal danger if he left, Joachim and Meta Gottschalk went into the kitchen with their son, turned on the gas oven, and waited there together until death came.

There were only a handful of people at the funeral, because orders had come over the radio to stay away. Brigitte and her husband and another couple who had been close friends made the arrangements. Because of Nazi racial laws, they had great difficulty finding a cemetery where the three could be buried together. At the funeral, to which she and her friends had brought "most of the flowers in Berlin," Brigitte remembers "the Gestapo was taking pictures of us, but we didn't care."

Brigitte made one more movie after the Gottschalks' suicide, then had a recurrence of her childhood tuberculosis, and spent the next three years in Switzerland recovering. She believes the Gottschalk tragedy was "part of the reason I became ill." Her husband meanwhile was imprisoned by the Nazis for a time. She had had a house in Babelsberg, near Potsdam, before the war, which she prized and fussed over. After the Russians occupied the eastern zone at war's end she never saw the house or her possessions again.

Karen wrote and sent money to Brigitte at the hospital where she was being treated in Zuoz, Switzerland. But until the war was over they couldn't see each other or even talk on the telephone. "When she telephoned me," Brigitte remembers, "I was still in bed in Zuoz, with my TB. I think it was one of the first calls put through from the States to Switzerland." The conversation cost "a fortune," according to Brigitte, because neither of them could bear to end it. Karen would say, "We have to say goodbye," then they would say goodbye, but neither of them would hang up. Then after a while one would say, "Hello?" And the other voice would come back, "Hello, are you still there?" "We were half an hour helloing."

In the summer of 1946 Karen and Brigitte were reunited in Switzerland. Karen met Brigitte's husband (soon to be her ex-husband) for the first time, and mother and daughter spent time together in the familiar and very beautiful little villages around Lake Maggiore. For the next six summers Karen spent a good part of her summer vacations in Switzerland with Brigitte.

If the Japan trip had come off as originally planned, in the summer of 1951, Brigitte wouldn't have come along. But when Karen applied for a passport renewal, she discovered to her surprise that the State Department wouldn't give her one. As a result, the trip was put off for a year. And in December of 1951 Brigitte decided, for reasons that are mysterious to her still, that she should spend some time with her mother in New York. "I came over when I had the feeling I had to. All of a sudden I was thinking that maybe she was much more lonely than I thought." Brigitte arrived in New York by boat on December 10, 1951. After she arrived she became her mother's constant companion. Gertrude Lederer-Eckardt was consigned to a minor role by the sometimes imperious Brigitte.

One of the very first things Brigitte and her mother did, predictably, was to buy still another house in the country. This one was in Rye, New York, on a quiet inlet of the sound. It was a modest little place but it had a picture window in the second-floor bedroom that looked out through the trees to the water. In the late afternoon the egrets were silhouetted in the sunset. And there was a hammock tied between two trees down near the shore. Brigitte and her mother loved spending weekends there together, eating (Brigitte was an excellent cook), drinking, and laughing a lot. One time, Brigitte remembers, she scolded her mother for taking her nap with her slippers on. "Mutti, how dare you go to bed with your shoes on!" she asked. To which Karen answered, "In a certain sense, these are not shoes." This became a running joke between them. "In a certain sense, this is not a suitcase" or "a chair" or whatever. Once, when they heard visitors coming up the drive and didn't want to see them, they ran out of the house and hid in the huge gnarled trunk of a tree until the visitors had left.[43] In contrast, when Rita Honroth Welte, the daughter of Karen's good friends from Berlin days, visited the Rye house with her two little boys aged three and six, Karen arrived to pick them up at the train station in a convertible, with a big branch full of cherries from a cherry tree in the yard in the backseat. Rita remembers the little boys' "delight at being able to eat cherries that had just come off a tree."[44]

When Brigitte came to New York, Karen, still hopeful that she could get a passport, was busy making plans to go to Japan the following summer. The idea was to travel with D. T. Suzuki to Zen monasteries, primarily in the area around Kyoto. In addition to Suzuki and Karen the group was to include Suzuki's assistant, Dick DeMartino, and Cornelius Crane, an adventurer and heir to his family's fortune from plumbing fixtures. And coming along because she too was interested in Zen was Cornelius Crane's ex-wife, Cathy, with whom he was on friendly terms. Cornelius Crane and Cathy Crane Bernatschke, as she was by then called, had both been Horney's patients. It was said to be Cathy Crane Bernatschke whose therapy provided Karen with the line she used in *Neurosis and Human Growth:* "If it were not for reality, I would be perfectly all right."[45] Paradoxically, it was Cathy Crane Bernatschke's very real and practical intervention that finally broke the impasse with the State Department over Karen's passport.

The imbroglio over the passport was puzzling to everyone at the time. Why should the State Department stand in the way of Karen Horney, a distinguished and completely apolitical psychiatrist with a sincere interest in Buddhism? Because of Freedom of Information laws it is now possible to provide an explanation. But it is an explanation that reveals much more about the FBI than it does about Karen Horney. There is nothing in the files to suggest that Horney was other than what she claimed to be. At the same time the file shows the FBI to be, in varying degrees, xenophobic, inefficient, and, most consistently, governed by the view that everyone extraordinary, including Horney, was a Communist until proven otherwise—or, in the case of Germans, if not a Communist, then a Nazi.

The FBI had begun keeping an eye on Karen Horney way back in November of 1940 when an informant had called in to file a report, accurately describing her history and noting that she was listed in the spring catalogue of the New School for Social Research. "This institution," the report noted, "is known to have communistic sympathies." The report ends by stating—apparently on the basis of the New School affiliation—that "Dr. Horney is listed as a communist or communist sympathizer."[46] In

March of the following year another informant wrote that Horney was probably a Nazi using the New School as camouflage. Evidence for this was the fact that her daughter "Brigida" was "absolutely nothing until the Nazis got going and since then she has become the big number," and that Karen Horney "spoke well of Rudolph Hess... as recently as four or five years ago." For this somewhat confused informant the "circle seemed... complete" when he learned that "a work of hers attacking Freud is the *only* book on psychiatry that the C.P. [Communist party] allows sold in its book shops" and that "Madame Horney's books sell fine" in Russia.[47] A month later J. Edgar Hoover himself wrote a letter passing along this information to another office.[48]

In the summer of 1942, during the first year of U.S. involvement in World War II, the postmistress for Monhegan Island, in Maine, began writing to the FBI about a woman named Karen Horney who was "outwardly" a psychologist and who had been vacationing on the island for a few weeks during the past several summers. The postmistress had learned from Horney's neighbor that she might have a "short wave radio set" and that "a plane went over the cottages a short time ago and, right away, she heard the dot-dash dot-dash... from the set... for a period of a few minutes after the plane went past; then it stopped and went into news." Her opinion was that the plane was sending "some sort of a message that these people could have received."[49]

Later that summer the postmistress wrote again, assuring the FBI that "with quite a few foreigners here—they may be Germans or Jews—I am on the alert, to the 'nth degree," and noting that Dr. Karen Horney "receives and sends a lot of mail.... She may be bona fide... and a real psychologist but she does seem to have goodly sums of money at her disposal" and had sent four hundred and fifty dollars of it to a bank in Mexico City. "Practically all of the foreign accent people here are of one party or seem to have known each other before coming here," the postmistress added. "I am apprehensive and shall continue to be."[50] Later that summer, the postmistress wrote once again, concluding that "the fact that at least some of them are Jews and that Dr. Horney is a writer of established reputation would seem to free them from suspicion and I have no definite proof that they are not what they assume [*sic*] themselves to be. But they do not fit into the picture, and, in view of the activities along the Atlantic coast, I shall feel easier if you know of their continued location here."[51] The FBI assured her that her efforts were "sincerely appreciated."[52]

Later the FBI added documents to Horney's file indicating that her books were found in a packet of Communist literature seized on a pier on the West Coast and that her name was on the letterhead of an organization called the American Committee for the Protection of the Foreign-Born. This committee, which had its offices in New York, worked against anti-alien laws and helped foreigners who had been denied U.S. citizenship to press their cases. Horney was one of a wide variety of prominent people, including Edward G. Robinson and Fannie Hurst, on the letterhead. But when she applied for a passport, it was viewed as evidence, along with her New School connection and membership in something called the New York Conference for Inalienable Rights, that she was probably a "communist or communist sympathizer."[53]

In June of 1952, with the McCarthy era in full swing, the Department of State issued a memo in response to Horney's renewed application for a passport. "After carefully reviewing this file it is my opinion that Dr. Karen Horney's record follows the familiar pro-Communist or fellow traveller pattern. Her membership and active participation in at least five pro-Communist organizations, it seems is sufficient evidence to prove that she was well aware of the objectives of these organizations and was not just innocently 'taken in.'" The report goes on to note that since Dr. Horney is "an author and psychologist," she will "with her background... follow the usual pattern of specialists in such subjects, and discuss in a favorable light socialist and communist theories."

For these reasons, the memo concludes, Horney shouldn't be allowed to go. "It is well known that the shock of Japan's defeat has left Japanese educators bewildered and confused, resulting in many becoming receptive to communism. It would appear that an American with Dr. Horney's record of active participation in several Communist front organizations visiting Japan at this critical time and discussing subjects with Japanese professors in which the subject of socialism and communism is certain to come up, could influence the thinking of these Japanese to the detriment of the American interests in the Far East. It is, therefore, recommended that she be denied a passport to visit Japan at this time."[54]

Karen Horney asked her influential friends to write letters on her behalf and wrote a long letter herself to Secretary of State Dean Acheson pleading her case. But what seems to have turned the tide was a personal connection Cathy Bernatschke had, possibly through her admiral father, with a woman named Ruth Shipley, who was chief of the Passport Division. Cathy went to Washington with Cornelius and stopped by Ruth Shipley's office to say hello. And on June 25 a memo went out stating that "one-time membership in Communist-front organizations should not prejudice a person for all time."[55] On July 21, 1952, a passport was finally issued. Soon after, Karen Horney, Brigitte, and Cathy Bernatschke boarded a Pan Am World Airways Flying Clipper and took off for Hawaii en route to Japan.

PART SIX

Japan
1952

20

Japan

Karen Horney's tour of Japan began inauspiciously on the last day of July 1952. Richard DeMartino, who drove her into Tokyo from the airport that day, remembers that the air was thick with the smell of human excrement, used by farmers to fertilize their crops. It was the hottest time of year in Japan and hotter even than usual that summer. The sickening smell and the heat made Horney wish —as she later told DeMartino—that she'd stayed behind in Hawaii.[1] Tokyo probably disappointed her too at first. Its history had been destroyed by American bombs, and the rebuilt city, a bustling metropolis again only seven years after surrender, looked almost entirely Occidental. The most Japanese-seeming building Horney saw that first day may well have been the Imperial Hotel, with its carved wood, lava rock, and bamboo furniture. The architect of the Imperial, however, had been Frank Lloyd Wright, an American reworking Japanese materials.

Still, when Akihisa Kondo, a Japanese psychiatrist who had studied at her institute in New York, welcomed Horney later that day in the Imperial Hotel lobby, she seemed "more vivacious and jovial than in New York. She was beaming." Her first words to Kondo, as she came out of the elevator with arms spread in greeting, were "At last I'm in Japan!"[2] It was exciting for a woman of her adventurous spirit to be in the Orient for the first time. And

the long delay over her passport must have made the arrival especially sweet. What's more, she was about to undertake the best
kind of journey: one with a purpose, in the company of stimulating and knowledgeable companions.

The seeds of the Japan trip had been planted sometime during
the winter of 1950–51, when Cathy Crane Bernatschke, a longtime patient of Horney's, attended a lecture given at the Church of
the Peace Union in New York by a diminutive scholar of Zen
Buddhism, Daisetz Suzuki. In either therapy or conversation (the
relationship with Horney seems to have allowed for both), Cathy
Bernatschke passed on her impressions. Karen Horney had known
of Suzuki's ideas at least five years before and had quoted from his
book *Zen Buddhism and Its Influence on Japanese Culture* in *Our Inner
Conflicts,* published in 1945. When Horney expressed an interest in
meeting Suzuki, Cathy called him up and invited him to dinner.
Suzuki accepted but explained that he didn't like to travel in New
York alone at night and asked to bring along his assistant, Richard
DeMartino. Cathy, for her part, invited her ex-husband, Cornelius
Crane, also a longtime patient of Horney's.

It was an improbable collection of people: an old Japanese
scholar and his young ex-GI assistant, a hostess given to enthusiasms and the millionaire husband she had divorced ten years before, and the therapist they had both relied on for nearly eighteen
years. Nonetheless, or perhaps as a result, the evening was a great
success. Suzuki found an important sponsor in Cornelius Crane.
And Karen Horney found in Suzuki an inspiring guide for a journey into a rich and remarkable new territory.

At the time of Cathy Bernatschke's dinner party Suzuki was
eighty years old—a small, wiry man with a wisp of a voice and
memorable eyebrows, "ferocious eyebrows," as Winthrop Sargant
wrote in a *New Yorker* profile some years later, "which project
from his forehead like the eyebrows of the angry demons who
guard the entrances of Buddhist temples in Japan."[3] Many who
met him or heard him lecture sensed some ineffable Buddha-like
quality in him. A British Orientalist, after hearing him speak at the
World Congress of Faiths in London in 1936, wrote that he "had
saturated his whole life with the teachings of Buddha and, in his
own way, he expressed those teachings so that everyone who saw
or heard him was drawn to him and disposed toward Buddhism."[4]

Suzuki lived a life of almost monkish simplicity: when he traveled he took only two small bags and then filled them mostly with
books. True to Zen precepts, he wasted nothing: old clothes were

carefully cut into squares for future dusting, and pieces of string and used envelopes were recycled whenever possible. Toward his late teacher, Soyen Shaku, he was deeply humble. "Might his spirit not for once be awakened from deep meditation and criticize the book now before the reader!" he wrote in a 1926 introduction to *Essays in Zen Buddhism.*[5] He could also show a warm interest in students, provided they were sincere. But when he was confronted with trivial questions he was capable of dramatic displays of Zen rudeness. Norman Kelman, who was intrigued by Zen, once questioned Suzuki at a cocktail party about an inconsistency in one of the many anecdotes that pervaded his books. Suzuki responded by closing his eyes and appearing to drop off into deep sleep. Kelman supposed that was "some kind of Zen master answer... it took me many years of experience before it began to make sense."[6]

In fact Suzuki was not himself a Zen master, or *roshi,* but a scholar and writer of great authority. His learning was formidable —he knew Sanskrit, classical Chinese, and Pali, as well as Japanese and English—but his most remarkable gift was his ability to explain Zen to the West. Using examples and anecdotes from Buddhist life and the arts, Suzuki wrote with lucidity about a subject that refuses to be contained in words. As he frequently acknowledged, writing about Zen was in itself an impossibility, since true enlightenment must come through direct personal experience. "Zen is not necessarily against words," Suzuki explained in the opening chapter of *Zen and Japanese Culture,* "but it is well aware of the fact that they are always liable to detach themselves from realities and turn into conceptions. And this conceptualization is what Zen is against.... Zen insists on handling the thing itself, not an empty abstraction." To illustrate this point Suzuki tells of the time a Zen monk encountered three monks from another Buddhist sect on a bridge arching over a river. When one of the three asked, "How deep is the river of Zen?" the Zen monk responded, "Find out for yourself," and started to throw the questioner into the water below.

What gives Suzuki's writings their unique authority, particularly in the eyes of practicing Zen Buddhists, is the fact that he immersed himself first in Zen practice and only later in scholarship. Suzuki was the son of a doctor of the samurai class, but he came into the world at a time when the samurai were being divested of their hereditary rights and annual grants of rice. As a result, he went to work right after secondary school as an English teacher in a remote fishing village. Later he did go to the Imperial University

in Tokyo. But his studies soon became secondary to the time he
spent as a novice at Engaku-ji, a temple in Kamakura, where he
became a favorite pupil of the Zen master Shaku Soyen. Suzuki
lived the life of a monk at Engaku-ji, a life of meditation, hard
physical work, and very few creature comforts. During that time
he had a profound enlightenment experience—known in Zen as
satori. His master conferred the dharma, or enlightened, name
"Daisetz" on him as a result, a name that Suzuki liked to translate
as "great stupidity" but that was given in the complimentary Zen
sense of "not-knowing"—unhindered by concepts and illusions.[7]
He used the name "Daisetz" for the rest of his life, a reminder,
perhaps, that all his writings, "my sins"[8] as he sometimes called
them, could not bring true enlightenment.

Soon after his enlightenment experience Suzuki's life as a scholar
began in earnest. While accompanying his master to the Parliament of Religions at the Chicago World's Fair in 1893, Suzuki met
a German-born American industrialist, Edward Hegeler, who invited him to stay on as a translator for his pet project, a publishing
house in nearby La Salle, Illinois, which was devoted to religious
and scientific works. The Open Court Publishing Company, as it
was called, published not only books but also a periodical that
attracted the writings of many prominent Orientalists. Suzuki's
job there was to translate from Japanese and Chinese into English;
he worked at it for eleven years, teaching himself Sanskrit and
writing his first important book in English, *Outlines of Mahayana
Buddhism,* in his spare time. On one of numerous tours of the
country he met an American woman named Beatrice Erskine
Lane, a Radcliffe graduate, who became his wife and an important
contributor to the quality of his writing in English. After the La
Salle years Suzuki returned to Japan, where he settled into married
life and taught, first in Tokyo and then for many years at the Otani
University in Kyoto. When his wife died, in 1938, he took up
traveling again. He was a frequent lecturer at the Jungian Eranos
conference in Ascona, Switzerland, and a memorable speaker at
the East-West Philosophers' Conference in Honolulu in 1949. By
the time Karen Horney met him he had landed at Columbia, under
a Rockefeller Foundation grant, and was living in rooms known,
appropriately, as the Prophets' Chambers.

It is easy to see why Karen Horney would have been attracted to
Suzuki, and to Zen Buddhism. She would have liked Suzuki's di-
rectness and his ability—not unlike her own—to explain himself.
She would have liked the deeply humorous strain in Zen and, per-

haps most of all, its refusal to embrace doctrine. "Truth, in the sense of reality," Buddha tells his disciple in the Diamond Sutra, "cannot be cut up into pieces and arranged into a system."[9] For a woman who had spent her life resisting orthodoxies, Zen's anti-doctrinaire spirit had natural appeal. But there was a deeper reason for her interest: during the last decade of her life she was drawn increasingly toward spiritual questions. Unlike some Westerners in the sixties, who took to Zen because it seemed exotic and the thing to do, Horney's attraction was part of a larger search. Well before she read Suzuki, she had admired William James, a psychologist who concerned himself with spiritual questions and whose *Varieties of Religious Experience* is, among other things, an argument for the inevitability of faith. "Over-beliefs in various directions are absolutely indispensable," James wrote in the concluding chapter of his great treatise, "and... we should treat them with tenderness and tolerance so long as they are not intolerant themselves.... The most interesting and valuable things about a man are usually his over-beliefs."[10]

Horney may not have been searching for personal faith—and certainly not for a sudden enlightenment—but her curiosity turned increasingly to ultimate questions. Her last two books draw on Kierkegaard's *The Sickness unto Death*[11] and particularly on Kierkegaard's depiction of the despair that comes with the loss of meaning. In addition to her conversations with theologian Paul Tillich, whose book *The Courage to Be*[12] was gestating around this time, Horney talked frequently with Gertrude Lederer-Eckardt's daughter Ursula, who taught philosophy at Hunter College, about Ursula's special interest in the ideas of Plato and Aristotle, and about the inadequacy of the Cartesian division of mind and body. There were even a few group meetings at Gertrude's house involving Karen Horney, Ursula, and other members of the philosophy department at Hunter.

Horney's reading also reflected these preoccupations. She developed an affection for a book called *The Perennial Philosophy,* compiled by Aldous Huxley. The title, as Huxley explained in the introduction, was taken from the Latin *philosophia perennis* and referred to "the metaphysic that recognizes a divine Reality substantial to the world of things and lives and minds."[13] The book consisted of brief excerpts from religious writings of Islam and varieties of Buddhism and Christianity, with commentary by Huxley. For the last four years of her life, Karen Horney read from *The Perennial Philosophy* almost every night.

The yearning for religious understanding that had characterized Karen Horney's early adolescence had returned. In girlhood the way to faith had been obstructed by the association of religion with her Bible-thumping, autocratic father and his fiery preacher-friend Pastor von Ruckteschell. But in her last years the need for some spiritual dimension—a need that she may have acquired from her father—led her toward non-Protestant sources. Perhaps it is not too farfetched to think of Suzuki as an alternative father in this regard, remote enough in background and belief from her own father to function as a spiritual mentor.

Karen Horney's search may have gained urgency as she grew older and closer to the boundary between life and death. Zen, like most religions, is deeply concerned with this boundary. And even before she got to know much about Zen, she was intrigued by the notion that mind can conquer matter. In *Our Inner Conflicts* she referred to a "most interesting paper"[14] of William James, "The Energies of Men,"[15] which discusses a number of instances in which spiritual training has helped people overcome illness. One was the case of a man James knew who took up Yoga and "by persistently carrying out for several months its methods of fasting from food and sleep, its exercises in breathing and thought-concentration, and fantastic posture-gymnastics, seems to have succeeded in waking up deeper and deeper levels of will and moral and intellectual power in himself, and to have escaped from a decidedly menacing brain-condition of the 'circular' type, from which he had suffered for years."[16] Another case of "mind-cure" cited in James's 1907 paper was of a woman with breast cancer whose "ideas have kept her a practically well woman for months after she should have given up and gone to bed."[17]

What distinguishes Zen ideas from the "mind-cures" James wrote about is that the goal of Zen meditation is not to cure ills but to transcend them through enlightenment, to enter through deep concentration into a state that Suzuki calls "isness," a sense of immediacy that allows one to "break the adhesive of one's constant train of conceptual thought about past, present and future."[18] True enlightenment, as Zen would have it, frees one from the fear of death, since one breaks through the boundaries of ego to a sense of union with the breathing universe. It was this that made Zen particularly attractive to samurai warriors, who were looking for fearlessness. If death ceased to have meaning, then acts of great daring were possible. Perhaps Karen Horney was looking for some of this fearlessness too. At the time of the Japan trip, although neither she nor anyone else was aware of it, she was fatally ill with cancer. It is possible that she had some sense, in her bones if not in her conscious mind, of danger.

The ostensible reason for Horney's journey to Japan was not personal but professional. She was interested in the way Zen might reaffirm or complement her own theory; her questions, according to Richard DeMartino, usually concerned such comparisons. But as Horney herself acknowledged in her last major paper before the trip, true understanding is, ultimately, personal. "Only that counts which is felt and experienced," she wrote in "The Paucity of Inner Experience." "Life," she claimed, citing Zen sources, "is not a problem to be solved but an experience to be realized."[19]

Suzuki was to lead Horney and the others on a tour of some of the most important Zen monasteries in Japan, located primarily in the old imperial cities of Kyoto and Nara, which had escaped the ravages of the war. They would spend about a month, and at least some of the time, they would be guests in the monasteries themselves.

No one was looking for miracles. And yet the trip *was* a sort of modern pilgrimage, long anticipated and undertaken with great expectations. The pilgrims, like those in Chaucer's *Canterbury Tales,* were a colorful lot who contributed in a variety of ways to the undertaking. Horney and Suzuki were the *éminences grises.* But everyone felt an obligation to Cornelius Crane, who was paying all the expenses. Since the costs would have been prohibitive for Suzuki and DeMartino, if not for the others, it was Crane's largesse that made the whole enterprise possible.

Cornelius Crane was the grandson of Richard Teller Crane, a machinist who founded the Crane Company in 1855, and the son of Richard T. Crane, Jr., who turned it into a multimillion-dollar producer of valves and plumbing fixtures during World War I. After the war Richard Crane, Jr., succeeded, through the largest advertising campaign in American history, in making America "want a better bathroom."[20] As a result of his efforts, lavish bathrooms by Crane began to appear in Cecil B. DeMille movies, as well as in the palace of King Hussein in Saudi Arabia and, coincidentally, in the Imperial Hotel in Tokyo. Not surprisingly, the Crane family lived a life of conspicuous opulence. In 1925, when Cornelius was about twenty, his parents built Castle Hill, a fifty-nine-room mansion on a high hill in Ipswich, Massachusetts, overlooking pristine beaches and islands off the Atlantic Coast. In its heyday Castle Hill—which is now used for public concerts—

was a true exemplar of the gilded age, a copy of the grand residences of seventeenth-century England, overlooking a *grand allée* that swept majestically down to the sea. The formal boxwood maze was fashioned after the one at Hampton Court. There was a casino with a salt-water swimming pool and Italian and rose gardens that were maintained by as many as a hundred caretakers at a cost of thirteen thousand dollars a year.

Cornelius liked Castle Hill enough to travel there with Horney and others on numerous occasions over the years. But he never became an active partner in the Crane Company, and he clearly wanted to use his inheritance to create another kind of life. While still in his twenties he developed an interest in the Museum of Natural History in Chicago, where he grew up. In 1928 he took a scientific team to the South Seas aboard his laboratory-equipped yacht *Illyria*. The expedition, staffed by museum and university scientists, returned after eleven months with thousands of specimens for the museum.[21]

The year after the trip around the world Cornelius married Catharine Parker. Two or three years after that he sought treatment with Karen Horney. At least one of Crane's difficulties was apparent: he suffered from asthma, severe enough so that he kept a small inhaler with him all the time on the Japan trip. There is no way of knowing what other problems he brought to therapy or whether Horney helped him. But one thing is clear: he developed a great attachment to her. She was "like a mother to him,"[22] according to the woman he married after Horney's death. Crane even tried to persuade his sister to go to Horney for therapy, but with little success. He was always eager to help bring Horney's message to the world—lending support to her institute and even offering to pay for extra advertising for her books. (The offer apparently was declined, on the advice of W. W. Norton.)[23] At the time of the Japan trip he lived on another floor of the building on Central Park South where she had her apartment.

Cornelius Crane's ex-wife Cathy had also played a pivotal role in the Japan undertaking—by getting everyone together in the first place and, later, by using her connections to get Horney a passport. Horney seems to have looked upon Cathy with benevolent amusement, though she sometimes lost patience with her because she was so frequently late for therapy appointments. Cathy and Cornelius had been divorced for twelve years at the time of the Japan trip. Her second marriage, to Bernatschke, seems also to have been behind her.

A fifth member of the traveling party, Akihisa Kondo, was more host than guest. Born and raised in Japan and trained first in Japanese psychiatry, Kondo had come to study at Karen Horney's institute without knowing anything of her interest in Zen. Yet, by coincidence or perhaps by intuition, he found that he had come to a place where his personal history made him an expert. For long before he became a psychiatrist Kondo had been deeply involved in Zen. In early adolescence, when an obsession with dying rendered him sleepless, he undertook Zen training. Later, during a period of depression that kept him in bed, he had a sudden awakening, or enlightenment experience, when he got up one day and saw light streaming down on a chrysanthemum outside his door. Kondo was a radio operator in the Japanese army during World War II and escaped death only by a lucky chance (he stayed back with an injury) when his entire company was wiped out at Okinawa. Back in Tokyo after the war, he vowed as he walked through the rubble that he would become a doctor and treat the sick. Later, because of his own mental struggles as a young man, he decided to go into psychiatry.[24]

Japanese psychiatry had little use for Freud's ideas, so Kondo learned instead how to practice a uniquely Japanese treatment called Morita therapy, which drew on Zen precepts. But when he heard that there were funds available, through the U.S. occupation government, to travel to the United States for postgraduate study, he jumped at the chance, came to New York, and, after exploring the alternatives, enrolled in Karen Horney's institute. Kondo saw many connections between Morita therapy and Horney's ideas. In particular, he thought her concept of the "real self" might be a means of "integrating the ideas of the East and the West." Along with his wife, he joined the traveling party for most of the trip. And since his English was excellent, he often found himself acting as interpreter.[25]

The youngest members of the party, Richard DeMartino and Brigitte Horney, were closely tied to the oldest. DeMartino acted as Suzuki's assistant, taking care of driving and details. DeMartino was also a serious student of Zen and participated in many of the discussions. Brigitte, of course, had come along to be with her mother and to take in the sights. But even she had prepared a little bit by attending some of Suzuki's lectures before they left. Her "primitive" version of meditation was that "you empty yourself like a sponge" and then "open up" to whatever element surrounds you. This interested her, because it corresponded to the actor's process in preparing to play a role. Brigitte was also a gifted amateur artist. Japan for such a person is a continual feast for the eyes. She never tired, she said later, of visiting the Zen temples because "it's never the same, it's always more beautiful."[26]

Suzuki, like most Japanese hosts, had taken pains to anticipate the needs of his guests. To help them recover from their long journey he took them first for a few days' rest away from the heat at a resort hotel on Lake Hakone. It was a setting that might have reminded Horney a little of Switzerland: spotless rooms full of sunlight, looking out over a beautiful lake encircled by mountains. The mountains, though, were distinctly Japanese, with sharp ridges and creases like crumpled paper, coated evenly with green, darkening to black in their many folds. On a clear day gray Mount Fuji, Japan's sacred mountain, loomed in the distance, its broad base and cratered, snow-capped summit reducing the lake and green mountains below to miniatures.

For stimulation during this interlude Akihisa Kondo had arranged for two of the leading proponents of Morita therapy, Dr. Takehisa Kora and Dr. Yoshiyuki Koga, to come to the Hakone Hotel and discuss their ideas with Karen Horney. This proved to be a useful orientation, since Horney was scheduled to speak at the Jikei-kai Medical School in Tokyo right after the rest in Hakone. In her talk at the medical school Horney was able to refer to a number of similarities between her ideas and those of Shomo Morita, the founder of Japan's indigenous psychotherapy.

Horney's favorable remarks about Morita therapy were welcomed and celebrated by the Japanese. Kondo wrote afterward that "it was the first time that Morita's ideas were commented on, particularly with regard to their similarities with the basic ideas of psychoanalysis, by such a distinguished person as Dr. Horney." Dr. Kora wrote in the *Japan Medical Journal:* "I was very much impressed by her openness, a dynamic flexibility of mind totally different from the hard, rigid attitude of the orthodox Freudians. . . . Attending her lecture, I felt that what she talked about was not only very close and similar to what Morita told us, but also was expressing in the content the same thing in a different language."[27]

This appears to have been wishful thinking—perhaps a response more to Horney's personality than to her ideas. For while it is possible to find broad similarities between Horney and Morita— both are optimistic about the possibilities for growth, for instance

—the differences are far more striking. Indeed, if ever proof were needed of Horney's thesis that cultural differences influence our views of neurosis and treatment, Morita therapy could provide it. Dr. Morita used the word *shinkeishitsu* (sometimes translated "nervosity") to describe a wide variety of ailments, including all kinds of phobias and psychosomatic complaints, as well as a very common Japanese condition in which the patient is overly sensitive, shy, prone to headaches and other stress-based symptoms, and preoccupied with concern about his faults. In Morita's view such complaints resulted from the patient's being too much a captive of his "subjectivity" and unable as a result to feel for others, to be aware of his environment, and to escape "egocentricity."[28]

The cure for these ills was a "training or drilling treatment" that borrowed extensively from Zen and encouraged the patients to cultivate "an attitude to life appropriate to things as they are." The treatment was usually undertaken in a hospital, where the patient was first confined to bed for four to seven days and encouraged to "endure worldly thoughts and all of the pain which accompanies them." No contact with the world was permitted, except a brief interview each day. In the second stage, which lasted three to seven days, the patient was allowed to do light work but no reading or associating with others. The patient kept a diary, which was read and commented on by the therapist. Patients were encouraged to "stop taking an attitude of being ill, but rather to pretend that they are healthy, and to dissolve their fascination with contrasting phenomena of pleasure and displeasure." The third stage was a period of chores which helped the patient to realize that "happiness lies, not far away, but in the immediate experience of daily life." In the fourth stage, the "period of complicated practical life," the patient was allowed to read books (but only nonfiction), go shopping, and perhaps go to work or school outside the hospital. The hope was that patients would learn to "fully experience their own lives and gradually realize what Morita called 'pure mind.'"[29]

Inevitably, those trained in the West were critical of Morita therapy's emphasis on repression rather than insight. Two American psychiatrists who visited Japan around the same time as Horney pointed out that Morita didn't "investigate the foundations and origins of neurotic behavior" or seek out "sources of conflict. . . . Suppression is the dominant theme in therapy; conformity the goal."[30] While Horney was against wallowing in self-pity or the past (and here might have had some sympathy with the Morita approach), she was nonetheless opposed to adaptation at all costs.

In one of her last interviews she was asked if "adjustment of the patient" was the goal in psychotherapy. She answered: "Adjustment *to what* is important. . . . If you want the patient to become more productive, then the word 'adjustment' is completely meaningless."[31] Certainly the idea that the patient should "stop self-observing feelings,"[32] as one writer on Morita therapy put it, was inimical to Horney, who had spent her life practicing and advocating self-observation.

If Horney had reservations about Morita therapy, however, she kept them to herself. And after her lecture at the Jikei-kai Medical School in Tokyo, they were no longer relevant. From then on the focus would be not on psychiatry but on Zen, where Horney was a beginner along with the rest of her traveling companions. Suzuki had planned visits to the oldest and most important Zen temples, in Kyoto and Nara. But in order to provide his guests with some understanding of Zen training he had planned a stop at a smaller place off the beaten track: Shogenji Temple in Minokamo, a small village at some distance from cities in the province of Gifu.

At Shogenji the travelers stayed in the monastery, sleeping on futons and sharing at least some of the thick green ceremonial tea and spartan vegetarian meals that were the monks' daily fare. It was probably at Shogenji that Karen and Brigitte attended prayers or meditation, filing into the prayer hall behind the monks in their gauzy, black, flowing robes. Someone had explained to Karen and Brigitte that they must sit in lotus position (or their best approximation) on the tatami-mat floor, each exactly in line with the row of shaven-headed monks in front of them. Perhaps Karen and Brigitte came at dawn when the monks chanted ancient sutras in monotone, in rhythm with the hollow tock of a gourd-shaped wooden drum. Or perhaps they sat with the monks during silent meditation. On such a warm August day the shoji screens along the wall of the prayer hall would have been slid open, revealing the garden beyond to wandering eyes. And it would have been difficult to keep the eyes from wandering. If they were like most novices, Karen and Brigitte had to focus a good deal of their energy that first day on just sitting still.[33] Karen, however, continued to be intrigued by meditation and asked a lot of questions about it as the journey progressed.

It was in the city of Gifu, not far from the monastery, that the group took a boat out onto the river at dusk and watched the ancient sport of cormorant fishing—a spectacular sight at night, with Japanese fishermen in small boats luring the fish with torches, then sending trained cormorants on leashes into the water to retrieve them. It was on this leg of the journey too that the group visited Pearl Island, where cultivation of pearls was perfected by Kokichi Mikimoto, also known as "the Pearl King." Brigitte remembers that they actually met the Pearl King (he was an old man by then and accompanied by his nurse) and were each given an oyster. By lucky chance (or could it have been by design?) the oysters had pearls in them.

For the most part the whole trip seemed to be blessed with such good fortune. As on any trip, there were a few problems here and there. Karen's bunions, exacerbated by all the walking, sent her to a doctor one day. And later, back in Tokyo, they were all swindled, in a minor way, by an art dealer whom everyone trusted because he was a friend of Suzuki's. The dealer laid out a fabulous feast for them, then sold them Japanese paintings that he claimed were executed by masters but that turned out to be "in the school of." The paintings, however, were beautiful, according to Brigitte, and the dealer's false claims weren't discovered until after the trip. The outing had been undertaken in great good humor anyway. Brigitte remembers that her mother didn't have enough cash and had to get permission to pay for the pictures by check. That gave her an excuse to buy them. "Well, we'll give him a check," she told Brigitte. "That's not real money."[34]

No one on the trip seems to have seen any evidence of the cancer that would prove fatal to Karen Horney within four months. What they remember instead is her wide-ranging curiosity, not only about Zen but about Japanese life in general. "I was very much impressed," Kondo wrote afterward, "by her tremendous interest in observing and participating in the life of the Japanese people. One day I found her cheerful and jubilant with her experience of . . . a festival some place around Kyoto. I remember she was almost ecstatic in telling her experience . . . with her daughter there."[35] On another occasion, DeMartino was out buying books late in the day near the red light district in Kyoto and noticed that prostitutes were beginning to take their places along the street in preparation for the evening's business. When he returned to the hotel and told Karen and Brigitte about it, they insisted on going back there with him to see. The Miyako Hotel, a first-class establishment for Westerners, provided them with a large limousine, and they cruised the red light district staring out the windows. Karen, DeMartino recalls, "got a tremendous kick out of it all."[36]

Horney's enthusiasm shows too in a series of photographs taken by Kondo as the group toured Zen temples in Kyoto and Nara. There is one photograph of her sitting on the wooden steps of a temple with Brigitte and Cathy Bernatschke in which she appears fragile and old—perhaps it is the cane she's holding or the unguarded, childlike look on her face. But it is atypical. Most of the pictures show a woman full of energy, looking plump but firm in her short-sleeved cotton dresses and "space" shoes, with her sensible black pocketbook at her side. A cone-shaped straw peasant's hat, which she acquired to protect her from the hot sun, adds a jaunty, mildly eccentric air. In a characteristic picture, Horney stands in the broad walkway approaching Horyuji, one of the oldest Nara temples, with Suzuki on one side and Cornelius Crane and DeMartino on the other. Suzuki holds his walking stick in one hand and gestures with the other as he explains something about the building before them. Horney stands, with hand on hip, listening and looking. Her face and posture are wide open, her lips half parted and smiling, as though she is breathing in the experience.

Visitors to Japan are often advised to forgo museums, since the temples contain many of the most important paintings and Buddhist sculptures. The temples themselves, like the cathedrals of Europe, are structures of great aesthetic power. And yet the look and feel of the temples are vastly different from those of the cathedrals. Instead of stone, there are tatami mats underfoot and warm, dark wood above. Above all, scale is different. There are some colossal Buddhas and great halls. But the tile-roofed temples lie relatively low, and the rooms inside are often intimate. The art is intimate too—screen paintings of willows in four seasons or a crane in flight, which are seen best from a sitting position a few feet away. What is perhaps most surprising and new to a Westerner is the central place of the garden in these religious structures. In the West gardens are a secular pursuit. But in Japan the gardens within temple walls are important reflections of Buddhist understanding. The garden is there for the same reason that the temple structure is unobtrusive: nature must be treated with great reverence, used and tamed but not overpowered.

Like most visitors, Horney was intrigued and moved by these gardens. There is a photograph of her staring out at the rock garden at Ryoan-ji, with DeMartino at her side; her look, as she surveys this stark, enigmatic garden made up entirely of fifteen rocks surrounded by raked gravel, is interested but quizzical. The garden she loved most was the far lusher one near another Kyoto temple, the Sambo-In garden at Daigo-Ji. Kondo photographed Horney in profile at Sambo-In, gazing serenely out at the garden from under her cone-shaped straw hat. The Sambo-In garden, which was designed about 1600, revolves around a spring-fed pond generously adorned with rocks and dotted with islands and small arched bridges of wood and stone and earth. At one end of the pond is a waterfall, designed in three tiers to produce a pleasing sound. It was explained to Karen and the rest that the emperor Hideyoshi, who supervised the design, required the waterfall to be rebuilt several hundred times before he was satisfied with the sound. Later Horney asked DeMartino to take her back to Sambo-In, "probably," he conjectures, to "get away from a lot of chitchat... and be by herself."[37] Sometime during the trip she sent Renate an enthusiastic card. "It is overwhelming," she wrote hurriedly in German: "the art of the gardens, the simplicity of the homes, the feeling of deep inner meaning in the monasteries."[38]

When it came time to leave Japan at the end of five weeks Karen Horney told DeMartino it had been one of the greatest experiences of her life. And in New York that fall she tried to prolong it. There had been ongoing conversations during the five-week journey about Zen and Buddhism. Most of the time Suzuki talked and Horney listened. "She didn't spew," DeMartino recalls. "If anything was said about Zen, she'd think it over, try to fit it in with her concepts. Then if it fit and she understood it she would say, 'Ja.' And if she didn't, she would ask a question."[39] Brigitte remembers them all sitting around trying describe the essence of meditation and arriving finally at the phrase "breaking through the shell of egocentricity."[40]

Back in the United States the conversations continued—in evening meetings at the institute and in social gatherings at Horney's apartment. That September, Cornelius Crane invited Horney, Suzuki, DeMartino, and Kondo to Castle Hill for the weekend, and they continued to mull over the Japan trip. They took picnic food out to one of the beautiful islands off the coast and argued over lunch about the relative merits of the Nō and Kabuki theater they had seen in Japan. DeMartino thought Kabuki sentimental, but Horney loved it. "Dick," she told him, "your head is better than your heart."[41]

What Horney kept returning to was the relationship between her psychology and Zen. At the very first dinner party at Cathy Bernatschke's she had given DeMartino a copy of the letter from a patient, published in the *American Journal of Psychoanalysis* in 1949, about an experience of finding the "real self."[42] Horney wanted to know if the question "What do you really want?," which was central to this patient's breakthrough, had anything to do with Zen enlightenment. "I think [Horney] was really trying to understand another approach to problems she was dealing with," DeMartino says in retrospect, "and sensing that there was some kind of solution there." After the Japan trip Horney's questions became more sophisticated. Returning from Castle Hill with DeMartino after their weekend there together, she asked if he thought her concept of "basic anxiety" was anything like the Buddhist idea of *dukkha,* which means suffering or pain in the sense of dislocation. That was when DeMartino sensed she was beginning to understand Zen Buddhism.[43]

Some people who knew her during the last year or two of her life believe Horney would have turned more and more to Zen in her writing if she had lived. According to DeMartino, her lectures that fall showed Zen's influence. And in her last months, she relied increasingly on the one person she knew who was familiar with both Zen and psychiatry, Akihisa Kondo. "Her experience in her trip in Japan was quite stimulating to her," Kondo wrote, "and a strong fermentation process was taking place in her. . . . She wanted my participation in her work in view of my experience and understanding of . . . Zen and also of my intimacy with her own ideas." Kondo spent several weekends with Horney at her Rye house so that they could work together. For Kondo it was a unique experience of "intellectual cooperation." They sat together in Horney's study looking out over the bay. "She sat in a chair behind a big table with a large-sized paper pad on it." Kondo sat a "fair distance from her" and looked out too. "From time to time, I noticed, she jotted down some words . . . seemingly at random. I realized it was her way of thinking. For after a while she turned to me and asked my opinion." At Horney's insistence, Kondo wrote and delivered a paper at the institute that fall on Morita therapy.[44]

As powerful as Horney's experience in Japan had been, however, she would have been hard put to integrate Zen into her psychology. In the blush of first acquaintance everyone stressed the similarities. Horney advocated wholeheartedness and authenticity, and so did Zen teachings. Horney believed that ignorance was the enemy and that it was possible, through insight, to rediscover a real self and nurture it. Zen too expressed this optimism: in Buddhism, ignorance, not sin, is the source of man's difficulties, and ignorance can be overcome by certain *teachable* techniques.[45] Enlightenment is always possible. In future millennia, as Suzuki told Winthrop Sargeant of the *New Yorker,* "we will all undoubtedly be Buddhas."[46]

The differences, however, are larger. They have to do with the cultural differences Horney had often stressed in earlier writings, and which were so brilliantly summarized in her colleague and friend Ruth Benedict's 1946 analysis of Japanese culture, *The Chrysanthemum and the Sword.* "The lenses through which any nation looks at life," as Benedict wrote, "are not the ones another nation uses. It is hard to be conscious of the eyes through which one looks . . . the tricks of focusing and of perspective which give to any people its national view of life seem to that people the god-given arrangement of the landscape."[47] Horney's psychology, like that in the West generally, concerned itself with relationships. When she wrote of "moving toward, moving away, moving against," she was talking about man's relationship to his fellow man. Later, when she wrote of self-effacing, expansive, or aggressive behaviors, she was writing about the *individual's* behavior in relation to others. This seems so obvious as to go without saying to a Western reader. But these ubiquitous themes of Western psychology are what Zen is *not* about. In order to reach enlightenment Buddha had to renounce his family. Detachment, casting off, is the first step toward wisdom. While Horney's and most Western psychologies examine the interpersonal, Zen is a method designed to help the practitioner transcend personal concerns and indeed to transcend personhood, or ego. Horney might have wished, toward the end of her life, for such transcendence. But it was never a goal, or even a possibility, in her psychology.

Had there been more time, there is no telling how Horney might have altered her views as the result of her new interest in Zen. But in October, less than two months after her return, she suddenly became ill with what appeared to be pleurisy. She had planned to have Suzuki, DeMartino, and Tillich come to her apartment on a Tuesday to talk about impressions of Japan. But on Monday she felt so ill that Norman Kelman insisted on taking her to Columbia Presbyterian Hospital, where she was admitted right away, first to a ward and later to a private room in Harkness Pavilion. Even at this late stage she was mocking illness. As she rolled by Norman Kelman on a stretcher en route to her private room, she was "holding a flower as though she were in a coffin, big smile on her face, making great fun."[48] The diagnosis, however, was serious: she was found to have cancer of the gall bladder, which had spread to the lungs.

In retrospect, all three of Horney's daughters could remember signs that she was not entirely well. In May of that year Renate had come from Mexico to pick up her oldest daughter, Karen, from boarding school in Massachusetts and visit her mother and Brigitte. When Renate arrived at the house in Rye she was surprised to find her mother in bed with a high, unexplained fever. Later that summer, when Karen and Brigitte were packing to go to Japan, Karen had felt suddenly ill and had had to leave the stuffy apartment to get some air. And in September, when Karen arrived in Washington for a visit with Marianne and her family, Marianne noticed something different about her mother's walk as she left the plane. "I said to myself it was the end."[49] During the visit, when she complained about her irregular pulse, Marianne urged her mother to go to a doctor. Karen, however, had always had a dread of doctors: the prospect of going to the dentist could ruin her day. Even at the end, when Norman Kelman told her she was looking jaundiced and needed to go to the hospital, Karen was reluctant, insisting the color change was caused by her home remedy, carrot juice concocted in a blender.[50]

When Karen finally arrived at the hospital, Brigitte took charge, allowing some visitors in and keeping others out in a way that left permanent resentments. Gertrude Lederer-Eckardt, who had in any case been eclipsed by Brigitte, was barred—and complained of it bitterly for the rest of her life. Harold Kelman too was denied access to Horney, as was his wife, Katie, who had been instrumental in realizing Horney's dream of a clinic. On the other hand, the young psychiatrist who had been Horney's patient and had become her lover was allowed to visit. And then of course Marianne, who came during the second week, took turns with Brigitte sitting with Karen as she clung to life under an oxygen tent.

Brigitte claims that she was only protecting her mother from people she didn't want to see. But those who were excluded have offered a number of other explanations for her behavior. Brigitte didn't want her mother to know she was fatally ill with cancer and may have kept Harold Kelman out because he "broached the question, when it was really obvious that she was dying, 'Don't you think Karen would want to know?' "[51] Or perhaps Brigitte was protecting her mother's secret relationship with the young psychiatrist, which would have been shocking to colleagues. Only Gertrude seems to have defied Brigitte's ban. "I said, 'No matter what you say or do I *am* going to visit Karen now,'" Gertrude recalled, "'because I know she wants to see me.' And I never in my life will forget the radiant smile when I entered the room in the hospital and she turned around to look and see who came in. There was such a radiant light in her face when she said, 'Oh, Trübel!' Every bit of bitterness was out of me when I saw that."[52]

One of the last people to talk with Horney was a young medical student named Robert Coles, who had been assigned to the ward she was in at Harkness Pavilion. The conversation began because Coles noticed that Horney was reading George Meredith's *The Egoist*—a remarkable fact in itself, since Meredith's prose is difficult even for a native English speaker in the best of health. Coles was familiar with the book from his undergraduate years as an English major at Harvard, and it turned out that Horney knew one of his Harvard professors. A conversation was begun and continued over the next two days. According to Coles, who years later wrote of the encounter, "She knew she was dying, and made no effort to conceal her knowledge from me, a stranger." On the third morning Coles and Horney had their "longest and last conversation." Rather surprisingly, given Horney's reticence on the subject until then, she asked Coles how many women were in his class at medical school. "When I told her there were three, out of a hundred or so, she asked me why I thought that was the case." This led to a discussion of all the difficulties of professional life for a woman, difficulties Horney had struggled with all her life but rarely discussed so directly: the personal challenge of combining marriage, motherhood, and medicine, the male doctors' resentment of women in the field, and, "most of all, the irony that a profession so dedicated to caring for people, nurturing them... should be so overwhelmingly made up of men. (At least in this country, she reminded me; in Russia things are far different.) Her last remark, as he got ready to leave, was 'You are young, and maybe when you reach my age the world will be quite different.'"[53]

During her second week in the hospital Karen Horney's condition worsened rapidly, and on December 4 Renate flew up from Mexico to say goodbye. But she was too late: her mother had died two hours before her arrival. She went to her mother's apartment on Central Park South and "found my sisters in much the same state as I was, consternation, numbness, a sense of such emptiness and of loss. The apartment seemed cold without her, she was there but not there. Her desk was covered with papers as if she would sit down and continue her work." Later, when the three daughters paid a visit to the Frank E. Campbell Funeral Home, on Madison Avenue, Renate was shocked to find her mother "laid out in an open coffin with her hair coiffed and make-up on.... I felt like screaming out, 'This is not she... she is not part of this at all!'" The three sisters left hurriedly and did something their mother might have done too under the circumstances: they took an elevator to the top of Rockefeller Center and stood out in the cold, fresh night air, looking down at the blurred lights of the city below.[54]

At the time of her death the institute Karen Horney had founded eleven years before was thriving: there were over sixty candidates in training and twenty-five teachers. And an old dream was about to be realized. Since the early days of her institute Horney had talked about forming a clinic that would offer low-cost psychoanalytic therapy to people of modest means. Finally, in 1952, Norman Kelman's wife, Katie, announced that a board had been assembled and funds had been raised for a foundation and clinic that would bear Karen Horney's name. Horney wrote Katie Kelman that the clinic represented "the most meaningful honor I ever received or might receive in my life."[55] The Karen Horney Clinic continues to thrive, along with the institute (renamed the Karen Horney Psychoanalytic Institute), at 329 East 62nd Street, in New York City. Sometime during her last years Horney spoke to Katie Kelman of her pride in another legacy: her three daughters. As a young girl, Horney told Kelman, she had wanted to be either a mother, an actress, or a doctor. "You see I'm already living on through my children."[56]

The funeral service took place at Campbell's two days after her death and was led by Paul Tillich, Karen Horney's old friend. Tillich told the large crowd gathered for the ceremony:

> One of the most powerful lives we have known came to an end, unexpectedly except in the last few weeks, unimaginably to most of us, even now after it has happened.... Few people whom one encountered were so strong in the affirmation of their being, so full of the joy of living, so able to rest in themselves and to create without cessation beyond themselves.... She was what the words of Jesus say, a light on a high stand which gave light to all in the house.... It was this light radiating from her being which we have experienced whenever we encountered her.... It was this light which gave light... to her friends, who knew that hours with Karen would count as good and often unforgettable hours in their lives.... She wrote books, but she

loved human beings. She helped them to throw light into the dark places of their souls."[57]

Karen Horney was buried in Ferncliff Cemetery, in Ardsley, a quiet suburban town in Westchester, north of New York City. Her grave is a simple rectangular slab of rough-cut granite, inscribed "Karen Horney, 1885–1952." Around her in the cemetery the graves lie in clusters, uniting families in death. Karen Horney's grave stands alone, but in a lovely spot shaded by fruit and fir trees. It is an appropriate, if subdued, resting place for a woman who lived much of her life alone in beautiful places. The minimal inscription makes sense too. At the time of her death, her editor Storer Lunt noted that Karen Horney's "influence on American readers has been... far-reaching."[58] Why bother with an epitaph when Horney's own voice lived on so vigorously in her books? And yet such a life surely deserves a summing up, some evocation of what Paul Tillich spoke of in the funeral service: "her being, her power to be, the well-founded balance of an abundance of striving and creative possibility."[59] Perhaps the right words are those she herself used to end one of her most personal books, *Self-Analysis*. "Life is a struggle and striving, development and growth," she wrote, "and analysis is one of the means that can help in this process. Certainly its positive accomplishments are important, but also the striving itself is of intrinsic value. As Goethe has said in *Faust:*

> *Whoe'er aspires unweariedly,*
> *Is not beyond redeeming."*[60]

Source Notes

Abbreviations Used Throughout the Notes

Works of Karen Horney:

FP: Feminine Psychology
NP: The Neurotic Personality of Our Time
NW: New Ways in Psychoanalysis
SA: Self-Analysis
OIC: Our Inner Conflicts
NHG: Neurosis and Human Growth
Diaries: The Adolescent Diaries of Karen Horney

Other sources:

Standard Ed: Sigmund Freud, *Complete Works*.

Brill: Archives of the A. A. Brill Library, New York Psychoanalytic Institute.

Cornell: Archives of Psychiatry of New York Hospital–Cornell Medical Center, David Levy papers.

When psychoanalytic articles were published in both English and German, the reference given is usually to the article in English only. Unless otherwise indicated, all English translations of German texts are by the author.

Prologue
1. Letter from Fritz Wittels to Lawrence Kubie, president of the New York Psychoanalytic Society, and to all other members, March 13, 1940: Brill.

2. Minutes of meeting, April 29, 1941: Brill.
3. Letter from Lawrence Kubie to Joanna Knobler, Dec. 28, 1971: Francis A. Countway Library of Medicine, Boston, MA.
4. Interview with Dr. Samuel Atkin by the author, May 16, 1983.
5. *The Adolescent Diaries of Karen Horney* (New York: Basic Books, 1980), p. 102—hereafter cited as *Diaries* with page numbers.

CHAPTER ONE *Home*

1. Birth certificate. A previous biography, by Jack Rubins (*Karen Horney: Gentle Rebel of Psychoanalysis* [New York: Dial Press, 1978]), identified Blankensee as Horney's birthplace, and at least one of Horney's daughters believed her to have been born in that much lovelier place—a town situated just above the Elbe where many sea captains lived. The source of this piece of misinformation is unknown.
2. *Diaries,* 252.
3. Unpub. introduction by Renate Horney Patterson to the diaries of Karen Horney.
4. Press release, Hapag-Lloyd Aktiengesellschaft, Oct. 3, 1972.
5. Walter Kresse, *Seeschiffs-Verzeichnis der Hamburger Reederein, 1824–1888,* pp. 6–9, and *Hamburger Seeschiffe 1889–1914,* pp. 49–51 (Hamburg Museum für Hamburgische Geschichte, 1969, 1974).
6. Personal communication to author from Arnold Kludas, Deutsches Schiffahrtsmuseum, Bremerhaven, West Germany.
7. Unpub. history of van Ronzelens, compiled by Ollie Gramberg-Danielsen.
8. Kristine v. Soden and Gaby Zipfel, eds., *70 Jahre Frauenstudium: Frauen in der Wissenschaft* (Köln: Phal-Rugenstein Verlag, 1979), p. 11.
9. Church record, Friedenskirche, Eilbek, Germany.
10. *Diaries,* 3.
11. *Diaries,* 13.
12. *Diaries,* 17.
13. *Diaries,* 4.
14. *Diaries,* 17.
15. Fritz Lachmund, *Alt-Hamburg durch die Camera* (Hamburg: Christians Verlag, 1971); Fritz Lachmund and Rolf Müller, *Hamburg: Seinerzeit zur Kaiserzeit* (Hamburg: Verlag Rolf Müller, 1976); Jörgen Bracker and Carsten Prange, eds., *Alster, Elbe und die See* (Hamburg: Verlag Rolf Müller).
16. Hermann Hinrichsen, *Vergangenes aus Eilbek und Hohenfelde* (Hamburg: M and K Hansa Verlag, n.d.).
17. Hamburg Address Books, 1885–1901, Hamburg Staatsarchiv.
18. Interview with Ellen Möller, May 1984, Hamburg.
19. Lachmund, *Alt-Hamburg,* p. 30.
20. *Diaries,* 27.
21. *Diaries,* 3.
22. *Diaries,* 5.
23. *Diaries,* 6.
24. *Diaries,* 8.
25. *Diaries,* 11.

26. Karen Horney, *Our Inner Conflicts* (New York: Norton, 1945), p. 219—hereafter cited as *OIC* with page numbers.
27. *Diaries*, 21.
28. *Diaries*, 13.
29. *Diaries*, 22.
30. *Diaries*, 33.
31. Pastor W. Remé, *Eilbek und seine Kirche* (pamphlet, Hamburg, 1947), p. 16.
32. Pastor Günther Severin, unpub. history of the Eilbek Friedenskirche, 1984.
33. *Diaries*, 4.
34. *Diaries*, 23.
35. Remé, *Eilbek und seine Kirche*, pp. 14–23.
36. Severin, unpub. history of the Eilbek Friedenskirche.
37. *Diaries*, 5.
38. *Diaries*, 18.
39. Remé, *Eilbek und seine Kirche*, pp. 18–19.
40. Severin, unpub. history of the Eilbek Friedenskirche.
41. *Diaries*, 12.
42. *Diaries*, 23–24.
43. *Diaries*, 25–26.
44. *Diaries*, 37.
45. Church record, Friedenskirche, Eilbek. Two days later 136 boys were confirmed.
46. *Diaries*, 37–38.
47. *Diaries*, 22.

CHAPTER TWO *School*

1. F. E. Chadwick et al., *Ocean Steamships: A Popular Account of Their Construction, Development, Management and Appliances* (New York: Scribners, 1891), p. 196.
2. Unpub. introduction by Renate Horney Patterson to the diaries of Karen Horney.
3. Chadwick et al., *Ocean Steamships*, p. 287.
4. Sigmund Freud, *Complete Works* (London: Hogarth Press, 1957), 11:84—hereafter cited as *Standard Ed.*
5. Lady Brassey, *A Voyage in the "Sunbeam"* (New York: Hippocrene Books, 1984). This adventurous Englishwoman's account of an 1876 sail around the tip of South America and beyond provided useful color.
6. *Diaries*, 28.
7. Karl May, *Winnetou*, trans. Michael Shaw (New York: Seabury Press, 1977).
8. *Diaries*, 35–36.
9. *Diaries*, 44.
10. *Diaries*, 9.
11. *Ibid.*
12. *Diaries*, 19.
13. Richard J. Evans, *The Feminist Movement in Germany 1894–1933* (London: Sage Publications, 1976).
14. Quoted *ibid.*, p. 23.

15. *Die Frauenbewegung,* Jan. 1, 1895, as excerpted in *Die Frauenfrage in Deutschland 1865–1915,* ed. Elke Frederiksen (Stuttgart: Philipp Reclam Jun., 1981), p. 54.

16. Evans, *The Feminist Movement in Germany.*

17. From *Der Jesuitismus im Hausstande* (1873), as quoted in *Die Frauenfrage in Deutschland,* ed. Frederiksen, p. 200.

18. Fanny Lewald, *Für und wider die Frauen* (Berlin: Otto Janke, 1870), excerpted in *Die Frauenfrage in Deutschland,* ed. Frederiksen, p. 204.

19. *Diaries,* 3.

20. *Diaries,* 19.

21. *Diaries,* 4.

22. *Diaries,* 10.

23. *Diaries,* 6.

24. *Ibid.*

25. *Diaries,* 7.

26. *Diaries,* 10.

27. *Diaries,* 20. The sentence about Dr. Karstens' peculiar speech is not in the translation.

28. *Diaries,* 21.

29. *Diaries,* 28.

30. *Hamburger Fremdenblatt,* Dec. 18, 1900.

31. Hamburg Address Book, 1904, Hamburg Staatsarchiv.

32. Lida Gustava Heymann and Anita Augspurg, *Erlebtes—Erschautes,* ed. Margrit Twellmann (Meisenheim am Glan, Germany: Anton Hain, 1972), as excerpted in *Die Frauenfrage in Deutschland,* ed. Frederiksen, pp. 239–242.

33. Hedwig Dohm, *Erziehung zum Stimmrecht der Frau* (Berlin: Preussischer Landesverien für Frauenstimmrecht, 1910), as excerpted in *Die Frauenfrage in Deutschland,* ed. Frederiksen, p. 233.

34. *Hamburger Fremdenblatt,* Jan. 20, 22, 24, 25, 29, 1901.

35. *Ibid.,* Feb. 13, 1901.

36. *Ibid.,* Dec. 18, 1901.

37. Hamburg Address Books, 1885–1901, Hamburg Staatsarchiv.

38. *Diaries,* 24.

39. *Ibid.*

40. *Diaries,* 24–25.

41. *Diaries,* 26.

42. *Ibid.*

43. *Diaries,* 27.

44. *Diaries,* 31.

45. *Ibid.*

46. *Diaries,* 29.

47. *Diaries,* 29–30.

48. *Diaries,* 36–37.

49. *Diaries,* 38.

50. *Diaries,* 38–39.

51. *Diaries,* 28.

52. *Diaries,* 34.

53. *Diaries,* 30.

CHAPTER THREE *"Karen Hamburgensis"*

1. *Diaries*, 121.
2. *Diaries*, 53.
3. Unpub. diary, 1903.
4. *Diaries*, 58.
5. *Diaries*, 39.
6. *Diaries*, 41.
7. *Diaries*, 44.
8. *Ibid.*
9. *Diaries*, 41.
10. *Diaries*, 42.
11. *Diaries*, 46.
12. *Ibid.*
13. *Diaries*, 47.
14. *Diaries*, 39.
15. *Diaries*, 103.
16. *Diaries*, 41.
17. *Diaries*, 45.
18. *Diaries*, 40.
19. *Diaries*, 48.
20. *Diaries*, 47.
21. *Diaries*, 60.
22. *Diaries*, 58–61.
23. *Diaries*, 60–61.
24. Émile Zola, *Nana* (New York: Modern Library, 1927), p. 248.
25. *Diaries*, 63–64.
26. Marie Madeleine, *Auf Kypros* (Berlin: Est-Est Verlag, n.d.), pub. in *Hydromel and Rue,* trans. Ferdinand E. Kappey (London: Francis Griffiths, 1907), pp. 37–40.
27. *Diaries*, 65.
28. Madeleine, *Hydromel and Rue*, p. 48.
29. *Diaries*, 64.
30. Heymann had also played a role in the Gymnasium-versus-Reformschule debate. Lida Gustava Heymann and Anita Augspurg, *Erlebtes—Erschautes,* ed. Margrit Twellmann (Meisenheim am Glan, Germany: Anton Hain, 1972), as excerpted in *Die Frauenfrage in Deutschland 1865–1915,* ed. Elke Frederiksen (Stuttgart: Philipp Redam Jun., 1981).
31. Richard J. Evans, *The Feminist Movement in Germany 1894–1933* (London: Sage Publications, 1976), p. 56.
32. *Die Frauenfrage in Deutschland*, ed. Frederiksen, p. 473.
33. Evans, *The Feminist Movement in Germany.*
34. *Diaries*, 73.
35. Evans, *The Feminist Movement in Germany*, p. 119.
36. *Ibid.*, p. 125.
37. *Ibid.*, p. 132.
38. Unpub. letter from Berndt to Sonni, May 7, 1907.
39. *Diaries*, 91–92.

40. *Diaries*, 61.
41. *Diaries*, 81–82.
42. *Diaries*, 61.
43. *Diaries*, 61–62.
44. *Diaries*, 42.
45. *Diaries*, 43.
46. *Diaries*, 42.
47. *Diaries*, 45.
48. *Diaries*, 49. The extra exclamation points are in the original German diary but not in the published version in English.
49. *Diaries*, 50.
50. *Diaries*, 49.
51. *Diaries*, 50.
52. *Diaries*, 49.
53. *Diaries*, 63–64.
54. *Diaries*, 66.
55. *Diaries*, 63.

CHAPTER FOUR *First Love*

1. *Diaries*, 55.
2. *Diaries*, 57.
3. *Diaries*, 55.
4. *Diaries*, 65–66.
5. Marie Madeleine, *Auf Kypros* (Berlin: Est-Est Verlag, n.d.), pub. in *Hydromel and Rue*, trans. Ferdinand E. Kappey (London: Francis Griffiths, 1907).
6. *Diaries*, 79.
7. *Diaries*, 82.
8. *Diaries*, 83.
9. *Diaries*, 88.
10. *Ibid.*
11. *Ibid.*
12. *Diaries*, 67–68.
13. *Diaries*, 88.
14. *Diaries*, 89.
15. *Diaries*, 71.
16. *Diaries*, 69–70.
17. *Diaries*, 71.
18. *Diaries*, 71, 72; see also 154.
19. *Diaries*, 74.
20. *Diaries*, 99.
21. *Diaries*, 74.
22. *Diaries*, 76.
23. *Diaries*, 74.
24. *Diaries*, 76.
25. *Ibid.*
26. *Diaries*, 80.
27. *Diaries*, 99.

28. *Diaries,* 62.
29. *Diaries,* 74.
30. *Diaries,* 77.
31. *Ibid.*
32. *Diaries,* 107.
33. *Diaries,* 88.
34. *Diaries,* 90–91.
35. *Diaries,* 93.
36. *Diaries,* 58.
37. *Diaries,* 101–102.
38. *Diaries,* 89.
39. *Diaries,* 120.
40. Thomas Mann, *Buddenbrooks* (New York: Vintage Books, 1984), p. 248.
41. *Diaries,* 120.
42. The translation in the published English version is "gay boys," which implies homosexuality in modern parlance. The German word is *Gecken,* probably more accurately translated as "dandies."
43. *Diaries,* 120–121.
44. *Diaries,* 121.
45. *Ibid.*
46. *Diaries,* 122.
47. *Diaries,* 95.
48. *Diaries,* 123.
49. *Diaries,* 123–124.
50. *Diaries,* 100.
51. *Diaries,* 198.
52. *Diaries,* 124–125.
53. *Diaries,* 82.
54. *Diaries,* 125.
55. *Diaries,* 122.
56. *Diaries,* 129.
57. *Diaries,* 123.
58. *Diaries,* 128.
59. *Diaries,* 141–142.
60. *Diaries,* 139.
61. *Diaries,* 126.
62. *Diaries,* 99.
63. *Diaries,* 103.
64. *Diaries,* 129.
65. *Diaries,* 134.
66. *Diaries,* 155.
67. *Diaries,* 137.
68. *Diaries,* 125.
69. *Diaries,* 128.
70. *Diaries,* 129–130.
71. *Diaries,* 131.
72. *Diaries,* 133.

73. *Diaries,* 134.
74. *Diaries,* 135.
75. *Diaries,* 136.
76. *Ibid.*
77. *Diaries,* 137.
78. *Diaries,* 144–145.
79. *Diaries,* 150.
80. *Diaries,* 151.
81. *Diaries,* 98.
82. *Diaries,* 151.
83. *Diaries,* 143.
84. *Diaries,* 140.
85. *Diaries,* 143.
86. *Diaries,* 117.
87. *Diaries,* 104.
88. *Diaries,* 127.
89. *Diaries,* 104.
90. *Diaries,* 95.
91. *Diaries,* 96.
92. *Diaries,* 99.
93. *Diaries,* 151.
94. *Diaries,* 99.
95. *Diaries,* 129.
96. *Diaries,* 98.
97. *Diaries,* 152–153.
98. *Diaries,* 154.
99. *Diaries,* 109.
100. *Diaries,* 176.
101. *Diaries,* 156–158.
102. *Diaries,* 107.
103. *Diaries,* 95.
104. *Diaries,* 142.
105. *Diaries,* 110–112.
106. *Diaries,* 131.
107. *Diaries,* 116.
108. *Diaries,* 118.
109. *Diaries,* 125.
110. *Diaries,* 155.
111. *Diaries,* 108–109.
112. *Diaries,* 159.
113. *Diaries,* 119.
114. *Diaries,* 117.
115. *Diaries,* 116.
116. *Diaries,* 118.
117. *Diaries,* 116–117.
118. *Diaries,* 147.

CHAPTER FIVE *"Myself in Every Part"*

1. *Diaries*, 240.
2. *Diaries*, 180.
3. Museum for Transportation Systems, Nürnberg.
4. *Diaries*, 184.
5. *Diaries*, 127.
6. *Diaries*, 147–148.
7. *Diaries*, 148.
8. *Diaries*, 190.
9. *Diaries*, 168.
10. *Diaries*, 172.
11. *Diaries*, 149.
12. *Diaries*, 173–174.
13. *Diaries*, 163.
14. *Diaries*, 202.
15. *Diaries*, 180.
16. Long after it was outlawed elsewhere in Europe, student dueling was a central fact of life in German universities. Historian Richard J. Evans has written that the two proofs of manhood in the German middle class were a visit or two to a brothel and a dueling scar. In 1906 the fraternity of dueling clubs and the bloody excitement of duels would still have been an important part of student life in Freiburg. See Evans, *The Feminist Movement in Germany 1894–1933* (London: Sage Publications, 1976), p. 17.
17. Peter Gay, *The Education of the Senses* (New York: Oxford Univ. Press, 1984), p.183. A degree from a German university, as the American educator M. Carey Thomas discovered in 1882, was out of the question. Thomas, armed with an undergraduate degree from Cornell and three years of study at the University of Leipzig, petitioned the University of Göttingen for permission to take the doctoral examination. Her request had to be presented to forty professors, each of whom would be "asked his opinion upon the woman question and if two or three disagreed my fate would be decided in the negative." Predictably, Thomas' petition was turned down; she left Germany to complete her studies in the more tolerant atmosphere of Zürich and, later, to become president of Bryn Mawr. See Marjorie Dobkin, ed., *The Making of a Feminist: Early Journals and Letters of M. Carey Thomas* (Kent State Univ. Press, 1979), p. 252.
18. E. Th. Nauck, *Das Frauenstudium an der Universität Freiburg im Breisgau* (Freiburg: Verlag Eberhard Albert Universitätsbuchhandlung, 1953), p. 23.
19. *Ibid.*, p. 55.
20. *Ibid.*, p. 58.
21. *Ibid.*, p. 25.
22. Arthur Kirchhoff, *Die akademische Frau* (1897), p. 124.
23. *Ibid.*, p. 33.
24. *Ibid.*, p. 73.
25. *Simplicissimus*, 7, No. 49 (1903).
26. *Ibid.*, 6, No. 5 (1901/2).
27. As quoted by Gay, *Education of the Senses*, pp. 256–257.

28. *Gartenlaube Kalender* (Berlin: Verlag von Ernst Keils, 1909).
29. *Die Frauenfrage in Deutschland 1865–1915,* ed. Elke Frederiksen (Stuttgart: Philipp Reclam Jun., 1981), p. 28.
30. "Ego" notebook (unpub.).
31. *Diaries,* 177–178.
32. *Diaries,* 183–185.
33. *Diaries,* 194.
34. *Diaries,* 227.
35. *Diaries,* 174.
36. *Diaries,* 179.
37. *Diaries,* 219.
38. *Ibid.*
39. University of Freiburg, *Matrikelbuch, Sommer-Semester 1906,* Freiburg University Archives.
40. Freiburg Address Book, 1906, Freiburg University Archives.
41. *Diaries,* 147.
42. *Ibid.*
43. *Diaries,* 148.
44. *Studien und Sitten Zeugnis,* Freiburg University Archives, 1906–8.
45. *Diaries,* 218.
46. *Diaries,* 211.
47. *Diaries,* 210.
48. *Diaries,* 149.
49. *Diaries,* 178.
50. *Diaries,* 197.
51. *Diaries,* 203.
52. *Diaries,* 170.
53. *Diaries,* 172.
54. *Diaries,* 178.
55. *Diaries,* 148.
56. *Diaries,* 149.
57. *Diaries,* 164.
58. *Diaries,* 164–165.
59. *Diaries,* 167.
60. *Diaries,* 148.
61. German universities divide the academic year into a summer semester, from mid-April to mid-August, and a winter semester, from October to March.
62. *Diaries,* 170.
63. *Diaries,* 167.
64. *Diaries,* 180.
65. Abraham Flexner, *Medical Education in Europe* (New York: Carnegie Foundation for the Advancement of Teaching, 1912), p. 254. According to Flexner, the German professor in those days "receive[d] his remuneration partly, sometimes largely, in the form of student fees," and relied on "large lecture groups" to make a decent living.
66. *Diaries,* 168..
67. Freiburg Address Book, 1907.
68. *Diaries,* 171–172, 173.

69. *Diaries,* 178.
70. Unpub. letter from Berndt to Sonni, June 23, 1907.
71. *Diaries,* 173.
72. *Diaries,* 185.
73. *Diaries,* 178.
74. *Diaries,* 169.
75. *Diaries,* 172.
76. *Diaries,* 174.

CHAPTER SIX *Courtship and Marriage*

1. *Diaries,* 179–181.
2. *Diaries,* 148. The *Jägerhäusle* seems to have been a destination on a hike in the Black Forest; it means, literally, "hunters' cottage."
3. *Diaries,* 182–183.
4. *Diaries,* 185.
5. *Diaries,* 186.
6. *Diaries,* 187.
7. Ibid.
8. *Diaries,* 188.
9. *Diaries,* 189.
10. Ibid.
11. *Diaries,* 190–191.
12. *Diaries,* 189.
13. *Diaries,* 192.
14. *Diaries,* 194.
15. *Diaries,* 192–193.
16. *Diaries,* 193.
17. *Diaries,* 198.
18. *Diaries,* 200.
19. *Diaries,* 205–206.
20. *Diaries,* 206.
21. *Diaries,* 214.
22. *Diaries,* 215.
23. *Diaries,* 216.
24. Ibid.
25. *Diaries,* 199.
26. *Diaries,* 204.
27. *Diaries,* 222.
28. *Diaries,* 209.
29. *Diaries,* 232.
30. Letter from Sonni to Berndt, Jan. 1, 1908.
31. Letter from Sonni to Berndt, Nov. 17, 1907.
32. *Diaries,* 66.
33. Letter from Sonni to Berndt, Jan. 1, 1908.
34. Letter from Berndt to Sonni, July 13, 1907.

35. Letter from Berndt to Sonni, July 28, 1907.
36. Letter from Berndt to Sonni, June 6, 1907.
37. Letter from Berndt to Sonni, June 23, 1907.
38. Letter from Berndt to Sonni, Aug. 23, 1907.
39. *Diaries*, 19.
40. Letter from Berndt to Sonni, Nov. 22, 1907.
41. Letter from Berndt to Sonni, May 19, 1908.
42. Letter from Berndt to Sonni, June 18, 1908.
43. *Diaries*, 240–241.
44. Letter from Berndt to Sonni, Dec. 31, 1908.
45. Unpub. letter from Karen and Oskar to Sonni, Jan. 1, 1909.
46. Letter from Berndt to Sonni, Sept. 27, 1909.
47. Letter from Berndt to Sonni, May 13, 1910.
48. *Diaries*, 166.
49. *Diaries*, 212.
50. *Diaries*, 169.
51. Karen Horney, *Self-Analysis* (New York: Norton, 1942), p. 55—hereafter cited as *SA* with page numbers.
52. Letter from Berndt to Sonni, Sept. 27, 1909.
53. *Diaries*, 19.

CHAPTER SEVEN *Psychoanalysis*

1. Edward Edgeworth, *The Human German* (New York: Dutton, n.d.), p. 95.
2. *Die Frauenfrage in Deutschland 1865–1915,* ed. Elke Frederiksen (Stuttgart: Philipp Reclam Jun., 1981), p. 27.
3. Gerhard Masur, *Imperial Berlin* (New York: Basic Books, 1970), p. 188.
4. Barbara Tuchman, *The Proud Tower* (New York: Macmillan, 1966), p. 308.
5. Masur, *Imperial Berlin,* p. 223.
6. *Ibid.*, p. 250.
7. Annemarie Lange, *Das Wilhelminische Berlin: Zwischen Jahrhundertwende und Novemberrevolution* (Berlin: Dietz Verlag, 1967), p. 157.
8. Ibid., p. 67.
9. Masur, *Imperial Berlin,* p. 74.
10. The address books for these years were found in the Staatsbibliothek in West Berlin and in the Boston Public Library.
11. Theodor Fontane, *Short Novels and Other Writings* (New York: Continuum Publishing Co., 1982).
12. Franz Alexander, *American Journal of Psychoanalysis,* 106, No. 11 (May 1950): 844.
13. H. C. Abraham and E. L. Freud, eds., *The Letters of Sigmund Freud and Karl Abraham 1907–1926* (New York: Basic Books, 1965), p. 81.
14. Hannah S. Decker, *Freud in Germany* (New York: International Universities Press, 1977), p. 41.
15. *Ibid.*, p. 25.
16. *Ibid.*, p. 41.
17. W. McGuire, ed., *The Freud/Jung Letters: The Correspondence Between Sigmund*

Freud and C. G. Jung, trans. R. Mannheim and R. F. C. Hull (Princeton: Princeton Univ. Press, 1974), p. 69.

18. *Standard Ed.*, 1:49.
19. *Standard Ed.*, 16:449.
20. Abraham and Freud, eds., *Letters of S. Freud and K. Abraham*, p. 46.
21. *Standard Ed.*, 15:67
22. *Standard Ed.*, 17:139 ff.
23. Abraham and Freud, eds., *Letters of S. Freud and K. Abraham*, p. 11.
24. *Ibid.*, p. 9.
25. *Ibid.*, pp. 9–10.
26. Decker, *Freud in Germany*, pp. 158–159.
27. Abraham and Freud, eds., *Letters of S. Freud and K. Abraham*, p. 16.
28. *Ibid.*, pp. 88–89.
29. "Ego" notebook (unpub.).
30. *Diaries*, 270.
31. Abraham and Freud, eds., *Letters of S. Freud and K. Abraham*, p. 114.
32. Unpub. diary, April 18, 1912.
33. Pub. in *Zeitschrift für Sexualwissenschaft*, 4 Bd., 7 u. 8 Heft (Okt./Nov. 1917), trans. in *American Journal for Psychoanalysis*, 28, No. 1 (1968): pp. 3–12.
34. Abraham and Freud, eds., *Letters of S. Freud and K. Abraham*, p. 134..
35. Decker, *Freud in Germany*, p. 64.
36. *Ibid.*, p. 328.
37. The thesis from which all this material is drawn is entitled in German *Ein kasuistischer Beitrag zur Frage der traumatischen Psychosen* (Berlin: Buchdruckerei Hermann Bode, 1915). It was further described, on the title page, as "Inaugural-Dissertation zur Erlangung der Doktorwürde der Hohen Medizischen Fakultät an der Friedrich-Wilhelms-Universität zu Berlin. Vorgelegt von Karen Horney, approb. Ärztin. Tag der Promotion: 14 Januar 1915."
38. *Diaries*, 102.
39. *Standard Ed.*, 14:7.
40. See n. 33, above.
41. Unpub. diary, April 9, 1912.

CHAPTER EIGHT *Love and Work*

1. Interview with Rita Honroth Welte, Oct. 8, 1984.
2. *Diaries*, 238.
3. *Diaries*, 242.
4. *Diaries*, 255.
5. *Diaries*, 247.
6. *Diaries*, 270.
7. Annemarie Lange, *Das Wilhelminische Berlin: Zwischen Jahrhundertwende und Novemberrevolution* (Berlin: Dietz Verlag, 1967), pp. 449–450.
8. Letter from Berndt to Sonni, Sept. 27, 1909.
9. *Diaries*, 245.
10. *Diaries*, 258.
11. *Diaries*, 254.
12. Unpub. diary, Jan. 3, 1911.

13. *Ibid.*, May 3, 1910.
14. *Diaries*, 249.
15. *Diaries*, 247.
16. *Diaries*, 263.
17. *Diaries*, 257.
18. *Diaries*, 238.
19. *Diaries*, 251.
20. *Diaries*, 259–260.
21. *Diaries*, 260.
22. Standard Ed., 7:116.
23. *Diaries*, 246.
24. *Diaries*, 245.
25. *Diaries*, 244.
26. Unpub. diary, April 16, 1912.
27. Standard Ed., 16:452.
28. *Diaries*, 238–239.
29. "The Technique of Psychoanalytic Therapy," pub. in *Zeitschrift für Sexualwissenschaft,* 4 Bd., 7 u. 8 Heft (Okt./Nov. 1917), trans. in *American Journal for Psychoanalysis*, 28, No. 1 (1968): 3–12.
30. From interviews with Sandor Rado, 1964–65, conducted by Bluma Swerdloff for the Oral History Research Office of Columbia University.
31. *Standard Ed.,* 7:115.
32. *Diaries*, 239.
33. *Standard Ed.,* 16:318.
34. Unpub. diary, April 18, 1910.
35. Unpub. diary, Jan. 3, 1911.
36. *Diaries*, 242.
37. Unpub. diary, April 25, 1910.
38. *Diaries*, 242.
39. *Diaries*, 243.
40. *Diaries*, 253.
41. *Diaries*, 236.
42. Unpub. diary, April 2, 1910.
43. Unpub. diary, Jan. 23, 1911.
44. *Diaries*, 262.
45. Unpub. diary, April 2. 1912.
46. Unpub. diary, June 24, 1912.
47. Unpub. diary, April 3, 1912.
48. Gustav Regler, *The Owl of Minerva* (New York: Farrar, Straus and Cudahy, 1966), p. 117.
49. Unpub. reminiscence of Rita Honroth Welte.
50. Unpub. diary, April 2, 1912.
51. *Ibid.*
52. Unpub. diary, April 18, 1912.
53. Unpub. diary, April 3, 1912.
54. Unpub. diary, April 20, 1912.
55. Unpub. diary, June 24, 1912.
56. Unpub. diary, June 20, 1912.

57. Karen Horney, *The Neurotic Personality of Our Time* (New York: Norton, 1937), pp. 103–104—hereafter cited as *NP* with page numbers.
58. Unpub. diary, April 2, 1912.
59. Unpub. diary, Easter Sunday, 1912.
60. *Diaries*, 260.
61. *Diaries*, 256.
62. Unpub. diary, Jan. 9, 1911.
63. *Diaries*, 256.
64. Unpub. diary, April 2, 1912.
65. Unpub. diary, July 7, 1912.
66. *SA*, 8.
67. Unpub. diary, May 4, 1912.
68. *Diaries*, 262–263.
69. *Diaries*, 265.
70. *Diaries*, 264–265.
71. *Diaries*, 266.
72. *Diaries*, 251–252.
73. *Diaries*, 254.
74. *Diaries*, 252.
75. Unpub. diary, Jan. 9, 1911.
76. *Diaries*, 262.
77. *Diaries*, 268.
78. Unpub. diary, April 10, 1911.
79. "The Flight from Womanhood," in *Feminine Psychology,* ed. Harold Kelman (New York: Norton, 1973), pp. 60–61. Hereafter *FP.* The article was first published in both the German and English versions of the *International Journal of Psycho-Analysis* in 1926.
80. *Ibid.*, p. 70.

CHAPTER NINE *Zehlendorf*

1. As quoted in John Willett, *Art and Politics in the Weimar Period: The New Sobriety 1917–1933* (New York: Pantheon Books, 1978), p. 23.
2. As quoted in Otto Friedrich, *Before the Deluge* (New York: Harper and Row, 1972), p. 37.
3. Paul Mebes, *Um 1800: Architektur und Handwerk im letzten Jahrhundert ihrer traditionellen Entwicklung* (Munich: F. Bruckmann, 1908), p. 12.
4. *Ibid.*, p. 17.
5. Ellen Key, *The Century of the Child* (New York: Putnam, 1909), p. 13.
6. *Ibid.*, p. 31.
7. *Ibid.*, p. 102.
8. *Standard Ed.*, 4:255.
9. Key, *The Century of the Child,* p. 173.

CHAPTER TEN *Separation*

1. Barbara Tuchman, *The Proud Tower* (New York: Macmillan, 1966), p. xiii.

2. As quoted in Otto Friedrich, *Before the Deluge* (New York: Harper and Row, 1972), p. 148.
3. Bruno Walter, *Theme and Variations* (New York: Knopf, 1946), p. 268.
4. Ives Hendrick, unpub. letter to his parents, Sept. 17, 1928, in the collection of the Boston Psychoanalytic Society and Institute.
5. As quoted in Peter Gay, *Weimar Culture: The Outsider as Insider* (New York: Harper and Row, 1968), p. 132.
6. Klaus Mann, quoted in Bernd Ruland, *Das War Berlin: Die Goldene Jahre 1918–1933* (Munich: Graupner and Partner GmbH, 1972), p. 239.
7. As quoted in Peter Gay, *Weimar Culture*, pp. 129–130.
8. George Grosz, *An Autobiography*, trans. by Nora Hodges (New York: Macmillan, 1983), p. 125.
9. As quoted in Gordon A. Craig, *Germany 1866–1945* (New York: Oxford Univ. Press, 1978), p. 452.
10. Unpub. letter written by Horney to Georg Groddeck, July 12, 1923.
11. Edward Edgeworth, *The Human German* (New York: Dutton, n.d.), p. 2.
12. Karen Horney, "The Distrust Between the Sexes," *FP*, 107–108.
13. *FP*, 109.
14. *FP*, 108.
15. Unpub. diary, Jan. 13, 1911.
16. Horney, "Problems of Marriage," *FP*, 121–122.
17. Renate Horney Patterson's unpub. reminiscences.
18. Interview with Henry and Yela Lowenfeld by the author, May 17, 1983.
19. Ernst Simmel, writing in *Zehn Jahre Berliner Psychoanalytisches Institut* (Wien: Internationaler Psychoanalytischer Verlag, 1930), p. 12. Translation by Sanford Gifford for "Remarks of Oral History Workshop on the History of Psychoanalytic Training, Berlin and Vienna, 1920–1928."
20. Sigmund Freud, in "Vorwort" to *Zehn Jahre Berliner Psychoanalytisches Institut*.
21. *Zehn Jahre Berliner Psychoanalytisches Institut*. H. C. Abraham and E. L. Freud, eds., *The Letters of Sigmund Freud and Karl Abraham 1907–1926* (New York: Basic Books, 1965).
22. *Internationale Zeitschrift für Psychoanalyse* (1925), p. 502.
23. From interviews conducted by Dr. Bluma Swerdloff, 1964–65, for the Oral History Research Office of Columbia University.
24. *Internationale Zeitschrift für Psychoanalyse*, 13 (1927): 247.
25. Renate Horney Patterson's unpub. reminiscences.
26. Nathan G. Hale, Jr., "From Berggasse XIX to Central Park West: The Americanization of Psychoanalysis, 1919–1940," *Journal of the History of the Behavioral Sciences*, 14 (1978): 302.
27. Josine Ebsen Müller's career was intertwined with Karen Horney's in many ways. She and Karen went to Gymnasium together and attended medical school at Freiburg together. Both were analyzed by Karl Abraham and became psychiatrists and members of the Berlin Psychoanalytic Institute. Furthermore, Josine married Karl Müller-Braunschweig, Oskar Horney's boyhood friend. And, finally, Josine wrote several papers on the genital phase in girls which questioned, like Horney's, whether the vagina was as insignificant as Freud maintained in early development. (See Josine Müller, "The

Problem of Libidinal Development of the Genital Phase in Girls," *International Journal of Psycho-Analysis,* 13 [1932]). Her creative years were cut short, however, by her premature death, in 1930. She died of a lung infection on a sea voyage to the Canary Islands.

28. Max Eitingon in "Korrespondenzblatt," *Internationale Zeitschrift für Psychoanalyse,* 17 (1931).
29. Report in *International Zeitschrift für Arztliche Psychoanalyse* (1919).
30. Ernst Freud, Lucie Freud, and Ilse Grubrich Simitis, eds., *Sigmund Freud: His Life in Pictures and Words* (New York: Norton, 1978), p. 200.
31. Interviews with Marianne Kris, 1972–73, for the Oral History series of the New York Psychoanalytic Institute.
32. Frederick S. Perls, *In and Out of the Garbage Pail* (Lafayette, Calif.: Real People Press, 1969), unnumbered pages.
33. Unpub. reminiscence by Gustav Hans Graber.
34. Interview with Henry and Yela Lowenfeld, May 17, 1983.
35. Franz Alexander, Samuel Eisenstein, and Martin Grotjahn, eds., *Psychoanalytic Pioneers* (New York: Basic Books, 1966), p. 188.
36. Obituary by Ernest Jones, *International Journal of Psycho-Analysis,* 24 (1943): 190–192.
37. "The Technique of Psychoanalytic Therapy," pub. in *Zeitschrift für Sexualwissenschaft,* 4 Bd., 7 u. 8 Heft (Okt./Nov. 1917), trans. in *American Journal for Psychoanalysis,* 28, No. 1 (1968): 3–12.
38. Horney, "The Problem of the Monogamous Ideal," *FP,* 84–98.
39. Horney, "Problems of Marriage," *FP,* 119–132.
40. Horney, "The Problem of the Monogamous Ideal," *FP,* 84.
41. *Standard Ed.,* 9:191 ff.
42. *Standard Ed.,* Vol 17, p. 168.
43. *Standard Ed.,* 9:197.

CHAPTER ELEVEN *Freud, Horney, and the Psychoanalytic View of Women*

1. See Paul Roazen, *Helene Deutsch: A Psychoanalyst's Life* (New York: Anchor Press/Doubleday, 1985).
2. Jones, Ernest, *The Life and Work of Sigmund Freud* (New York: Basic Books, 1955), 387.
3. *Standard Ed.,* 3:100.
4. *Standard Ed.,* 3:272.
5. *Standard Ed.,* 2:103.
6. *Standard Ed.,* 2:232.
7. *Standard Ed.,* 11:205.
8. *Standard Ed.,* 11:99.
9. *Standard Ed.,* 14:91.
10. *Standard Ed.,* 13:15.
11. *Standard Ed.,* 12:323.
12. *Standard Ed.,* 3:109.
13. *Standard Ed.,* 7:151.
14. *Standard Ed.,* 9:215.

15. *Standard Ed.*, 16:333.
16. *Standard Ed.*, 3:13.
17. *Standard Ed.*, 21:241.
18. Karl Abraham, "Manifestations of the Female Castration Complex," *International Journal of Psycho-Analysis*, 3, Pt. 1 (1922): 1–29.
19. *Ibid.*
20. Karen Horney, "On the Genesis of the Castration Complex in Women," *International Journal of Psycho-Analysis*, Vol. 5, Pt. 1 (1924). The title of the paper as presented in German was "Zur Genese des weiblichen Kastrationskomplexes."
21. *Standard Ed.*, 19:32.
22. *Standard Ed.*, 19:256.
23. *Standard Ed.*, 19:142.
24. *Standard Ed.*, 19:179.
25. *Standard Ed.*, 19:37.
26. *Standard Ed.*, 19:142.
27. *Standard Ed.*, 19:145.
28. Simmel anticipated some of the ideas of Carol Gilligan, *In a Different Voice: Psychological Theory and Women's Development* (Cambridge, MA.: Harvard Univ. Press, 1982), and Jean Baker Miller, *Toward a New Psychology of Women* (Boston: Beacon Press, 1976). Guy Oakes, in an introduction to his recent translation of the writings of Georg Simmel, *Georg Simmel: On Women, Sexuality, and Love* (New Haven: Yale Univ. Press, 1984), notes that "the conclusions of Gilligan's research—and especially her thesis that there is a paradigmatic male ethic of justice and a paradigmatic female ethic of responsibility that qualify as irreducibly different and incommensurable modes of social experience and interpretation—support the main claims of Simmel's essays Female Culture" and "The Relative and the Absolute in the Problem of the Sexes" (p. 47).
29. Franz Alexander, Samuel Eisenstein, and Martin Grotjahn, eds., *Psychonalytic Pioneers* (New York: Basic Books, 1966), p. 310.
30. Georg Groddeck, *The Book of the It: Psychoanalytic Letters to a Friend* (New York and Washington: Nervous and Mental Disease Publishing Co., 1928), p. 108.
31. *Ibid.*, p. 91.
32. *Standard Ed.*, 19:23.
33. Alexander, Eisenstein, and Grotjahn, eds., *Psychoanalytic Pioneers*, p. 311.
34. Carl M. Grossman and Sylvia Grossman, *The Wild Analyst: The Life and Work of Georg Groddeck* (New York: George Braziller, 1965), pp. 98–99.
35. Groddeck, *The Book of the It*, p. 89.
36. *Ibid.*, pp. 11–12.
37. Unpub. letter written by Horney to Groddeck from Juist, on the North Sea, July 12, 1923.
38. Paul Roazen, in his biography *Helene Deutsch: A Psychoanalyst's Life* (p. 261), quotes a 1926 letter from Deutsch to her husband in which she complains of "rigid adherence to the phantom of 'Freudian Method,' which, as I now realize, I must regard as an *area of research* and not as a therapeutic method.... To give psychic treatment, yes—but with full awareness that success is only

minimally connected with the uncovering of infantile libido fixations and with transference agencies. The short-sightedness of these established views is clear to me in a theoretical sense as well."

39. *Ibid.*, p. 178.
40. *Ibid.*, p. 193.
41. Helene Deutsch, "The Psychology of Women in Relation to the Functions of Reproduction," *International Journal of Psycho-Analysis*, 6 (1925): 405–418.
42. Karen Horney, "Book Reviews," *ibid.*, 7 (1926): 92–100.
43. *Standard Ed.*, 19:258.
44. Unpub. letter from Karen Horney to Georg Groddeck, Feb. 7, 1926.
45. Karen Horney, "The Flight from Womanhood," *International Journal of Psycho-Analysis*, 7 (1926): 324–339. The paper was part of a *Festschrift* of original papers dedicated to Freud on his seventieth birthday. German title: "Die Flucht aus der Weiblichkeit."
46. Ernest Jones, "The Early Development of Female Sexuality," *International Journal of Psycho-Analysis*, 8 (1927): 459.
47. *Standard Ed.*, 21:243.
48. *Standard Ed.*, 21:229–230.
49. *Standard Ed.*, 21:230.
50. Jeanne Lampl de Groot, "The Evolution of the Oedipus Complex in Women," *International Journal of Psycho-Analysis*, 9 (1928): 332.
51. Karen Horney, "The Denial of the Vagina: A Contribution to the Problem of the Genital Anxieties Specific to Women," *FP*, 147–161 (*International Journal of Psycho-Analysis*, 14 [1933]: 57). German title: "Die Verleugnung der Vagina: Ein Beitrag zur Frage der spezifisch weiblichen Genitalangst."
52. Horney, "Book Reviews," *International Journal of Psycho-Analysis*, 7 (1926): 92–100.
53. Horney, "On the Genesis of the Castration Complex in Women," *International Journal of Psycho-Analysis*, 5, Pt. 1 (1922): 1–29.
54. Karen Horney, "Inhibited Femininity," *FP*, 71–83; originally pub. as "Gehemmte Weiblichkeit: Psychoanalytischer Beitrag zum Problem der Frigidität," *Zeitschrift für Sexualwissenschaft*, 13 (1926–27), 67–77.
55. *Ibid.*
56. Karen Horney, "The Distrust Between the Sexes," *FP*—read before the Berlin-Brandenburg branch of the German Women's Medical Association on Nov. 20, 1930, and subsequently published as "Das Misstrauen zwischen den Geschlechtern" in *Die Arztin.*
57. Unpub. letter to Groddeck, July 12, 1923.
58. Karen Horney, "The Dread of Women: Observations on a Specific Difference in the Dread Felt by Men and by Women Respectively for the Opposite Sex," *International Journal of Psycho-Analysis*, 13 (1932): 348–360. German title: "Die Angst vor der Frau: Über einen spezifischen Unterschied in der männlichen und weiblichen Angst vor dem anderen Geschlecht."
59. *Standard Ed.*, 18:274.
60. Horney, "The Dread of Women," pp. 348–360.
61. Horney, "The Denial of the Vagina," pp. 147–161.
62. *Standard Ed.*, 22:112–135.
63. *Standard Ed.*, 22:116.

64. Letter to Karl Müller-Braunschweig, July 21, 1935, pub. in *Psychiatry*, 34 (Aug. 1971).

65. Zenia Odes Fliegel, "Feminine Psychosexual Development in Freudian Theory," *Psychoanalytic Quarterly*, 12 (1973): 385–408.

66. Robert Coles, in Jean Strouse, ed., *Dialogues on Psychoanalytic Views of Feminity: Women and Analysis* (New York: Grossman, 1974), p. 191.

67. Unpub. letter written by Horney to Groddeck from Juist, on the North Sea, July 12, 1923.

68. As told by Alix Strachey to James Strachey in a letter, December 14, 1924, in *Bloomsbury/Freud: The Letters of James and Alix Strachey, 1924–1925*, eds. Perry Meisel and Walter Kendrick (New York: Basic Books, 1985), p. 146.

69. Horney, "The Dread of Women," p. 355.

70. Geoffrey Cocks, *Psychotherapy in the Third Reich: The Göring Institute* (New York: Oxford Univ. Press, 1985), p. 6.

71. From interviews conducted by Dr. Bluma Swerdloff, 1964–65, for the Oral History Research Office of Columbia University.

72. *Ibid*.

73. Karen Horney, XVIII, in "Discussion on Lay Analysis," *International Journal of Psycho-Analysis*, 8 (1927): 255–259.

74. Karen Horney, "Der Kampf in der Kultur: Einige Gedanken und Bedenken zu Freuds Todestreib und Destruktionstreib," in *Das Problem der Kultur und die ärtzliche Psychologie*, Vortrage Institut für Geschichte der Medizin (Leipzig: Thieme Verlag, 1931). Trans. in *American Journal of Psychoanalysis*, 20 (1960): 130–138.

75. *International Journal of Psycho-Analysis*, 13 (1932), p. 392.

76. Interview with Jack Rubins, Horney's previous biographer (*Karen Horney: Gentle Rebel of Psychoanalysis* [Dial Press, 1978]), May 25, 1973.

77. Smiley Blanton, *Diary of My Analysis with Sigmund Freud* (New York: Hawthorn Books, 1971), p. 65.

78. Gordon A. Craig, *Germany* (New York: Oxford Univ. Press, 1978), p. 543.

79. George Grosz, *An Autobiography*, trans. Nora Hodges (New York: Macmillan, 1983), p. 150.

80. In *Bilder aus der Grossen Stadt* (Berlin: Staatliche Museen Preussischer Kulturbesitz, 1977), No. 115.

81. As quoted by Henry Pachter in "On Being an Exile: An Old-Timer's Personal and Political Memoir," *Salmagundi*, No. 10–11 (Fall 1969–Winter 1970), p. 16.

82. There is no evidence in the minutes of the congress at Wiesbaden that Karen Horney attended. Renate, however, believes she attended a congress (although she places it in England), and Harold Kelman later reported that she attended the Wiesbaden congress. Also, the date of her arrival in the United States would suggest that she attended the congress.

83. From "Report of the Twelfth International Congress," *Bulletin of the International Psycho-Analytical Association*, 1932.

84. Christopher Isherwood, *Berlin Stories* (New York: New Directions, 1935), p. 203.

85. As quoted in Ernest Jones, *The Life and Work of Sigmund Freud*, 3 (New York: Basic Books, 1957): 298.

86. The statistics on the fate of German psychoanalysts are from *"Hier geht das Leben auf eine sehr merkwürdige Weise weiter..."*: *Zur Geschichte der Psychoanalyse in Deutschland,* ed. Karen Brecht, Volker Friedrich, Ludger M. Hermanns, Isidor J. Kaminer, and Dierk H. Juelich (Hamburg: Verlag Michael Kellner, 1985), a collection of documents presented in coordination with an exhibit at the Thirty-fourth Psychoanalytic Congress in Hamburg in 1985. The congress was the first to be held in Germany since the Nazi period.

87. See *"Hier geht das Leben"* (above), and, for a different view, Cocks, *Psychotherapy in the Third Reich.*

CHAPTER TWELVE *Psychoanalysis in the New World*

1. From Declaration of Intention to Immigrate, provided by the U.S. Immigration and Naturalization Service.

2. As quoted in *Keesing's Contemporary Archives,* weekly diary of important world events, 1 (Sept. 1932): 474.

3. Renate Horney Patterson's unpub. reminiscences.

4. *The Complete Essays of Mark Twain,* ed. Charles Neider (New York: Doubleday, 1963), p. 89.

5. *As Others See Chicago: Impressions of Visitors 1673–1933,* ed. Bessie Louise Pierce (Chicago: Univ. of Chicago Press, 1933), p. 508.

6. Henry Pachter, "On Being an Exile: An Old-Timer's Personal and Political Memoir," *Salmagundi,* No. 10–11 (Fall, 1969–Winter 1970), p. 30.

7. Harold M. Mayer and Richard C. Wade, *Chicago: Growth of a Metropolis* (Chicago: Univ. of Chicago Press, 1969), p. 360.

8. George Grosz, *An Autobiography,* trans. Nora Hodges (New York: Macmillan, 1983).

9. *As Others See Chicago,* ed. Pierce, p. 500.

10. Renate Horney Patterson's unpub. reminiscences.

11. Henry Pachter, "On Being an Exile," p. 31.

12. Nathan G. Hale, Jr., *Freud and the Americans: The Beginnings of Psychoanalysis in the United States* (New York: Oxford Univ. Press, 1971), p. 183.

13. *Standard Ed.,* 11:5.

14. Ernest Jones, *The Life and Work of Sigmund Freud,* 2 (New York: Basic Books, 1957): 57.

15. Hale, *Freud and the Americans,* p. 19.

16. Max Eitingon's characterization of Brill at the Wiesbaden congress in 1932, in "Report of the Twelfth International Congress," *Bulletin of the International Psycho-Analytical Association,* 1932.

17. Frederick J. Hoffman, *Freudianism and the Literary Mind* (Baton Rouge, LA: Louisiana State Univ. Press, 1945), p. 49.

18. *Ibid.,* p. 50.

19. *Ibid.,* p. 52.

20. *Ibid.* p. 56.

21. Laura Fermi, *Illustrious Immigrants* (Chicago: Univ. of Chicago Press, 1968), pp. 144–145.

22. From interviews conducted by Dr. Bluma Swerdloff, 1964–65, for the Oral

History Research Office of Columbia University.

23. Jones, *Life and Work of Freud*, 3:111.
24. Interview with Dorothy Blitsten by the author, March 14, 1983. Dorothy Blitsten was married to Lionel Blitzsten during this period. Since then she has simplified the spelling of her name.
25. Dorothy Blitsten, "Lionel Blitzsten and the Chicago Psychoanalytic Scene 1932–42" (unpub. memoir).
26. Franz Alexander, *The Western Mind in Transition* (New York: Random House, 1960), pp. 102–103.
27. Interview with Leon Saul by the author, April 3, 1982.
28. Paul Roazen, *Helene Deutsch: A Psychoanalyst's Life* (New York: Anchor Press/Doubleday, 1985), pp. 274–275.
29. Alexander, *The Western Mind in Transition,* p. 94.
30. From "A Statement of Purpose and Scope of the Institute" in a brochure issued in Oct. 1932.
31. *Ibid.*
32. *Ibid.*
33. Letter from Alfred K. Stern to Max Eitingon, Nov. 26, 1932.
34. Interview with Leon Saul, April 3, 1982.
35. Interview on videotape with Dr. Helen McLean by Dr. Lucia Tower, Fall 1974, from the Maxwell Gitelson Film Library of the Chicago Institute.
36. Interview with Leon Saul, April 3, 1982.
37. *Review for the Year, 1932–1933,* a brochure put out by the Institute for Psychoanalysis, Chicago.
38. Anthony Heilbut, *Exiled in Paradise* (New York: Viking Press, 1983), p. 57.
39. Karen Horney, "Psychogenic Factors in Functional Female Disorders," *American Journal of Obstetrics and Gynecology,* 25, No. 5 (May 1933): 694 ff.
40. Letter from Alfred K. Stern to Max Eitingon, Nov. 26, 1932.
41. Interview on videotape with Dr. Helen McLean by Dr. Lucia Tower, Fall 1974.
42. Interview with Leon Saul, April 3, 1982.
43. Interviews with Renate Horney Patterson by the author, Aug. 28 and 29, 1982.
44. Renate Horney Patterson's unpub. reminiscences.
45. Interviews with Renate Horney Patterson, Aug. 28 and 29, 1982.
46. Heilbut, *Exiled in Paradise,* p. 61.
47. Grosz, *An Autobiography,* p. 228.
48. Interviews with Brigitte Horney Swarzenski by the author, June 7 and 10, 1983, July 7, 1983, and April 4, 1984.
49. Interview with Dorothy Blitsten, March 14, 1983.
50. *Ibid.*
51. Letter from Alfred K. Stern to Max Eitingon, Nov. 26, 1932.
52. Interview with Heinz Kohut by the author, on March 29, 1980, for an article in the *New York Times Magazine.*
53. As quoted by Henry Pachter in "On Being an Exile," p. 51.
54. Heilbut, *Exiled in Paradise,* p. 69.
55. Interview with Henry and Yela Lowenfeld by the author, May 17, 1983.

56. *Diaries,* 226–227.
57. *Diaries,* 238.
58. *Diaries,* 116.
59. *Diaries,* 147.
60. This story was told in its fullest form by Roy Grinker in an interview with Horney's previous biographer, Jack Rubins, in 1976. Partial corroboration was provided to me by Lucia Tower's interview with Helen McLean (see n. 35, above) and by a subsequent telephone conversation with Dr. Tower, as well as by a letter from Dr. Karl Menninger in response to my inquiry, on Dec. 12, 1985. No one except Dr. Grinker, however, stated with certainty that a "seduction" of a sexual kind occurred. Dr. Grinker's response to me when I wrote him asking for an interview was that he "never knew her [Horney], even to say hello."
61. Interview with Leon Saul, April 3, 1982.
62. Karen Horney, "Maternal Conflicts," *American Journal of Orthopsychiatry,* 3, No. 4 (Oct. 1933): 455–461; rptd. in *FP,* 175–181.
63. Karen Horney, "The Overvaluation of Love: A Study of a Common Present-Day Feminine Type," *Psychoanalytic Quarterly,* 3 (1934): 605; rptd. in *FP,* 182–213.
64. Dorothy Thompson, "Room to Breathe In," *Saturday Evening Post,* June 24, 1933.
65. Renate Horney Patterson's unpub. reminiscences.
66. *Ibid.*
67. Interview with Dorothy Blitsten, March 14, 1983.
68. Horney, "The Overvaluation of Love" (see n. 64, above).
69. *Review for the Year, 1932–1933,* a brochure put out by the Institute for Psychoanalysis, Chicago.
70. Letter from Harold Lasswell to Horney's previous biographer, Jack Rubins, July 22, 1974.
71. Interview with Margaret Mead, by Jack Rubins, March 17, 1976.
72. Helene Deutsch, "Der feminine Masochismus und seine Beziehung zur Frigidität," *Internationale Zeitschrift für Psychoanalyse,* 2 (1930). In English: "The Significance of Masochism in the Mental Life of Women," *International Journal of Psycho-Analysis,* 11 (1930): 48–60.
73. Sandor Rado, "Fear of Castration in Women," *Psychoanalytic Quarterly,* 2 (1932): 425–475.
74. Karen Horney, "The Problem of Feminine Masochism," *Psychoanalytic Review,* 22, No. 3 (July 1935); rptd *FP,* pp. 214–233.
75. Letter from A. A. Brill to Ernest Jones, May 7, 1934, archives of the British Psycho-Analytical Society, London.
76. Letter from Ernest Jones to A. A. Brill, Nov. 21, 1934, archives of the British Psycho-Analytical Society, London.
77. Letter from Brill to Jones, Dec. 8, 1934, archives of the British Psycho-Analytical Society, London.
78. Letter written to Lionel Blitzsten in Feb. 1932, as quoted by Dorothy Blitsten in an unpub. history.
79. Alexander, *The Western Mind in Transition,* p. 109.
80. Interview with Leon Saul, April 3, 1982.

81. Interview on videotape with Dr. Helen McLean by Dr. Lucia Tower, Fall 1974.
82. Interview with Dorothy Blitsten, March 14, 1983.

CHAPTER THIRTEEN *New York Energy*

1. Brill.
2. Interview with Ernest Schachtel by Jack Rubins, 1973.
3. Erich Fromm's *Escape from Freedom* (New York: Farrar and Rinehart, 1941) refers repeatedly to Horney's work, and his idea of individual powerlessness in modern culture is closely related to Horney's idea that "basic anxiety" stems from a sense of powerlessness. Horney, however, stresses individual childhood experiences, while Fromm stresses historical and cultural determinants.
4. As quoted in Wolf von Eckardt and Sander L. Gilman, *Bertolt Brecht's Berlin* (New York: Anchor Press/Doubleday, 1975), p. xviii.
5. Interview with Hannah Tillich by the author, April 9 and 10, 1983.
6. Hannah Tillich, *From Time to Time* (New York: Stein and Day, 1973), p. 184.
7. Interview with Hannah Tillich, April 9 and 10, 1983.
8. The poem was entitled "Der Gläserne Traum" and had been written in Germany before the Tillichs came to New York.
9. Tillich, *From Time to Time,* p. 172.
10. *Ibid.*, p. 176.
11. Interview with Hannah Tillich, April 9 and 10, 1983.
12. Peter Rutkoff and William B. Scott, *New School: A History of the New School for Social Research* (New York: Free Press, 1986), p. 89.
13. Henry Pachter, "On Being an Exile: An Old-Timer's Personal and Political Memoir," *Salmagundi,* No. 10–11 (Fall 1969–Winter 1970), p. 34, n. 84.
14. Interview with Hans Speier by the author, April 13, 1983.
15. Marie Jahoda, "The Migration of Psychoanalysis: Its Impact on American Psychology," *The Intellectual Migration,* ed. Donald Fleming and Bernard Bailyn (Cambridge, MA: Harvard Univ. Press, 1969), pp. 432–433.
16. Alexander Reid Martin, in the oral history portrait of Karen Horney sponsored by the American Academy of Psychoanalysis, Dec. 5, 1975.
17. Interviews with Marianne Horney Eckardt, March 26, April 16, Dec. 18, 1982, and April 17, Oct. 16, 1983.
18. Alexander Reid Martin, in the oral history portrait of Karen Horney sponsored by the American Academy of Psychoanalysis, Dec. 5, 1975.
19. Karen Horney, *NP,* 252.
20. Jack Rubins, *Karen Horney: Gentle Rebel of Psychoanalysis* (New York: Dial Press, 1978), p. 3.
21. Interview with Katie Sugarman (formerly Kelman) by the author, Dec. 18, 1983.
22. Statistics provided by W. W. Norton and Company, Inc.
23. Nathan G. Hale, Jr., "From Berggasse XIX to Central Park West: The Americanization of Psychoanalysis, 1919–1940," *Journal of the History of the Behavioral Sciences,* 14 (1978): 305.
24. As quoted in Helen Swick Perry, *Psychiatrist of America: The Life of Harry*

Stack Sullivan (Cambridge, MA: Harvard Univ. Press, 1982), p. 205.

25. *Ibid.*, pp. 201–203. Thompson's account of that occasion is an example of the zany, provocative humor that made trouble for her in orthodox circles. "I was giving the first paper of my life," she remembers, "which was on 'Suicide and Psychotics,' and I had a temperature of 105 and had typhoid fever, but nobody knew it. Apparently I looked like hell, and I was scared to death in addition, and Sullivan saw me and he thought, 'My God, that woman is schizophrenic—I must know her!'... A few months later he got in touch with me and found out to his dismay I wasn't as schizophrenic as he thought. (I won't say I wasn't schizophrenic!)"

26. Clara Thompson seems to have given him a sort of secondhand Ferenczi treatment after her return from Hungary.

27. Douglas Noble, M.D., and Donald L. Burnham, M.D., "History of the Washington Psychoanalytic Society and the Washington Psychoanalytic Institute," 1969 (unpub.).

28. Interview with Esther Spitzer by Jack Rubins. It is unclear whether Sullivan was speaking literally or metaphorically, since there is some evidence that he did have a schizophrenic episode earlier in his life. See the discussion of this question in Perry, *Psychiatrist of America.*

29. Letter from A. A. Brill to Ernest Jones, Dec. 8, 1934, archives of the British Psycho-Analytical Society, London.

30. From interviews conducted by Dr. Bluma Swerdloff, 1964–65, for the Oral History Research Office of Columbia University.

31. Alix Stachey in *Bloomsbury/Freud: The Letters of James and Alix Strachey 1924–1925,* eds. Perry Meisel and Walter Kendrick (New York: Basic Books, 1985), p. 127.

32. Letter from Lawrence Kubie to David M. Levy, Nov. 17, 1939: Cornell.

33. Franz Alexander, Samuel Eisenstein, and Martin Grotjahn, eds., *Psychoanalytic Pioneers* (New York: Basic Books, 1966), p. 241.

34. Telephone interviews with Harmon (Saul) Ephron by the author, Oct., Nov. 1983.

35. Edward Glover, Theodor Reik, Ella Freeman Sharpe, and Wilhelm Reich.

36. Karen Horney, "Conceptions and Misconceptions of the Analytical Method," *Journal of Nervous and Mental Disease,* 81, No. 4 (April 1935): 399–410.

37. Karen Horney, "The Problem of the Negative Therapeutic Reaction," *Psychoanalytic Quarterly,* 5 (1936): 29–44.

38. Anna Freud, *The Ego and the Mechanisms of Defence* (New York: International Universities Press, 1936, 1946).

39. Merton Gill, ed., *The Collected Papers of David Rapaport* (New York: Basic Books, 1967), p. 206.

CHAPTER FOURTEEN The Neurotic Personality of Our Time

1. Letter from Karen Horney to Smith Ely Jeliffe, March 7, 1936: Brill.
2. Brochure of the Baltimore-Washington Psychoanalytic Society for 1935–36.
3. Letter from Karen Horney to Adolph Stern, March 4, 1937: Brill.
4. Letter from Karen Horney to Adolph Stern, April 7, 1937: Brill.
5. Letter from Adolph Stern to Karen Horney, June 14, 1937: Brill.

6. Letter from Lawrence Kubie to Jack Rubins, July 11, 1972.
7. Interview with Alexander Wolf, by Jack Rubins.
8. Letter to the author from Alexander Wolf, July 3, 1984.
9. Interview with Alexander Wolf, by Jack Rubins.
10. Letter to the author from Alexander Wolf, July 3, 1984.
11. Interview with Alexander Wolf, by Jack Rubins.
12. Interview with Judd Marmor, conducted by Jack Rubins, March 21, 1977.
13. Alexander Reid Martin, in the oral history portrait of Karen Horney sponsored by the American Academy of Psychoanalysis, Dec. 5, 1975. In 1951 Horney gave a series of seven lectures on psychoanalytic technique, five of which have been preserved on tape. The lectures, which were the last she gave before her death, are scheduled for publication by W. W. Norton.
14. As quoted in the Tacoma, Washington, *Ledger,* July 18, 1935.
15. Interview with Ruth Moulton, by Jack Rubins.
16. From an evaluation of her work by a supervisor, Bernard Robbins, Association for the Advancement of Psychoanalysis (AAP) file.
17. Interviews with Brigitte Horney Swarzenski by the author, June 7 and 10, 1983, July 7, 1983, and April 4, 1984.
18. *Ibid.*
19. *New York Times,* June 25, 1938.
20. *Ibid.*, Oct. 1, 1938.
21. *Ibid.*, May 6, 1939.
22. *Ibid.*, May 27, 1939.
23. *Ibid.*, Jan. 22, 1938.
24. *Ibid.*, May 6, 1939.
25. Walter Laqueur, *Weimar: A Cultural History* (New York: Putnam, 1974), p. 231.
26. *New York Times,* Sept. 1, 1939.
27. *Ibid.*, May 6, 1939.
28. Interviews with Brigitte Horney Swarzenski, June 7 and 10, 1983, July 7, 1983, and April 4, 1984.
29. Unpub. reminiscences of Renate Horney Patterson.
30. Interview with Margaret Mead, by Jack Rubins, March 17, 1976.
31. Written from Tanco, Mexico, on Aug. 19, 1936: Rare Book and Manuscript Library, Columbia University.
32. *NP,* 36.
33. *NP,* 286.
34. *NP,* 223.
35. *NP,* 225.
36. *Psychoanalytic Quarterly,* 6, No. 4 (1937): 536–540.
37. *Psychoanalytic Review,* 25 (1938): 279–284.
38. As quoted in Jane Howard, *Margaret Mead: A Life* (New York: Simon and Schuster, 1984), p. 199.
39. *NP,* 19.
40. *NP,* 14–15.
41. Ernest R. Groves, *Social Forces,* 16 (Oct. 1937): 138–140.
42. Kimball Young, *American Journal of Sociology,* 43 (Jan. 1938): 654.
43. *NP,* 161.

44. *NP,* 80.
45. Ernest Jones, *International Journal of Psychoanalysis,* 19, 1938.
46. Robert Knight, *Survey,* 13 (Aug. 1937): 269.
47. J. F. Brown, *Nation,* July 3, 1937, p. 21.
48. Clara Thompson, "The History of the William Alanson White Institute," a speech delivered on March 15, 1955, in the collection of the William Alanson White Institute Library.
49. Letter to the author, Dec. 12, 1985.

CHAPTER FIFTEEN *New Ways In Psychoanalysis*

1. Telephone interviews with Harmon (Saul) Ephron by the author, Nov. 1983.
2. Telephone interview with Judd Marmor by the author, Jan. 21, 1986.
3. *NW,* 18.
4. *Ibid.*
5. *NW,* 21.
6. *NW,* 23–24.
7. *NW,* 33.
8. *NW,* 37.
9. *NW,* 38.
10. *NW,* 41.
11. *NW,* 42.
12. *NW,* 62.
13. *NW,* 61–62.
14. *NW,* 71.
15. *NW,* 70–71.
16. *NW,* 85.
17. *NW,* 86.
18. *NW,* 131.
19. Letter to Miss Lincoln, W. W. Norton's assistant, Dec. 18, 1938: Rare Book and Manuscript Library, Columbia University.
20. *NW,* 187.
21. *NW,* 190.
22. *NW,* 188–189.
23. Letter to W. W. Norton, March 29, 1938: Rare Book and Manuscript Library, Columbia Unviersity.
24. *NW,* 11.
25. *NW,* 46.
26. *NW,* 68.
27. *NW,* 185.
28. Merton Gill, ed., *The Collected Papers of David Rapaport* (New York: Basic Books, 1967), p. 617.
29. *Ibid.,* p. 359.
30. Letter to W. W. Norton, Jan. 12, 1938: Rare Book and Manuscript Library, Columbia University.
31. *NW,* 65–66.
32. Arnold Cooper, "Narcissism," *American Handbook of Psychiatry,* 7, "Advances

and New Directions," ed. Silvano Arieti, H. Brodie, and H. Keith, pp. 297–316.

33. *NW*, 215–217.
34. Others were Alfred Adler and Harry Stack Sullivan. See Cooper, "Narcissism," and Gill, ed., *The Collected Papers of David Rapaport.*
35. *American Sociological Review*, 4 (Dec. 1939): 876.
36. *American Journal of Sociology*, 44 (May 1939): 997.
37. *New York Times*, May 7, 1939.
38. *Psychoanalytic Quarterly*, 9 (1940): 114–121.
39. *New Republic*, Jan. 8, 1940, p. 57.
40. *Psychoanalytic Quarterly*, 9 (1940): 114–121.
41. Gill, ed., *The Collected Papers of David Rapaport*, p. 750.
42. *NW*, 299.
43. *NW*, 286.
44. *Nation*, Sept. 23, 1939, p. 328.
45. *NW*, 118.
46. Letter to Katherine Barnard at Norton, March 4, 1939: Rare Book and Manuscript Library, Columbia University.
47. "On the Americanization of Martin Grotjahn," *The Home of the Learned Men;* a symposium on the immigrant scholar in America, ed. John Kosa, New Haven College and University Press, 1968, p. 55.
48. Interview with Antonia Wenkart by the author, May 18, 1983.
49. Interview with Edith Jacobson by Dr. David Milrod, April 27, 1971: Brill.
50. Interview with Rose Tannenbaum, MSW, by Jack Rubins.
51. Interview with Rita Honroth Welte by the author, Oct. 8, 1984.
52. Geoffrey Cocks, *Psychotherapy in the Third Reich: The Göring Institute* (New York: Oxford Univ. Press, 1985), p. 90.
53. Letter from Karen Horney to Miss Lincoln at Norton, June 15, 1937.
54. *Journal of Adult Education*, 9, No. 2 (1939): 129–132.

CHAPTER SIXTEEN *The Split*

1. *Psychoanalytic Quarterly*, 6, No. 3 (1937): 274.
2. *Ibid.*, 7, No. 1 (1938): 166.
3. Cornell.
4. Cornell.
5. Letter from Sandor Rado to Franz Alexander, May 27, 1938: Cornell.
6. *Psychoanalytic Quarterly*, 8 (1939): 406–407.
7. Letter from Lawrence Kubie to David Levy, Nov. 11, 1939: Cornell.
8. Letters from Lawrence Kubie to Jack Rubins, July 11, 1972, and Aug. 9, 1972.
9. Sam Atkin, "The New York Psychoanalytic Society and Institute: Its Founding and Development," a paper presented on the sixty-fifth anniversary of the New York Psychoanalytic Society, 1976.
10. Telephone interviews with Harmon (Saul) Ephron by the author, Oct., Nov. 1983.
11. Telephone interview with Judd Marmor by the author, Jan. 21, 1986.

12. All of the foregoing details regarding the student committee and the larger society are from the archives of the A. A. Brill Library.
13. Letter from David M. Levy to Bertram D. Lewin, Sept. 18. 1939: Cornell.
14. Letter from Karen Horney to David Levy, Dec. 1. 1932: Cornell.
15. Letter from Karen Horney to David Levy, Dec. 18, 1934: Cornell.
16. Interview with Harmon Ephron by Jack Rubins, 1972.
17. David Goldfarb, M.D., Ph.D., "In Memoriam," *American Journal of Psychiatry,* 134 (Aug. 1977): 8.
18. Alvin Johnson, *Pioneer's Progress* (New York: Viking Press, 1952).
19. Letter from David Levy to Bertram Lewin, Sept. 20, 1939: Cornell.
20. Letter from educational committee to Karen Horney, Sept. 1939: Brill.
21. Letter from Karen Horney to educational committee, Sept. 15, 1939: Brill.
22. Letter from educational secretary to committee, Sept. 19, 1939: Brill.
23. Dr. Leon Blumgart, minutes of meeting, Oct. 17, 1939: Brill.
24. Interview with Sam Atkin by author, May 16, 1983.
25. Letter from Abram Kardiner to Lawrence Kubie, Oct. 24, 1939: Brill.
26. Letter from Lawrence Kubie to David Levy, Nov. 11, 1939: Cornell.
27. *Ibid.*
28. Letter from Levy to Kubie, Nov. 14, 1939: Cornell.
29. Letter from Kubie to Levy, Nov. 17, 1939: Cornell.
30. Minutes of "special subcommittee" meeting, Jan. 16, 1940: Brill.
31. *Standard Ed.* 19:286–287.
32. Fritz Wittels, *The Jeweller of Bagdad* (New York: George H. Doran, 1927).
33. Letter from Fritz Wittels to the president of the New York Psychoanalytic Society, March 13, 1940; copies sent to all members of the society: Brill.
34. Letter from Lawrence Kubie to Fritz Wittels, March 20, 1940: Brill.
35. Minutes of interval meeting, March 26, 1940: Brill.
36. Minutes of educational committee, April 4, 1940: Brill.
37. Minutes of Student Organization, Oct. 22, 1940: Brill.
38. Letter from Lawrence Kubie to Sandor Rado, June 28, 1940: Cornell.
39. Letter from Lawrence Kubie to Sam Atkin, Dec. 11, 1940: Cornell.
40. "Appendix *re* Educational Director," attached to Kubie's letter to Atkin, Dec. 11, 1940: Cornell.
41. Letter from the Student Organization of the Psychoanalytic Institute to Gregory Zilboorg, Jan. 9, 1941: Cornell.
42. From an interview with Harold Kelman by David Levy, Feb. 8, 1941: Cornell.
43. Minutes of interval meeting, fall 1934: Brill.
44. This account of Zilboorg's behavior is based on material in the archives of the Brill Library. Much of it is taken from the testimony of the patient himself. At least one analyst on the investigating committee claimed that the patient was "not a reliable witness," but both Franz Alexander and David Levy believed his story.
45. Letter from Gregory Zilboorg to Karen Horney, Jan. 14, 1941.
46. Minutes of a special meeting of the society, Feb. 11, 1942.
47. Minutes of a meeting of the society, Feb. 25, 1941.
48. Letter to Drs. Kelman and Wiggins, officers of the Student Organization of

the New York Psychoanalytic Institute, from Gregory Zilboorg, chairman of the educational committee, March 11, 1941: Cornell.

49. *Ibid.*

50. *Resolutions* submitted to the New York Psychoanalytic Society, March 25, 1941: Cornell.

51. Report by Zilboorg to the Society, minutes of meeting, March 25, 1941: Brill.

52. Minutes of the meeting of the Society, March 25, 1941: Brill.

53. Interview with Dr. Ruth Moulton by the author, May 18, 1983.

54. Interview with Abram Kardiner by Dr. Bluma Swerdloff for the Columbia Oral History project, 1963. According to him: "Horney put herself through a degrading experience in order to get Rado to consent to join her in the formation of the new group. He sat listening to her like a Buddha, didn't open his mouth, and at the end of a two-hour harangue by her, he simply said, 'I will think it over and let you know,' and the answer was no."

55. Questionnaire written by David M. Levy, dated Feb. 14, 1941. All the subsequent quotes are taken from the questionnaire responses unless cited otherwise: Cornell.

56. Letter from Janet Rioch to David Levy, Feb. 19, 1941: Cornell.

57. Based on copies of Gregory Zilboorg's two letters to Herman Selinsky on March 20 and March 26, 1941, which were sent by Selinsky to David Levy.

58. Letter from David Levy to members of the New York Psychoanalytic Society, April 14, 1941: Cornell.

59. Letter from Lawrence Kubie to David Levy, March 28, 1941: Cornell.

60. Letter from David Levy to Lawrence Kubie, March 31, 1941: Cornell.

61. Meeting of the education committee, April 7, 1941: Brill.

62. Minutes of the meeting of the Society, April 29, 1941: Brill.

63. Ibid.

64. Letter dated May 1, 1941: Brill.

65. Telephone interview with Judd Marmor by the author, Jan. 21. 1986.

66. Letter dated June 14, 1941: Cornell.

67. See n. 45, above.

68. Letter of resignation, March 20, 1941.

69. From an earlier draft of the letter of resignation, dated March 16, 1941, but never sent: Cornell.

CHAPTER SEVENTEEN *A New Institute*

1. Interview with Henry and Yela Lowenfeld by the author, May 17, 1983.

2. M. R. Green, *Interpersonal Psychoanalysis: The Selected Papers of Clara M. Thompson* (New York: Basic Books, 1964), p. 362.

3. Jan. 8, 1942: from the archives of the Vernon B. Alden Library at Ohio University, Athens.

4. As quoted in Ralph Crowley and Maurice Green, "Revolution Within Psychoanalysis: A History of the William Alanson White Institute" (unpub.).

5. *American Journal of Psychoanalysis,* 1, No. 1 (1941).

6. *Ibid.*, 2, No. 1 (1942).

7. As quoted in Crowley and Green, "Revolution Within Psychoanalysis."

8. Telephone interviews with Harmon (Saul) Ephron by the author, Oct., Nov. 1983.

9. Interview with Edwin Kasin, M.D., by Jack Rubins.

10. Interview with Walter Bonime by the author, May 18, 1983.

11. Interview with Ruth Moulton by the author, May 18, 1983.

12. Ruth Moulton, "History of the William Alanson White Institute: Notes on the Origin of the Institute and Its Founders," prepared for the fortieth-anniversary celebration in 1983.

13. Karen Horney, "Understanding of Individual Panic," *American Journal of Psychoanalysis*, 2, No. 1 (1942): 40–41.

14. Letter from Lawrence Kubie to Adolph Stern, early 1942: Brill.

15. Lionel Trilling, "The Progressive Psyche," *Nation*, Sept. 12, 1942, pp. 215–217.

16. *SA*, 27.

17. Telephone interviews with Harmon (Saul) Ephron by the author, Oct., Nov. 1983.

18. Trilling, "The Progressive Psyche," 215–217.

19. Edward E. Harkavy, review of *Self-Analysis* in *Psychoanalytic Quarterly*, 11, No. 4 (1942): 580.

20. Bertram D. Lewin, "Forces in Neurosis," *Saturday Review of Literature*, June 13, 1942, p. 19.

21. J. F. Brown, "The Inward View," *New Republic*, July 27, 1942, p. 125.

22. Brill.

23. Statement dated Nov. 25, 1941, *Psychoanalytic Review*, 29 (1942): 222–226.

24. Letter from LeRoy M. A. Maeder to Lawrence Kubie, Feb. 5, 1942: Brill.

25. Letter from O. Spurgeon English to Kubie, Feb. 6, 1942: Brill.

26. Letter from Ralph Crowley to Kubie, Feb. 19, 1942: Brill.

27. Letter from Crowley to Kubie, March 1942: Brill.

28. Letter from Kubie to Crowley, March 18, 1942: Brill.

29. Letter from the senior attorney, New York State Department of Education, to Kubie, Feb. 14, 1942: Brill.

30. "Statement of Correction by the New York Psychoanalytic Society and Institute" (typed communication): Cornell.

31. Telephone interviews with Harmon Ephron by the author, Oct., Nov., 1983.

32. "Presidential Address" to the American Psychoanalytic Association, delivered May 18, 1942, in Boston, *Psychoanalytic Quarterly*, 11, No. 3 (1942): 287–300.

33. Clara Thompson, "The History of the William Alanson White Institute," a speech delivered on March 15, 1955, in the collection of the William Alanson White Institute Library.

34. Telephone interview with Judd Marmor by the author, Jan. 21, 1986.

35. Marianne Horney Eckardt, in a chapter entitled "Organizational Schisms in American Psychoanalysis," in *American Psychoanalysis: Origins and Development*, ed. Eric T. Carlson, M.D., and Jacques M. Quen, M.D. (New York: Brunner/Mazel, 1978), writes that a second split with the New York Psychoanalytic a year later had a happier ending. In June of 1942 Sandor Rado and ten others wrote a letter complaining of "an atmosphere of bickering, slander, and gossip [in the society]" and declared their intention of withdrawing.

Partly because of the group's careful diplomacy, the American Psychoanalytic Association ultimately changed the rules and accepted the Rado group (based at Columbia and called the Association for Psychoanalytic Medicine) into the American in 1946. Among those who worked toward inclusion of the Rado group were Karl Menninger, Franz Alexander, and Bertram Lewin. David Levy, who had resigned earlier in protest over the Zilboorg and Horney affairs, joined the Rado group at Columbia.

36. Interview with Irving Bieber by Jack Rubins.

CHAPTER EIGHTEEN *Dissension Within*

1. This account is derived from many sources. See Chap. 14, n. 48, Chap. 17, n. 12 and 35, as well as the William Alanson White Newsletter (Fall 1972), and "Scientific Proceedings of the First Interinstitute Candidate Forum," June 15, 1971.
2. Ruth Moulton, "Memories of My Analytic Training" (unpub.).
3. Letter from Ralph Rosenberg to Ruth Moulton, April 1943.
4. Marianne Horney Eckardt, in a chapter entitled "Organizational Schisms in American Psychoanalysis," in *American Psychoanalysis: Origins and Development,* ed. Eric T. Carlson, M.D., and Jacques M. Quen, M.D. (New York: Brunner/Mazel, 1978).
5. Five-page typewritten statement on the split written by Clara Thompson, April 1943; courtesy of Jack Rubins.
6. Ruth Moulton in a talk at "Scientific Proceedings of the First Interinstitute Candidate Forum," June 15, 1971.
7. As quoted by Marianne Horney Eckardt in "Organizational Schisms," *American Psychoanalysis.*
8. Five-page typewritten statement on the split, written by Clara Thompson, April 1943.
9. Interview with Marie Levy by Jack Rubins, Oct. 3, 1972.
10. *OIC,* 81, 85–86.
11. Interview with Ernest Schachtel by Jack Rubins, 1973.
12. Interview with Lawrence Kubie by Jack Rubins.
13. "Reflections on What Helps a Patient," a talk by Marianne Horney Eckardt, unpub.
14. Interview with Marianne Horney Eckardt by Jack Rubins, Feb. 12, 1973.
15. *Ibid.*
16. Letter from Ruth Moulton to Karen Horney, May 2, 1943.
17. Letter from Ralph M. Crowley to Frances Arkin, secretary of the AAP, April 25, 1943.
18. Judd Marmor in the WAW Newsletter (Fall 1968).
19. Minutes of a meeting of faculty members of the AAP at the apartment of Karen Horney, Dec. 1, 1943.
20. *American Journal of Psychoanalysis,* 4 (1944): 1.
21. Letter from Stephen P. Jewett to Elizabeth Kilpatrick, secretary of the AAP, Feb. 18, 1944.
22. Judd Marmor, "The Pre-History and the Founding of the Comprehensive

Course in Psychoanalysis," Newsletter, Society of Medical Psychoanalysts, 5 (1964): 1–3.
23. Harold Kelman, at American Academy Oral History Colloquium, Dec. 5, 1975.
24. Harold Kelman, *Helping People: Karen Horney's Psychoanalytic Approach* (New York: Science House, 1971), p. 21.
25. Interview with Henry Holt by the author, May 15, 1983.
26. Interview with Esther Spitzer by Jack Rubins.
27. Telephone interviews with Harmon Ephron by the author, Oct., Nov. 1983.
28. Interview with Janet Frey by Jack Rubins.
29. Telephone interview with Judd Marmor by the author, Jan. 21, 1986.
30. Interview by Jack Rubins with Marianne Horney Eckardt, Feb. 12, 1973.
31. Harold Kelman, in the oral history portrait of Karen Horney sponsored by the American Academy of Psychoanalysis, Dec. 5, 1975.
32. Interview with Morris Isenberg by Jack Rubins.
33. In addition to his own book *Helping People,* Kelman edited *Feminine Psychology.*
34. Interviews with Marianne Horney Eckardt by the author, March 26, April 16, Dec. 18, 1982, and April 17, Oct. 16, 1983.

CHAPTER NINETEEN *Solo Flight*

1. Harry Gershman, in the oral history portrait of Karen Horney sponsored by the American Academy of Psychoanalysis, Dec. 5, 1975.
2. Interview with Norman Kelman by Leo Berman, American Academy oral history interviews.
3. Ibid.
4. Interview with Norman Kelman by the author, Dec. 15, 1982.
5. Interview with Norman Kelman by Leo Berman, American Academy oral history interviews.
6. Interview with Louis DeRosis by Jack Rubins.
7. Interviews with Gertrude Weiss by the author, Nov. 2 and 9, 1982.
8. Interview with Marie Levy by the author, Nov. 1985.
9. *Contemporary Psychotherapists Examine Themselves,* ed. Werner Wolff (Springfield, IL: Charles C. Thomas, 1956), p. 87.
10. The source of this information and the name of the young lover must remain confidential. The fact of the affair, however, has been confirmed by two people who were very close to Karen Horney at the end of her life.
11. All of the foregoing is based on Gertrude Lederer-Eckardt's unpub. reminiscences, written in 1958.
12. Interview with Morris Isenberg by Jack Rubins.
13. *American Journal of Psychoanalysis,* 9, No. 1 (1949): 3.
14. Personal communication from Westcott's husband to the author.
15. Interview with Norman Kelman by the author, Dec. 15, 1982.
16. Gertrude Lederer-Eckardt's unpub. reminiscences.
17. Harold Kelman, *Helping People: Karen Horney's Psychoanalytic Approach* (New York: Science House, 1971), p. 25.
18. Renate Horney Patterson's unpub. reminiscences.

19. Gertrude Lederer-Eckardt's unpub. reminiscences.
20. *OIC*, 15.
21. *OIC*, 16.
22. *OIC*, 16.
23. *OIC*, 98.
24. This phrase actually appears for the first time in the book Horney would write next, *Neurosis and Human Growth*.
25. *OIC*, 98.
26. *OIC*, 115.
27. *OIC*, 116.
28. *OIC*, 241.
29. Letter from Storer B. Lunt to Karen Horney, Oct. 9, 1946: Rare Book and Manuscript Library, Columbia University.
30. Letter from Karen Horney to Storer B. Lunt, Oct. 14, 1946: Rare Book and Manuscript Library, Columbia University.
31. Postcard from Karen Horney to Storer B. Lunt, Aug. 17, 1949: Rare Book and Manuscript Library, Columbia University.
32. Ashley Montagu, in *New York Herald Tribune,* Nov. 5, 1950, p. 20.
33. Letter from Storer B. Lunt to Karen Horney, June 13, 1947: Rare Book and Manuscript Library, Columbia University.
34. Karen Horney, *Neurosis and Human Growth* (New York: Norton, 1950), p. 15—hereafter cited as *NHG* with page numbers.
35. Karen Horney, "Der Kampf in der Kultur: Einige Gedanken und Bedenken zu Freuds Todestreib und Destruktionstreib," in *Das Problem der Kultur und die ärtzliche Psychologie,* Vortrage Institut für Geschichte der Medizin (Leipzig: Thieme Verlag, 1931). Trans. in *American Journal of Psychoanalysis,* 20 (1960): 130–138.
36. *OIC*, 187.
37. Lionel Trilling, "The Progressive Psyche," *Nation,* Sept. 12, 1942, pp. 215–217.
38. Paul L. Wachtel, *New Republic,* Jan. 6, 1979. See also Herbert Marcuse, *Eros and Civilization: A Philosophical Inquiry into Freud* (Boston: Beacon Press, 1955).
39. *NHG*, 190.
40. *NHG*, 187.
41. *NHG*, 38.
42. *OIC*, 162–163.
43. Interviews with Brigitte Horney Swarzenski by the author, June 7 and 10, 1983, July 7, 1983, and April 4, 1984.
44. Unpub. reminiscence of Rita Honroth Welte.
45. *NHG*, 37.
46. Internal security report, FBI, made in October, 1941. The name of the reporter has been blacked out.
47. Report filed March 27, 1941. The name of the reporter has been blacked out.
48. Letter from J. Edgar Hoover to E. J. Connelly, assistant director, April 19, 1941.
49. Letter from the postmistress of Monhegan Island to J. Edgar Hoover, July 17, 1942.

50. Letter from the postmistress to J. Edgar Hoover, Aug. 6, 1942.
51. Letter from the postmistress to J. Edgar Hoover, Aug. 13, 1942.
52. Letter from J. Edgar Hoover to the postmistress, Aug. 27, 1942.
53. Report filed by assistant chief of staff, Intelligence, Military District of Washington, Aug. 6, 1951.
54. Memo from a Mr. Lory to a Mr. Warner, June 19, 1952.
55. Memo from a Mr. Young to Ruth Shipley, June 25, 1952.

CHAPTER TWENTY *Japan*

1. Interview with Richard DeMartino by the author, Nov. 11, 1983.
2. "Recollections of Dr. Horney," by Akihisa Kondo (unpub.).
3. Winthrop Sargeant, "Great Simplicity," *New Yorker,* Aug. 31. 1957.
4. *Ibid.*
5. *Essays in Zen Buddhism* (New York: Harper, 1949).
6. Interview with Norman Kelman by the author, Dec. 15, 1982.
7. Peter Matthiessen, *Nine-Headed Dragon River: Zen Journals 1969–1982* (Boston: Shambhala Publications, 1985), p. 11.
8. Sargeant, "Great Simplicity."
9. Aldous Huxley, comp., *The Perennial Philosophy* (New York: Harper, 1945) p. 263.
10. William James, *The Varieties of Religious Experience* (New York: Modern Library, 1936), p. 505.
11. Søren Kierkegaard, *The Sickness Unto Death* (Princeton: Princeton Univ. Press, 1941).
12. Paul Tillich, *The Courage to Be* (New Haven: Yale Univ. Press, 1952).
13. Huxley, comp., *The Perennial Philosophy,* p. vii.
14. *OIC,* 158.
15. William James, *Memories and Studies* (New York: Longmans, Green, 1911).
16. *Ibid.*, p. 252.
17. *Ibid.*, p. 260.
18. Nancy Wilson Ross, *Buddhism: A Way of Life and Thought* (New York: Knopf, 1980), p. 159.
19. Karen Horney, "The Paucity of Inner Experiences," *American Journal of Psychoanalysis,* 21, No. 1 (1952): 3.
20. 1986 Program, Castle Hill.
21. Obituary, *New York Times,* July 10, 1962, p. 33.
22. Interview with Sawahara Crane by Jack Rubins.
23. Letter from W. W. Norton to Karen Horney, July 3, 1945. Norton wrote: "I have a feeling that if it ever got out that Mr. Crane had contributed to actual advertising, it would not be good for you or for us."
24. Interview with Akihisa Kondo by the author, June 19, 1986.
25. "Recollections of Dr. Horney," by Akihisa Kondo (unpub.).
26. Interviews with Brigitte Horney Swarzenski by the author, June 7 and 10, 1983, July 7, 1983, and April 4, 1984.
27. In *Japan Medical Journal,* as translated by Kondo in "Recollections of Dr. Horney."
28. This explanation of Morita therapy is drawn from Akihisa Kondo, "Morita

Therapy: A Japanese Therapy for Neurosis," *American Journal of Psychoanalysis,* 13, No. 1 (1953): 31–37; Momoshige Miura and Shin-ichi Usa, "A Psychotherapy of Neurosis: Morita Therapy," *Yonago Acta medica,* 14, No. 1, Feb. 17, 1970: 1–17; and Daniel Goleman, "In Japan Gratitude to Others Is Stressed in Psychotherapy," *New York Times,* June 3, 1986.

29. Miura and Usa, "A Psychotherapy of Neurosis: Morita Therapy."

30. *Ibid.*

31. *Contemporary Psychotherapists Examine Themselves,* ed. Werner Wolff (Springfield, IL: Charles L. Thomas, 1956) p. 90.

32. Miura and Usa, "A Psychotherapy of Neurosis: Morita Therapy," p. 9.

33. These observations are based on the author's visit to Tofukuji, in Kyoto, for the recitation of morning prayers, June 28, 1986.

34. Interviews with Brigitte Horney Swarzenski by the author, June 7 and 10, 1983, July 7, 1983, and April 4, 1984.

35. Recollections of Dr. Horney by Akihisa Kondo (unpub.).

36. Interview with Richard DeMartino by the author, Nov. 11, 1983.

37. *Ibid.*

38. Postcard in the possession of Renate Horney Patterson.

39. Interview with Richard DeMartino by the author, Nov. 11, 1983.

40. Interviews with Brigitte Horney Swarzenski.

41. Interview with Richard DeMartino.

42. *American Journal of Psychoanalysis,* 9 (1949): 3–7.

43. Interview with Richard DeMartino.

44. "Recollections of Dr. Horney," by Akihisa Kondo (unpub.).

45. Ross, *Buddhism.*

46. Winthrop Sargeant, "Great Simplicity."

47. Ruth Benedict, *The Chrysanthemum and the Sword* (New York: New American Library, 1946), p. 14.

48. Interview with Norman Kelman by Leo Berman, American Academy oral history interviews.

49. Interview with Marianne Horney Eckardt by Jack Rubins, Feb. 12, 1973.

50. Interview with Norman Kelman by Leo Berman, American Academy oral history interviews.

51. *Ibid.*

52. Gertrude Eckardt Lederer's unpub. reminiscences.

53. Robert Coles, in Jean Strouse, ed., *Dialogues on Psychoanalytic Views of Femininity: Women and Analysis* (New York: Grossman, 1974), p. 188–189.

54. Renate Horney Patterson's unpub. reminiscences.

55. Jack Rubins, *Karen Horney: Gentle Rebel of Psychoanalysis* (New York: Dial Press, 1978), p. 329.

56. Interview with Katie Sugarman (formerly Kelman), Dec. 8, 1983.

57. Paul Tillich, funeral oration, Dec. 6, 1952.

58. Letter of tribute, courtesy of Jack Rubins.

59. Paul Tillich, funeral oration, Dec. 6, 1952.

60. *SA,* 276.

Bibliographical Essay

PART I: *Girlhood*

Hamburg
1885–1906

The most important source for these chapters was *The Adolescent Diaries of Karen Horney.* All three of Karen Horney's daughters played important roles in the translation and publication of the diaries. Renate Horney Patterson was the first to reread them in the early 1970s and realize their wonderful immediacy and value. Renate, who was living in Mexico at the time, began the work of translation, with the help of Mrs. Crena de Iongh. Brigitte Horney, then living in Germany, made important suggestions for revision and contributed the letters to Oskar Horney that inform Part II of this biography. Finally, Marianne Eckardt, by then living in New York, worked with Jane Isay, an editor at Basic Books, on the excellent final translation and wrote brief introductory notes to each diary. I have also had access during this project to the original diaries, handwritten in German; they have consistently demonstrated to me the great care and accuracy of the translation in all but a few small instances (see notes).

For a visual picture of Hamburg and Eilbek at the turn of the century I have relied on period postcards and collections of photographs, particularly Fritz Lachmund, *Alt Hamburg durch die Camera,* Fritz Lachmund and

Rolf Müller, *Hamburg: Seinerzeit zur Kaiserzeit,* and Hermann Hinrichsen, *Vergangenes aus Eilbek und Hohenfelde.* In addition, I have referred to a book edited by Jörgen Bracker and Carsten Prange, *Alster, Elbe und die See,* which brings together paintings, drawings, and watercolors of Hamburg's port from the Museum of Hamburg History.

Two residents of Hamburg provided important additional information. Pastor Günther Severin, the current minister at the Friedenskirche in Eilbek, where Karen Danielsen was baptized and confirmed, showed me the evidence of those events in the church records and in addition provided excerpts from his history of the church which gave a vivid picture of Pastor von Ruckteschell. Pastor Severin also produced an old photograph of the apartment house at 64 Papenstrasse (where Karen lived with her family). I also talked with Ellen Möller, the daughter of a sea captain, who, by happy chance, had as a girl actually lived at 64 Papenstrasse. I am also grateful to the Hamburg Staatsarchiv, which provided period newspaper material, address books, and information about the Hamburg Gymnasium for girls and about Captain Danielsen's voyages to South America. A recently reissued account of a voyage around the tip of South America in 1876, Lady Brassey's *A Voyage in the "Sunbeam,"* provided South American color for Chapter 2.

I found *Die Frauenfrage in Deutschland 1865–1915,* a collection of primary texts put together by Elke Frederiksen, to be a useful source of feminist opinion of the time. But by far the most important source, for the discussion of women's rights and education and for information about the Hamburg controversy regarding prostitution, and about the Mutterschutz movement, was Richard J. Evans' excellent history, *The Feminist Movement in Germany 1894–1933.* For general history and background throughout the book I relied on Gordon A. Craig, *Germany 1866–1945.*

PART II: *University Life*

Freiburg and Göttingen
1906–9

Once again, the most important single source was *The Adolescent Diaries of Karen Horney,* particularly the letters of Karen Danielsen to Oskar Horney. In addition, these chapters draw for the first time on unpublished letters and notebooks. The "Ego" notebook, begun on Christmas Eve of 1906 and continued into the Berlin years, provides valuable evidence of Karen's wide-ranging reading and energetic note-taking, which fills ninety-seven pages. Unlike the "Ego" notebook, which I worked with in its original form, the letters exchanged between Berndt and Sonni were available only in a typed transcription in German. Both were provided by members of the family.

The Freiburg University Archives provided important proofs of Karen Horney's enrollment and course of study, as well as photographs and historical background on the medical school in that period. A second important source of information about German medical education was the American Abraham Flexner's 1912 report to the Carnegie Foundation, *Medical Education in Europe.* In addition, I found valuable facts and supporting documents regarding women at the university in *Das Frauenstudium an der Universität Freiburg im Breisgau,* by E. Th. Nauck. Arthur Kirchhoff's *Die akademische Frau* provided vivid opinions of the male medical establishment in regard to women interlopers. Peter Gay's *The Education of the Senses,* particularly the chapter entitled "Offensive Women and Defensive Men," provided both details and insights.

PART III

Berlin
1909–32

For background on Wilhelmine Berlin (Chapters 8 and 9) before World War I, I relied primarily on two texts: Gerhard Masur's *Imperial Berlin* and Anne Marie Lange's *Das Wilhelminische Berlin: Zwischen Jahrhundertwende und Novemberrevolution.* In addition, the English journalist Edward Edgeworth's *The Human German* provided a witty outsider's view of imperial Berlin. *The Proud Tower,* by Barbara Tuchman, provided historical anecdotes. Finally, the fiction of Theodor Fontane gave insight into the social fabric of the times. For a visual sense of the period I made use of a collection of postcards, *Herrliche Zeiten* (Berlin: Rembrandt Verlag, 1970), and *"Mein Milljöh": Neue Bilder aus dem Berliner Leben* (Hannover: Fackelträger Verlag, 1977), a collection of the comic art of Heinrich Zille.

In these chapters I also drew on unpublished sections of Karen Horney's fifth and last diary and on two unpublished notebooks—the "Ego" notebook and the little book in which Horney entered her observations about her small daughters. I am grateful to Richard Lentschner and Sabine Schulte for their help in translating these documents.

The beginnings of the psychoanalytic movement in Berlin are chronicled, informally, in the correspondence between Freud and his Berlin emissary, Karl Abraham, in *The Letters of Sigmund Freud and Karl Abraham.* Hannah Decker, in *Freud in Germany,* provided a historical context in which to place psychoanalysis.

The Weimar period in Berlin (Chapters 10, 11, and 12) has been profusely documented in words and pictures. I made use of many reminiscences of the period, most notably George Grosz, *An Autobiography;* Harry Kessler, *In the Twenties: The Diaries of Harry Kessler;* Gustav Regler, *The Owl of Minerva;* and Carl Zuckmayer, *A Part of Myself.* Finally, I found Christopher Isherwood's *Berlin Stories* to be wonderfully evocative. Peter Gay's *Weimar Culture: The Outsider as Insider* was also useful, as were several retrospective books on the period: *Das war Berlin,* by Bernd Ruland; *Bertolt Brecht's Berlin,* by Wolf von Eckardt and Sander L. Gilman; and *Weimar: A Cultural History,* by Walter Laqueur. For a visual understanding of the Weimar period I relied on *Bilder aus der Grossen Stadt,* published by the Staatliche Museen Preussischer Kulturbesitz; *Art and Politics in the Weimar Period,* by John Willett; and, finally, *Berlin 1910–1933* (New York: Rizzoli, 1982), by Eberhard Roters et al.

For factual and background material on the Berlin Psychoanalytic Institute in the twenties and thirties I found the correspondence of Alix and James Strachey in *Freud/Bloomsbury,* along with the unusually thorough notes by the editors, Perry Meisel and Walter Hendrick, very revealing. I was also grateful for the detailed news of events provided by the Berlin group to the international journal in its various incarnations: first the *Zentralblatt,* then the *Internationale Zeitschrift für Ärztliche Psychoanalyse,* then the *Internationale Zeitschrift für Psychoanalyse,* and, in both English and German editions, *The International Journal of Psycho-Analysis.* In addition, the ten-year report of the Berlin Psychoanalytic Institute in 1930 (*Zehn Jahre Berliner Psychoanalytisches Institut*) provided a wealth of detail about education and treatment. And finally, *"Hier geht das Leben...,"* the book prepared for the Thirty-fourth Psychoanalytic Congress in Hamburg in 1985, was a sad testament, in documents and photographs, to the institute's demise in the Fascist period.

Several biographical works provided useful background as well: *Psychoanalytic Pioneers,* edited by Alexander, Eisenstein, and Grotjahn; Carl and Sylvia Grossman's *The Wild Analyst: The Life and Work of George Groddeck;* Paul Roazen's *Helene Deutsch: A Psychoanalyst's Life;* Myron Sharaf's *Fury on Earth: A Biography of Wilhelm Reich* (New York: St. Martin's Press/Marek, 1983); and Phyllis Grosskurth's *Melanie Klein: Her World and Her Work* (New York: Knopf, 1986). I have made use often of Ernest Jones's three-volume *The Life and Work of Sigmund Freud.*

For my account of the debate concerning women and psychoanalysis I relied, of course, on the writings of the participants. While there is certainly merit to the recent criticism of Strachey's translation of Freud, I found the *Standard Edition* to be a remarkable work of documentation. In particular, a final volume, with its array of bibliographies and indexes, was invaluable. Another editor, Harold Kelman, performed an important service by bringing together most of Horney's writings on women (some of it in English translation for the first time) in *Female Psychology.* Jean Strouse's collection of essays *Dialogues on Psychoanalytic Views of Femininity: Women and Analysis* gave me a first insight into the significance of Horney's work, and Zenia Odes Fliegel's article "Feminine Psychosexual Development in Freudian Theory," in the *Psychoanalytic Quarterly,* remains, fifteen years after its publication, the best historical overview I have found. I also benefited from the thoughtful comparisons of theory made by Nellie Buckley in her dissertation, *Women, Psychoanalysts and the Theory of Feminine Development: A Study of Karen Horney, Helene Deutsch, and Marie Bonaparte* (UCLA, 1982), as well as a recent paper by William I. Grossman, "Freud and Horney: A Study of Psychoanalytic Models via the Analysis of a Controversy" in *Psychoanalysis: The Science of Mental Conflict*, ed. Charles Brenner (Hillsdale, N.J.: The Analytic Press, 1986).

Finally, in this chapter I have relied for the first time on the memories of living persons. In two instances there were written reminiscences to draw on. Renate Horney Patterson, Karen Horney's youngest daughter, has written a lengthy memoir (unpublished) and has kindly provided me with a copy, which I have quoted extensively in these and subsequent chapters. In addition, in this section I made use of the briefer reminiscences of Rita Honroth Welte, the daughter of Lisa and Walther Honroth. Interviews with Dr. Welte, Dr. Marianne Eckardt, Brigitte Horney Swarzenski, and Renate Horney Patterson, as well as with Drs. Henry and Yela Lowenfeld, also informed these chapters.

PART IV

Chicago
1932–34

For a general understanding of the immigrant experience I found Anthony Heilbut's *Exiled in Paradise* informative. I have also drawn repeatedly on a wonderful essay by Henry Pachter in *Salmagundi*, "On Being an Exile: An Old-Timer's Personal and Political Memoir." For the history of psychoanalysis in America I relied on Laura Fermi, *Illustrious Immigrants;* Nathan G. Hale, Jr., *Freud and the Americans: The Beginnings of Psychoanalysis in the United States;* and Frederick J. Hoffman, *Freudianism and the Literary Mind.*

Interviews and personal reminiscences were essential to this chapter. In particular, I depended on the written and spoken memories of Renate Horney Patterson, who was with her mother throughout these two years. Some of the memories were corroborated by Marianne Horney Eckardt. In addition, the written history by Dorothy Blitsten, as well as a personal interview, were invaluable, as was the interview with Leon Saul. I am indebted to the Chicago Institute, the Oral History Research Office at Columbia, and the British Psycho-Analytical Society for the McLean-Tower interview, the Sandor Rado interview, and the Brill-Jones correspondence respectively.

PART V

New York
1934–52

Peter Rutkoff and William B. Scott's recent *New School: A History of the New School for Social Research* was a valuable resource for my discussion of that institution. The essay of Nathan Hale, Jr., "From Berggasse XIX to Central Park West: The Americanization of Psychoanalysis, 1919–1940," and Marie Jahoda's "The Migration of Psychoanalysis: Its Impact on American Psychology" provided insight into the social history of psychoanalysis in New York. I found Quen and Carlson's *American Psychoanalysis: Origins and Developments* to be useful, particularly the article on schisms in American psychoanalysis by Marianne Horney Eckardt. A biography, *Psychiatrist of America: The Life of Harry Stack Sullivan,* by Helen Swick Perry, and an autobiography, *From Time to Time,* by Hannah Tillich, also provided useful information. *The Feminist Legacy of Karen Horney,* by Marcia Westcott (New Haven: Yale Univ. Press, 1986), stimulated my thinking about connections between Horney's early papers on women and her later work.

Most of the material for these chapters, however, came from unpublished sources. I am thankful to all those within psychoanalysis who have taken the trouble to document its development. Specifically, I have relied on histories of the New York Psychoanalytic Society and Institute by Sam Atkin and, more recently, Theodore J. Jacobs, as well as on a history of the Washington Psychoanalytic Society and Institute by Douglas Noble and Donald L. Burnham. For an understanding of the splits within the Horney group I have found reminiscences by Clara Thompson and Ruth Moulton to be particularly helpful. I am grateful to Ruth Moulton as well for her work in putting together a history of the William Alanson White Institute for a fortieth-anniversary celebration. The interviews and Oral History Portrait sponsored by the American Academy of Psychoanalysis were also of enormous value.

For my account of the split at the New York Psychoanalytic I drew heavily on two sources: the archives of the A. A. Brill Library, at the New York Psychoanalytic Institute, and the David Levy papers, in the Archives of Psychiatry of New York Hospital-Cornell Medical Center. I am also indebted to the Rare Book and Manuscript Library at Columbia University for the extensive correspondence between Horney and her publisher, W. W. Norton. A final source and one for which I feel particularly grateful was the personal archive of Horney's previous biographer, Jack Rubins. Dr. Rubins conducted extensive interviews for his 1978 biography, many of them with subjects who had died before I began my project, and took verbatim notes in his own shorthand. I have relied on his notes in many instances.

In addition to the written reminiscences of Renate Horney Patterson, in Chapter 19 I made use of the writings of Karen Horney's friend Gertrude Lederer-Eckardt. I have also made extensive use of interviews with Karen Horney's three daughters, Renate, Marianne, and Brigitte, and with others who knew her: Sam Atkin, Walter Bonime, George Daniels, Helen De Rosis, Saul Ephron, Henry Holt, Norman Kelman, Gertrude Lederer-Eckardt, Marie Levy, Henry and Yela Lowenfeld, Judd Marmor, Ruth Moulton, Herman Selinsky, Hans Speier, Katie Sugarman, Alexandra Symonds, Hannah Tillich, Gertrude Weiss, Antonia Wenkart, and Wanda Willig.

PART VI

Japan

Nancy Wilson Ross's *Buddhism: A Way of Life and Thought* provided an excellent introduction to Zen, along with Suzuki's extensive writings, most notably *Zen and Japanese Culture* and *Essays in Zen Buddhism*. Peter Mathiessen's *Nine-Headed Dragon River* gave insight into a Westerner's experience with Zen over time and in depth. And, finally, I made extensive use of Winthrop Sargeant's wonderful portrait of Suzuki in the *New Yorker*. Ruth Benedict's *The Chrysanthemum and the Sword* is a remarkable document still and an excellent introduction to Japanese mores.

For an understanding of Morita therapy I relied on two articles, one written by Akihisa Kondo for the *American Journal of Psychoanalysis* and the other, by Momoshige Miura and Shin-ichi Usa, written for a Japanese journal.

My most important resource for this chapter was a trip to Japan in the summer of 1986, during which I attempted to retrace Karen Horney's footsteps. While there I met not only with Akihisa Kondo but also with two Zen masters, Keido Gensho Fukishima, *roshi* at Tofukuji, and Nanrei Kobori, chief priest of the seventeenth-century temple Ryoko-In. Kobori had been a young monk when Karen Horney visited, and he appears in one of the pictures of her touring the monasteries. Both priests increased my understanding of Suzuki and of the varieties and complexities of Zen.

Once again, in this chapter I made extensive use of interviews and reminiscences. The memories of Brigitte Horney Swarzenski, along with those of Richard DeMartino and Akihisa Kondo, were indispensable, as were Kondo's written "Recollections."

Works of Karen Horney

1915 Ein kasuistischer Beitrag zur Frage der traumatischen Psychosen (A Case History *re* the Question of Traumatic Psychoses). Doctoral thesis. Berlin: H. Bode.

1917 Die Technik der psychoanalytischen Therapie, *Zeitschrift für Sexualwissenschaft* 4. The Technique of Psychoanalytic Therapy, *American Journal of Psychoanalysis* 5 (1968): 3.

1923 Zur Genese des weiblichen Kastrationskomplexes, *Internationale Zeitschrift für Psychoanalyse* 9:12. On the Genesis of the Castration Complex in Women, *International Journal of Psycho-analysis* 5 (1924): 50. Also in *Feminine Psychology*, ed. Harold Kelman, New York: W. W. Norton, 1966.

1926 Review of "Zur Psychologie der weiblichen Sexualfunktionen" by Helene Deutsch, *Internationale Zeitschrift für Psychoanalyse*. Also *International Journal of Psycho-Analysis* 7:92.

1926 Die Flucht aus der Weiblichkeit, *Internationale Zeitschrift für Psychoanalyse*, 12: 360. The Flight from Womanhood, *International Journal of Psycho-Analysis*, 7 (1926): 324. Also in *Feminine Psychology*.

1926 Gehemmte Weilbichkeit: Psychoanalytischer Beitrag zum Problem der Frigiditat, *Zeitschrift für Sexualwissenschaft* 13 (1926): 67. Inhibited Femininity: A Psychoanalytic Contribution to the Problem of Frigidity in *Feminine Psychology*.

1927 Der Männlichkeitskomplex der Frau [The Masculinity Complex of Women], *Archiv für Frauenkunde* 13:141.

463

1927 Diskussion der Laienanalyse, *Internationale Zeitschrift für Psychoanalyse*. Discussion on Lay Analysis, *International Journal of Psycho-Analysis* 8 (1927): 255.

1927 Psychische Eignung und Nichteignung zur Ehe [Psychological Suitability and Unsuitability for Marriage], *Ein biologisches Ehebuch,* ed. M. Marcuse, Berlin: Marcus & Weber.

1927 Über die psychischen Bestimmungen der Gattenwahl [On the Psychological Condition for Choice of Marriage Partner], *Ein Biologisches Ehebuch,* ed. M. Marcuse, Berlin: Marcus & Weber.

1927 Über der psychischen Wurzeln einiger typische Ehekonflikte [On the Psychological Roots of Typical Marriage Conflicts], *Ein biologisches Ehebuch,* ed. M. Marcuse, Berlin: Marcus & Weber

1927 Die monogame Forderung, *Internationale Zeitschrift für Psychoanalyse* 13 (1927): 397. The Problem of the Monogamous Ideal, *International Journal of Psycho-Analysis,* 9:18. Also in *Feminine Psychology.*

1928 The Problem of the Monogamic Statute, *Psychoanalytic Review* 15:92.

1930 Die specifische Problematik der Zwangsneurose im Lichte der Psychoanalyse [Specific Problems of Compulsion Neurosis in Light of Psychoanalysis], *Archiv für Psychoanalyse* 91:597.

1930 Die Einrichtungen der Lehranstalt: Zur Organisation [The Establishment of the Educational Program: On Organization], *Zehn Jahre Berliner Psychoanalytisches Institut,* Wien: Internationaler Psychoanalytischer Verlag.

1930 Das Misstrauen zwischen den Geschlechtern, *Die Ärztin* 7 (1931): 5. The Distrust Between the Sexes, *Feminine Psychology.*

1931 Die prämenstruellen Verstimmungen, *Zeitschrift für Psychoanalyse pädagogik* 5:1. Premenstrual Tension, *Feminine Psychology.*

1931 Der Kampf in der Kultur: Einige Gedanken und Bedenken zu Freuds Todestreib und Destruktionstreib in *Das Problem der Kultur und die ärztliche Psychologie* in *Vortrage Institut für Geschichte der Medizin* 4:105. Culture and Aggression: Some Thoughts and Doubts About Freud's Death Drive and Destruction Drive, *American Journal of Psychoanalysis* 20 (1960): 130.

1932 Zur Problematik der Ehe, *Psychoanalytische Bewegung* 4:212. Problems of Marriage, *Feminine Psychology.*

1932 Die Angst vor der Frau: Über einen spezifischen Unterscheid in der männlichen und weiblichen Angst vor dem anderen Geschlecht, *Internationale Zeitschrift für Psychoanalyse* 18:5. The Dread of Woman: Observations on a Specific Difference in the Dread Felt by Men and by Women for the Opposite Sex, *International Journal of Psycho-Analysis* 13:348. Also in *Feminine Psychology.*

1932 Die Verleugnung der Vagina: Ein Beitrag zur Frage der spezifisch weiblichen Genitalangst, *Internationale Zeitschrift für Psychoanalyse* 19:372. The Denial of the Vagina: A Contribution to the Problem of Genital Anxieties in Women, *International Journal of Psycho-Analysis* 14 (1933): 57. Also in *Feminine Psychology.*

1932 On Rank's *Modern Education:* A Critique of Its Fundamental Ideas (book review), *Psychoanalytic Quarterly* 1:349.

1933 Psychogenic Factors in Functional Female Disorders, *American Journal of Obstetrics and Gynecology* 25:694. Also in *Feminine Psychology.*

1933 Research in Female Psychology, Institute for Psychoanalysis, *Review for the Year, 1932–33,* p. 31.

1934 Maternal Conflicts, *American Journal of Orthopsychiatry* 3:455. Also in *Feminine Psychology.*

1934 Concepts and Misconcepts of the Analytic Method, *Archives of Neurology and Psychiatry* 32:880.

1934 Restricted Applications of Psychoanalysis to Social Work, *The Family* 15:169.

1935 The Overvaluation of Love: A Study of a Common Present-Day Feminine Type, *Psychoanalytic Quarterly* 3 (1934): 605. Also in *Feminine Psychology.*

1935 The Problem of Feminine Masochism, *Psychoanalytic Review* 22:241. Also in *Feminine Psyhology.*

1935 Personality Changes in Female Adolescents, *American Journal of Orthopsychiatry* 5:19. Also in *Feminine Psychology.*

1935 On Difficulties in Dealing with the Transference, Newsletter, American Association of Psychiatric Social Workers 5:1.

1935 Conceptions and Misconceptions of the Analytical Method, *Journal of Nervous and Mental Disease* 81:399.

1936 The Problem of the Negative Therapeutic Reaction, *Psychoanalytic Quarterly* 5:29.

1936 Culture and Neurosis, *American Sociological Review* 1:221.

1937 Das neurotische Liebesdurfnis, *Zentralblatt für Psychotherapie* 10:69. The Neurotic Need for Love, *Feminine Psychology.*

1937 *The Neurotic Personality of Our Time,* New York: W. W. Norton.

1939 Can You Take a Stand? *Journal of Adult Education* 11:129.

1939 What Is a Neurosis? *American Journal of Sociology* 45:426.

1939 *New Ways in Psychoanalysis,* New York: W. W. Norton.

1942 *Self-Analysis,* New York: W. W. Norton.

1945 *Our Inner Conflicts,* New York: W. W. Norton.

1946 *Are You Considering Psychoanalysis?,* ed. Karen Horney, New York: W. W. Norton. Articles by Horney: "What Does the Analyst Do?" and "How Do You Progress After Analysis?" In German, "Was tut eigentlich der Psychoanalytiker?" *Psyche* 4 (1950): 1.

1946 The Future of Psychoanalysis, *American Journal of Psychoanalysis* 6:66.

1947 Inhibitions in Work, *American Journal of Psychoanalysis* 7:18. Arbeitshemmungen, *Psyche* 3:481. Inhibitions dans le Travail, *Psyche* 4 (1949): 581.

1947 Foreword to Gymnastics and Personality by Gertrude Lederer-Eckardt, *American Journal of Psychoanalysis* 7:48.

1947 Maturity and the Individual, *American Journal of Psychoanalysis* 7:85.

1948 The Value of Vindictiveness, *American Journal of Psychoanalysis* 8:3. La Valeur de la Vengeance, *Psyche* 6.

1949 Foreword to a Letter: Finding the Real Self, *American Journal of Psychoanalysis* 9:3.

1950 A Morality of Evolution, *American Journal of Psychoanalysis* 10:64.

1950 *Neurosis and Human Growth,* New York: W. W. Norton.

1950 The Search for Glory, *Pastoral Psychology* 1:13.

1950 Speech on the Tenth Anniversary of the Association for the Advancement of Psychoanalysis, *American Journal of Psychoanalysis* 11 (1951): 3.

1951 On Feeling Abused, *American Journal of Psychoanalysis* 11:5.

1951 Ziele der analytischen Therapie (Goals of Analytic Therapy), *Psyche* 7:463.

1952 The Paucity of Inner Experiences, *American Journal of Psychoanalysis* 12:3.

Index

About the Author

Susan Quinn grew up in Ohio and graduated from Oberlin College. She has written for numerous periodicals including *The New York Times Magazine* and *The Atlantic Monthly*. In addition to *A Mind of Her Own,* she is the author of a book on the theater. Ms. Quinn has lectured on Karen Horney at the Boston Psychoanalytic Society. She lives with her family in Brookline, Massachusetts.